THE CHILD'S JOURNEY THROUGH CARE

THE CHILD'S JOURNEY THROUGH CARE

Placement Stability, Care Planning, and Achieving Permanency

Edited by

Dorota Iwaniec

Queen's University, Belfast

John Wiley & Sons, Ltd

Copyright © 2006   John Wiley & Sons Ltd, The Atrium, Southern Gate, Chichester,
West Sussex PO19 8SQ, England

Telephone (+44) 1243 779777

Email (for orders and customer service enquiries): cs-books@wiley.co.uk
Visit our Home Page on www.wiley.com

Other Wiley Editorial Offices

John Wiley & Sons Inc., 111 River Street, Hoboken, NJ 07030, USA

Jossey-Bass, 989 Market Street, San Francisco, CA 94103-1741, USA

Wiley-VCH Verlag GmbH, Boschstr. 12, D-69469 Weinheim, Germany

John Wiley & Sons Australia Ltd, 42 McDougall Street, Milton, Queensland 4064, Australia

John Wiley & Sons (Asia) Pte Ltd, 2 Clementi Loop #02-01, Jin Xing Distripark, Singapore 129809

John Wiley & Sons Canada Ltd, 6045 Freemont Blvd, Mississauga, ONT, L5R 4J3, Canada

Wiley also publishes its books in a variety of electronic formats. Some content that appears in print
may not be available in electronic books.

Library of Congress Cataloging in Publication Data

The child's journey through care : placement stability, care planning, and achieving
    permanency / edited by Dorota Iwaniec.
      p.   cm.
    Includes bibliographical references and index.
    ISBN-13: 978-0-470-01137-9 (cloth : alk. paper)
    ISBN-10: 0-470-01137-8 (cloth : alk. paper)
    ISBN-13: 978-0-470-01138-6 (pbk. : alk. paper)
    ISBN-10: 0-470-01138-6 (pbk. : alk. paper)
    1. Child welfare – Government policy – Great Britain.   2. Child care – Research – Great Britain.
    3. Children – Services for – Great Britain.   I. Iwaniec, Dorota.
    HV751.A6C587 2006
    362.70941 – dc22   2006009321

British Library Cataloguing in Publication Data

A catalogue record for this book is available from the British Library

ISBN-13 978-0-470-01137-9 (ppc)   978-0-470-01138-6 (pbk)
ISBN-10 0-470-01137-8 (ppc)   0-470-01138-6 (pbk)

Typeset in 10/12pt Palatino by Integra Software Services Pvt. Ltd, Pondicherry, India
Printed and bound in Great Britain by Antony Rowe Ltd, Chippenham, Wiltshire
This book is printed on acid-free paper responsibly manufactured from sustainable forestry
in which at least two trees are planted for each one used for paper production.

CONTENTS

LIST OF ILLUSTRATIONS

FIGURES

TABLES

ABOUT THE CONTRIBUTORS

Jane Aldgate AcSS is Professor of Social Care at the Open University and Honorary Professor of Social Work at Queen's University Belfast. She has researched and written about many aspects of child welfare. Her current research includes a study on kinship care commissioned by the Social Work Inspectorate of the Scottish Executive and an evaluation of services for children with challenging behaviour for Children 1st, Scotland, funded as part of the Scottish Executive's prevention of youth crime initiative. With Jane Tunstill, in 2006, she will also be publishing a study on family centres, the final book in the DfES's Supporting Parenting Initiative. She has just published a co-edited book on child development for the DfES: J. Aldgate, D. Jones, W. Rose, & C. Jeffery (2006) *The Developing World of the Child*, London: Jessica Kingsley.

Theresa Donaldson qualified as a social worker in 1984 and worked in the voluntary and statutory child-care sector as a practitioner and manager before being appointed Deputy Director of the newly established Northern Ireland Guardian ad Litem Agency in December 1996. As well as developing a career as a practitioner and manager, she also maintained academic interests through achieving a Masters degree by thesis in 1992, and doctorate in July 2003, having been awarded a Research Fellowship from the Research and Development Office for Northern Ireland. Theresa was appointed Director of Policy and Service Development with the Northern Ireland Legal Services Commission in September 2004. She has also held the position of Chair to a Health and Personal Social Services Research Ethics Committees since January 2004.

Stan Houston is a Senior Lecturer in the School of Sociology, Social Policy, and Social Work at Queen's University Belfast. He has worked for over 20 years in child and family social work in Belfast in a range of posts, including practitioner, trainer, and manager before moving to higher education in 1997. His academic interests lie in the application of critical social theory to social work practice.

Dorota Iwaniec AcSS is Emeritus Professor of Social Work and founder and former Director of the Institute of Child Care Research (ICCR) at Queen's University Belfast. She has had extensive clinical and research experience in child care and child protection, and has written wide-ranging studies on these subjects. She is internationally known for her work on emotional abuse and neglect and on children who fail to thrive. Her book *Children Who Fail to Thrive: A Practice Guide* (2004) was awarded High Commendation by the British Medical Association, and her book *The Emotionally Abused and Neglected Child: Identification, Assessment, and Intervention* (1995 – translated into several languages) came out in a new, extended, second edition in 2006. She is co-Chair of the International Residential Care Group and co-editor of the book *Residential Care of Children: International Perspectives* (in press, Oxford University Press). She also practises as an Expert Witness.

Greg Kelly is a Senior Lecturer in Social Work at Queen's University Belfast. He is chair of the Adoption Forum for Northern Ireland and a member of the Management Board of the Northern Ireland Guardian ad Litem Agency. His main research interests are in fostering and adoption and he has published widely in these areas including an edited book entitled *Issues in Foster Care: Policy, Practice and Research.*

Rosemary Kilpatrick is Director of the Institute of Child Care Research (ICCR) at Queen's University Belfast. Prior to this, she was a Senior Lecturer in the Graduate School of Education in the same university with special responsibility in the field of children with emotional and behavioural problems. She is a chartered forensic psychologist and has a vast amount of professional experience in the juvenile justice and care systems in Northern Ireland as well as in the voluntary sector. Her particular area of interest is children and young people who are at risk of being socially excluded and much of her research has been on this topic, with findings having been used to inform policy and practice within both the education and child-care sector.

Emma Larkin is a Research Fellow at the Institute of Child Care Research (ICCR) at Queen's University Belfast. Since joining the ICCR, Emma has worked on a range of research projects. These include the 'Multiple Placements' study (2003) which investigated the extent of stability in the care careers of younger looked-after children, and the 'Counting the Costs' study (2004) which examined the costs that are incurred by children when social services use the courts to resolve disputes with families about the care of their children. She is currently a co-investigator on the 'Pathways to Permanency' project which is examining pathways to permanency (home, adoption, or long-term foster care) and the subsequent social, emotional, and behavioural outcomes for children in care. In 2003, she completed a PhD entitled 'A Longitudinal Study of Parent–Infant Bonding' that investigated parent–infant bonding in the first year of life with a focus on the multiple parent, child, contextual, and temporal factors that influence this process.

Una Lernihan is Principal Social Worker for looked-after children in the Eastern Health Social Services Board, Northern Ireland. Qualifying as a professional social worker in 1980, she has worked extensively in family and child-care social work and training in North and West Belfast for 21 years. She completed her research on kinship foster care in Northern Ireland while seconded as a Research Fellow to the School of Social Work at Queen's University Belfast.

Colette McAuley lectures in the School of Sociology, Social Policy, and Social Work at Queen's University Belfast. From 2002 to 2005, she was Head of Research in the School of Social Work. Her research interests include evaluating outcomes for looked-after children, researching children's perspectives, and evaluating support services for young families under stress. Her recent publications include McAuley, C., Knapp, M., Beecham, J., McCurry, N., & Sleed, M. *Young Families Under Stress: Outcomes and Costs of Home-Start Support* (York: Joseph Rowntree Foundation, 2004), McAuley, C. *Pathways and Outcomes: A Ten Year Follow-Up Study of Children Who Have Experienced Care*, and McAuley, C., Pecora, P., & Rose, W. (eds) *Enhancing the Well-Being of Children and Families through Effective Interventions: International Evidence for Practice* (London: Jessica Kingsley, 2006). Prior to joining QUB, Dr McAuley worked in child-care practice and management including being a team leader for fostering and post-adoption fostering. She is a founding member of the International Association for Outcome-Based Evaluation and Research on Family and Children's Services.

Dominic McSherry is a chartered psychologist and Senior Research Fellow at the Institute of Child Care Research (ICCR) at Queen's University Belfast. He began working in the School of Social Work (QUB) in 1999, following the completion of his PhD in cognitive psychology (QUB). Since then he has been almost exclusively involved in foster care and adoption research. He was Principal Investigator on a study entitled 'Counting the Costs: the Children (NI) Order, Social Work, and the Courts'. This had a particular focus on the impact that care proceedings can have upon children's chances of attaining a permanent placement (with birth or alternative parents). He is currently Principal Investigator on the ongoing 'Pathways to Permanency Study: the Carers' Perspective' at the ICCR. He has developed a keen interest in the lives of looked-after and adopted children.

Helga Sneddon is a developmental psychologist at ICCR, who is particularly interested in how early experiences shape later behaviour. Helga's research interests lie in the effects of early environments on later development with special foci on parenting, the prenatal period, child maltreatment, and substitute care. Her research has included examining the care planning for adolescents living in residential or foster care, the effects of parenting on young children's growth, learning and development, and outcomes of a community-based parent-training programme.

Tom Teggart is Consultant Clinical Psychologist with the Child and Adolescent Mental Health Service in Craigavon and Banbridge Health and Social Services Trust in Northern Ireland. He has also been involved in adult mental-health services, has been a clinical psychology trainer, and continues to teach Critical Community Psychology for the DClinPsych training course at Queen's University Belfast. Dr Teggart provides psychology consultancy to the Southern Health and Social Service's intensive support unit for looked-after children with challenging behaviours, and has published research investigating the mental-health needs of looked-after children. Other areas of research interest include autistic spectrum disorder, and the impact of bullying on young people's mental health.

He has also been a supporter of action research and has published both discussion and research papers on user involvement in mental-health services.

Karen Winter has been a qualified social worker since 1992 and has spent her social work career working with children and their families as a social worker, team manager, and most recently as a guardian ad litem. She has a particular interest in the participation rights of 'looked-after' children. She is completing a PhD regarding this issue and has several related publications.

PREFACE

After implementation of the Children Act (1989) in England and Wales, and its equivalents in Northern Ireland and Scotland (1995), many research projects were commissioned by the Department of Health to examine the effectiveness (or otherwise) of legislation in terms of improvements in children's welfare and protection from harm.

The results of empirical investigations regarding comparisons of children in need of help who lived in the community and those who were looked after by the State showed many shortcomings, and, as far as children in State care were concerned, were alarming. In the midst of organisational and policy changes, children in residential and foster care have tended to be forgotten, under-resourced, and their plight ignored. Research findings identified serious problems that required urgent attention and demanded considerable revision of policies, practice, rules, regulations, ideology, and resource allocation associated with children in substitute care. A high level of placement breakdown was found in foster care, and many children drifted from one home to another, without being given professional help or with little or no possibility of ever being able to return to any of them, least of all to their 'natural' homes. In such cases, adoption clearly could have been the better solution to provide permanence, security, identity, and possibilities to develop lifelong attachments to members of one family. The plight of children in residential care emerged as even worse. In addition to the social services' lack of interest, commitment, and resources to make residential care more effective and successful, sexual abuse (often inflicted by the residential staff) added to the horrors of badly run and badly managed residential settings. Many scandals regarding abuse, as well as peculiarly ill-informed methods of behaviour management, led to many public inquiries and a subsequent collapse of confidence in residential child care. Research results also indicated that children in State care were not prepared for independent living, and that many of them had been emotionally damaged by their experiences *prior* to coming into public care (which, at times, was clearly no better [and possibly worse] than living with their own dysfunctional natural families), and that, instead of being helped, their behaviour and well-being tended to deteriorate.

In response to these disturbing research findings concerning the ways in which children in State care fared, the government issued a White Paper entitled *Quality Protects* (1998), introducing major reforms to service provision, inspections, and resource allocation in order to improve the quality of care and to ensure better outcomes for such children. Following the introduction of *Quality Protects*, many research projects have been funded to evaluate the effectiveness and suitability of the services created to implement the recommended changes and provide better outcomes for 'looked-after' children.

This book aims to provide readers with information and findings arising from recent and current research, addressing various needs, policies, practice, and service provision for children in substitute care, following the publication of *Quality Protects* in England and Wales and *Children Matter* in Northern Ireland. It discusses how 'looked-after' children fare, and whether care planning is based on better-informed practice and adequate resource allocation. It also examines legal processes and the consequences of delay in decision-making. Each chapter should enhance knowledge and understanding about the current state of play regarding children in State care, and whether recommendations regarding change have been adequately implemented.

Dorota Iwaniec
Holywood, Co. Down, 2006

EDITOR'S ACKNOWLEDGEMENTS

First of all, my husband, Professor Emeritus James Stevens Curl, has my gratitude for his help and advice during the onerous task of editing this book. My thanks are also due to Mrs Maura Dunn for her efforts in producing a clean text for the publishers, and to the Research and Development (R&D) Office in Belfast for financing many of the research projects, the findings of which are discussed in the book. Funding was also provided by the Social Work Inspectorate and by the Health and Social Services Trusts. My thanks go to my former colleagues in the Institute of Child Care Research and the School of Social Work at Queen's University Belfast.

Part I

The Need for a Good Start in Life
Attachment, Bonding, and Children's Rights

CHAPTER 1

INTRODUCTION: AN OVERVIEW OF CHILDREN IN PUBLIC CARE

Dorota Iwaniec

INTRODUCTION

UNICEF stated in its millennium report, *The State of the World's Children*, that although huge advances have been made globally in recognising and responding to the needs and rights of children during the twentieth century, there is still a significant population of children who grow up in unacceptable conditions and do not reach their potential.

One group of children of particular concern consists of those who cannot be cared for by their parents or extended family. Often in these cases the responsibility falls to the State, whose main approved alternatives are adoption, fostering, residential care, or boarding schools for children with various disabilities. Some children and young people are looked after by the State or voluntary sector with the agreement of their parents who are temporarily, or permanently, unable to provide such care, but others, in order to protect them from neglect or abuse (inflicted, as a rule, by their parents), require the intervention of the State through legal powers implemented by a court system. For some children, orphaned as a consequence of natural disasters (such as the tsunami of Christmas, 2004, in South-East Asia, war, or civil conflict), the loss of parents may mean that the State has to take over parenting, or direct responsibility of parenting to the philanthropic child-care agencies, but keep quality control and inspection of these institutions to safeguard children's welfare. Such powers place the State, or an agent of the State, *in loco parentis* with the responsibility for determining most of the major issues in relation to a child's welfare.

It is difficult to discover comprehensive information on the number of children currently being looked after by States or by agents of States. In the developed world they usually constitute somewhere between 5 to 20 children in every 1,000, although this figure varies from country to country (UNICEF, 2004). For example, there are over 75,000 children and young people in care in the United Kingdom (Wilson et al., 2004) and 500,000 in the USA. This variation in prevalence may result from how the countries compile their statistics (or do not keep statistics at all), the criteria used when planning interventions for these children, and how resources are prioritised and allocated. Thresholds differ substantially between countries partly due to cultural, religious, economic, and general ideological reasons. Welfare States and developed countries have somewhat better organised systems and policies than those which have no social policies at all regarding the welfare of children.

According to Rushton and Minnis (2002), in the United Kingdom, after a steady fall, the number of children in care has been rising again from 45 in 10,000 in 1995, to 49 in 10,000 in 1999. Most children (65%) are in foster homes and 12% are in children's homes. The number of children in residential care in England and Wales fell by 80% from the late 1970s to the 1990s, but for the past five years the foster/residential care ratio has been constant. The general trends in North America, Australia, and Europe are reduction of residential placements and reduction of time spent there. Some Scandinavian countries, like Sweden, have almost completely eliminated children's homes from their child-care system, and others have reduced residential provision to the bare minimum. There were several reasons for the drastic reduction of residential care in the UK over the years. Firstly, the theoretical base for bringing up children in institutions became, at best, confusing, and, at worst, condemning, which affected the ways children's homes were run and the way children were looked after. Secondly, the cost of running residential establishments was considered to be too high and gave poor value for money. Thirdly, difficulties in recruiting well-trained, skilful, and experienced staff – but above all well-organised, theoretically sound, and skilful leaders – resulted in constant changes of personnel, and an incoherent philosophy as to how to run the homes and to deal with the very needy residents. Fourthly, the infiltration of residential homes by paedophiles and highly unsuitable characters (often having criminal records) led to serious and frequent scandals, resulting in numerous public inquiries, damaging the image of children's homes and blaming the local authorities for their lack of proper inspection, recruitment criteria, failure to listen to the children, and general professional shortcomings. Berridge and Brodie (1996) drew attention to the plight of children in residential care, pointing to the fundamental lack of interest, commitment, and resources in making residential care effective and successful. Residential care suffered, of course, from a collapse of confidence because of the abuse of children by the residential child-care workers, malpractice in behaviour management, and lack of theoretical bases.

Even though many countries have signed the UN Convention on the Right of the Child, there are huge variations in how children are perceived and valued in different societies. It should also be noted that there are some children who should be under the care of the State, but who are not. For example, in some South American, African, and Asian countries, and in parts of Europe (including the UK), there are many children without familial support who end up living on the streets. Interventions with these 'street-children', when they occur, tend to be inappropriate or ineffective, and often the shame associated with the problem distracts attention from the issues that drove the children onto the streets in the first place. We have children living on the streets in the UK and other European countries, in spite of these States' considerable wealth and sophisticated public policies. Interventions when dealing with such children tend to be reactive rather than proactive and, as a result, focus on short-term rather than long-term solutions (Department of Health, 1998a). Many homeless young people living on the streets come from residential or foster homes. They are usually totally unprepared for independent living after leaving care, and they have nobody to turn to for help. Additionally, they have many mental-health problems, which have not been addressed sufficiently and adequately when in State care. Chronic lack of suitable resources and a paucity of highly skilled professional assistance (at the required frequency and intensity) have not helped to solve these problems.

The situation of children without adequate familial support requires special attention, regardless of where they live. Their vulnerability is compounded by the extent of their dependence. Unlike other children, services to this group are generally not mediated through the informal social care networks of family, friends, and neighbours. They are reliant on the commitment and best practice of policy-makers and planners within the government and its agencies to protect and promote their welfare. Some of these children have often been let down by the State and by agents of the State.

It is all too easy to underestimate the needs and vulnerability of children once they become looked after by the local authority or other agencies, even though they are often damaged and deprived compared with their peers. Unfortunately, many children in foster or residential care experience poor service provision that fails to provide the stability and continuity necessary for a contented childhood in which to thrive and realise their developmental potential (Department of Health, 1998a; Parker et al., 1991; Sinclair & Gibbs, 1998; Triseliotis et al., 1995).

PROBLEMS AND DILEMMAS WITH FOSTERING AND RESIDENTIAL CARE

Most children in need of care and protection living away from home in the United Kingdom are placed in foster homes. The shift from residential to foster care in the past two decades or so has been both ideological and financial. There is a strong belief that foster care is a better option for children living away from home as it provides a family model of everyday life and greater opportunity to build warm relationships with the foster family which can last for a long time after leaving care. Foster care is also much cheaper, and that was another reason for the development of the foster care placements policy. While foster care provides an excellent service, especially for infants and young children, it is not free of problems. Cases of abuse and neglect have been reported which were inflicted by the foster parents as well as their children, or foster parents' children being sexually abused by a foster child. Again, older fostered children, especially those with a history of sexual abuse, abused other children in the family. The isolated nature of foster care means that children placed there might be at risk. Given the young age of children in foster care who are unable to report what is happening to them, the scale of possible ill-treatment is not clear. Again, children with learning disabilities, whether in foster homes or residential care, are particularly vulnerable and require special attention (Rushton & Minnis, 2002).

Many foster placements break down: this can be due to many factors. More disturbed children are placed in foster homes than before, yet the nature of children's problems is not fully communicated to foster parents who often do not fully understand what they are taking on, or how best to deal with children's difficulties. They are not given sufficient training and support; they are not always treated as equal partners with the professionals involved; and, at times, they take on a fostering role for the wrong reasons. Various reviews on fostering and research reports on both sides of the Atlantic indicate the necessity for appropriate selection procedures, regular reviews of performance and suitability, and independent inspection of foster homes (Sinclair et al., 2005b; Utting, 1997). It is also recommended that children should be seen alone when visited by social workers, and those visits should be more frequent; children should have access to a telephone and to information; and parental participation and visits should be facilitated whenever appropriate (Berridge & Cleaver, 1987). A child's personality structure and his or her attributes also require study and sympathetic assessment (which is often overlooked). At the same time, the characteristics of foster parents or key carers should be taken into consideration so that care-givers and children can be beneficially matched and unnecessary discord, friction, and confrontation avoided. For example, a quiet, withdrawn, frightened child, lacking in self-confidence, will need to be matched to a carer capable of emotional demonstrativeness, with a warm, tolerant, and patient personality, while a more robust, but stubborn, moody, and highly active child will need a carer offering firm, consistent (but fair) routines and rules. Far too often, stress resulting from a mismatch between the carer's temperament (including the threshold of tolerance) and the child's behaviour structure sets the scene for inevitable discord, conflict, nervous exhaustion, anger, confrontation, guilt, and disappointment, eventually leading to the breakdown of the placement. Informed choices and careful assessment can help to prevent a child's sense of rejection and a carer's feeling of failure (Sinclair et al., 2005a, 2005b).

In order to protect and properly care for children living away from home there is a need to examine objectively how far the requirements of regulations and statutory-based guidance are met, and the effectiveness with which they are monitored and enforced. Regulations and guidance which are not put into practice create a false sense of security which adds to the risk faced by the very children they are intended to protect. Selection and recruitment of residential staff and foster parents, regular visits and inspections, comprehensive and regular reviews of the care plans, and children's participation in planning their lives – and where possible with their parents – will not only help children, but also those who care for them (Utting, 1997).

Choice of placement is a vital factor in meeting the assessed needs of children. Sadly, children are often placed on the basis of vacancy and not suitability, and seldom is a child's wish heard as to where he/she prefers to be placed. If we seriously want to take on board children's wishes and rights, and treat them with respect, as stated in the Children's Act and the Rights of Children as postulated by the United Nations Convention on the Rights of the Child, we need a variety of settings to accommodate children living away from home. Children old enough and capable of making decisions should be allowed a choice as to where they want to live. Older children might prefer residential care, as they often feel that they already have a family. But residential care (if it is to help teenagers) has to change considerably in terms of the helping philosophy, selection of residence and staff, and the building of a positive image as a place of care and help – and not a dumping ground for difficult cases. Amazing loyalty and a sense of belonging are demonstrated by some children even though they were often badly treated, suffered abuse, and were persistently neglected by their parents. Some are so grossly disturbed that no single family could cope with their behaviour: they are simply unfosterable. Attempts to do so only lead to placement breakdown and consequently to more problems for everybody concerned.

Yet we also know that some children want to belong to a family and to be a part of a normal family unit which, in turn, can provide a model of healthy family functioning. For some to live in an institution, regardless of how good it might be, is degrading and stigmatising. Young children are better off in foster care as well. The fact is that we need both if we are to make informed decisions about children's lives and help them recover from harm or various forms of disadvantage they have experienced prior to becoming looked after. We can all learn a great deal and put in place better policy and practice if we listen to children and young people and take on board messages based on their experiences while in care. The past few years have witnessed positive movements in that direction. Indeed, organisations have begun to emerge whose membership includes children who have been in, or are in care, as partners who can inform, advise, and participate in promoting positive changes. For instance, The Voice of Young People in Care in Northern Ireland, Voices from Care in Wales, and an equivalent group in Scotland have done much work to hear and to listen to children, and many research projects included children as participants (*see* Kilpatrick, Chapter 4, and Winter, Chapter 14, in this volume).

Sir William Utting, in his (1997) report *People Like Us: The Report of the Review of the Safeguards for Children Living Away from Home*, brings to our attention how children felt when they entered the care system. There were positive and negative responses. Quite often they felt lost, bewildered, left to their own devices, unsupported, and became the victims of delinquent peers. They felt that they had little control over their destinies (for example, in the choice of placement, location, school, social worker, or with whom they lived). Young people felt their views were not taken into account, and that they were not involved in decision-making, quite often becoming helpless and cynical about their lives and the way things were planned for them. However, a number of them considered that when they had a key worker who would take them under his or her wing, offering protection, answering questions, lowering anxiety, and showing concern for them, they settled down more easily, and made sense of their new life and circumstances. Listening to children, and asking them what they think and feel about their lives, difficulties, aspirations, dreams, and how they could be helped are important to explore in order to get them involved in a consciously chosen problem-solving strategy. Recent publications by Sinclair et al. (2005a, 2005b) discuss reasons why foster placements succeed and why they fail, as well as movements and destinations from the foster home (e.g. going back home, being adopted, and permanence planning).

LOOKED-AFTER CHILDREN IN THE UNITED KINGDOM

Many research projects in the United Kingdom showed continually and categorically that looked-after children constitute one of the most severely troubled and disturbed groups in the general child and youth population (Frost et al., 1999; Hobbs et al., 1999; McCann et al., 1996; Parker, 1966; Quinton et al., 1998; Rowe et al., 1984; Sinclair & Gibbs, 1998). There is also growing evidence that the problems and the associated behaviours displayed by these children and young people have become more acute in recent years (Berridge & Brodie, 1998; Ray et al., 2000; Sinclair et al., 2005a; Utting, 1997).

During the 1970s and 1980s, there was an almost complete concentration on the protection of children. As a consequence, vast resources were devoted to 'policing' families and admitting children into care through a very expensive legal process. These children were often provided with a very unstable and highly unsatisfactory care experience before being discharged back into the community, frequently to those same parents who had abused or neglected them in the first place, and who remained under-resourced, unsupported, and whose behaviour had not changed to justify discharging them back home (Parker et al., 1991; Sinclair et al., 2005a).

With the introduction of the Children Act (1989) in England and Wales, and its equivalent in Scotland and Northern Ireland (1995), the focus began to shift from child protection to family support. This new 'child-care philosophy' contains the belief that children are best looked after by their families, and every effort should be made to make this possible by providing help and family support for as long as necessary. Only in serious cases would children be removed from parental care.

The Children Act (1989) stated that local authorities should make appropriate use of services available to them to meet the needs of children being cared for by them. The Children Act required from the local authorities not only provision of care (which would protect looked-after children from further harm) but that they should provide enhanced opportunities for these children in educational attainments, social skills learning, self-help skills, and training for jobs, provide interactional and relationship-building opportunities, and teach them what is right and wrong, in order to prepare them for life and to take responsibility for their behaviour and actions.

In spite of comprehensive reforms in child-care law, such as the Children Act (1989), and the availability of many associated regulations and guidelines to inform policy and practice, they have not produced the desired outcomes, especially for looked-after children. The messages which emerged from Social Services Inspections (Department of Health, 1998a, 1998b; Ray et al., 2000; Rushton & Minnis, 2002; Utting, 1997), and independent reports such as from the Who Cares? Trust's *Remember My Messages* (Shaw, 1998), indicated serious shortcomings in the quality of care provided for children in foster and residential care, and extremely poor developmental outcomes for these children.

The legacy of failure within the relatively advanced UK system makes for grim reading. For example, Warren (1999) found that children in foster care were found to be more likely than their peers to be excluded from school; twelve times more likely to leave school with no qualifications; four times more likely to be unemployed; sixty times more likely to join the ranks of the young homeless; fifty times more likely to suffer from mental illness; and their children were sixty-six times more likely than the children of their peers to need public care. On leaving care, many of these young people found themselves unprepared for their adult responsibilities and the challenges of living independently. Some children in care have nobody to turn to when in difficulties and when they are in need of support.

The outcomes of children in residential care were found to be even worse. In addition to similar problems experienced by children in foster care, a greatly increased likelihood of disadvantage in residential care was noted (Utting, 1997), such as: vulnerability to involvement in prostitution; early and unwanted pregnancies; poor parenting of their own children; loss of contact with their families and communities of origin; social exclusion through unemployment and poverty; attempted suicides; drug and alcohol abuse; homelessness; and progression to different and more serious forms of institutional care as time goes on (e.g. hospitalisation for mental illness or imprisonment).

The Utting Report (1997), Warner (1992), Audit Commission (1994), Fraser (1993), Social Services Inspectorate (1985) and Shaw (1998), among others, on the basis of their research of 'looked-after' children, have made rather concerning comments about their findings. They stated that there is a high level of placement breakdown, especially in foster care. It was estimated by Who Cares? Trust that an average child was moved to five different foster families, and that 9% of the 11-year-olds and younger children reported being moved more than 10 times. Of those who had been in care for five or more years, nearly a quarter (24%) had been in 11 or more different placements. For many of these children who drifted from one home to another with little or no possibility of ever being able to return home, adoption clearly would have been the best option to provide permanence, security, stability, identity, and development of lifelong attachment to a family. Choice of placement and appropriate matching according to the children's needs were found to be extremely poor. Children were put where there was a vacancy rather than taking into account suitability, which led to frequent placement breakdown and, at times, abuse.

Education of looked-after children required urgent attention and collaborative efforts between social services and education departments, and more under-standing and tolerance from the schools (Jackson, 1994). More than 33% of children in care were not receiving an education, and one in four of those aged 14–16 did not regularly attend school. Many were excluded from school, and had no regular educational placement. At the point of leaving care, three out of four teenagers had no qualifications, and eight out of ten had no job to which to go (Utting, 1997).

It was also worrying that, in spite of legal requirements, only just over half of the children in substitute care had a care plan, and some were unaware of a care plan as nobody had discussed it with them. Equally, only two-thirds of young people knew how to make an official complaint about the way they were looked after in care (Shaw, 1998). Helga Sneddon, in this volume (Chapter 10), and Dominic McSherry (Chapter 13) examine to what degree care planning has improved and whether it has been properly recorded and acted upon.

The lamentable outcomes outlined in many research projects, highlighted by several scandals, and exposed by public inquiries into the abuse of children in residential care, forced the Department of Health to make fundamental changes to policy and practice regarding children in public care. *Quality Protects*, published by the DoH (1998a), and its equivalent in Northern Ireland, put forward new money, new ideas, rules, and regulations to safeguard 'looked-after' children's welfare, with particular emphasis on leaving care (Department of Health, 2000). This book will discuss the findings of the studies carried out after *Quality Protects* was issued, to examine if the changes recommended by the government have taken place and the effect they have had on looked-after children.

ABUSE OF CHILDREN IN CARE

It is impossible to discuss the experiences of children in public care without referring to widespread abuse. Many 'looked-after' children have been physically, sexually, and emotionally abused. The scandals of children abused by residential workers are well known, and have resulted in various public inquiries (Iwaniec, 2006). The Welsh Office reported widespread abuse in Welsh children's homes, and in 1992 serious, and long-lasting, sexual abuse was reported in Leicester's children's homes orchestrated by Frank Beck or the 'pin-down' regime in Stafford later on.

Hobbs et al. (1999) have compared abuse in foster and residential care with the general urban population. Children in foster care were seven to eight times, and in residential care six times, more likely to be physically or sexually abused in comparison with the general population of children. Vulnerability to being abused in these two care settings (apart from by foster or residential staff) included abuse by their natural families during access visits and by other children in care. Lindsay (1999) found that 91% of children in residential care who sexually abused others also had histories of being sexually abused themselves, thus exposing vulnerable children to further molestation.

Sadly, the available evidence tells us that some children are still at risk of being abused or bullied while under the protection of State care, even after being removed from the abusive home environment: this particularly applies to children with physical and learning disabilities. In effect, the abusing family member is replaced by an abusing carer within the institution or foster home. This problem is not unique to the UK, but has been reported in many different countries in recent years (Rushton & Minnis, 2002). The abuse of trust and power by those responsible for protecting the child not only blights the childhood of the victims, but leaves scars that maim their adult lives.

THE PURPOSE AND ORGANISATION OF THE BOOK

This book is based on recent research and contemporary policy, practice, and theoretical deliberations, addressing many problems and dilemmas as well as possible solutions for looked-after children. The chapters are concerned with children in substitute care, and with what happens to them. Do they become happier, better adjusted to social demands, more stable in emotional expressions, better prepared for life in terms of learning skills, and are they adequately socialised, educated, and competent in social and economic functioning? Different routes, and often complex and painful processes, are described to illustrate children's journeys to presumed stable and helpful placements. For some, these journeys are very difficult and unhelpful, while for others they are more enjoyable and successful. Why this is the case is the subject of discussion in the chapters that follow.

Each chapter is written as a separate piece of empirical or theoretical research, connected one way or another with issues associated with children in substitute care and the processes involved in getting there. Each chapter has to be read, therefore, as a separate piece of work covering different areas of looked-after children's lives, taking into account their needs, care plans, rights, and participations in decision-making. Management, in terms of resource allocation, competence, and suitability of care staff, as well as the philosophy and theoretical bases governing policies and procedures of children in need of care and protection when living away from home are also discussed. The book is organised into five Parts and contains 15 chapters.

Part I, entitled 'The Need for a Good Start in Life: Attachment, Bonding, and Children's Rights', deals with the fundamental needs of children to become attached to their parents and carers, to survive in infancy, and to lay the foundations for the future development of relationships with adults and peers. Chapter 1 gives a brief overview of foster and residential care and describes the organisation of the book. Jane Aldgate, in Chapter 2, discusses the theory of attachment and how new attachments can be built with substitute carers. Additionally, she emphasises the importance of promoting resilience by identifying protective factors in each looked-after child, the environment in which it lives, and how it might make the best out of life.

In Chapter 3, Emma Larkin brings to our attention the importance of early bonding between parents (primarily mothers) and a baby, and discusses how an emotional link based on commitment, love, and sacrifice helps the child to build trust in people and to see the world around as friendly and good. What stands in the way of bond development and how adoptive or foster parents can build an emotional link lasting a lifetime are discussed.

Chapter 4 addresses the rights of children, specifically those in substitute care. Rosemary Kilpatrick discusses what stands in the way of successful and meaningful implementation of the Convention on the Rights of the Child and puts forward ways in which children might be seen as human beings capable of expressing opinions, feelings, and wishes to be respected and taken seriously into consideration.

Part II, 'Pathways to Permanency', consists of three chapters covering: a 10-year follow-up study on children in long-term foster care; kinship foster care; and permanency through adoption. In Chapter 5, Colette McAuley shares the outcomes of a small-scale study of a cohort of young people and their perspectives of being brought up in foster homes. The implications for policy and evidence-based practice are discussed. Chapter 6 brings to our attention the positives and negatives of being fostered by the extended family. Una Lernihan and Greg Kelly argue that kin-foster care offers a family for life and, therefore, should be advocated and promoted whenever possible and appropriate. Dominic McSherry and Emma Larkin look at the outcomes of adopted children in Chapter 7. Dominic McSherry and Emma Larkin also argue that residential care is needed for some hard-to-place and very disturbed teenagers, but the way it is managed, staffed, and resourced has to change. They explore recent moves towards specialised residential provision within Northern Ireland and other parts of the UK.

Part III, 'Residential and Mixed Care', explores the state of residential care in the UK, and the serious shortcomings in the quality and intensity of helping strategies for very needy children. Impoverished resources, lack of appropriate selection of trained staff, and unsuitable allocation of placements for youngsters with specific problems requiring expert attention are explored. Abuse and bullying, and the high cost of running residential institutions, as well as the general perceptions and theoretical framework that residential care is bad for the children are discussed in Chapter 8 by Dominic McSherry and Emma Larkin. This chapter will examine the level of permanency (adoption, long-term foster care, and return home) achieved over a two-year period for a population (n = 384) of children in

Northern Ireland who were looked after (on Care Order or Accommodated) on 31 March 2000. A key issue examined is the extent to which this reflects a placement geographical lottery in Northern Ireland, i.e. the child's placement being dependent upon the particular policies of the Trust that has responsibility for them. This raises major issues in terms of ensuring that all looked-after children have the same opportunities to gain the types of long-term placement that are best suited to their long-term needs. In Chapter 9, Tom Teggart explores the mental-health needs of looked-after children, shares research outcomes pointing to the wide range of factors contributing to the development of mental-health problems, and debates to what extent the mental-health needs of these children are being met. He also reflects on models of service that may best deliver suitable help.

Chapter 10 explores the care planning of over 100 looked-after children and the decision-making processes regarding their assessed needs, such as developmental attainments, health, education, and leisure. Helga Sneddon shares research findings regarding the existence, suitability, and implementation of care plans while in State care, comparing identified needs at the time of removal from home, and after a year of being looked after in either residential or foster care.

Stan Houston, in Chapter 11, writes about the use of positive psychology to help young people overcome some of their deep-seated emotional and behavioural problems. He makes some suggestions as to how residential staff can become more skilled and confident when dealing with young people with challenging behaviour in residential care. He explores various theories such as emotional intelligence and their application to inform practice, policy, and service planning.

Part IV, 'Court and Family Support Pathways to Substitute Care', is concerned with the process leading to substitute care such as: accommodation of children in need of care and protection provided on a voluntary basis; compulsory care proceedings; the length and cost of court proceedings, and effects on children and their families; and participation of children in decision-making regarding their future.

In Chapter 12, Theresa Donaldson examines difficulties in the management of cases inside and outside the court process. She discusses the role played by legal and social work practitioners in situations where children become looked after through voluntary and compulsory interventions. Case studies are provided to illustrate enforced accommodation as a means to start court proceedings, the consequences for these children, and the effects on their families.

Chapter 13 deals with the consequences of prolonged delays in care proceedings. Dominic McSherry discusses the results of the research project examining 'no delay and the child welfare is paramount' principles in decision-making when cases go through the courts. Apart from the cost to the children, he looks at the financial cost to the social services and questions the necessity for such expense.

In Chapter 14, Karen Winter examines the participation of looked-after children in public law proceedings. She explores the reasons and importance of increased emphasis on children's participation; the perceived benefits of participation; and looked-after children's experiences in this area, including their feelings and wishes. She explores the suitability of methods and techniques in communicating with children and ways of enabling and encouraging them to express their preferences and wishes. Attention is drawn to the absence of children in the court process which, she argues, requires active action for positive change.

Part V, 'Messages from Research', contains one integrative chapter that pulls together messages arising from research as discussed in different parts. Some recommendations are put forward, based on current understanding of what are the needs of children entering substitute care and how these needs are being met; what resources, skills, training, and support are required to assist children and families in need; and what changes are needed in the perceptions and attitudes of service providers, policy-makers, and practitioners regarding children in substitute care.

REFERENCES

Audit Commission for Local Authorities and the National Health Service in England and Wales (1994). *Seen But Not Heard: Co-ordinating Community Child Health and Social Services for Children in Need: Detailed Evidence and Guidelines for Managers and Practitioners.* London: HMSO.

Berridge, D., & Brodie, L. (1996). Residential child care in England and Wales: The enquiry and after. In M. Hill & J. Aldgate (eds), *Child Welfare Services: Developments in Law, Policy, Practice, and Research.* London: Jessica Kingsley.

Berridge, D., & Brodie, I. (1998). *Children's Homes Revisited.* London: Jessica Kingsley.

Berridge, D., & Cleaver, H. (1987). *Foster Home Breakdown*, 2nd edn. Oxford: Blackwell.

Department of Health (1998a). *Quality Protects: Framework for Action.* London: Social Care Group, Department of Health.

Department of Health (1998b). *Caring for Children Away from Home: Messages from Research.* Chichester: John Wiley & Sons, Ltd.

Department of Health (2000). *Guidance on the Education of Children and Young People in Public Care.* London: Department for Education and Employment.

Fraser, C. (1993). *Corporate Parents: Inspection of Residential Child Care Services in Eleven Local Authorities.* London: Social Services Inspectorate.

Frost, N., Mills, S., & Stein, M. (1999). *Understanding Residential Child Care.* Aldershot: Ashgate.

Hobbs, G., Hobbs, C., & Wynnes, J. (1999). Abuse of children in foster and residential care. *Child Abuse and Neglect*, **23**, 1239–1252.

Iwaniec, D. (2006). *The Emotionally Abused and Neglected Child*, 2nd edn. Chichester: John Wiley & Sons, Ltd.

Iwaniec, D., & Hill, M. (2000). *Child Welfare Policy and Practice: Issues and Lessons Emerging from Current Research.* London: Jessica Kingsley.

Jackson, S. (1994). Educating children in residential and foster care. *Oxford Review of Education*, **20**(3), 267–279.

Lindsay, M. (1999). The neglected priority: Sexual abuse in the context of residential child care. *Child Abuse Review*, **8**, 418.

McCann, J.B., James, A., Wilson, S., & Dunn, G. (1996). Prevalence of psychiatric disorders in young people in the care system. *British Medical Journal*, **313**, 1529–1530.

Parker, R.A. (1966). *Decision in Child Care: A Study of Prediction in Fostering*. London: Allen & Unwin.

Parker, R., Ward, H., Jackson, S., Aldgate, J., & Wade, P. (1991). *Assessing Outcomes in Child Care*. London: HMSO.

Quinton, D., Rushton, A., Dance, C., & Mayes, D. (1998). *Joining New Families: A Study of Adoption and Fostering in Middle Childhood*. Chichester: John Wiley & Sons, Ltd.

Ray, P., Rutter, M., & Pickles, A. (2000). Institutional care: Risk from family background or pattern of rearing? *Journal of Child Psychology and Psychiatry*, **41**, 139–149.

Rowe, J., Caine, M., Hundleby, M., & Keane, A. (1984). *Long-term Foster Care*. London: Batsford Academic and Educational in association with British Agencies for Adoption and Fostering.

Rushton, A., & Minnis, H. (2002). Residential and foster family care. In M. Rutter & E. Taylor (eds), *Child and Adolescence Psychiatry*, 4th edn. Oxford and Malden, MA: Blackwell Science.

Shaw, C. (1998). *Remember My Messages: The Experiences and Views of 2000 Children in Public Care in the UK*. London: Who Cares? Trust.

Sinclair, I., Baker, C., Wilson, K., & Gibbs, I. (2005a). *Foster Children: Where They Go and How They Get On*. London: Jessica Kingsley.

Sinclair, I., & Gibbs, I. (1998). *Children's Homes: A Study in Diversity*. Chichester: John Wiley & Sons, Ltd.

Sinclair, I., Wilson, K., & Gibbs, I. (2005b). *Foster Placements: Why They Succeed and Why They Fail*. London: Jessica Kingsley.

Social Services Inspectorate (1985). *Inspection of Community Homes*. London: Department of Health and Social Security.

Triseliotis, J., Sellick, C., & Short, R. (1995). *Foster Care: Theory and Practice*. London: Batsford in association with British Agencies for Adoption and Fostering.

Utting, W. (1997). *People Like Us: The Report of the Review of the Safeguards for Children Living Away from Home*. London: HMSO.

Warner, N. (1992). *Choosing with Care: The Report of the Committee of Inquiry into the Selection, Development, and Management of Staff in Children's Homes*. London: HMSO.

Warren, D. (1999). Adoption and fostering. *Child Welfare*, **23**(2), 48–56.

Wilson, K., Sinclair, I., Pithouse, A., & Sellick, C. (2004). *Fostering Success: An Exploration of the Research Literature in Foster Care*. London: Social Care Institute for Excellence, Policy Press.

CHAPTER 2

ORDINARY CHILDREN IN EXTRAORDINARY CIRCUMSTANCES

Jane Aldgate

INTRODUCTION

Children looked after by the State are just ordinary children with the same range of developmental needs as other children. At the same time, because they have come to be cared for by the State, they find themselves in circumstances which demand from them extraordinary inner resources. A childhood as a looked-after child should be a time of pleasure and positive challenge. We know from two decades of research with young people who have left the care system that being looked after has more often been a time of anxiety and adversity (Dixon & Stein, 2005; Stein & Carey, 1986). Rather than improving experiences and outcomes for children, the care system has often contributed to their adversity by providing care that is less than adequate.

CHILDREN IN NEED

In different parts of the UK, many children become looked after because of abuse and neglect, sometimes attributed to parental substance misuse. These children have not had an auspicious start to their young lives. In many cases, their care will have been chaotic and uncertain, undoubtedly affecting their development. Every child who is looked after by the State is a child in need of services. Some may be looked after on a compulsory basis; others may be in voluntary arrangements. Legislation across the different countries of the UK broadly agrees on the definition of children in need. The Scottish definition, for example, talks of children who are unlikely to achieve or maintain a reasonable standard of health or development without the provision of local authority services (Children (Scotland) Act 1995, 93 (3)). The appropriate response of those providing services is to make sure the health and development of children in need is not impaired.

The Child's Journey Through Care: Placement Stability, Care Planning, and Achieving Permanency. Edited by D. Iwaniec.
Copyright © 2006 John Wiley & Sons, Ltd.

There is a growing body of theory and research which is helpful in identifying key factors that are necessary for children's development, no matter what their circumstances (Aldgate et al., 2006; Daniel et al., 1999). Understanding what is helpful for all children gives a good foundation from which to assess the needs of individuals.

Policy-makers have increasingly tried to spell out the ambitions of the State in relation to the health and well-being of all children. There are similar initiatives across the different countries of the UK. The Scottish Executive's vision for Scotland's children, outlined in the policy document *Getting It Right for Every Child* (Scottish Executive, 2005), for example, spells out its ambitions. It stresses the need for children to have a positive and rewarding childhood experience, even if they cannot be with their own families. Children should also have access to high-quality services to help them overcome disadvantage and inequality. Children need to be safe, nurtured, healthy, achieving, active, respected, responsible, and included (Scottish Executive, 2005). This vision applies to each looked-after child as well as to any other child, and is a useful foundation for thinking about the aspects of children's development that need to be addressed by the local authority acting as corporate parent.

RECENT CHILD-DEVELOPMENT THINKING

Theories about how children develop are complex. There are many different ways that child development can be approached. Some commentators take a traditional developmental view, which states that children go through stages of development, not necessarily at the same time but they all go through them in the same order (Mussen et al., 1990). Others criticise this approach and consider it is too deterministic. There is a large body of work, for example, that emphasises the impact of different social expectations of child rearing on children's development (see, for example, Woodhead, 1999). Attachment behaviour in children may differ between cultures, according to what is expected socially (Quinton, 1994). There are also differences in the concept of relationships between self and others, influenced by the cultural expectations of how far adults should be autonomous individuals or should base their identity on being seen having an obligation to a group (Owusu-Bempah & Howitt, 2000).

This chapter takes what may broadly be described as a developmental–ecological approach to children's development (Aldgate, 2006; Jones & Ramchandani, 1999). Such an approach recognises that dissimilar pathways can arrive at similar destinations in terms of the experiences of the developing child. Conversely, similar pathways can have quite diverse outcomes because of factors within children, such as temperament. Further, development is a process that involves interactions between the growing child and his or her social environment.

The developmental–ecological model gives scope to identify and assess the range of positive and negative influences which may have an impact on outcome in terms of a child's development. This has relevance to looked-after children, especially where child maltreatment has been the main reason for admission to the care system. Jones and Ramchandani suggest that:

> Once abuse has occurred there are a number of intervening factors which influence outcome. These include the individual child's coping skills and strategies, parental and family support, and societal influence including the impact of child protection procedures and, where offered, psychological treatment.
>
> (1999, pp. 3–4)

Although Jones and Ramchandani are clear about the potential for change, they also urge caution in recognising that change may be slow. Where there are severe developmental problems caused by child maltreatment, recovery, though not insurmountable, may be more difficult. Cicchetti and Lynch (1993), for example, assert that there are serious differences in developmental disadvantage between abused and non-abused children. What happens when children enter the care system, therefore, will be critical to their long-term developmental outcomes.

This chapter selects aspects of children's development of special relevance to looked-after children: these include attachment, separation, socio-genealogical connectedness, attainment, and stability. It begins by placing developmental thinking in the context of the ecological perspective, the strengths and resilience approaches in developmental psychology, and the part played by children in their own development.

THE ECOLOGICAL PERSPECTIVE

The ecological perspective is a useful approach to identifying the complex influences on children's development. First advanced by Bronfenbrenner in 1979, it has gained much credibility in child welfare policy (see, for example, Department of Health, 2000). The study of a child's ecology suggests there are different sources of influence on development. Some factors are within children, such as genetic factors. Others are outwith the child and include family, community, and culture (Bronfenbrenner, 1979, 1986). The ecological system also allows for the impact of government policies on child care and family life (Daniel et al., 1999). Children themselves play a part in shaping their own development (see Aldgate et al., 2006). Different parts of the system can interact with each other. There can be compensatory elements, for example, a stressful home can be compensated for by excellent and unstressful experiences at school.

In the best circumstances, children's ecology will be positive across most, if not all, aspects of their development, but children in need, by definition, are likely to have some challenges within their ecology as well as positive inputs. An ecological approach to assessing children's development looks at both strengths and weaknesses in the ecology and provides a model whereby negative factors in some areas can be compensated for by positive inputs from elsewhere. Such an approach is helpful because it sets the role of children's birth-parents in context, recognising that their influence, albeit important, is only one part of the ecology (Schaffer, 1992).

When children become looked after, it should, in theory, be possible to ask how the experience can enhance the positive aspects of their development. Indeed, such evidence has to be provided in a care plan for all looked-after children, but especially where there are compulsory proceedings within family courts or children's hearings (Hunt & McLeod, 1999; Scottish Office, 1997). Further, plans have to identify how the care system, far from reinforcing any sense of failure or lack of self-esteem, should help to promote children's welfare and effect optimal developmental outcomes for every looked-after child.

The ecological perspective has been incorporated into the framework for the assessment of children originating in England and Wales, and has become familiar through the Department of Health's triangle, which has safeguarding and promoting the child's welfare at its centre, surrounded by three domains of the child's developmental needs, parenting capacity, and family and environ-mental factors (Department of Health et al., 2000). Recent work in Scotland on the development of a similar assessment and recording framework has kept an ecological perspective but has modified the triangle to take into account a child's view of the world, with three domains. These are identified as: 'how I grow and develop', 'what I need from people who look after me', and 'my wider world' (Scottish Executive, 2005).

Both approaches are relevant to the development of looked-after children. Both approaches acknowledge the complexity of influences on children's development. The Scottish triangle brings a child-centred view of development and focuses on the child's present needs. Writers such as Ben-Arieh (2002) have stressed the importance of seeing the 'here' and 'now' as a significant phase for every child. To this end, Ben-Arieh distinguishes between concepts of children's *well-being* in the 'here' and 'now', and their *well-becoming* as adults (Ben-Arieh, 1997). A main theme of this chapter is that attention to present well-being will predict positive well-becoming.

RECOGNISING THE UNIQUENESS OF INDIVIDUAL CHILDREN

Perhaps, most importantly, the ecological approach allows for a view of the individual child that moves away from defining groups of children as 'different' or 'abnormal'. Rather, it creates a context in which each individual child can be accepted and valued as unique. The aim surely is to ensure looked-after children move towards a status of being ordinary children. As Coleridge (1993, p. 73) suggests:

> integration is ultimately about removing barriers, not normalisation, cure, or care. Reha-bilitation conducted within a comprehensive social framework is about the removal of barriers and attitudinal barriers in society at large.

THE WELL-NESS APPROACH

Apart from emphasising that all children are to be valued as individuals, looking at children's development through an ecological lens has also helped to reframe attitudes to assessment and intervention. Looking at any deficits is balanced by looking at strengths. This more balanced view of both children and families reflects general trends in developmental psychology towards looking at 'well-being' and 'well-ness' rather than illness. Such an approach does not deny the negative experiences and their legacies but concentrates on strengths to identify what can be done to improve matters. As Kelly suggests:

> The work of psychologists is moving from an emphasis upon the troubles, the anxieties, the sickness of people, to an interest in how we acquire positive qualities, and how social influences contribute to perceptions of well-being, personal effectiveness, and even joy. There will be signs that, in the future, psychologists less and less will be viewing us as having diseases. Instead the psychological view will be one of persons in process over time and as participants in social settings.
>
> (Kelly, 1974, p. 1, quoted in Lorion, 2000, p. 5)

This approach is very helpful in moving away from a success/failure model of development to one which allows for permutations of well-ness. As Aldgate (2006, p. 11) suggests: 'Most of us will never achieve the ideal but that does not matter. The agenda here is "to process" and, it could be argued, make progress, not to be labelled as ill or failed.'

RESILIENCE AND STRENGTHS

The most powerful application of the ecological perspective for looked-after children is that it provides the possibility of a compensatory model of care, where negative influences in the past can be compensated by protective factors in the future. If protective factors can outweigh negative ones, this will help children become resilient. Resilience has been defined by Fonagy and colleagues (1994, p. 231) as 'normal development under difficult conditions'.

Resilient children are likely to do better than their past circumstances might predict. The application of resilience in practice has been developed by several key writers, such as Gilligan (2001), Seligman (1995), and Daniel and Wassell (2002). Gilligan suggests a list of protective factors influencing the development of resilience. Children will become more resilient to adverse circumstances if they have the following:

- supportive relationships with at least one person;
- supportive relationships with siblings and grandparents;
- a committed adult other than a parent who takes a strong interest in the young person and serves as a long-term mentor and role model;
- a capacity to develop and reflect on a coherent story about what has happened and is happening to them;

- talents and interests;
- positive experiences in school;
- positive friendships;
- a capacity to think ahead and plan in their lives.

(Gilligan, 2001, pp. 189–191)

There are examples of how the theory of resilience has been translated into practice tools. Seligman, for example, has developed a programme aimed at overcoming depression in childhood. He stresses the role that adults can play in helping children learn from and utilise difficult experiences (Seligman, 1995). Daniel and Wassell (2002) have developed a useful guide to assessing and promoting resilience in children across the different stages of childhood.

Gilligan has written about the importance of schools and achievement in building self-esteem, self-efficacy, and resilience (1998, 2000). Gilligan (1998) believes that children's experiences at school have a deep and lasting effect on their social and educational development. Success can also be defined in terms of other kinds of achievements, such as being good at sport or being creative in the arts. Ben-Arieh (2002) believes one of the most important areas for developing children's sense of self-esteem is to make a contribution to their communities. Achieving success in any area can promote self-esteem and self-efficacy. This develops a sense of control and empowerment and an ability to adapt and respond positively to life-challenges at a later stage (Daniel et al., 1999; Rutter, 1985). As Daniel et al. comment: 'Children with high self-esteem see successes due to their own efforts, resources and abilities but are realistic, and have a sense of personal control over successes and failures' (1999, p. 216).

AN OPTIMISTIC VIEW OF CHILD DEVELOPMENT

Although the caveats suggested by Jones and Ramchandani (1999) about the difficulties of improving developmental outcomes for abused children must be remembered, both the ecological perspective and the recognition that children can be resilient in the face of adversity suggest a much more optimistic view of childhood. This is summed up by Schaffer (1992). His view is very relevant to meeting the developmental needs of looked-after children:

> We now know that whatever stresses an individual may have encountered in the early years, he or she need not be for ever more at the mercy of the past. There are survivors as well as victims; children's resilience must be acknowledged every bit as much as their vulnerability; single horrific experiences, however traumatic at the time, need not lead to permanent harm but can be modified and reversed by subsequent experiences; children who miss out on particular experiences at the usual time may well make up for them subsequently; and healthy development can occur under a far wider range of circumstances than was thought possible at one time.

(Schaffer, 1992, p. 40)

CHILDREN AS ACTORS IN THEIR OWN DEVELOPMENT

So far, in this chapter, there has been an emphasis on the inputs by others that can make a difference to children's development. Increasingly, writers on the subject recognise that children themselves play a major part in shaping their own childhoods, including their relationships with other children and adults in their world. Children's individuality, their temperaments, and their actions are significant in influencing how others interact with them. As Aldgate suggests:

> It used to be thought that children were 'blank slates' upon which the influence of those around them could be imprinted. Now it is recognised that there are *transactions* between each individual child and his or her environment. This can occur in several ways. Children will elicit positive or negative responses in adults. Children's individual temperament and their behaviour will shape the responses they elicit in those who influence their lives.
>
> (2006, p. 11)

Schaffer believes that children actively select and shape environments that are appropriate to their own characteristics:

> Children themselves seek out and construct compatible environments and in this way help to determine which settings will have an opportunity to influence their own development – surely a much more dynamic and truly reciprocal view of the social influence process.
>
> (Schaffer, 1992, p. 46)

Even very young children can shape the responses of others to them (Murray & Andrews, 2000). Lansdown further suggests that 'children can, when empowered to do so, act as a source of expertise, skill and information for adults and contribute towards meeting their own needs' (2001, p. 93).

The children's rights and participation movement has also been instrumental in demonstrating that children may be capable of advanced social behaviour at early ages (see, for example, Clark & Moss, 2001; Hill et al., 2004; Prout & Hallett, 2003; Tisdall & Davis, 2004). The right of children to be involved in decision-making which affects their lives (as spelt out by Section 12 [1] of the *United Nations Convention on the Rights of the Child* [United Nations, 1989]) is now embedded in child-welfare legislation within the UK. The establishment of children's commissioners within the different countries of the UK is further testament to the awareness of children's potential contribution to all matters that are likely to affect their development and well-being.

Children's right to be involved in decisions that affect them has special resonance for looked-after children, where serious decisions are being made about where they should live and what should happen to them. Looked-after children have told researchers that they value being involved in planning and review, but that this inclusion needs to be child-friendly (Aldgate & Statham, 2001; Grimshaw & Sinclair, 1997). In terms of children's development, genuine empowerment of children is a way of increasing their social skills, self-esteem, and self-efficacy.

ASPECTS OF CHILDREN'S DEVELOPMENT OF SPECIAL RELEVANCE TO LOOKED-AFTER CHILDREN

Clearly, every aspect of children's development is as important for looked-after children as it is for any other child. Much has been written about the poor outcomes in the health of looked-after children, suggesting that their physical and mental health are often very poor in comparison with their peers (Chambers et al., 2003). Substance misuse in adolescence is a major contributory factor. The poor outcomes are clearly an indictment of the looked-after system.

If developing problems in children's physical and mental health do not receive timely attention, they can undoubtedly affect other aspects of their physical, social, and emotional development, which will become manifest in their behaviour (Meltzer et al., 2004; Ward et al., 2002). This fact provides a context for looking in more detail at aspects of emotional and social development that have special relevance in relation to looked-after children. There are three fundamental questions which all looked-after children should be able to answer:

- Who am I?
- Who do I belong to?
- What is going to happen to me?

The rest of this chapter explores four different but related aspects of children's emotional and social development, all relating to the three questions posed above. It looks at attachment (including new thinking on multiple attachments for children) and then examines the impact on children's development of separation and loss, and goes on to look at children's genealogical connections with attachment-figures. It suggests that stability or instability within the care system can provide a positive environment for children's development, and ends with implications for policy and practice.

CHILDREN'S ATTACHMENTS

It is impossible to talk about attachment in children without reference to John Bowlby, whose seminal work over three decades from the 1950s to the 1980s remains pivotal in understanding the importance of attachment in children's development. Bowlby has been much quoted and misquoted. He has been criticised for being mother-focused, neglecting fathers, and not being aware about cultural diversities in patterns of attachment. Many of these criticisms do not hold up in the light of the wording of Bowlby's own texts, and in the context of subsequent cross-cultural research (see Aldgate & Jones, 2006). In some of his earliest writing, Bowlby (1958) uses the term 'principal attachment figure' or 'mothering figure' rather than the term 'mother'. He recognised that the nature and behaviour of that figure are more important than its designated status. He also described how children could have multiple attachment-figures ([1969] 1982).

WHAT IS ATTACHMENT?

Bowlby's thesis, which still holds today, but in a different cultural and social context, is based on the idea that attachment is a biological response which arises from a desire of an individual (either adult or child) to seek security and protection from harm through proximity to an attachment-figure (who is seen as stronger and wiser), with the ultimate aim of survival from predators, and, thereby, preservation of the species. This biological approach to attachment is, in Bowlby's view, an evolutionary adaptation to self-preservation. Today, attachment-behaviour is considered 'a normal and healthy characteristic of humans throughout the life span, rather than a sign of immaturity that needs to be outgrown' (Cassidy, 1999, p. 5). Attachments, therefore, can last over time, and can be formed at any stage of the life-cycle.

It is generally thought that attachment-behaviour in children occurs from around seven months (Aldgate & Jones, 2006; Mussen et al., 1990). All children will show affectional behaviour towards their carers from much earlier (Murray & Andrews, 2000). Sometimes, this has been mistaken for attachment-behaviour. Attachment is only one part of a complex system of emotional and sociable development: it is closely related to the exploratory behavioural system and the fear behavioural system. When children are afraid, they will display attachment-behaviour. The aim of this behaviour is not the person to whom they turn as an attachment-figure, but it is to regain a state of equilibrium. When a young child feels safe, that child will be sociable and curious. A child's exploratory system will be suppressed when attachment-behaviour is activated.

Attachment refers only to a specific aspect of a child–care-giver relationship, and is activated through fear. It does not refer to the whole of the affectional relationship between child and parenting figure. This distinction is critical to an understanding of attachment-behaviour in looked-after children. Furthermore, attachment between child and adult is one-way only. It refers to the child seeking adult protection when he or she is frightened. Children may employ behaviours (such as signalling, calling out, or moving) to be in proximity to attachment-figures. Attachment-behaviours will to some extent be culturally determined (Quinton, 1994). Children learn to behave according to the response of their care-givers whom they see as attachment-figures.

Attachment-behaviour in the child is separate from, but parallel to, the behaviour of the care-giver who is seen by a child as an attachment-figure. This is a fundamental point – that the care-giver system is separate from the attachment-system in the child, although the two are closely related. The care-giving system needs to be seen as working in parallel with the attachment-system. It provides behaviour on the part of the care-giver that ideally responds to and pre-empts the child's attempts to gain protection. So care-givers need to be sensitive to children. A child who does not get a consistent response when engaging in seeking security will learn that the care-giver/attachment-figure is unreliable. The child is then likely to transfer this learning to other significant people in his or her world, such as siblings, friends, and adults, like childminders or teachers (see Berlin & Cassidy, 1999), resulting in behaviour which can be seen as problematic.

The care-giver can indeed have an affectional relationship with the child but it is the child who is attached and the care-giver who provides care-giving behaviour which enables the child to feel secure. So, in relation to looked-after children, it is not necessary for foster carers initially to feel an emotional connection with the children they are looking after so long as their care-giving behaviour is consistent with a sensitive response to the attachment-needs of those children. The care-giving response for many looked-after children will call for heightened sensitivity and persistence, especially in cases where children have learnt that the world is unsafe and that they cannot trust anyone. This has implications for securing adequate training and support for foster carers and residential staff.

Attachment-patterns develop early in childhood. Over time, children will develop a strong and lasting attachment-bond but this cannot exist on its own, and is embedded in an enduring affectional relationship. Children learn to respond to the actions of their care-givers to them. Usually the primary carer will be a parent, but this is not always so. Children's patterns of attachment will be influenced by what the care-giver does, not who the care-giver is. Children internalise their care-givers' responses into an internal working model. This initially sets a pattern of expectation for subsequent experiences but, as suggested later, patterns of attachment can be disconfirmed by later experiences. It is generally agreed that there are four patterns of attachment: secure; ambivalent; avoidant; and disorganised (see Howe, 1995, 2001).

Children in need may well have experienced inconsistent or rejecting care-giving behaviour. Those who have learnt the avoidant pattern may often be very self-reliant, finding that seeking an attachment-figure elicits little response, and that they have to rely instead on themselves. Those whose attachments have been ambivalent or disorganised may display behaviours such as helplessness, aggression, or attention-seeking (Howe, 2001). It is because patterns of attachment can have such a serious effect on behaviour and on children's perception of those in their world that they are so important to children's well-being and development.

CHILDREN AND MULTIPLE ATTACHMENTS

Of considerable interest for the looked-after child is recent thinking on children who experience multiple attachments. A leading researcher on attachment in the USA (Howes, 1999) has suggested that it is more helpful to look at children's networks of attachment-relationships rather than concentrating on a hierarchy or primary attachment-figure. In today's diverse family life-styles, that view about hierarchy of attachments has been revised, influenced by a greater understanding about attachment in different cultures across the world. It is now suggested that children who have multiple carers may have patterns of attachment that are spread more evenly among them. Children's internal working models will relate to the quality of all the attachment-relationships in their network. This new line of thinking suggests that children who experience multiple carers from early on will give equal weight to each experience: the quality of attachment will influence outcome, and two secure attachments, for example, will be more powerful than one that is secure.

Howes (1999, p. 673) proposes that the following questions need to be asked in order to identify attachment figures in multiple care situations:

- Does this person provide physical and emotional care?
- Is this person a consistent presence in the child's social network?
- Is this person emotionally invested in the child?

It is possible to fit immediate and extended family, foster carers, and residential carers into this line of questioning. Although foster carers and residential staff may not be *emotionally connected* to children, their roles demand they have an *emotional investment* in wanting a child to flourish.

A further refining of this idea is that each attachment-relationship is *independent* in its quality and influence. Different attachment-relationships may predominately have an effect on one domain of development. Such a pattern has been evident for many years in cultures where adults are ascribed special roles in relation to one aspect of children's development. The new independent model of attachment suggests, for example, a mother may influence a child's sense of competence while attachment to a father may influence how a child deals with conflict (Howes, 1999). A grandparent, who does not see a child every day, may help a child recognise the qualitative dimension of attachment. This new thinking, though still in its developmental stage, has positive implications for the roles and tasks of carers of looked-after children (for further reference, see Aldgate & Jones, 2006; Howes, 1999).

CONTINUITIES AND DISCONTINUITIES OF WORKING MODELS

Related to the positive potential of multiple attachments is the evidence from studies of continuities and discontinuities between patterns of attachment learned in early childhood and subsequent discontinuities of those experiences. Although there is still a widely held view that childhood patterns will be carried into adult life and will influence care-giver behaviour towards the next generation (see, for example, Howe et al., 1999), it is now known that the pattern of those relationships is not fixed: they can be 'discontinued' and children and adults can 'disconfirm' or change the way they have learnt to see others. Inter-generational research on parenting has shown that many intervening experiences (including relationships with new carers, professionals, and adult partners) can influence individuals' working models and their states of mind, both through childhood and into adulthood (Berlin & Cassidy, 1999; Bowlby, 1953;

Rutter, 1985; Rutter & Quinton, 1984). Howe reflects the interest in discontinuities in attachment throughout the life-cycle:

> A lifespan approach is now taken to attachment theory. There is great interest in the continuities and discontinuities that affect attachment styles and internal working models from childhood to adulthood. In their attempts to promote children's welfare. social workers seek to disconfirm children's insecure working models, either by improving the quality of their close relationships with parents and peers, or by providing them with new care-giving relationships in substitute families.
>
> (2001, p. 205)

Contemporary approaches aimed at helping practitioners assess the impact of childhood attachment on adults are moving towards the line taken by Main in the USA. Main's tool for assessing attachment in adults (see Hesse, 1999; Howe et al., 1999) stresses that it is what individuals have made of experiences of attachment rather than the experiences themselves that are important (see Aldgate & Jones, 2006).

Information about how discontinuities occur is also emerging. Recent research in the USA on attachment between small children and alternative carers (such as extended family and foster carers) suggests that the process of making new attachments is similar, whenever it occurs. In other words, children construct their attachment-relationships on the basis of repeated and frequent interactions with new care-givers. Children are able to reorganise their attachment-behaviour on the basis of being with sensitive care-givers who respond consistently to their needs (Aldgate & Jones, 2006; Howes, 1999).

It is, however, not so easy for some children to make new attachments. Those who have had repeated experience of feeling emotionally unsafe will find it very hard to show trust in new relationships with adults. This is one of the key factors that make recovery from serious maltreatment so difficult (Jones & Ramchandani, 1999). The care-giver (such as a foster carer), who looks after a toddler with previous experiences of inconsistent care-giving, may find that the child will not trust her for a very long time until the child has learned from repeated testing out of attachment-behaviour that this person can be a consistent and safe attachment-figure.

THE IMPACT OF LOSS ON CHILDREN'S DEVELOPMENT

Children who come into the care system are very much at risk of harm from loss of their attachment-figures. As Stevenson suggested in the 1960s (Stevenson, 1968), such an event will break the lifeline of the developing child. One of the main criticisms of the care system over at least two decades has been that the system itself creates further instability and change for children.

Placement instability emerges as a significant problem in two decades of research in the UK (see, for example, Berridge & Cleaver, 1987; Department of Health,

1991; Department of Health and Social Security, 1985; Kelly, 1995; Ward et al., forthcoming). The scale of the problem in different parts of the UK is not reliably known but recent research by Ward et al. (forthcoming) suggests that there is an increase in babies being admitted to the care system and that some of those have on average up to six moves in one year.

Owusu-Bempah (1995) urges acknowledgement of the complexity of the psycho-social mechanisms involved in children's adjustment to separation and loss. Children separated from adult attachment-figures will go through a process of protest, despair, and detachment (Bowlby, 1969, 1973). How children recover from such loss will depend on what happens next. A short parental absence may cause distress, but trust and positive attachments can be restored if the child is returned quickly to sensitive care-givers. The most enduring images of such experiences come from the films made by the Robertsons in the 1950s (see, for example, Robertson, 1952) which showed graphically the strength of children's emotions on separation and the mixture of equally strong emotions on return, including anger, clinging, and ignoring the parents.

Where children have a permanent loss of an attachment-figure through death or adoption, they need to be allowed to grieve that loss in an age-appropriate way. Above all, they need to have very sensitive care-giving which allows them to express their grief and to find replacement attachment-figures (see Aldgate, 1991; Jewett, 1984).

The most vulnerable children are those with avoidant or disorganised patterns of attachment before they came into the care system. If such children are subject to further separations, which may easily happen, since children with such patterns of attachment are likely to test the staying power of the majority of carers, this will only increase children's sense of being unlovable. Children's behaviour in these cases is likely to present considerable challenges to their carers and professionals (Howe et al., 1999). It used to be thought that such children were avoiding new relationships solely because they were in conflict within themselves about previous attachments and wished to avoid further pain. Green has suggested that the problems for many children with multiple losses also emanate from their never having learned to be attached securely in the first place. The behaviour of these children is likely to be influenced by the fact that their development is impaired in the basic under-standing of social relationships or social communication (Green, 2003). Children whose attachments have been damaging to their development need to have those attachments discontinued: they need experienced care-givers, who are themselves secure in their adult attachments, and to have living circumstances where children can gain the attention and consistent response they need. In some cases, children will have to learn how to be social beings almost from scratch.

The new thinking on multiple attachments and the increasing body of research confirming that changes in attachment-patterns can be modified (Aldgate &

Jones, 2006) give practitioners a direction in which to work. However, although damage may be repaired, it would be better for it to be minimised in the first place. Recognising this fact has led policy-makers to stress the importance of children maintaining connections with their kin (e.g. Department of Health, 1990; Scottish Office, 1997) and the need to create stability in the care system (Berridge, 2000).

COUNTERACTING THE IMPACT OF LOSS AND SEPARATION WITH CONTACT AND CONNECTEDNESS

Contact between looked-after children and their families has consistently been shown to be the key to reunification (Aldgate, 1980; Cleaver, 2000; Pine et al., 2002). Cleaver's research showed that looked-after children tend to have more contact than they used to, and that this appears to be associated with placement stability and general well-being (Cleaver, 2000; Thoburn, 1994), but the association between children's patterns of attachment to their parents prior to being looked after and the quality of contact is unclear. However, quality of contact is associated with stability in the placement (Thomas, 2005). Thomas suggests that contact can bring to the surface painful feelings about separation with the result that children try to avoid contact or show their aversion through their behaviour.

In sympathy with the ideas on the potential of multiple attachments to promote children's emotional health and social development, Fahlberg (1994, p. 168) suggests that 'minimizing the trauma of separations and losses and working to facilitate the development of new attachments are complementary rather than competitive tasks'. In the same vein, current thinking on reunification suggests that there is room for a flexible definition of a successful reunification aimed at:

> helping each child and family to achieve and maintain, at any given time, their optimal level of reconnection – from full reentry of the child into the family system to other forms of contact, such as visiting, that affirms the child's membership of the family.
> (Warsh et al., 1994, p. 3)

Little work has been done on looking specifically at the relationship between children's patterns of attachments with their parents and reunification, although it has been suggested that it is harder to reunify children with emotional and behavioural difficulties (Pine et al., 2002). Programmes of intensive preparation of both children and parents have been found to be effective in the USA (Pine et al., 2002).

Research with young people who have left the care system suggests that the maintenance of attachments and ties with parents, siblings, and the wider family is important to young people's sense of identity and belonging (Marsh & Peel, 1999; McAuley, 2004).

ATTACHMENTS AND SOCIO-GENEALOGICAL CONNECTEDNESS

A different way of looking at attachment (which has considerable relevance to looked-after children who, for whatever reason, cannot maintain contact with their kin) comes from the theory of socio-genealogical connectedness. Both constructs make similar assumptions about attachment and children's emotional health, but socio-genealogical connectedness puts less emphasis on actual contact and more on the information about attachment-figures that children possess (Owusu-Bempah, 2005; Owusu-Bempah & Howitt, 1997):

> The notion of socio-genealogical connectedness refers to the extent to which children identify with their birth parents' biological and social backgrounds, it refers to the extent to which a child sees him/herself as an offshoot of his/her parents' backgrounds, both in the biological and social sense. A basic tenet of the theory is that the degree to which children identify with their parents' backgrounds is dependent on the amount and quality of information they possess about their parents... An equally fundamental assumption is that the greater a child's sense of connectedness is, the better adjusted the child will be.
>
> (Owusu-Bempah & Howitt, 1997, p. 201)

This theory is a useful map through the minefields of attachment and contact for all children who live in separation from one or both parents. It also offers a way of dealing with situations where coming face to face with parents is likely to cause children further significant emotional harm. It has special relevance for all children who are in permanent placements without face-to-face contact.

Socio-genealogical connectedness does not see contact as a *sine qua non* in promoting the retention of attachments, rather it complements attachment-theory in suggesting that children's knowledge of significant, absent attachment-figures will influence their internal working models of themselves and those around them. Both theories recognise that the modifying of internal working models is important to 'increase children's potential to deal with their emotional, interpersonal and behavioural problems' (Owusu-Bempah & Howitt, 1997, p. 205).

Socio-genealogical connectedness also fits with an ecological approach to development, allowing for the influences of the wider family and environment to enhance a child's sense of continuity and general well-being, and thereby compensate for the negative impact of an absent parent or other primary attachment-figure (Owusu-Bempah & Howitt, 1997).

The theory has relevance to any child who is in need of a permanent placement, including a child in kinship care. Provided kin do not impart negative information about parents to children, which can happen (Lernihan, 2003), Owusu-Bempah (2005) suggests that maintaining connectedness through relationships with family members and other significant adults can give children continuity to enhance their emotional well-being. Research would support these arguments. Marsh and Peel (1999), for example, noted the significance of belonging to a family in their study of young people leaving care, even if there had been no contact with family members for several years.

COUNTERACTING THE IMPACT OF SEPARATION WITH STABILITY

It has already been suggested that instability continues to be a major problem in the care system. If children move frequently, they lose not only their carers, but access to social supports within their communities, relationships with peers, and continuity in school. This catalogue of losses will deprive children of the opportunity of enhancing self-esteem and self-efficacy from social interactions and achievements.

There are many causes of instability, but the most common reasons for unplanned change are the child's behaviour problems, rivalry in relationships between foster children and the family's own children, contact with birth-parents, and events within the foster family (Aldgate & Hawley, 1986; Berridge, 2000; Berridge & Cleaver, 1987; Kelly, 1995). Kinship care breaks down less frequently than 'stranger' care, irrespective of its planned length (Broad, 2001; Lernihan, 2003), but when it does, it can be devastating for all concerned since children face yet another rejection by their families. The problem of placement stability seems to be greatest for older children and those with serious behavioural problems (Berridge, 2000).

There are several ways that stability can be enhanced. Studies have shown that the characteristics of carers are important. According to Berridge (2000, p. 4), foster carers providing the greatest stability are felt to do the following:

- enjoy being with children;
- be flexible but firm;
- be emotionally resilient;
- communicate openly and honestly;
- be amenable to outside support.

It is also noted that foster placements where there are proper salaries, training, and support for carers seem to work best for children of all ages (Berridge, 2000).

Residential care remains an important option for older looked-after children, but Berridge suggests that there are complexities in creating stability in residential homes. Often children arrive in an emergency, and there is sometimes the challenge of group dynamics. In spite of this, changing the young persons' eco-system by moving them from their destructive and deviant influences can break the cycle of participating in delinquent networks (Berridge, 2000).

One major problem for children's development is that when they move placements they have tended to move school (Berridge, 2000), resulting in poor motivation and poor attendance, because the school places and placements are not found at the same time. Solutions are not easy: there may be difficult choices to be made between long journeys (to maintain continuity with a school) or facing the challenge of making new relationships and starting over again.

Although, as suggested earlier, school can be a positive influence for children, writers such as Hunt (2000) have identified several factors that inhibit looked-after children's educational opportunities. There are, for example, myths that looked-after children have learning difficulties because of their life experiences: teachers and social workers may have low expectations about such children's potential. Children may be placed in homes where there is little emphasis on carers' abilities to help children with educational progress (Hunt, 2000). Jackson and Martin (1998) suggest that a fundamental change is needed in relation to the education of looked-after children. Policy-makers across the UK have begun to give more attention to the educational attainment of looked-after children by setting targets for attainment, allocating financial resources, and appointing teachers with special responsibilities for looked-after children (Department for Education and Skills and Department of Health, 2000; Scottish Executive, 2002). The outcome of these measures on the well-being and development of children is not yet known.

A PERMANENCY PLANNING APPROACH

This chapter has emphasised the part children's circumstances, attachment, connections, and stability play in the positive development of looked-after children. Primary legislation relating to the upbringing of children across the different countries of the UK in the 1980s and 1990s pushed towards policies which, in theory, offered a range of permanency options, including strengthening family support and more trenchant planning in relation to compulsory measures (see Aldgate & Statham, 2001; Hill & Aldgate, 1996). In practice, it has proved very difficult to retain the balance between giving children the stability of the parental home and creating stability in different ways away from home (Aldgate & Statham, 2001). Permanency planning is as much about offering family support and planned periods of short-term care as it is about offering long-term foster or residential placements and adoption. Above all, a permanency planning approach to services needs to have at the forefront the developmental needs of children at different stages of childhood.

WHAT CAN HELP PROMOTE CHILDREN'S DEVELOPMENT IN PRACTICE?

If children's development is to count for more in the planning and delivery of child-welfare services for looked-after children, several things need to happen.

Firstly, there needs to be a multi-disciplined workforce, whose members understand the impact on children's development of attachment-relationships, a child's ecology, and building resilience. Such a workforce needs key workers (who will usually be social workers but who could also be carers or teachers) who will commit themselves to be children's champions, acting as good parents would do, ensuring children feel cherished and secure, and making a point of championing children's achievements. Wherever possible, workers should stay the course with children as long as possible. If they leave, transitions should be made as smoothly as possible, using techniques for saying goodbyes such as those advocated by Jewett (1984).

Secondly, there is a case for a new approach to working with looked-after children which pays attention to all aspects of their development. Petrie (2004) has suggested that much could be gained from adopting a social pedagogy perspective embracing every aspect of children's development:

> As used in continental Europe, the word 'pedagogy' relates to the overall support for children's development. In pedagogy, care and education meet. To put it another way, pedagogy is about bringing up children, it is 'education' in the broadest sense of that word...

> Parents are sometimes referred to as the first pedagogues, but pedagogy is also a foundational concept that informs many sorts of services, providing a distinctive approach to practice, training and policy. In continental Europe, the terms 'education' and pedagogy imply work with the whole child: body, mind, feelings spirit and creativity. Crucially, the child is seen as a social being, connected to others and at the same time with their own distinctive experiences and knowledge.
>
> (Petrie, 2004)

Thirdly, the skills of social workers in relation to children and their families must improve. Planning and reviewing of children should have meaning and purpose and should consider the impact of change on children's development. Planning for new attachments can be positive and may mark a turning-point for some children, who should be consulted about their wishes and feelings. There is an urgent need to reinstate direct work with children as an essential part of the social work role. Direct work can be effective in helping children to move from one place to another and to manage loss and change. A recent review of social work in Scotland (Social Work Review Team, Scottish Executive, 2005) commented on the damage the change of role from direct worker to care-manager had done to practice. Until recently, direct work as described in the early 1990s (see, for example, Aldgate & Simmonds, 1991) seemed to have become lost to mainstream social work practice. Recent developments have indicated a renaissance of manuals of guidance for this kind of work (see Aldgate et al., 2006). It is imperative that direct work is reclaimed in order to help children come to terms with their past and move on.

Fourthly, if the care system is to take seriously its mandate in law to safeguard and promote the welfare of children in need, attention needs to be paid to strengthen the roles and tasks attached to corporate parenting. Local authorities can never replicate children's families, but they can delegate roles and accountability to individuals to ensure that every child in care is given the best possible environment in which to develop positively. High on the list should be enduring positive relationships with adults who can make a difference to children's lives and help build resilience.

Finally, there needs to be a sea-change in attitudes of social workers and others working with children. Practice should embrace the optimism of contemporary developmental psychology, and there is an urgent need to depart from the idea that vulnerable children will be held back by their pasts. Furman, for example, has written extensively about how children survive abuse and adversity. His work emphasises how attitudes can influence the reappraisal of past adversities and can contribute to quality of life:

> It's natural to think that our past has an effect on how our future will turn out, but we rarely look at it the other way round. The future – that is what we think it will bring – determines what the past looks like.
>
> (Furman, 1997, p. 81)

Looked-after children need help to overcome past adversities, but becoming looked after should be a significant turning-point to provide the circumstances in which they can flourish. Looked-after children need the good parenting that is the right of ordinary children so that they can grow up in stable, loving relationships with adults committed to championing their present and future. This kind of ecology will give them the opportunity to achieve their developmental potential. In other words, they have the right to be extraordinary children in ordinary circumstances.

REFERENCES

Aldgate, J. (1980). Factors influencing children's stay in care. In J. Triseliotis (ed.), *New Developments in Foster Care and Adoption*. London: Routledge & Kegan Paul.

Aldgate, J. (1991). Attachment theory and its application to child care social work – an introduction. In J. Lishman (ed.), *Handbook of Theory for Practice Teachers in Social Work*. London: Jessica Kingsley.

Aldgate, J. (2006). The developing child. In J. Aldgate, D. Jones, W. Rose, & C. Jeffery (eds), *The Developing World of the Child*. London: Jessica Kingsley.

Aldgate, J., & Hawley, D. (1986). *Recollections of Disruption: A Study of Foster Home Breakdown*. London: National Foster Care Association.

Aldgate, J., & Jones, D. (2006). The place of attachment in children's development. In J. Aldgate, D. Jones, W. Rose, & C. Jeffery (eds), *The Developing World of the Child*. London: Jessica Kingsley.

Aldgate, J., Jones, D., Rose, W., & Jeffery, C. (eds) (2006). *The Developing World of the Child*. London: Jessica Kingsley.

Aldgate, J., & Simmonds, J. (eds) (1991). *Direct Work with Children*. London: Batsford.

Aldgate, J., & Statham, J. (2001). *The Children Act Now – Messages from Research*. London: The Stationery Office.

Ben-Arieh, A. (1997). Introduction: measuring and monitoring the state of children. In A. Ben-Arieh & H. Wintersberger (eds), *Monitoring and Measuring the State of Children beyond Survival*. Vienna: European Centre for Social Welfare Policy and Research.

Ben-Arieh, A. (2002). Evaluating the outcomes of programs versus monitoring well-being. In T. Vecchiato, A. Maluccio, & C. Canali (eds), *Evaluation in Child and Family Services*. New York: Aldine de Gruyter.

Berlin, L., & Cassidy, J. (1999). Relations among relationships contributions from attachment theory and research. In J. Cassidy & P.R. Shaver (eds), *Handbook of Attachment: Theory, Research and Clinical Applications*. New York and London: The Guilford Press.

Berridge, D. (2000). *Placement Stability*, Quality Protects Research Briefing No. 4. London: Department of Health, research into practice, Making Research Count.

Berridge, D., & Cleaver, H. (1987). *Foster Home Breakdown*. Oxford: Blackwell.

Bowlby, J. (1953). *Child Care and the Growth of Love*. Harmondsworth: Penguin.

Bowlby, J. (1958). The nature of the child's tie to its mother. *International Journal of Psycho-Analysis*, **39**, 350–353.

Bowlby, J. ([1969] 1982). *Attachment and Loss*, vol. 1. *Attachment*. New York: Basic Books.

Bowlby, J. (1973). *Attachment and Loss*, vol. II. *Separation Anxiety and Anger*. New York: Basic Books.

Broad, B. (2001). *Kinship Care: The Placement Choice for Children and Young People*. Lyme Regis: Russell House Publishing.

Bronfenbrenner, U. (1979). *The Ecology of Human Development*. Cambridge, MA: Harvard University Press.

Bronfenbrenner, U. (1986). Ecology of the family as a context for human development: Research perspectives. *Developmental Psychology*, **22**(6), 723–742.

Cassidy, J. (1999). The nature of the child's ties. In J. Cassidy & P. Shaver (eds), *Theory, Research and Clinical Applications*. New York and London: The Guilford Press.

Chambers, H., Howell, S., Madge, N., & Olle, H. (2003). *Healthy Care: Building an Evidence Base for Promoting the Health and Wellbeing of Looked After Children and Young People*. London: National Children's Bureau.

Cicchetti, D., & Lynch, M. (1993). Towards an ecological transactional model of community violence and child maltreatment: Consequences for children's development. *Psychiatry*, **56**(1), 96–118.

Clark, A., & Moss, P. (2001). *Listening to Young Children: The Mosaic Approach*. London: National Children's Bureau.

Cleaver, H. (2000). *Fostering Family Contact: A Study of Children, Parents and Foster Carers*. London: The Stationery Office.

Coleridge, P. (1993). *Disability, Liberation and Development*. Oxford: Oxfam.

Daniel, B., & Wassell, S. (2002). *Assessing and Promoting Resilience in Vulnerable Children* (3-volume set: the early years, the school years, adolescence). London: Jessica Kingsley.

Daniel, B., Wassell, S., & Gilligan, R. (1999). *Child Development for Child Care and Protection Workers*. London: Jessica Kingsley.

Department for Education and Skills and Department of Health (2000). *Guidance on the Education of Children and Young People in Public Care*. London: Department for Education and Skills and Department of Health.

Department of Health (1990). *Principles and Practice in Guidance and Regulations*. London: HMSO.

Department of Health (1991). *Patterns and Outcomes in Child Placement*. London: HMSO.

Department of Health (2000). *Assessing Children in Need and their Families: Practice Guidance*. London: The Stationery Office.

Department of Health and Social Security (1985). *Social Work Decisions in Child Care*. London: HMSO.

Department of Health, Department for Education, and Home Office (2000). *Framework for the Assessment of Children in Need and Their Families*. London: The Stationery Office.

Dixon, J., & Stein, M. (2005). *Leaving Care: Throughcare and Aftercare in Scotland*. London: Jessica Kingsley.

Fahlberg, V. (1994). *A Child's Journey Through Placement*. London: British Agencies for Adoption and Fostering.

Fonagy, P., Steele, M., Steele, H., Higgit, A., & Target, M. (1994). The theory and practice of resilience. *Journal of Child Psychology and Psychiatry*, **35**, 231–257.

Furman, B. (1997). *It's Never Too Late to Have a Happy Childhood: From Adversity to Resilience*. London: BT Press.

Gilligan, R. (1998). The importance of schools and teachers in child welfare. *Child and Family Social Work*, **3**, 13–25.

Gilligan, R. (2000). Adversity, resilience and young people: The protective value of positive school and spare time experiences. *Children and Society*, **14**, 37–47.

Gilligan, R. (2001). *Promoting Resilience: A Resource Guide on Working with Children in the Care System*. London: British Agencies for Adoption and Fostering.

Green, J. (2003). Concepts of child attachment. Paper given at the President's Interdisciplinary Conference, Dartington Hall, 12–14 September.

Grimshaw, R., & Sinclair, R. (1997). *Planning to Care: Regulations, Procedure and Practice Under the Children Act 1989*. London: National Children's Bureau.

Hesse, E. (1999). The adult attachment interview: Historical and current perspectives. In J. Cassidy & P. Shaver (eds), *Theory, Research and Clinical Applications*. New York and London: The Guilford Press.

Hill, M., & Aldgate, J. (eds) (1996). *Child Welfare Services: Developments in Law, Policy, Practice and Research*. London: Jessica Kingsley.

Hill, M., Davis, J., Prout, A., & Tisdall, K. (2004). Moving the participation agenda forward. *Children and Society*, **18**, 77–96.

Howe, D. (1995). *Attachment Theory for Social Work Practice*. Basingstoke: Macmillan.

Howe, D. (2001). Attachment. In J. Horwath (ed.), *The Child's World: Assessing Children in Need*. London: Jessica Kingsley.

Howe, D., Brandon, M., & Schofield, G. (1999). *Attachment Theory, Child Maltreatment and Family Support*. London: Macmillan.

Howes, C. (1999). Attachment relationships in the context of multiple carers. In J. Cassidy & P.R. Shaver (eds), *Handbook of Attachment: Theory, Research and Clinical Applications*. New York and London: The Guilford Press.

Hunt, J., & McLeod, A. (1999). *The Best Laid Plans: Outcomes of Judicial Decisions in Child Protection Proceedings*. London: The Stationery Office.

Hunt, R. (2000). *The Educational Performance of Children in Need and Children Looked After*, Quality Protects Research Briefing No. 1. London: Department of Health, research into practice, Making Research Count.

Jackson, S., & Martin, P.Y. (1998). Surviving the care system: Education and resilience. *Journal of Adolescence*, **21**, 569–583.

Jewett, C. (1984). *Helping Children Cope with Separation and Loss*. London: Batsford.

Jones, D.P.H., & Ramchandani, P. (1999). *Child Sexual Abuse: Informing Practice from Research*. Oxford: Radcliffe Medical Press.

Kelly, G. (1995). Foster parents and long-term placements: Key findings from a Northern Ireland study. *Children and Society*, **9**(2), 19–29.

Kelly, J.G. (1974). Towards a psychology of healthiness. Ichabod Spencer lecture, Union College.

Lansdown, G. (2001). Children's welfare and children's rights. In P. Foley, J. Roche, & S. Tucker (eds), *Children in Society*. Basingstoke: Palgrave/Open University Press.

Lernihan, U. (2003). Kinship foster care: Equal but different challenges for policy and practice. PhD thesis, Queen's University Belfast.

Lorion, R.P. (2000). Theoretical and evaluation issues in the promotion of wellness and protection of 'well enough'. In D. Cicchetti, J. Rappaport, I. Sandler, & P. Weissberg (eds), *The Promotion of Wellness in Children*. Washington, DC: Child Welfare League of America.

Marsh, P., & Peel, M. (1999). *Leaving Care in Partnership: Family Involvement with Care Leavers*. London: The Stationery Office.

McAuley, C. (2004). *Pathways and Outcomes: A Ten Year Follow Up of Children who Have Experienced Care*. Belfast: Department of Health, Social Services, and Public Safety.

Meltzer, H., Gatward, R., Corbin, T., Goodman, R., & Ford, T. (2004). *The Mental Health of Young People Looked After by Local Authorities in Scotland*. Edinburgh: The Stationery Office.

Murray, L., & Andrews, L. (2000). *The Social Baby*. Richmond, Surrey: C.P. Publishing.

Mussen, P.H., Canger, J.J., Kagan, J., & Huston, A.C. (1990). *Child Development and Personality*. New York: HarperCollins.

Owusu-Bempah, K. (1995). Information about the absent parent as a factor in the wellbeing of children of single-parent families. *International Social Work*, **38**, 253–257.

Owusu-Bempah, K. (2005). Socio-genealogical connectedness: knowledge and identity. In J. Aldgate, D. Jones, W. Rose, & C. Jeffery (eds), *The Developing World of the Child*. London: Jessica Kingsley.

Owusu-Bempah, K., & Howitt, D. (1997). Socio-genealogical connectedness, attachment theory, and childcare practice. *Child and Family Social Work*, **2**, 199–207.

Owusu-Bempah, K., & Howitt, D. (2000). *Psychology beyond Western Perspectives*. Leicester: BPS Books.

Petrie, P. (2004). *Pedagogy – A Holistic, Personal Approach to Work with Children and Young People, Across Services: European Models for Practice, Training, Education and Qualification*, Briefing Paper. London: Thomas Coram Research Unit, Institute of Education, University of London.

Pine, B.A., Healy, L.M., & Maluccio, A.N. (2002). Developing measurable program objectives: A key to evaluation of family reunification programs. In T. Vecchiato, A.N. Maluccio, & C. Canali (eds), *Evaluation in Child and Family Services*. New York: Aldine de Gruyter.

Prout, A., & Hallett, C. (eds) (2003). *Hearing the Voices of Children: Social Policy for a New Century*. London: Falmer Press.

Prout, A., & James, A. (1997). A new paradigm for the sociology of childhood? Provenance, promise and problems. In A. James & A. Prout (eds), *Constructing and Reconstructing Childhood*. London: Routledge Falmer.

Quinton, D. (1994). Cultural and community influences. In M. Rutter & D.F. Hay (eds), *Development Through Life: A Handbook for Clinicians*. Oxford: Blackwell Science.

Robertson, J. (1952). *A two-year-old goes to hospital* (Film: 16mm: 45min.; sound. Distributors: Tavistock Child Development Research Unit. London; New York University Film Library; United Nations, Geneva).

Rutter, M. (1985). Resilience in the face of adversity: Protective factors and resistance to psychiatric disorder. *British Journal of Psychiatry*, **147**, 598–611.

Rutter, M., & Quinton, D. (1984). Long-term follow-up of women institutionalised in childhood: Factors promoting good functioning in social life. *British Journal of Developmental Psychology*, **2**, 191–204.

Schaffer, H.R. (1992). Early experience and the parent–child relationship: Genetic and environmental interactions as developmental determinants. In B. Tizard & V. Varma (eds) (2000), *Vulnerability and Resilience in Human Development*. London: Jessica Kingsley.

Scottish Executive (2002). *Report on Educational Attainment of Looked after Children*. Edinburgh: Scottish Executive.

Scottish Executive (2003). *Improving Health in Scotland: The Challenge*. Edinburgh: Scottish Executive.

Scottish Executive (2005). *Getting It Right for Every Child: Proposals for Action*, parts 1–4. Edinburgh: Scottish Executive.

Scottish Office (1997). *The Children (Scotland) Act 1995, Regulations and Guidance*, vol. 2, *Children Looked After by Local Authorities*. Edinburgh: The Stationery Office.

Seligman, M.E.P. (1995). *The Optimistic Child*. New York: Harper Perennial.

Social Work Review Team, Scottish Executive (2005). *21st Century Review of Social Work: Interim Report*. Edinburgh: Scottish Executive.

Stein, M., & Carey, K. (1986). *Leaving Care*. Oxford: Blackwell.

Stevenson, O. (1968). Reception into care: Its meaning for all concerned. In R.J.N. Tod (ed.), *Children in Care*. London: Longmans.

Thoburn, J. (1994). *Child Placement Theory and Practice*. Aldershot: Arena.

Thomas, N. (2005). *Social Work with Young People in Care*. Basingstoke: Palgrave Macmillan.

Tisdall, K., & Davis, J. (2004). Making a difference? Bringing children's and young people's views into policy-making. *Children and Society*, **18**, 131–142.

United Nations (1989). *UN Convention on the Rights of the Child*. Geneva: United Nations.

Ward, H., Jones, H., Lynch, M., & Skuse, T. (2002). Issues concerning the health of looked after children. *Adoption and Fostering*, **26**(4), 8–18.

Ward, H., Macdonald, I., & Skuse, T. (forthcoming). *Looking After Children: Longitudinal Cohort Study – Final Report to the Department of Health*. Loughborough: University of Loughborough.

Warsh, R., Maluccio, A.N., & Pine, B.A. (1994). *Teaching Family Reunification: A Source-book*. Washington, DC: Child Welfare League of America.

Woodhead, M. (1999). Reconstructing developmental psychology – some first steps. *Children and Society*, **13**, 3–19.

CHAPTER 3

THE IMPORTANCE OF DEVELOPING EMOTIONAL BONDS BETWEEN PARENTS AND CHILDREN

Emma Larkin

INTRODUCTION

There is no doubt that the concept of parent–infant bonding has experienced a confusing and somewhat controversial theoretical evolution (Goulet et al., 1998; Sluckin et al., 1983). Indeed, while certain aspects of bonding theory have passed in and out of favour (including debate as to the existence and nature of a critical or sensitive period in which the bonding process occurs and even as to the value of the concept in the first place [e.g. Eyer, 1992]), the concept has achieved and retained wide popular appeal. In addition to being explored by various health-care professionals to help parents and their children, the bonding concept is also widely used among social work and other professionals who work in the family and child-care arena, whether with high-risk parental populations or with foster and adoptive parents. This chapter will introduce the concept of bonding, and explore the relationship between bonding and attachment. Factors that have been shown to influence the bonding process will also be discussed. The first half of this chapter will primarily refer to findings based on research with birth-parents and their children. Ways in which this information can and has been applied to alternative care providers such as long-term foster and adoptive parents will then be explored. Finally, ways in which the bonding process can be facilitated for foster and adoptive parents will be presented.

WHAT IS BONDING?

Although embedded in popular culture, the bonding construct has been relatively under-researched in recent decades and large gaps exist in our knowledge of the processes and mechanisms involved. At a basic level, confusion even exists as to

The Child's Journey Through Care: Placement Stability, Care Planning, and Achieving Permanency. Edited by D. Iwaniec.
Copyright © 2006 John Wiley & Sons, Ltd.

what 'bonding' means, although the earliest and simplest definition of bonding is as 'a tie from parent to infant' (Klaus & Kennell, 1982, p. 2).

Bonding research began in response to an observed phenomenon whereby premature infants in intensive-care units appeared to be more vulnerable to non-organic failure to thrive, abuse, and neglect. Researchers began investigating whether early post-natal separation led parents to miss out on a critical period for the bonding process. Such research appeared to show evidence for a sensitive period for bonding as extended post-partum contact was associated with both long- and short-term consequences for the parent, the child, and the parent–child relationship (e.g. Klaus et al., 1972; Ringler et al., 1975). Multiple pieces of research carried out in the 1970s appeared to provide evidence for a sensitive period (Brody, 1993). Further, the research climate at the time paved the way for widespread acceptance of bonding theory. For example, Bowlby's (1953) maternal deprivation hypothesis suggested that maternal deprivation leads to retarded development and emotional and mental-health problems. In addition, ethological research (e.g. Lorenz, 1970) claimed to show the existence of a short critical period post-birth with long-term consequences for development of attachment. As early bonding theory appeared to fit in with such thinking, it was received in a positive manner and recommendations were made to facilitate extra contact between parents and neonates. Bonding theory also began to inform family and child-care theory and practice.

However, the popularity of early bonding research was short-lived, and sensitive-period hypothesis research spanned just one decade. In addition to criticism of the methods used by researchers such as Klaus and Kennell (e.g. Klaus et al., 1972), early conceptualisations of bonding were also criticised. Definition of bonding as a unidimensional 'tie' from parent to infant did not recognise the role that fathers or the infants themselves played in the process and, importantly, failed to accommodate for parents who did not have early post-natal contact. Further, the notion of a critical or sensitive period during which bonding must occur was discredited as it was not sufficiently robust to take into consideration alternative early parenting scenarios such as those experienced by long-term foster or adoptive parents.

A number of definitional changes emerged in keeping with evolving conceptualisation of the theory. The term 'maternal attachment' began to replace the term 'bonding' in a move away from adherence to a sensitive-period approach (Mercer, 1990). The role of fathers in the process was later acknowledged through use of the term 'parental attachment' (e.g. Mercer & Ferketich, 1990). The contribution of the child and of the timing of the relationship was also recognised when bonding was defined as a bi-directional, reciprocal process that develops over time (e.g. Goulet et al., 1998; Mercer & Ferketich, 1994).

There remains considerable confusion and a general lack of uniformity in definitions of the terms 'parent–child bonding' and 'parent–child attachment' (Goulet et al., 1998). For example, based on a review of over 40 articles introducing nurses to the concept, Eyer (1992) found that there was no common definition and that the words 'attachment' and 'bonding' were used interchangeably. Distinctions between the concepts of parent–child bonding and parent–child attachment tend to be based on a view that 'bonding' represents the early and more limited conceptualisation of bonding as a unidirectional parent–infant response occurring in the post-partum period, while 'parent–child attachment' represents 'reformed' conceptualisation. However, others have argued for the continued use of the term 'bonding'. Klaus and Kennell, for example, justified their continued use of the term 'bonding' based on the premise that the word was so widely known (Klaus & Kennell, 1982). The term 'bonding' has a further advantage as it is more clearly distinguishable from the child–parent attachment phenomenon.

Bonding is generally believed to be a bi-directional, reciprocal process. It has also been defined as a cognitive and social process that develops through positive feedback and satisfying experiences between the attachment dyad (Mercer, 1990). This process is viewed as beginning during pregnancy and continuing after birth, and can be documented by observable quantifiable behaviours including seeking and maintaining close proximity to, and exchanging gratifying experiences with, the child (Mercer & Ferketich, 1990). 'Bonding' has also been defined as the extent to which a parent feels that a child occupies an essential position in his/her life and to which the interests of a child take precedence over the interests of the parent (Iwaniec et al., 2002).

Indicators of bonding serve to maintain contact and to exhibit affection and include behaviours such as cuddling and prolonged gazing (Klaus & Kennell, 1982; Mercer & Ferketich, 1990). Components of bonding have been described as including feelings of warmth, affection, love, sacrifice, a sense of possession and belonging, devotion, protection, and concern for the child's well-being, positive anticipation of prolonged contact, exchange of rewarding experiences, and a desire to maintain proximity (Iwaniec et al., 2002; Klaus & Kennell, 1982; Mercer, 1990).

In their concept-analysis of 'parent–infant attachment', Goulet et al. (1998) outline what they perceive to be three essential defining characteristics of the concept. These include proximity, reciprocity, and commitment. Proximity is described as the physical and psychological experience of the parent or carer being close to his or her child. Reciprocity is described as a process involving sensitivity and responsiveness of the parent or carer towards the child whereby the child plays an active role in eliciting parental response. Finally, commitment refers to the centrality of the child in the parent or carer's life, together with incorporation of the parental identity into the self-identity.

BONDING AND ATTACHMENT

While bonding and attachment share an evolutionary function of promoting behaviours that facilitate protection and survival, bonding is based around care-giving and security-promoting parental or carer behaviours, while attachment is based around care-seeking and security-seeking child behaviours. Bonding is one aspect of the care-giving behavioural system which is believed to be reciprocal and to operate in parallel to the attachment-behavioural system. These mutually beneficial interactive systems are viewed as having evolved to facilitate protection, survival, and reproductive fitness (Bowlby, [1969] 1982).

Both bonding and attachment are said to be regulated by strong emotions and are believed to be activated and deactivated by internal and external cues with a related repertoire of resulting behaviours. For example, bonding, as part of the care-giving system, is believed to be activated by cues associated with situations perceived as frightening, stressful, or dangerous (e.g. separation, child-engagement, and a child's verbal and non-verbal signals of discomfort or distress) (Bowlby, [1969] 1982; George & Solomon, 1999; Heard & Lake, 1997). Once the care-giving system is activated, a repertoire of behaviours comes into play including retrieval, proximity, carrying, calling, following, and smiling (George & Solomon, 1999). As with the attachment-system, it is believed that the care-giving system can also be deactivated by physical or psychological proximity (Bowlby, [1969] 1982).

Miller and Rodgers (2001) have mapped out an overview of systems that underlie all forms of bonding which is useful as it points to how the bonding process fits into and interacts with other sets of behaviours. Their ontogenic bonding system (OBS) divides the area of human bonding into four components that work together to form a 'suprasystem'. These four components include a soccorant (or an attachment) system that serves to bond a child to his or her parent, an affiliative bonding system that serves to promote friendships, a sexual bonding system that serves to promote romantic and sexual relationships, and finally, but of most importance to bonding theory, a nurturant bonding system that functions to bond a parent to her or his child and to promote care-giving.

The OBS is said to operate sequentially across the life-course, and each system is said to elicit responses from and to be responsive to each other system. The nurturant and soccorant systems are believed to form a complementary pair of systems that together influence the parent–child dyad. Because individuals are viewed as functioning within multiple flexible and interlinked behavioural spheres, other behavioural systems can complement, conflict with, or override the bonding system. Parents must, therefore, balance between the need to protect and care for their child and pursuing alternative behaviours (George & Solomon, 1999).

WHAT INFLUENCES THE BONDING PROCESS?

The bonding process is influenced by multiple biological, psychological, and social factors relating to the parent(s) or carer(s), the timing of the relationship, and context in which the relationship occurs. When looking at the ways in which bonding might be influenced, it is helpful to look at available models of parenting. One particularly useful model of parenting was provided by Belsky (1984) who argued for a continuum of influence in parenting determinants and provided three general conclusions: first, that parenting is multiply determined; second, that characteristics of the parent, of the child, and of the social context are not equally influential; and third, that developmental history and personality indirectly shape parenting, by first influencing the broader context in which parent–child relations exist.

The context in which parenting occurs is influential. For example, conditions in which parental investment may be reduced have been described as including poverty, famine, lack of support, very young parental age, short birth-spacing, child weakness, illness, or deformity, and questioned paternity (Simpson, 1999).

Factors that have been shown to facilitate or inhibit the bonding process for birth-parents include risk status during pregnancy, intendedness or wantedness of the pregnancy, fathers' acceptance of the pregnancy and support, extent of ante-partal worry, foetal movement, positive events of labour and delivery, sex, and health status of the newborn, and early parent–infant contact. Additional factors that have been indicated to influence the bonding process for parents and carers include previous attachments, experienced bonding style, parental competence, parental self-efficacy, support (perceived and actual), marital status, parity, parental stress, and parental preoccupation (Goulet et al., 1998; Larkin, 2003; Mercer et al., 1986; Trowell, 1982; Tulman, 1981). The ways in which psychosocial factors such as experienced bonding style, social support, parental stress, depression, and parental self-efficacy exert an influence upon the bonding process will be explored in more detail below.

Experienced Bonding Style

Bowlby postulated that early attachment-experiences and early experienced bonding styles become internalised as internal working models that act to influence future interpersonal relationships, cognitions, and affective style, and influence the capacity to form meaningful emotional bonds with others. Indeed, it has been well documented that the quality of relationships experienced in childhood can exert an effect on later interpersonal functioning (e.g. Drayton et al., 1998; Howe, 1995).

An individual's style of parenting can be influenced by his or her parents' style (Iwaniec & Sneddon, 2002). Higher levels of experienced emotional warmth have been found to be an important determinant of the quality of prenatal attachment (Siddiqui & Hagglof, 2000). It is also believed that sensitive, responsive care-giving promotes attachment-security in children who are believed to subsequently be more likely to be described as engaging in high-investment parenting in later life (Simpson, 1999).

Social Support

Another factor believed to be important for the bonding process is social support: this refers to the social, emotional, and other supports that are provided by an individual's social contacts (Weinman et al., 1995). Social support has been found to greatly assist parental functioning by buffering the effects of negative stressors, enhancing parents' psychological well-being, and providing the parent with additional resources (Ceballo & McLoyd, 2002). While an absence of support contributes to loneliness, depression, and despair, the presence of support can raise self-esteem and lighten the burden of everyday life (Howe, 1995). It also has a positive impact on factors including depression (Gelfand et al., 1996), parenting stress (Harmer et al., 1999), and parental self-efficacy (Bandura, 1997), and buffers the effects of poverty on negative parenting behaviours (Hashima & Amato, 1994).

Higher levels of social support have been associated with increased parent–child sensitivity, responsivity, consistency, and an increased frequency of nurturing and accepting behaviour, together with a reduced frequency of harsh and rejecting parental behaviours and less use of scolding and ridiculing (McLoyd, 1990; Taylor & Roberts, 1995; Weinraub & Wolf, 1983). In contrast, low social support and social isolation have been found to negatively impact on parenting. Social isolation not only deprives a family of the social structures and networks which provide behavioural patterns, feedback, support, and the resources to cope with the negative effects of stress, but it also leaves a number of individual needs unfulfilled, including the need for affiliation, membership, respect, affection, and social recognition (Gracia & Musitu, 2003).

Research has shown that social support (or lack thereof) can act together with other factors to directly or indirectly facilitate or inhibit bonding. While social isolation has been linked to bonding failure, social support has been shown to enhance the bonding process (Crouch, 2002; Mercer et al., 1986; Mercer & Ferketich, 1990; Palkovitz, 1992).

Social support during pregnancy appears to enhance antenatal and post-natal bonding for birth-parents (Condon & Corkindale, 1997; Cranley, 1981; Klaus & Kennell, 1982, 1993; Leifer, 1977) and is thought to also facilitate the bonding process between adoptive parents and their children (Smith & Sherwen, 1998).

Parental Stress

Parenting stress is another factor that may influence the bonding process and may be defined as the extent to which parents or carers perceive themselves as having access to the resources required to carry out the parenting role (Morgan et al., 2002). Difficulties in the parenting domain induce parenting stress by acting as stressors, with higher levels of perceived difficulty leading to higher levels of parenting stress (Kwok & Wong, 2000; Shek & Tsang, 1993). Such stress together with other psychosocial influences may negatively impact on the parent–child relationship.

Pregnancy, childbirth, and the transition to parenthood represent major life-events. The arrival of a child requires adaptation to new roles and responsibilities for family members (Rice, 1999). This is also true for a new adoptive or foster placement. Research has indicated that stress prior to, during, and after birth (or the arrival of a child) can inhibit the development of bonding (e.g. Kazdin, 1990). Stress has been found to exert effects on parents' psychological and physiological health (Kwok & Wong, 2000) and consequently has been associated with increased child-directed hostility, negatively expressed emotion, coercive parent–child interaction styles, lack of warmth and availability, and child maltreatment (Abidin, 1995; Calam et al., 2002; Downey & Coyne, 1990; Rodgers, 1998).

Mercer and colleagues (1986) found that stress from negative life-events had an indirect negative impact on bonding, after first affecting a number of mediating variables (including self-esteem, health status, social support, parental competence, anxiety, and depression). The extent of ante-partal worry has also been identified as an inhibitor of bonding (Mercer & Ferketich, 1990), as has stress related to traumatic delivery (Condon & Dunn, 1988). Stress can also interfere with the bonding process between parents and their adopted children. Smith and Sherwen (1998) found, for example, that, together with characteristics of both the mother and child, environmental stressors played a part in the bonding process for these dyads.

While stress has been found to contribute to difficulties in bonding, the reverse is also true. The relationship between parenting stress and bonding appears to be bi-directional, as failure or difficulty in developing an emotional bond to a child has been documented to cause considerable parental distress and stress (Feldman et al., 1999; Sluckin, 1998).

Depression

Certain characteristics of parental depression potentially interfere with relationship-building and bond formation (Downey & Coyne, 1990; Jameson et al., 1997). Depression has been found to have a negative impact on parent–child interaction styles (e.g. Field et al., 1996; Murray et al., 1996). It is associated with reduced warmth, availability, and sensitivity, slower responsivity, reduced frequency and intensity of speech, together with increased helplessness, irritability, hostility, inconsistency, unpredictability, and poor sensitivity (Ainsworth et al., 1978; Radke-Yarrow et al., 1985). Characteristics of depressed parents' behaviour that may interfere with bonding include: sad and anxious facial expressions and posture; depressed speech; reduced frequency and intensity of speech; less frequent gazing behaviour; less sensitive attunement to infants; less affirmation; increased hostility and irritability; and more negation of infant experience (Downey & Coyne, 1990; Murray et al., 1996).

Depressed mothers can provide inappropriate stimulation during interaction with their children, show flat affect, and can provide little contingent responsivity, together with depressed affect and activity levels (Field et al., 1990; Righetti-Veltema et al., 2002). Depression has been theorised to have a negative effect on the bonding process (both during pregnancy and after birth), while mediating the influence of a number of additional factors (Condon & Corkindale,

1997; Mercer et al., 1986). For example, 'maternity blues' have been found to influence 'core maternal attachment' and 'anxiety regarding children' in an investigation of attachment to children in mothers of full-term infants (Nagata et al., 2000). Mercer and Ferketich (1990) also found that depression, together with anxiety, had direct effects on bonding both one week post-partum, and eight weeks after the birth. Evidence for a strong relationship between depression and the development of bonding was further compounded by Feldman et al. (1999) who found a link between depression, anxiety, and reduced bonding behaviours.

Parental Self-efficacy

Parental self-efficacy is concerned with parents' perceptions and expectations of their ability to competently and effectively perform parenting tasks and their perceived ability to exercise a positive influence on the behaviour and development of their children. This construct has been described as a guiding force behind much of the parenting experience (Coleman & Karraker, 1997; Teti & Gelfand, 1991). Once formed, efficacy beliefs play an important role in mobilising motivation to carry out and maintain behaviour and are believed to be strongly related to the parents' ability to foster a healthy, happy, and nurturant child-rearing environment (Bandura, 1997; Coleman & Karraker, 1997; Teti & Gelfand, 1991).

Parental self-efficacy has been found to mediate the relationship between social support, child temperament, and attachment (Donavan & Leavitt, 1985). It has also been associated with greater satisfaction with parenting, warmer, more nurturing care-giving interactions, and more positive perceptions of children's emotionality and sociability (Coleman & Karraker, 2000). In one of the few studies directly connecting self-efficacy and bonding, Williams et al. (1987) found that higher perceived care-giving self-efficacy during pregnancy was associated with parental ratings of closer attachment to their baby.

THE BONDING PROCESS AND CARE CAREERS

Significance of Bonding for Care Planning

The permanency planning movement (e.g. Maluccio et al., 1986) focused upon ensuring a sense of belonging and secure, positive, lifelong relationships for looked-after children (Thompson, 1998). This movement was driven by the belief led by attachment-theory that impermanent substitute care, multiple placements, and, particularly, absence of an early positive relationship can impair a child's ability to form subsequent relationships (Monck et al., 2003).

While attachment-theory has been widely applied to the organisation of alternative-care provision, less attention has been paid to how the bonding process might also be significant with respect to placement stability and permanence. This is despite the fact that (as described above) both attachment and bonding are believed to form a complementary pair of behavioural systems that together influence the parent/carer–child dyad (Miller & Rodgers, 2001).

Several potential adverse consequences have been identified for children of parents who encounter bonding difficulties. These include: reduced capacity to form meaningful emotional bonds with others; development of a fragile sense of self with resultant interpersonal difficulties; tendency towards negative self-evaluation; dysfunctional cognitions; and an impaired repertoire of defences and coping strategies (Bowlby, [1969] 1982; Drayton et al., 1998; Ingram et al., 2001). Less than optimum experienced bonding style has been associated with an increased risk of developing psychological disorders such as schizophrenia, borderline personality, conduct disorder, depression, anxiety, drug addiction, alcoholism, and obsessionality (Cosden & Cortez-Ison, 1999; Mohr et al., 1999).

The bonding process has also been found to exert a significant impact on parents. For example, perceived difficulty with the bonding process is potentially a distressing and isolating experience (Sluckin, 1998). Based on available knowledge of the components of bonding, it is linked to factors such as the parents' ability to view the child as their 'own'; ability to view the child as rewarding and exchanges with the child as satisfying; motivation to care for the infant; willingness to invest effort in meeting and prioritising the child's needs; willingness to make sacrifices on the child's behalf; and, importantly, motivation to prevent or avoid relationship breakdown in the face of multiple child or parent problems (Iwaniec et al., 2002; Klaus & Kennell, 1982; Larkin, 2003; Mercer, 1990).

Thus the bonding process may have implications not only for the quality of the parent–child relationship but also for placement stability and permanence. Indeed, placement outcome has been linked to individual differences not only in the child's expectations and preparedness to accept the new family, but also in individual differences in the new family's tolerance and commitment regarding the child (Dance et al., 2002).

Because the bonding process is linked to factors such as commitment and motivation to prevent or avoid relationship breakdown, it may be helpful to look at factors that have been identified to contribute to placement breakdown. Child factors associated with vulnerability to placement breakdown have been found to include: gender (Kemp & Bodonyi, 2000); older age at placement (Andersson, 1999); child satisfaction with the placement (Pinderhughes, 1998); ethnicity (Courtney, 2000); and reason for the placement (Wells & Guo, 1999). Additional factors include: quality of previous relationships (Thoburn, 2002); previous experience of placement breakdown (Fahlberg, 1985); prior experience of abuse or neglect (Browne et al., 2000); pre-natal exposure to drugs or alcohol, disabilities, and health problems (Frame, 2002); presence of special needs (Rutter, 2000); and behavioural problems (Dance et al., 2002).

Vulnerability to placement breakdown has also been linked to factors such as foster/adoptive parents' age, motivation, composition of the family, co-operation, and relationships between foster parents and supervisor (Strijker et al., 2002); birth-parent satisfaction with the placement (Pinderhughes, 1998); and the number and severity of problems experienced by the care-giver (Maluccio et al., 1996). Divorce or separation (Andersson, 1999) and presence of children of a similar age (Parker, 1966) have also been linked to placement breakdown. Place-ment stability is also threatened if carers believe that the well-being of their birth-children is put at risk by the behaviour of foster children (Triseliotis, 1989). Carer characteristics that have been shown to decrease the likelihood of place-ment breakdown include emotional resilience, amenability to outside support, flexibility, firmness, and having a strong marriage or partnership, and a desire to be a parent to the child (Berridge, 2000; Thoburn, 2002).

What Influences the Bonding Process in Substitute Care?

According to Smith and Sherwen (1988), the bonding process in adoptive families develops through dynamic interaction and is influenced by support systems and environmental stressors in addition to characteristics of both the adoptive parent and the child. These authors found that the bonding process between mothers and their adopted children was aided by factors such as the degree of mental preparation for the adoption of the child, physical closeness, nurturing, and joint activities. Destructive or negative behaviour, detachment or rejection by the child, and depletion of energy and resources hindered the bonding process. The bonding between adoptive mother and child was also influenced by what the child brought to the relationship in terms of history, age, background, culture, language, and past attachments (Smith & Sherwen, 1988).

Previous Experience of Placement Breakdown

Previous experience of placement breakdown is a well-recorded risk factor for subsequent placement difficulties for children (e.g. Browne, 1998) and may also affect the bonding process for alternative care-providers. While parents may be able to understand and rationalise placement breakdown to a greater extent than children can, it has been shown to create a sense of failure for both children and parents and can be distressing to both parties (Minty, 1999). Previous negative placement experiences involving a sense of failure may have a negative influ-ence on parental self-efficacy, a factor that has, in turn, been shown to play an important role in the bonding process (Larkin, 2003).

The 'Claiming' Process

Parental reports suggest that an important feature of the bonding process is the identification of the child as their 'own' and the feeling that the child 'belongs' to them (Larkin, 2003). A number of factors associated with alternative care provision may operate to facilitate or inhibit parental ability to view a child as their 'own' and may consequently influence bonding. Such factors may include lack of clarity as to the length or permanency of the placement. For example, how does the bonding process develop if a placement initially agreed to on a short-term basis develops into a 'long-term' short-term placement? The Quality Protects initiative, which was driven by the permanency planning movement as described above, measures success in terms of providing a child with a 'family for life' in addition to a sense of permanence, stability, and a sense of personal and cultural identity (Thoburn, 2002). However, a corresponding emphasis on the importance for the bonding process of a sense of permanency, or having a 'child for life' as opposed to a 'child for now', has not been explored to a great extent. It is worth noting that, in the past, development of a close relationship between a short-term foster parent and a foster child was seen as inappropriate because of the possibility of the child being moved to a long-term foster or adoptive placement or being returned home.

Relationships with Birth-parents

It is also possible that a foster or adoptive parent's relationship with a child's birth-parents may influence the bonding process. For example, it has been found that mutual agreement and acceptance between birth- and foster parents can facilitate a sense of permanence for foster parents (Andersson, 1999). This raises questions as to the impact on the bonding process of a birth-parent's disapproval of a placement, particularly in cases where contact occurs in contested adoptive placements.

Commitment to Meeting a Child's Needs and Associated Rewards

Parental motivation, responsibility, commitment, and willingness to make personal sacrifices to address a child's needs have all been linked to the bonding process (Iwaniec et al., 2002; Larkin, 2003). By effectively meeting a child's needs, not only is the bonding process enhanced, but the child also learns that he or she can trust the parent as an effective care-giver and the attachment process will also be facilitated (Fahlberg, 2001). However, it is also important for the bonding process that parents feel as though their investment, commitment, and personal sacrifices are affirmed.

The bonding process has been linked to both the demands placed upon parents by a child, and the rewards associated with care-giving (Larkin, 2003). Such rewards include: feeling recognised as an important care-giver, and feeling needed. Together with facilitating bonding, such rewards can enhance a parent's self-esteem and parental self-efficacy. However, if rewards are not forthcoming (e.g. if the child is blank, unresponsive, or not consistent with parental expectations), then the bonding process may be inhibited and care-giving efforts may not be reinforced (Denehy, 1992). This can cause problems for parents of children who are perceived to be unrewarding (due to difficult behaviour or lack of apparent interest in, recognition of, or affection for the parent). In addition to not affirming parental input, a child perceived to be unrewarding (with difficult behaviour and an apparent lack of interest or affection for the parents) may be more difficult for parents to 'claim', and this may have consequences for the bonding process. Children with previous negative care-giving experiences who find it difficult to form positive relationships with new carers may be more vulnerable in this respect.

Reciprocity

Bonding has been described as an interactive reciprocal process that develops through satisfying parent–child interactions (Goulet et al., 1998; Mercer & Ferketich, 1990). It is important for parents to feel as though they are part of a two-way reciprocal relationship and to have a sense that emerging bonds are bi-directional (Larkin, 2003). As important as it is for parents to go through a claiming process with a child, i.e. have a sense of knowing the baby and a sense that the baby is theirs, it is also important for parents to believe that their child engages in a similar identification process, i.e. identifies and recognises the parent as his or her parent (Fahlberg, 2001). In this sense, carers' feelings of bonding are affirmed when they see signs of the child being attached to them in return. A child's early attachment relationships and his or her ability to form healthy subsequent attachments to alternative care-givers may, in this way, have a positive or negative influence on a parent's or carer's ability to form a healthy bond with a child. It may be that interventions designed to help children resolve attachment issues may also facilitate the bonding process. However, as Fahlberg (2001) points out, it is also important to remember that it is part of a foster or adoptive parent's role to help the child in this process and to create an environment in which a child is facilitated to develop trust in others, and form healthy attachment relationships.

Learning Cues and Signals

Bonding is also linked to a parent's or carer's ability to appropriately interpret and respond to a child's cues and signals (Brazelton, 1979). This has implications for carers of children whose cues and signals may be confusing. It may also apply to carers who either have not yet learnt how to interpret and respond to a child's cues and signals, due to being in the process of getting to know a child, or who find it difficult to learn how to interpret and respond to these although the child has been placed with them for some time.

Mental Preparation for Placement

Egeland and Farber (1984) point out that a parent's perception of his/her infant and their relationship appears to influence the parent–child relationship to a greater extent than any single factor. An important part of bonding in relation to alternative care arrangements has been shown to be the process of mental preparation for the placement and the match between the carer's preconceived images of the child and the real child (Klaus & Kennell, 1993; Leifer, 1977; Smith & Sherwen, 1988).

Inclusive planning and involvement in the decision-making process have been shown to be important factors in determining placement stability and may also assist alternative carers in their mental preparations for the placement. Preparing a parent for a placement by providing as complete a picture of the child as possible (including aspects of the child's background, personality, and likely needs) will also aid mental preparation for the placement. Such preparations may also ensure that the needs and characteristics of a child are appropriately matched to the skills, expectations, and characteristics of a potential care-giver and may also benefit the bonding process by facilitating a sense of knowing and identifying with a child (Larkin, 2003; Sluckin, 1998). However, care planning is often constrained by insufficient resources (McSherry et al., 2004). Waterhouse and Brokelsby (2001), for example, point out that placement planning and preparation can fall victim to a combination of a crisis-led approach and a lack of choice of placements due to a shortage of available carers.

FACILITATING THE BONDING PROCESS FOR ALTERNATIVE CARE-PROVIDERS

Ensure that Carers are Supported at All Stages of Placement

While the presence of support has been shown to enhance the bonding process, a number of factors may influence the effectiveness of support provided. For example, while support perceived as encouraging and accepting or 'autonomy-supportive' is likely to enhance psychological well-being and feelings of control, support perceived as controlling or coercive may undermine feelings of competency or efficacy (Ryan & Solky, 1996). We know that it is the quality rather than quantity of support that is important in endeavours to promote adequate functioning and that satisfaction with support may be more influential than the quantity of support available (Condon & Corkindale, 1997; Thompson, 1995). This knowledge is useful when designing interventions to promote and support bonding in foster or adoptive placements.

Foster parents can be supported in their mental preparations for the placements and for resultant role and identity changes. Carers may also be supported prior to a placement by provision of information regarding the child and his/her background. Insight into how the child's background and previous attachment relationships might impact upon the child's behaviour, development, and ability to form secure attachment-relationships may also support the bonding process.

Promote Awareness of Diversity in Bonding Experience

It is important that carers are made aware that bonding is a very individual process that appears to progress at different rates, at different times, and can potentially be affected by situational factors. Awareness of a lack of uniformity regarding the bonding experience may help to calm fears and anxiety relating to the bonding process, and reassure carers whose experiences are not perceived to match expectations. Difficulty in the bonding process has been found to cause feelings of anxiety, guilt, disappointment, and isolation. As factors such as stress and anxiety have been found to negatively impact on bonding, such worries may be just as damaging for the carer–child relationship as the bonding failure itself. By providing more information on the full spectrum of bonding experiences, carers may experience less distress and isolation if difficulties in bonding occur.

Address the Cognitive Components of Bonding

Cognitive factors have been implicated regarding the progression of bonding over time, particularly in relation to parents' interpretation of, and response to, events (Larkin, 2003). Parental perceptions of the parent–child relationship and beliefs in their parenting skills have been shown to be hugely influential (Egeland & Farber, 1984). Therefore, interventions that aim to promote parental self-efficacy may be of use to promote bonding in alternative-care placements. A number of techniques can be used to enhance parental self-efficacy (based on Bandura, 1984) including verbal persuasion and encouragement, providing experiences of success, modelling behaviour, and addressing emotional arousal.

Adopt a Holistic Approach

We know that multiple variables interact to exert an influence on a carer's ability to bond with a child. For example, a pattern has been identified whereby bonding tends to be enhanced when parents are equipped with higher levels of social support, parental self-efficacy, and experience of a caring early relationship. It has also been found that bonding tends to be impaired when parents have higher levels of parenting stress, depression, and parenting anxiety (Larkin, 2003). This knowledge could be used to address ways in which multiple variables interact, to exert an influence on a carer's ability to bond with a child.

SUMMARY

While the care-planning movement has explored the concept of attachment in great detail, the concept of bonding has been afforded much less depth of consideration. However, it is useful for practitioners to be aware of the importance of the bonding process for alternative care-providers and of factors that may facilitate or inhibit it. Having first examined what bonding is, and the relationship between bonding and attachment, this chapter then explored how the bonding process relates to psychosocial variables such as social support, parental stress, depression, parental self-efficacy, and parents' own bonding style. Factors that may influence the bonding process in substitute care were also explored. Finally, recommendations were made regarding ways in which professionals may assist alternative care-providers in the bonding process with their adopted or long-term foster children.

REFERENCES

Abidin, R.R. (1995). *Parenting Stress Index: Professional Manual*, 3rd edn. Florida: Psychological Assessment Resources, Inc.

Ainsworth, M.D.S., Blehar, M.C., Waters, E., & Wall, S. (1978). *Patterns of Attachment: A Psychological Study of the Strange Situation*. Hillsdale, NJ: Lawrence Erlbaum.

Andersson, G. (1999). Children in permanent foster care in Sweden. *Child and Family Social Work*, **4**, 175–186.

Bandura, A. (1984). Recycling misconceptions of perceived self-efficacy. *Cognitive Therapy and Research*, **8**, 231–255.

Bandura, A. (1997). *Self-Efficacy: The Exercise of Control*. New York: W.H. Freeman & Co.

Belsky, J. (1984). The determinants of parenting: A process model. *Child Development*, **55**, 83–96.

Berridge, D. (2000). *Placement Stability: Providing Stability and Continuity for Looked After Children is Essential for Their Personal Development and Achievement*. Quality Protects Research Briefing No. 2. London: Department of Health, Research in Practice, Making Research Count.

Bowlby, J. (1953). *Child Care and the Growth of Love*. Harmondsworth: Penguin.

Bowlby, J. ([1969] 1982). *Attachment and Loss*, vol. 1. *Attachment*. London and New York: Basic Books.

Brazelton, T.B. (1979). Behavioral competence of the newborn infant. *Seminars in Perinatology*, **33**, 35–44.

Brody, S. (1993). The concepts of attachment and bonding. In T.B. Cohen, M.H. Etezady, & B.L. Pacella (eds), *The Vulnerable Child*, vol. 1. Madison, CT: International Universities Press, Inc.

Browne, D.C. (1998). The relationship between problem disclosure, coping strategies and placement outcome in foster adolescents. *Journal of Adolescence*, **21**, 585–597.

Browne, D.C., Moloney, A., & Taylor, M. (2000). Examining issues of child abuse in Irish foster children. *Irish Journal of Psychology*, **21**(1–2), 32–49.

Calam, R., Bolton, C., Barrowclough, C., & Roberts, J. (2002). Maternal expressed emotion and clinician ratings of emotional maltreatment potential. *Child Abuse and Neglect*, **26**, 1101–1106.

Ceballo, R., & McLoyd, V.C. (2002). Social support and parenting in poor, dangerous neighbourhoods. *Child Development*, **73**, 1310–1321.

Coleman, P.K., & Karraker, H. (1997). Self-efficacy and parenting quality: Findings and future applications. *Developmental Review*, **18**, 47–85.

Coleman, P.K., & Karraker, H. (2000). Parenting self-efficacy among mothers of school-age children: Conceptualisation, measurement, and correlates. *Family Relations*, **49**, 13–24.

Condon, J.T., & Corkindale, C. (1997). The correlates of antenatal attachment in pregnant women. *British Journal of Medical Psychology*, **70**, 359–372.

Condon, J.T., & Dunn, D.J. (1988). Nature and determinants of parent-to-infant attachment in the early postnatal period. *Journal of the American Academy of Child and Adolescent Psychiatry*, **27**, 293–299.

Cosden, M., & Cortez-Ison, E. (1999). Sexual abuse, parental bonding, social support, and program retention for women in substance abuse treatment. *Journal of Substance Abuse Treatment*, **16**, 149–155.

Courtney, M. (2000). Research needed to improve the prospects for children in out-of-home placement. *Children and Youth Services Review*, **22**(9/10), 743–761.

Cranley, M. (1981). Development of a tool for the measurement of maternal attachment during pregnancy. *Nursing Research*, **30**, 281–284.

Crouch, M. (2002). Bonding, postpartum dysphoria, and social ties: A speculative inquiry. *Human Nature*, **13**, 363–382.

Dance, C., Rushton, A., & Quinton, D. (2002). Emotional abuse in early childhood: Relationships with progress in subsequent family placement. *Journal of Child Psychology and Psychiatry*, **43**(3), 395–407.

Denehy, J.A. (1992). Interventions related to parent–infant attachment. *Nursing Clinics of North America*, **27**, 425–443.

Donavan, W.L., & Leavitt, L.A. (1985). Simulating conditions of learned helplessness: The effects of interventions and attributions. *Child Development*, **60**, 594–603.

Downey, G., & Coyne, J.C. (1990). Children of depressed parents: An integrative review. *Psychological Bulletin*, **108**, 50–76.

Drayton, M., Birchwood, M., & Trower, P. (1998). Early attachment experience and recovery from psychosis. *British Journal of Clinical Psychology*, **37**, 269–284.

Egeland, B., & Farber, I.A. (1984). Infant–mother attachment: Factors related to its development and changes over time. *Child Development*, **55**, 753–771.

Eyer, D. (1992). *Mother–Infant Bonding: A Scientific Fiction*. New Haven, CT: Yale University Press.

Fahlberg, V. (1985). *Attachment and Separation*. London: British Agencies for Adoption and Fostering.

Fahlberg, V. (2001). *A Child's Journey Through Placement*. London: British Agencies for Adoption and Fostering.

Feldman, R., Weller, A., Leckman, J., & Kuint, J. (1999). The nature of the mother's tie to her infant: Maternal bonding under conditions of proximity, separation, and potential loss. *The Journal of Child Psychology and Psychiatry*, **40**, 929–939.

Field, T., Healy, B., Goldstein, S., Perry, S., & Gutherz, M. (1990). Behavior state matching and synchrony in mother–infant interactions in depressed versus non-depressed dyads. *Developmental Psychology*, **26**, 7–14.

Field, T., Lang, C., Maartinez, A., Yando, R., Pickens, J., & Bendall, D. (1996). Preschool follow-up of dysphoric mothers. *Journal of Clinical Child Psychology*, **25**, 272–279.

Frame, L. (2002). Maltreatment reports and placement outcomes for infants and toddlers in out-of-home care. *Infant Mental Health Journal*, **23**(5), 517–540.

Gelfand, D.M., Teti, D.M., Seiner, S.A., & Jameson, P.B. (1996). Helping mothers fight depression: Evaluation of a home-based intervention program for depressed mothers and their infants. *Journal of Clinical Child Psychology*, **25**, 406–422.

George, C., & Solomon, J. (1999). Attachment and caregiving: The caregiving behavioural system. In J. Cassidy & P. Shaver (eds), *Handbook of Attachment: Theory, Research and Clinical Applications*. New York: The Guilford Press, pp. 141–162.

Goulet, C., Bell, L., St-Cyr Tribble, D., Paul, D., & Lang, A. (1998). A concept analysis of parent–infant attachment. *Journal of Advanced Nursing*, **28**, 1071–1081.

Gracia, E., & Musitu, G. (2003). Social isolation from communities and child maltreatment: A cross-cultural comparison. *Child Abuse and Neglect*, **27**, 153–168.

Harmer, A.L., Sanderson, J., & Mertin, P. (1999). Influence of negative childhood experiences on psychological functioning, social support, and parenting for mothers recovering from addiction. *Child Abuse and Neglect*, **23**, 421–433.

Hashima, P., & Amato, P.R. (1994). Poverty, social support, and parenting behaviour. *Child Development*, **65**, 394–403.

Heard, D., & Lake, B. (1997). *The Challenge of Attachment for Caregiving*. London: Routledge.

Howe, D. (1995). *Attachment Theory for Social Work Practice*. Basingstoke: Macmillan.

Ingram, R.E., Overbey, T., & Fortier, M. (2001). Individual differences in dysfunctional automatic thinking and parental bonding: Specificity of maternal care. *Personality and Individual Differences*, **30**, 401–412.

Iwaniec, D., Herbert, M., & Sluckin, A. (2002). Helping emotionally abused and neglected children and abusive carers. In K. Browne, H. Hanks, P. Stratton, & C. Hamilton (eds),

Early Prediction and Prevention of Child Abuse: A Handbook. Chichester: John Wiley & Sons, Ltd, pp. 249–265.

Iwaniec, D., & Sneddon, S. (2002). The quality of parenting of individuals who had failed to thrive as children. *British Journal of Social Work*, 32, 283–298.

Jameson, P.B., Gelfand, D.M., Kulscar, E., & Teti, D.M. (1997). Mother–toddler interaction patterns associated with maternal depression. *Development and Psychopathology*, 9, 537–550.

Kazdin, A.E. (1990). Premature termination from treatment among children referred for antisocial behavior. *Journal of Child Psychology and Psychiatry and Allied Disciplines*, 31, 415–425.

Kemp, S., & Bodonyi, J.M. (2000). Infants who stay in foster care: Child characteristics and permanency outcomes of legally free children first placed as infants. *Child and Family Social Work*, 5, 95–106.

Klaus, M., Jerauld, P., Kreger, N., McAlpine, W., Steffa, M., & Kennell, J. (1972). Maternal attachment: Importance of the first postpartum days. *New England Journal of Medicine*, 286(9), 460–473.

Klaus, M.H., & Kennell, J.H. (1982). *Parent–Infant Bonding*, 2nd edn. St Louis, MO: The C.V. Mosby Company.

Klaus, M.H., & Kennell, J.H. (1993). Care of the parents. In M.H. Klaus, A.A. Fanaroff, & W.B. Saunders. *Care of the High Risk Neonate*, 4th edn. Philadelphia, PA: W.B. Saunders Company.

Kwok, S., & Wong, D. (2000). Mental health of parents with young children in Hong Kong: The roles of parenting stress and parenting self-efficacy. *Child and Family Social Work*, 5, 57–65.

Larkin, E. (2003). A longitudinal study of parent–infant bonding. Unpublished doctoral dissertation, Queen's University Belfast.

Leifer, M. (1977). Psychological changes accompanying pregnancy and motherhood. *Genetic Psychology Monographs*, 95, 55–96.

Lorenz, K. (1970). *Studies in Animal and Human Behaviour*. London: Methuen.

Maluccio, A., Abramczyk, L.W., & Thomilson, B. (1996). Family reunification of children in out-of-home care: Research perspectives. *Children and Youth Services Review*, 18(4/5), 287–305.

Maluccio, A., Fein, E., & Olmstead, K.A. (1986). *Permanency Planning for Children*. New York: Tavistock.

McLoyd, V.C. (1990). The impact of economic hardship on black families and children: Psychological distress, parenting, and socioemotional development. *Child Development*, 61, 311–346.

McSherry, D., Iwaniec, D., & Larkin, E. (2004). *Counting the Costs: The Children (Northern Ireland) Order (1995), Social Work and the Courts*. Belfast: Institute of Child Care Research.

Mercer, R.T. (1990). *Parents at Risk*. New York: Springer Publishing Co.

Mercer, R.T., & Ferketich, S.L. (1990). Predictors of parental attachment during early parenthood. *Journal of Advanced Nursing*, 15, 268–280.

Mercer, R.T., & Ferketich, S.L. (1994). Maternal-infant attachment of experienced and inexperienced mothers during infancy. *Nursing Research*, 43, 344–351.

Mercer, R.T., May, K.A., Ferketich, S., & DeJoseph, J. (1986). Theoretical models for studying the effect of antepartum stress on the family. *Nursing Research*, 35, 339–346.

Miller, W.B., & Rodgers, J.L. (2001). *The Ontogeny of Human Bonding Systems: Evolutionary Origins, Neural Bases, and Psychological Manifestations*. Norwell, MA: Kluwer Academic Publishers.

Minty, B. (1999). Annotation: Outcomes in long-term foster family care. *Journal of Child Psychology and Psychiatry*, 40(7), 991–999.

Mohr, S., Preisig, M., Fenton, B.Y., & Ferrero, F. (1999). Validation of the French version of the parental bonding instrument in adults. *Personality and Individual Differences*, **26**, 1065–1074.

Monck, E., Reynolds, J., & Wigfall, V. (2003). *The Role of Concurrent Planning: Making Permanent Placements for Young Children*. London: British Association for Adoption and Fostering.

Morgan, J., Robinson, D., & Aldridge, J. (2002). Parenting stress and externalising child behaviour: Research review. *Child and Family Social Work*, **7**, 219–225.

Murray, L., Fioro-Cowley, A., Hooper, R., & Cooper, P. (1996). The impact of postnatal depression and associated adversity on early mother–infant interactions and later infant outcomes. *Child Development*, **67**, 2512–2526.

Nagata, M., Nagai, Y., Sobajima, H., Ando, T., Nishide, Y., & Honjo, S. (2000). Maternity blues and attachment to children in mothers of full-term normal infants. *Acta Psychiatrica Scandinavica*, **101**, 209–217.

Palkovitz, R. (1992). Changes in father–infant bonding beliefs across couples' first transition to parenthood. *Maternal-Child Nursing Journal*, **20**, 141–154.

Parker, R.A. (1966). *Decision Making in Child Care: A Study of Prediction in Fostering*. London: Allen & Unwin.

Pinderhughes, E.E. (1998). Short term placement outcomes for children adopted after age five. *Children and Youth Services Review*, **20**(3), 223–249.

Radke-Yarrow, M., Cummings, E.M., Keuzynski, L., & Chapman, M. (1985). Patterns of attachment in two- and three-year-olds in normal families and families with parental depression. *Child Development*, **56**, 884–893.

Rice, P.L. (1999). *Stress and Health*, 3rd edn. London: International Thompson Publishing, Inc.

Righetti-Veltema, M., Conne-Perreard, E., Bousquet, A., & Manazo, J. (2002). Postpartum depression and mother–infant relationship at three months old. *Journal of Affective Disorders*, **70**, 291–306.

Ringler, N.M., Kennell, J.H., Jarvella, R., Navojosky, B.J., & Klaus, M.H. (1975). Mother-to-child speech at two years: Effects of early postnatal contact. *Journal of Developmental and Behavioural Pediatrics*, **86**, 141–144.

Rodgers, A.Y. (1998). Multiple sources of stress and parenting behaviour. *Children and Youth Services Review*, **20**, 525–546.

Rutter, M. (2000). Children in substitute care: Some conceptual considerations and research implications. *Children and Youth Services Review*, **22**(9–10), 685–703.

Ryan, R.M., & Solky, J.A. (1996). What is supportive about social support? On the psychological needs for autonomy and relatedness. In G.R. Pierce, B.R. Sarason, & I.G. Sarason (eds), *Handbook of Social Support and the Family*. New York: Plenum Press, pp. 249–268.

Shek, T.L.D., & Tsang, K.M.S. (1993). *Care-Givers of Preschool Mentally Handicapped Children in Hong Kong: Their Stress, Coping Resources and Psychological Wellbeing*. Hong Kong: Heep Hong Society for Handicapped Children.

Siddiqui, A., & Hagglof, B. (2000). Does maternal prenatal attachment predict postnatal mother–infant interaction? *Early Human Development*, **59**, 13–25.

Simpson, J.A. (1999). Attachment theory in modern evolutionary perspective. In J. Cassidy & P. Shaver (eds), *Handbook of Attachment: Theory, Research and Clinical Applications*. New York: The Guilford Press, pp. 115–140.

Sluckin, A. (1998). Bonding failure: 'I don't know this baby, she's nothing to do with me'. *Clinical Child Psychology and Psychiatry*, **3**, 11–24.

Sluckin, W., Herbert, M., & Sluckin, A. (1983). *Maternal Bonding*. Oxford: Blackwell.

Smith, D.W., & Sherwen, L.N. (1988). *Mothers and their Adopted Children: The Bonding Process* (2nd edn). New York: Tiresias Press.

Strijker, J., Zandberg, T.J., & Van der Meulen, B.F. (2002). Indicators for placement in foster care. *British Journal of Social Work*, **32**, 217–231.

Taylor, R.D., & Roberts, D. (1995). Kinship support and maternal and adolescent well-being in economically disadvantaged African American families. *Child Development*, **66**, 1585–1597.

Teti, D.M., & Gelfand, D.M. (1991). Behavioral competence among mothers of infants in the first year: The mediational role of maternal self-efficacy. *Child Development*, **62**, 918–929.

Thoburn, J. (2002). *Adoption and Permanence for Children Who Cannot Live Safely with Birth Parents or Relatives*. Quality Protects Research Briefing No. 5. London: Department of Health, Research in Practice, Making Research Count.

Thompson, R. (1995). *Preventing Child Maltreatment Through Social Support*. Thousand Oaks, CA: Sage.

Thompson, S. (1998). Perspectives on permanence: An attachment perspective. *Representing Children*, **11**(3), 187–199.

Triseliotis, J. (1989). Foster care outcomes: A review of key research findings. *Adoption and Fostering*, **13**(3), 518–524.

Trowell, J. (1982). Effects of obstetric management on the mother–child relationship. In C.M. Parkes & J. Stevenson-Hinde (eds), *The Place of Attachment in Human Behaviour*. London: Tavistock.

Tulman, L.T. (1981). Theories of maternal attachment. *Advances in Nursing Science*, **3**, 7–14.

Waterhouse, S., & Brocklesby, E. (2001). Placement choice in temporary foster care: A research study. *Adoption and Fostering*, **25**(3), 38–46.

Weinman, J., Wright, S., & Johnston, M. (1995). *Measures in Health Psychology: A User's Portfolio. Social Support*. Windsor: NFER-NELSON.

Weinraub, M., & Wolf, B.M. (1983). Effects of stress and social support on mother–child interactions in single and two parent families. *Child Development*, **54**, 1297–1311.

Wells, K., & Guo, S. (1999). Reunification and re-entry of foster children. *Children and Youth Services Review*, **21**(4), 273–294.

Williams, T.M., Joy, L.A., Travis, L., Gotowiec, A., Blum-Steele, M., Aiken, L.S. et al. (1987). Transition to motherhood: A longitudinal study. *Infant Mental Health Journal*, **8**, 251–265.

CHAPTER 4

CHILDREN IN ALTERNATIVE CARE: ARE THEIR RIGHTS BEING MET?

Rosemary Kilpatrick

INTRODUCTION

This chapter will explore the lives of children and young people in alternative care from the perspective of the UN Convention on the Rights of the Child (CRC) and highlight any gaps, problems, and difficulties in the protection, promotion, and implementation of their rights as well as identifying where these rights are underplayed or ignored. The chapter is based on research that was commissioned by the Northern Ireland Commissioner for Children and Young People (NICCY) and for that reason it focuses on Northern Ireland.[1] The research, which will be referred to as the NICCY research, was conducted between January–September 2004, and drew on a range of sources including secondary data and documentary evidence, primary data collected from policy-makers, a wide range of professionals and representatives of organisations that work with young people in care, and of course the children and young people themselves. The chapter also draws on the Periodic Reports of the CRC (also referred to as the concluding observations) for the United Kingdom of Great Britain and Northern Ireland in 1995 and 2002 (http://www.unhchr.ch). Such observations are available for all countries that have ratified the CRC and, although the chapter is based on Northern Ireland, there are undoubtedly parallels that can be drawn with other Western countries.

By way of introduction the chapter will first of all outline the background to the CRC and identify the articles that are particularly pertinent to children in care. This will be followed by an overview of the process that leads to a care order and an exploration of three different types of care, namely, foster care, residential care, and secure accommodation. In each of these sections the legal situation, policy, and practice are briefly described and examined in light of the findings from the NICCY research. The concluding section then explores the extent to which the rights of children in care in Northern Ireland are being met and considers selected

The Child's Journey Through Care: Placement Stability, Care Planning, and Achieving Permanency. Edited by D. Iwaniec.
Copyright © 2006 John Wiley & Sons, Ltd.

issues that need to be addressed if the CRC is to be successfully implemented in this jurisdiction.

CHILDREN'S RIGHTS

The UN Convention on the Rights of the Child (which is the most widely ratified international human rights treaty in the world) celebrated its sixteenth anniversary on 20 November 2005. It applies to 'every human being below the age of 18 years, unless, under the law applicable to the child, majority is attained earlier'. Every child's rights must be secured in full compliance with the Convention's fundamental provisions of non-discrimination (Article 2), best interests of the child (Article 3), and the right to be involved in decision-making which concerns the child (Article 12). Additionally, the child's civil rights and freedoms are protected by articles such as the child's right to privacy (Article 8), freedom of expression (Articles 12, 13), religion (Article 14), and association (Article 15), as well as rights to health care (Article 24) and adequate standard of living (Article 27). These principles are reinforced by several provisions in the CRC that emphasise the State's obligation to protect and promote the rights of children and young people to a family, in the family, on family breakdown, or where alternative care is needed to ensure the child's care and protection.

Article 43 of the CRC establishes a Committee on the Rights of the Child to examine the progress made by State Parties in 'achieving the realization of the obligations undertaken in the present Convention'. The Committee bases its assessment of progress on Reports submitted by State Parties, supplementary requests for information, and oral examination of government officials and representation from non-government organisations from each country.

The European Convention on Human Rights (ECHR), which was incorporated into domestic law in the United Kingdom (UK) via the Human Rights Act, 1998, also provides for the rights of children, their parents/guardians, and the State. Together, the CRC and the ECHR not only set out the individual rights of children and young people within the family, but promote an active partnership between children, their carers, and the State. This partnership approach is supported in England and Wales by the Children Act 1989, and in Northern Ireland law by the Children (NI) Order 1995 (the Children Order), and the Scottish Children Act (1995) and its guidance and regulations. Additionally, key principles of both the Children Act and the Children Order relate to the paramountcy of the best interests of the child. The Children Order represented a root and branch reform of the existing law relating to children between private individuals, usually parents/carers (the *private* provisions) and between parents and the State (the *public* provisions). It was intended to be a comprehensive legislative basis to guide decision-making about disputed family affairs and state intervention in family life.

However, despite its impressive substantive content and high moral force, the CRC has weak enforcement mechanisms at local level since its approach is advisory and non-adversarial with success relying on diplomacy rather than on legal sanctions (McCarney, 2005). Until children's rights and particularly the Convention's guiding principles are protected in legislation in individual countries, it is difficult to see how such international standards can be fully effective (Kilkelly et al., in press). Furthermore, it is argued by Lundy (2005) that the capacity of such international human rights standards to effect change within individual countries is made even more difficult by the indeterminacy and resource dependence of such rights standards. By indeterminacy, Lundy is referring to the fact that many international human rights provisions are worded in very general terms, sometimes to the point of vagueness, especially when talking about socio-economic rights. In relation to the resource-dependence nature of children's rights, Lundy argues that the CRC is limited as it requires States to implement economic and social rights 'to the maximum extent of their available resources and, where needed within the framework of international cooperation' (Article 4). This then begs the question as to whether rights are so contingent upon resources that they are 'deprived of any normative significance' (Alston & Quinn, 1987). It is within these limitations of the CRC that the following overview of the implementation of children's rights in alternative care in Northern Ireland is examined.

ARTICLES ASSOCIATED WITH ALTERNATIVE CARE

While all of the articles in the CRC are relevant for all children and therefore apply to those living in alternative care as much as those living in everyday family situations, there are several that are specific to children who are separated from their parents for a variety of reasons and these are as follows.

Article 20

1. A child who is temporarily or permanently deprived of his or her family environment or, in whose best interests cannot be allowed to remain in that environment, shall be entitled to special protection and assistance provided by the State.
2. State Parties shall in accordance with their national laws ensure alternative care for such a child.
3. Such care could include, *inter alia* foster placement, *kalfalah* of Islamic law, adoption or if necessary placement in suitable institutions for the care of children. When considering solutions, due regard shall be paid to the desirability of continuity in a child's upbringing and to the child's ethnic, religious, cultural, and linguistic background.

Article 9 (1–3)

1. State Parties shall ensure that a child shall not be separated from his or her parents against their will, except when competent authorities, subject to judicial

review determine, in accordance with applicable law and procedures, that such separation is necessary for the best interests of the child. Such determination may be necessary in a particular case such as one involving abuse or neglect of the child by the parents, or one where the parents are living separately and a decision must be made as to the child's place of residence.

2. In any proceedings pursuant to paragraph 1 of the present article, all interested parties shall be given an opportunity to participate in the proceedings and make their views known.

3. State Parties shall respect the right of the child who is separated from one or both parents to maintain personal relations and direct contact with both parents on a regular basis, except if it is contrary to the child's best interests.

Article 19

1. State Parties shall take all appropriate legislative, administrative, social and educational measures to protect the child from all forms of physical or mental violence, injury or abuse, neglect or negligent treatment, maltreatment or exploitation, including sexual abuse while in the care of parent(s), guardian(s), or any other person who has the care of the child.

2. Such protective measures should, as appropriate, include effective procedures for the establishment of social programmes to provide necessary support for the child and for those who have the care of the child, as well as for others, of prevention and for identification, reporting, referral investigation, treatment and follow-up of instances of child maltreatment described heretofore, and, as appropriate for judicial involvement.

Article 25

State Parties recognise the right of a child who has been placed by the competent authorities for the purposes of care, protection or treatment of his or her physical or mental health, to a periodic review of the treatment provided to the child and all other circumstances relevant to his or her placement. Additionally, Article 8 of the European Convention on Human Rights further reinforces the child's right to family life by stating that:

1. Everyone has the right to respect for his private and family life, his home, and his correspondence.

2. There shall be no interference by a public authority with the exercise of this right except such as is in accordance with the law and is necessary in a democratic society in the interests of national security, public safety or the economic well-being of the country, for the prevention of disorder or crime, for the protection of health or morals, or for the protection of the rights and freedoms of others.

Given that looked-after children are a vulnerable group and therefore in need of support, it is useful to point out here that within the CRC there is a need to ensure that for all children there are effective, child-sensitive procedures available to them and their representatives, including child-friendly information, advice and advocacy as well as support for self-advocacy. There must also be access to independent complaints procedures and to the courts, accompanied by the necessary legal and other assistance (*UNCRC General Comments No. 5:8*).

PROCESSES LEADING TO CARE ORDERS

Legislation and the statutory framework for public law proceedings allowing children or young people to be removed from their family are found in the Children Order which is underpinned by associated regulations and guidance. In care cases, the Health and Social Services Trust (HSST) usually commences the proceedings and cases may be heard in one of two specialist classes of courts, namely, Family Care Centres or Family Proceedings Courts. Where delay may prejudice the welfare of the child, cases can be transferred to higher courts if specific criteria are met. However, despite the Children Order establishing the 'no-delay' principle, court proceedings which determine children's futures have become an increasingly lengthy and expensive process (COAC, 2003; McSherry et al., 2004). These continued delays clearly have implications for all concerned but especially the children and young people who are the subject of Care Orders in the first place. Ironically, it was suggested by social workers and legal professionals in the McSherry et al. study (2004) that delays may be exacerbated by the process of trying to balance the parent's right to a fair trial and family life as set out by Article 8 of the Human Rights Act (1998) with the no delay principle of the Children Order. Similarly, professionals who participated in the NICCY research expressed some apprehension that the Children Order was being interpreted in too paternalistic a manner within the courts, thereby tipping the balance in favour of parents over the child. They further highlighted a concern regarding the intimidating nature of the courts and suggested that the emotional and psychological impact that any child is likely to experience as a result of being separated from his/her parents may be heightened by this. It would seem that court proceedings, while attempting to protect the child, may, in certain cases, work against this and further place the child at risk of emotional abuse. While there is clearly a danger of the child's perspective getting lost within the court process, this might be counter-balanced by the Guardian ad Litem (GAL) service which the child has access to in public court proceedings.

The role of the GAL, following consultation with all the parties, including the child and his/her parents, is to represent the best interests of the young person to the court. It is important to note here that what the GAL perceives to be the child's best interests may not always match with the child's wishes and in such cases the child can have an independent legal representative to present his/her wishes and instructions to the court. The GALs are seen as playing a major part in allowing children and young people to have a say in the decision-making process.

CARE ORDERS

Where a child is judged by the court to be suffering or likely to suffer significant harm, it may give a Health and Social Services Trust (HSST) parental responsibility for the child through a Care or interim Care Order, or an emergency Child Protection Order. In such situations, the Trust can decide to what degree parents will exercise their parental responsibility over their child, even when the HSS Trust decides to remove the child from the care of the family and place him/her in alternative care. Care Orders may be on a voluntary or a compulsory basis. In the case of the former, parental responsibility remains exclusively with the parents, while in the latter, it is the Trust that acquires parental responsibility for the child. This can be shared with the child's parents, although the Trust has the right to decide to what degree parents may exercise their parental responsibilities for the child and effectively the HSS Trusts have corporate responsibilities for all children whom they accommodate.

Placement options available to HSSTs are foster care, including placement with kinship carers, a residential children's home, or secure care accommodation. In a small number of cases, adoption may be sought for children who can no longer be cared for by their birth-families; this is the only means by which parental responsibility is permanently removed from birth-parents. For all Care Orders, the Trust is required by the Children Order to ensure the continued contact with the child's birth-parents (unless it is judged not to be in the best interest of the child), to prepare an individual care plan, and to review placements, thus upholding Article 9(3) and Article 25 of the CRC. However, in the case of parental contact and reviews, there is no specification as to how often this should take place and, generally, this is left to the discretion of the individual HSST, thus leading to vagueness and uncertainty from the child's perspective.

In research conducted by Toal (2003), the question of family contact was raised by young people in care, with many pointing out that they felt such contact was not regular enough and they did not feel that it was given priority by either social workers or residential care staff, whom they believed could work towards making such contact more meaningful for them. In the same research, the issue of reviews was also raised, with one of the most frequent concerns raised by the young people being a lack of feeling genuinely involved in them. Rather, they felt that reviews were used to *'put you down'* and that they were rarely relevant to the issues important to the young person. It was stated that no matter what was said, the decision-makers did not listen or *'had already made their minds up anyway'*. Thus, while the young people believed that reviews were the most important venue for making decisions, some of them reported that *'they talk about the same stuff at them but there's never any action'* and *'they talk in the meeting as if you're not there'*. Children, therefore, sometimes chose not to attend them because they felt so uncomfortable. This is particularly concerning when considered alongside the social workers' reports (see Sneddon, Chapter 10, in this volume) and the fact that social workers believe that they do involve young people in the planning and review process.

To further protect children who are removed into care, the Children Order requires HSS Trusts, voluntary organisations, and privately run children's homes to establish procedures for considering representations and complaints about children's services. Research by Cousins et al. (2003) reports that 104 Children Order complaints were made in the year 2000–2001. Fifty-four of these were made by children themselves and, of these, 50 were from children in residential care, and four from children in foster care. The majority of these complaints were about rules and regulations of the accommodation. Of the 50 complaints that were made by adults on behalf of children, the majority concerned professional practice and judgment in the decision-making process. Many NGO representatives and workers in the NICCY research expressed the view that both the complaints and the advocacy arrangements for looked-after children need to be improved through strengthened access to independent advocacy, and the provision of independent visitors for all looked-after children.

The number of looked-after children in Northern Ireland has remained relatively stable in the past decade at around 2,500 children (2,446 on 31 March 2003), representing approximately 0.5% of the population of children aged under 18. The majority of children are placed with foster carers (64.5%) and a small proportion (12.1%) are in residential care. There is also a significant proportion of looked-after children who are placed with their family of origin as foster carers, though there is little information available regarding the needs and support that this group of children and their carers are receiving. Reasons for removal into care can vary, though it is most commonly sought for child protection reasons. Other factors include concerns over parental misuse of drugs and/or parenting deficits.

FOSTER CARE

The percentage of looked-after children who are fostered has grown steadily over the past 30 years. It remains, therefore, the dominant form of placement. In 2003, 65% of all looked-after children were cared for in foster care, compared to 12% in residential care, and 22% placed with their parents. The percentage of children placed in foster care is a result of consistent government policy since the 1940s, and a strong foster care culture in child care in Northern Ireland. A higher proportion of girls (66.6%) than boys (62.5%) are placed in foster care with the average length of a foster placement being 2.2 years. However, the number of foster carers has not grown in parallel with the increased demand for places. In a survey conducted by the Fostering Network (Northern Ireland) for the development of the Fostering Strategy (2004), 257 children were found to be waiting for foster placements. Social workers reported that long-term placements were non-existent and that access to placements in an emergency was difficult. Furthermore, it was almost impossible to place adolescents in foster care. This shortage of placements was also reflected in Mooney and Fitzpatrick's study (2003) where 93% of the social workers reported 'insufficient' placement availability. Some 64% also reported that the lack of availability of suitable placements 'affected decisions they made about admitting a child to public care or on the type of placement chosen for the child'. Taken together, these two reports reflect a general concern regarding the prospects of recruiting carers to meet the current needs. The Fostering Network Northern Ireland describes this as a 'crippling shortage' and such factors may well influence the decision to apply for a Care Order in the first instance (Mooney & Fitzpatrick, 2003). It also means that trying to ensure that the young person's wishes are met is not easy.

While the shortage of foster placements has been identified, there is less information available on placement stability in foster care and the last comprehensive review in Northern Ireland was that of the Social Services Inspectorate in 1997 (SSI, 1998a). This report makes two points in relation to the figures. Firstly, there was considerable variation in placement stability between Trusts, and, secondly, the overall level of instability was higher than that reported for England and Wales. A more recent study (see McSherry and Larkin, Chapter 7, this volume) examined the care careers of young children under 5 years of age over a two-year period and reported that 68% of the children had high stability (less than three placements) and 32% had low stability (more than three placements). While these findings are more encouraging, the study did not include older children and adolescents whose placements are known to disrupt most frequently (see, for example, Sneddon, Chapter 10, in this volume).

The main issues emerging from the primary data in the NICCY research were the variation in placement provision and stability, alongside the difficulty in placing children with foster parents of similar background. A number of policy-makers also commented on the wide variation in the range of options available across the Trusts, but all professionals reinforced the fact that, sometimes, placement depends on what is available at the time rather than what is best suited to meet the needs of the child. McAlister and Toal (2003) discussed with young people who were, or had been, in foster care what their ideal foster placement would be, and from this study it emerged that above all these young people wanted a choice in the family that they would be placed with and that it should be: 'Near your school and near your friends and the community you are used to' and as far as possible 'matched to the individual' with 'brothers and sisters being kept together'. These young people also stressed that they wanted to feel part of the family, to be treated normally, and do the same things as their peers, such as staying at their friends' house as well as having a say in relation to rules in the home.

The provision of an adequate foster care service is clearly a positive and beneficial means of providing for children who cannot be cared for by their own families as it provides them with the experience of family life necessary for their future development. Unfortunately, the scarcity of places has meant that there is little scope for placement choice either on the part of the social worker or the child. This raises concerns as to whether foster care is implemented in a manner consistent with the child's best interests and may well result in children's wishes on such matters being meaningless, thus denying them their rights under Article 3 and Article 12 of the CRC.

Since the current research was conducted, there have been developments in Northern Ireland which should improve this situation, though whether or not this initiative will bring about the substantial increase in places required remains to be seen. While this change is welcomed, the reported past failure to provide a fully resourced foster care service in an area where there is relative prosperity must still raise concern with respect to the government's duty to meet the best interests of such children under both the CRC (Article 20) and the ECHR (Article 8).

RESIDENTIAL CARE

In addition to the rights to which all children in alternative care are entitled, children in residential care are particularly vulnerable and thus additional safeguards may need to be put in place to ensure their rights are adequately protected. In particular, their right to have their voices heard (under Article 12 CRC) means that they have a right to be involved in decisions made regarding their care, they have a right to independent representation in both administrative and legal proceedings, and they have a particular right to access relevant information on their rights as well as independent advocacy services to realise those rights.

Volume 4 of the guidance and regulations for the Children Order provides specific direction in relation to the children's residential sector. There have been several recent developments in this area in Northern Ireland prompted primarily by the review of residential child care which identified the then stock of children's homes as outdated and often institutionalised, and recommended the development of small domestic homes located within the community. This resulted in the *Children Matter* report (SSI, 1998b) which recommended, among other things, an increase in the supply of places, the development of more specialist residential services, and the replacement of residential units which are no longer functional (SSI, 2001). In keeping with the CRC, young people in residential care can access additional support through mentoring and befriending schemes provided by non-government organisations (NGOs).

As of 31 March 2003, 12% (296) of all children who were looked after in Northern Ireland lived in a residential child-care setting. These residential care places are provided for in one of 40 children's homes. The vast majority (80%) of these children were in children's homes provided by a Health and Social Services Trust, a voluntary child-care agency or a private provider. Some 15% were accommodated in the Regional Care Centres, and 5% in Secure Accommodation.[2] For a number of children, residential care is provided by specialist units outside Northern Ireland, such as specialist therapeutic communities in England. For some children, residential care is the preferred placement choice, while for others, they are placed in residential care because there is no suitable alternative placement, such as fostering, adoption, or living with family members. Children in residential care tend to be older than those placed in foster care, with almost half of them being over 12 years of age. They are also the children who present the looked-after system with the greatest challenges as they frequently have complex social, behavioural, and psychological needs (see Teggart, Chapter 9, and Sneddon, Chapter 10) and are also likely to have difficulties with their educational careers (Kilpatrick & Barr, 2005; Kilpatrick & Harbinson, 2003; LACE, 2002).

Young people in residential care are a highly vulnerable group and it was often suggested in the NICCY research that the lack of placement choice in residential provision, combined with the challenging nature of the behaviour of the young people themselves, made it difficult for residential establishments to deliver good outcomes for these children, particularly where admissions are not in keeping with the unit's 'statement of purpose and function'. It was also pointed out that the situation is not helped by the fact that the specialist and therapeutic provision necessary to support the complex needs of this group is not always available. Additionally, in some cases, the young people themselves are unwilling to avail themselves of these services, which are generally provided by outside agencies.

The inappropriate mix of young people placed in residential settings was often reported as having a negative impact on the entire group, sometimes leading to placement disruptions and bullying. This was especially difficult when staff, despite their clear concern for the young people, were inexperienced and lacked sufficient specialist training to manage difficult situations. Given the range and number of potentially stressful factors, it might be envisaged that staff would experience 'burn-out', but recent research (Campbell & McLaughlin, 2005) has reported that both staff qualifications and morale are remarkably high in residential care in Northern Ireland and better than that of residential care staff in England. However, this does not negate the concern raised by many professionals in the NICCY study regarding the recruitment and retention of appropriately qualified and experienced staff, which often makes it hard for relationships between young people and their key workers to be established and consistent. Concern also was expressed that many newly qualified social workers are being asked to deal with complex child protection cases without the necessary experience and training. One example given here was of staff who were untrained to deal with mental-health issues responding inappropriately to young people following a self-harm incident. Such instances must raise questions regarding the State's commitment to these young people and are particularly pertinent in relation to Article 19 of the CRC.

Drawing on the perspective of the young people themselves who had experienced residential care, a range of views was expressed and these seemed to depend to some extent on the relationship with residential care staff and social workers, descriptions of whom ranged from 'my social worker is great' through to 'my social worker is an answering machine'. Additionally, comments were made regarding the rules and regulations in different homes with some young people feeling that these were too restrictive, while others felt they were not set clear enough boundaries. In both cases the young people did not feel that they were properly involved in developing the rules and regulations of the unit and this was also the impression of the NGO befrienders and mentors who participated in the NICCY research. There are also recent and exciting developments in this area in one

Health and Social Services Board in Northern Ireland. These include an initiative to involve young people in the setting and writing of standards for residential care (Goodman, 2004) and an on-going pilot project involving care-experienced young people as peer inspectors of children's homes (Goodman, 2005).

The State has a duty to ensure that all Convention rights are fully implemented within residential care settings. Given the above concerns, it is clear that children in residential care face particular challenges to the protection and promotion of those rights. The recent developments in the form of an increase in residential provision and the updating of standards for residential care are encouraging, as are the exciting initiatives of Goodman outlined above. However, there is a danger of not addressing current concerns simply because it is believed that the proposed developments will improve the situation. This is no reason for failing to address issues such as those outlined above more urgently. Furthermore, given the concerns regarding the lack of specialist and experienced staff, attention should be paid to ensuring that there are enough people with the therapeutic skills to staff the new support units that are being proposed.

SECURE ACCOMMODATION

While the CRC does not contain specific provisions on the rights of children detained for their own protection, it is clear from Article 37 that detention should only be imposed as a measure of last resort and that every child deprived of liberty must be treated with humanity and respect for the inherent dignity of the human person, and in a manner which takes into account the needs of persons of his or her age. Children in secure care have a right not to be deprived of their liberty arbitrarily, and have a right both to challenge the lawfulness of their detention at reasonable periods and to a regular review of their situation (Article 5 ECHR; Article 20 CRC).

The relevant legislative provision for restricting a child's liberty is found in Article 44 of the Children Order. Secure accommodation is defined in the legislation as 'accommodation for restricting liberty' and an unreported decision of the Family Division of the High Court of Northern Ireland ruled that secure accommodation was defined by its purpose rather than being a place (Higgins, J. RE AK: 11/12/98). Article 44 provides that restriction of liberty cannot be justified unless: the child or young person has a history of absconding and is likely to abscond from any other form of accommodation AND if they abscond, they are likely to suffer significant harm; OR if they are kept in any other description of accommodation, they are likely to injure themselves or others. Trusts have a duty to remove a child from the secure setting as soon as these criteria cease to apply. Further provisos are found in the Children (Secure Accommodation) Regulations (NI) 1996, including additional safeguards in respect of the restrictions on placement in secure care of those under the age of 13.

Currently, there are two secure units in Northern Ireland providing accommo-dation for 15 young people at any one time. During 2002–2003, 51 young people were admitted, approximately half boys and half girls with the average age being 14 and 15 years old respectively. In total, there were 58 placements since some of the young people were admitted more than once. The existing facilities in the secure accommodation in Northern Ireland were reported to be inadequate to support the work of either the social work or the teaching staff team (SSI and ETI, 2002) and as a result some £6m has been set aside to replace the existing provision and the new building is due to be completed in December 2005.

The demand for secure accommodation places at the regional centre always exceeds supply. For every young person who is offered a place by the Secure Accommodation Admissions Panel, three young people who meet the criteria are refused a regional place. The fact that all beds at the regional centre are full does not remove from a Trust the duty to restrict the child's liberty in some other way when it has been determined that the child requires such an intervention. The question remains, therefore, what do Trusts do for the young people who are not placed in one of the 15 available regional places? Little is known about those young people, with the exception of the secure care inspection which considered eight cases of children who were not admitted. However, there has been no long-term follow-up undertaken to compare the outcomes for those young people admitted or not admitted to secure care.

A young person in secure accommodation has the opportunity to speak to an independent representative (a service provided NGOs), who can advocate on their behalf and offer them support. In the NICCY research, the issues raised by the young people with these volunteers were reported to be everyday practical issues such as the quality and choice of food, and the no-smoking policy. Addi-tionally, the independent representatives felt that the young people had little say in most things that affected their daily lives – 'they just have to fit into the regime'. While this is an important mechanism, which allows young people to have their concerns represented by an independent advocate, independent repre-sentatives are understandably not always successful in resolving complaints, and may encounter hostility from staff at the centres who need training as to the importance of the independent representative's role. Also, independent represen-tatives are not trained to provide young people with information on their rights and there is currently a gap in the service in this regard.

In contrast, an extremely innovative way in which young people have been involved in decision-making was the invitation to VOYPIC (Voice of Young People in Care) to assist in the design and development of the new secure unit. As a result, a consultation with young people was carried out by VOYPIC (Toal, 2003), and a young person was trained to participate in the discussions with the planners and architects, including involvement in their appointment.

In addition to the deprivation of liberty, a young person placed in secure accom-modation also risks being denied the enjoyment of additional rights such as: the right to play and leisure, the right to health and health services, the right to education, and the right to family life. On these matters, the Social Services Inspectorate and the Education and Training Inspectorate (SSI & ETI, 2002) in their report on secure accommodation stated that the facilities for play and leisure in the current facilities were inappropriate, particularly for those young people who had to spend lengthy periods in such accommodation. The report also suggests that proper health assessments were not carried out on residents and that the inspectors were particularly concerned about the young people's access to Child and Adolescent Mental Health Services (CAMHS). In relation to education, it was reported that the curriculum was limited and that there was no training available to those young people who were over the compulsory school age. The same report also raised concerns about the length of time taken to acquire secure accommodation orders, and the use of interim orders, which meant it was unlikely that meaningful work could be undertaken with the young person concerned. The independent representatives who participated in the NICCY research two years after the SSI and ETI inspection remained concerned about the education provision (especially for those in the post-16 age group), the restricted leisure facilities, and associated health issues and were uneasy about the limited provision for females.

Secure accommodation raises significant issues in relation to the CRC. To deny young persons their right to liberty is one of the most serious penalties that can be imposed, yet there is little knowledge as to how effective this is in meeting their needs. The demand for secure accommodation always exceeds supply, yet there has been no long-term follow-up research undertaken to compare the outcomes for those young people admitted to secure care and those who were refused it. This opportunity to assess the effectiveness of secure accommodation which presents itself would clearly inform the children's rights debate and provide valuable information on the impact of the denial of liberty. A further issue in this context is that Schedule 2 of the Children Order requires HSS Trusts to develop other services to obviate the need for secure accommodation, and the *Children Matter* report (SSI, 1998a) notes also that the lack of a proper infrastructure of services places increased demands on the secure care sector.

CONCLUSION

In each of the alternative care settings described above, and throughout the court proceedings, there are examples of children's rights being underplayed or ignored, both in considering the protection of children's rights when removed from the family home and in relation to the key principles of best interests, non-discrimination, and participation in decision-making.

The scarcity of foster placements of all types results in a lack of choice for children when being placed and thus the child's wishes, best interests, and/or needs are not being met. Lack of places also leads to difficulties in ensuring that the child's ethnic, religious, cultural, and linguistic backgrounds are appropriately taken into account. Similarly, in residential care, lack of places has been shown to result in inappropriate groupings of children and young people in the same unit which places highly vulnerable children at risk. Furthermore, the high turnover of staff in these settings, combined with the shortage of skilled practitioners who are adequately trained, further exacerbates the situation. This gives particular rise for concern in relation to the safety of these children, for whom the State is responsible, and is counter to Article 19 of the CRC. For the young people in secure accommodation, a similar situation exists, and the limited number of places again means that demand outstrips supply, as well as similar staffing issues. Given their extreme situation, a particular concern was expressed regarding these young people's access to advocacy services, and problems of inconsistency with the ECHR was also noted. It is important to be aware here that the European Court of Human Rights has made it clear that administrative problems, such as the lack of available places, can play only a secondary role in decisions made about the child's alternative care. The child's best interests must be the paramount consideration.[3]

It could be argued that the described limitations in meeting the rights of looked-after children in Northern Ireland are solely the result of insufficient resources rather than a lack of commitment to the CRC and that the State is implementing the Convention 'to the maximum extent of available resources' (Article 4). However, this clause in Article 4 should not be used as a defence for ignoring or underplaying children's rights standards, but rather viewed as a means of ensuring that wealthy nations, like the United Kingdom, spend more because they can afford to do so. The link between the economic well-being of the country and the extent of the duty to protect and promote the rights of its children is clear. More-over, Article 4 also requires progressive realisation of rights, meaning that progress must continuously be made towards further implementation of the Convention, and always ensuring higher standards of children's rights protection. It also means that existing resources must not be employed in a discriminatory manner.

That these young people are marginalised and discriminated against, not only because of lack of resources but by societal attitudes, was frequently highlighted by respondents in the NICCY research with the point being summarised in the following quote from an NGO representative:

> Society has a very negative attitude towards young people in care. They seem to see them as undesirable and so don't want them. You talk about rights . . . these young people have the right to live in communities, they have a right to be themselves and not be judged and they do not get that right . . . society doesn't want them.

There was also much evidence that young people in alternative care did not feel that they were fully and genuinely involved in the decision-making process. One of the obvious difficulties here is that if this is to be addressed, it will require a funda-mental attitudinal shift among adults who hold the balance of power in the rela-tionship dynamic with young people. As one NGO representative put it: *'this is not just about raising awareness of rights'* but also *'about creating cultures of understanding'.* Both are necessary before meaningful progress will be made in the implementation of Article 12. But, just as the mountain to climb is daunting, so too is what is at stake and the prize that awaits society as a whole, as well as young people, is great. To quote a worker from an alternative education provision project:

> *Some of the young people I've met are really disheartened by life, you know. Really broken. They feel that they live in a community that doesn't listen to them, in a family that don't listen to them, in a system that didn't listen to them.*

The successful implementation of the Convention on the Rights of the Child is about exercising political power and choices, and making policy and legal decisions in a manner informed by the duty to protect and promote the rights of all children. This is not only a duty but a moral imperative, because children are not only the most vulnerable and the largest voiceless minority group in society, they are the only group of which everyone was once a member. They represent the society of tomorrow. There are, therefore, no arguments to the contrary.

ACKNOWLEDGEMENTS

The research described in this chapter in part of a large-scale study commissioned by the Northern Ireland Commissioner for Children and Young People and conducted in collaboration with Ursula Kilkenny (University of Cork), Laura Lundy (Queen's University Belfast), Linda Moore (Human Rights Commission, Northern Ireland), and Phil Scraton (Queen's University Belfast). The research team was also more than ably assisted by Ciara Davey, Clare Dwyer, and Siobhan McAlister. The study would not have been possible without the overwhelming support from all the voluntary and statutory agencies approached and the willing involvement on the part of all the schools, combined with the enthusiasm and eager engagement of the children and young people. The research team is indebted to all those who gave so freely of their time.

NOTES

1 A hard copy of the report will be available from NICCY (Northern Ireland Commissioner for Children and Young People) in the Summer 2006.
2 Secure accommodation refers to accommodation provided for the purpose of 'restricting liberty'.
3 Olsson v Sweden, no 10465/83, Series A no 130, 11 EHRR 259.

REFERENCES

Alston, P., & Quinn, G. (1987). The nature and scope of state parties' obligations under the International Covenant on Economic, Social and Cultural Rights. *Human Rights Quarterly*, **9**, 159–229.

Campbell, A., & McLaughlin, A. (2005). *Views that Matter: Staff Morale, Qualifications and Retention in Residential Childcare in Northern Ireland: September 2003–March 2004*. London: National Children's Bureau and Social Education Trust.

Children Order Advisory Committee (2003). *Children Order Advisory Committee Fourth Report*. Belfast: Northern Ireland Court Service.

Cousins, W., Milner, S., & McLaughlin, E. (2003). Listening to children, speaking for children: Health and social services complaints and child advocacy. *Child Care in Practice*, 9(2), 109–116.

Fostering Network (Northern Ireland) (2004). Regional fostering strategy for Northern Ireland. Unpublished report commissioned by four Health and Social Services Boards. Belfast, Fostering Network (Northern Ireland).

Goodman, F. (2004). Little voices – big dreams: An exploration of what LAC who live in residential care in the Southern Health and Social Services Board area consider to be good quality residential care. Unpublished research project submitted in partial fulfilment for the award of Masters in Advanced Social Work. Queen's University Belfast and University of Ulster at Jordanstown.

Goodman, F. (2005). A model for the inspection of children's services within the Southern Health and Social Services Board incorporating peer inspectors. Unpublished dissertation submitted in partial fulfilment for the award of Masters in Advanced Social Work, Queen's University Belfast and University of Ulster at Jordanstown.

Kilkelly, U., Kilpatrick, R., Lundy, L., Moore, L., Scraton, P., Davey, C. et al. (in press). *Children's Rights in Northern Ireland and the UN Convention on the Rights of the Child*. Northern Ireland Commissioner for Children and Young People (downloadable copy available at http://www.niccy.org/).

Kilpatrick, R., & Barr, A. (2005). School exclusion: Reversing the trend? In C. Donnelly, P. McKeown, & R.D. Osbourne (eds), *Devolution and Pluralism in Education in Northern Ireland*. Manchester: Manchester University Press.

Kilpatrick, R., & Harbinson, D. (2003). *Juvenile Justice Education Project: Educational Histories and Provision*. Bangor: Department of Education, Northern Ireland.

LACE (2002). *Branded a Problem? A Participative Research Project on the Educational Experiences of Children and Young People in Care*. Belfast: Include Youth.

Lundy, L. (2005). Pupils and health in international human rights law. In N. Harris & P. Meredith (eds), *Children, Education and Health: International Perspectives on Law and Policy*. Aldershot: Ashgate.

McAlister, K., & Toal, A. (2003). *Regional Consultation on the Fostering Strategy, Foster Care: Views and Experiences of Young People*. Belfast: Voice of Young People in Care (VOYPIC).

McCarney, W. (2005). Implementing the CRC: the challenge for judges. In R. Joyal, J.-F. Noël, & C.C. Feliciata (eds), *Final Report of Making Children's Rights Work: National and International Perspectives Conference*, Montreal, 18–20 November 2004. Montreal: Éditions Yvon Blais.

McSherry, D., Iwaniec, D., & Larkin, E. (2004). *Counting the Costs: The Children (Northern Ireland) Order 1995 and the Courts*. Belfast: Institute of Child Care Research, Queen's University Belfast.

Mooney, E., & Fitzpatrick, M. (2003). *Determinants of Residential and Foster Care Placements Research Report*. Belfast: Social Services Inspectorate.

SSI (Social Services Inspectorate) (1998a). *Fostering in Northern Ireland: Children and their Carers*. Belfast: SSI.

SSI (Social Services Inspectorate) (1998b). *Children Matter: Review of Residential Child Care Services in Northern Ireland*. Belfast: DHSS and SSI.

SSI (Social Services Inspectorate) (2001). *Report of the Children Matter Task Force: Phase One 2001–2003: The Development of Residential Child Care: A Regional Plan*. Belfast: DHSSPS.

Social Services Inspectorate & Education and Training Inspectorate (2002). *Secure Care: An Inspection of Secure Accommodation at Shamrock House and Linden House*. Belfast: DHSSPS.

Toal, A. (2003). *Proposed New Secure Accommodation Unit: Views, Experiences and Aspirations of Young People*. Belfast: Voice of Young People in Care (VOYPIC).

United Nations Convention on the Rights of the Child (CRC) available at the Office of the High Commissioner for Human Rights website: http://www.ohchr.org/english/bodies/crc/ last accessed 2 August 2005.

United Nations Convention on the Rights of the Child (CRC) guidance comments: http://www.unhchr.ch/tbs/doc.nsf/(symbol)/CRC.GC.2003.3 last accessed 2 August 2005.

United Nations Convention on the Rights of the Child (CRC) concluding observations for UK: http://www.unhchr.ch/tbs/doc.nsf/(Symbol)/981284eaf88fd518c12569fc00485004 last accessed 2 August 2005.

Part II

Pathways to Permanency

CHAPTER 5

OUTCOMES OF LONG-TERM FOSTER CARE: YOUNG PEOPLE'S VIEWS

Colette McAuley

A significant proportion of children who become looked after will not be able to return to their families, do not want to be adopted and have no realistic possibility of being so. Many of these children want to live with foster carers who act as parental figures and who could offer a life-long relationship.

(Sinclair, 2005, p. 123)

INTRODUCTION

Almost 78,000 children are currently looked after within the UK. While many stay in the care system only for brief periods, a considerable number spend a significant proportion of their childhood in care (DfES, 2005b; DHSSPS, 2004; National Assembly for Wales, 2005; Scottish Executive, 2004). Since the introduction of the Children Act 1989, government policy concerning these children has concentrated on increasing the stability and quality of placements offered to them, alongside improving outcomes for individual children to enhance their chances as adults. Long-term foster care remains an important form of substitute care which can provide both stable care and supportive relationships into adulthood (Sinclair, 2005).

Looked-after children could well be described as children in extraordinary circumstances (Aldgate, Chapter 2, in this volume). Legislative imperatives coupled with changing notions of childhood have made us much more aware of the importance of learning about childhood from children themselves. This is even more the case with children in extraordinary circumstances. There is a developing literature on children's experiences of living in step-families (Smith, 2004), following divorce (Butler et al., 2003), and being young carers (Gorin, 2004).

The Child's Journey Through Care: Placement Stability, Care Planning, and Achieving Permanency. Edited by D. Iwaniec.
Copyright © 2006 John Wiley & Sons, Ltd.

Children's accounts of their experiences of being looked after are also emerging (Cleaver, 2000; Shaw, 1998; Skuse & Ward, 2003).

In this chapter, the results of a small research study of a cohort of young people and their perspectives on the outcomes of long-term foster care will be discussed. It will begin by looking at government policy on improving outcomes for children and then examining the literature on the outcomes of long-term foster care. Issues relating to researching young people's views are considered. Key messages from the interviews with children in care are then shared and placed within the context of wider studies. Finally, the implications for policy and evidence-based practice are discussed.

IMPROVING OUTCOMES FOR LOOKED-AFTER CHILDREN

At 31 March 2004, approximately 61,000 children (55 per 10,000 children aged under 18 years) were looked after in England. Some 64% were the subject of compulsory care orders. Around 65% were in the 5–15 year age range. Some 55% were boys. The majority (80%) of children were white, while 8% were of mixed heritage, 8% were black or black British, and the remaining 4% were Asian or Asian British and from other ethnic groups (DfES, 2005b). Overall, in the UK, there are almost 78,000 looked-after children (DfES, 2005b; DHSSPS, 2004; National Assembly for Wales, 2005; Scottish Executive, 2004).

Throughout the UK, the most frequent substitute care option for looked-after children is foster care. In England, in 2004, around 68% of all looked-after children were placed in foster families while almost 13% were looked after in children's homes (including secure units) (DfES, 2005b). While many children who enter the care system stay only for brief periods, a considerable number of children spend a significant portion of their childhood in care. Some 57% of children in England in the year ending March 2002 had been looked after for over six months, and of these children, 12% had been looked after for five years or more.

Since the introduction of the Children Act 1989, government policy has been concerned with improving placement quality and stability through initiatives such as Quality Protects and Choice Protects, and on improving outcomes for individual children to enhance their chances in adult life. There has also been a welcome increase in the amount and quality of statistical information available, comparing the progress of these children relative to that of children in the general population, providing valuable inter-departmental information for children's services planners. For example, recent statistical information has estimated that children in substitute care are almost nine times as likely to hold a statement of special educational needs compared to children in the general population. Again, looked-after children of the age of criminal responsibility are three times more likely to be cautioned or convicted of an offence than others (Rose et al., 2006).

OUTCOMES OF LONG-TERM FOSTER CARE

Large-scale studies in the UK (Rowe et al., 1989) and the USA (Fein et al., 1990) have confirmed that long-term foster care remains an important form of substitute care. However, a consistent concern has been the high rate of breakdown in long-term placements. Triseliotis' recent overview (2002) estimated the overall breakdown rate for all age groups of children and between two and five years after placement to be 43%. However, there is evidence of a decrease in the rate over time, with earlier studies in the 1960s finding rates of 60% (George, 1970; Parker, 1966), whereas more recent studies have reported a rate of 27% (Thoburn, 1991). Moreover, it is well recognised that the population of children entering long-term foster care recently are much more likely to have experienced abuse and difficulties in relating to their families and hence pose greater challenges to their carers (Sinclair, 2005). Hence it has been argued that nowadays carers are managing to maintain placements of much more challenging young people.

Increasing placement stability is a key objective of recent government policy and understanding what is more or less likely to make that happen has been the subject of research. Earlier studies have identified a number of risk factors related to the children. Two of the most often quoted are the age of the child at placement – the older child being associated with a greater likelihood of breakdown (Berridge & Cleaver, 1987; Rowe et al., 1989), and the presence of child behavioural problems (Fratter et al., 1991; Rowe et al., 1989). It has also been found that where foster carers believe that the well-being of their own children is at risk, the stability of the placement may be threatened (Triseliotis, 1989). Recent research highlights the complex interplay of factors involved in a placement. The child, his or her carers, and the relationship between them all contribute to placement outcomes. The school, social workers, and the child's birth-family also play a part (Sinclair et al., 2005).

Improving outcomes for individual children to enhance their chances in adult life is another current government concern. Studies have, for some time, highlighted the relatively poor academic achievements of many looked-after children and the high level of emotional and behavioural difficulties experienced by them. Many of these problems have been found to exist prior to admission to care and among children in contact with social services but not in care (Aldgate et al., 1992; St Clair & Osborn, 1987). Hence it is recognised that children's experiences prior to care are likely to influence outcomes. However, the impact of care in terms of addressing the major difficulties of these young people over time has quite rightly become the focus of attention.

Current thinking concerning looked-after children focuses on individual progress and developmental outcomes. The availability of national data on looked-after children relative to youth in the general population has been a very signifi-cant recent step. Annual data collection on educational performance of looked-after children relative to the general population (ONS, 2005) has provided clear evidence of the extent of the problem and provides the means to monitor change over time. Recent surveys across Great Britain have also provided us with information on the prevalence of mental-health disorders among looked-after children relative to the national population (Meltzer et al., 2000, 2003, 2004a, 2004b). We appear to be at the stage of elucidating the nature and extent of these problems while still searching for evidence of effective approaches to improve matters. Nevertheless, such data are particularly useful for children's services planners and provide the basis for arguing for additional resources to effect change.

Studies of outcome in adult life of children who have been in long-term foster care have generally been positive (Dumaret et al., 1997; Maluccio & Fein, 1985; Schofield, 2003). Many were found to be in employment and were well integrated socially. Those admitted younger and remaining longer were more likely to have better outcomes. However, follow-up studies of young people who have recently left care (all types) are much less positive. Alongside poor educational attainments, high levels of unemployment and homelessness have been found (Biehal et al., 1995; Broad, 1998; Jackson, 1994; Stein & Carey, 1986). It has been suggested that the difference in outcomes can be attributed to the fact that the latter young people were more likely to have been admitted to care later, spent less time in care, and to have lived in residential rather than foster care (Minty, 1999). The intention of the recently implemented Children (Leaving Care) Act 2000 was to focus attention and resources to assist young people in the transition from care to improve their life chances (Wade, 2006).

The relative merits of long-term foster care and adoption have been examined. Breakdown rates for adoption are generally lower, although increasing age at placement narrows the differential. It has been argued that the main difference appears to be the higher levels of emotional security, sense of belonging, and general well-being expressed by those growing up as adopted compared with those fostered long term (Triseliotis, 2002). Yet Schofield (2002) argues that long-term foster care can provide a secure base, psychologically and socially, for children. The recent Department of Heath review of fostering studies concluded that 'foster care can provide long-term stable care in which children remain in contact with their foster family in adulthood. This is particularly so when the placement is intended to be permanent from the start' (Sinclair, 2005, p. 30).

CHILDREN'S RIGHTS AND RESEARCHING CHILDREN'S VIEWS

Children's rights to express their views on important matters affecting their lives are now well accepted. Legislative imperatives coupled with changing notions of childhood have made us much more aware of the importance of learning about childhood from children themselves. The United Nations Convention on the Rights of the Child (UNCRO) aimed to secure participatory rights for children and young people. Despite criticisms about inconsistencies in implementation of the Convention, it has been a notable landmark in declaring the rights which children in our society can expect. Under Article 12, children's rights to express their views and participate in decisions affecting their lives are underlined.

Conceptualisations of childhood in the social sciences have also changed significantly over the past decade. Children have been increasingly seen as social actors in their own right (James et al., 1998; Jencks, 1996; Qvortrup et al., 1994) with the capacity to influence their environment (Mason & Fattore, 2005; Willow et al., 2003).

With the introduction of the Children Act 1989 and the Children (NI) Order (1995), the wishes and feelings of children who come before the courts have to be ascertained and considered in the making of any court order. Social workers also have a responsibility to seek out children's views and to take them into account when making any decisions affecting their lives.

Alongside these developments, research studies which consult children and young people are on the increase. However, the involvement of children raises many issues. Useful discussions of the methodological and ethical challenges (Hill, 1997; McAuley, 1998; Morrow & Richards, 1997; Thomas & O'Kane, 1998) as well as research illustrations (Alderson, 2001; Christensen, 2004) are now available.

THE PATHWAYS AND OUTCOMES STUDY

This small study traced a cohort of 19 young people who had lengthy care experience in Northern Ireland and who had taken part in an earlier study. Sixteen agreed to participate in the follow-up. They were aged between 17 and 24 years at the time of interview. With their consent, file searches were also carried out (McAuley, 2005).

These individuals had been the subject of an earlier study of primary-school-aged children entering planned long-term foster care placements. The cohort consisted of all children aged 4 to 11 who were being placed in new, planned long-term foster placements in a seven-month period between 1988 and 1989 in Northern Ireland. Twelve boys and seven girls were included. The majority of the sample had been admitted to care on a compulsory basis several years prior to the commencement of the study. Most had been admitted as the result of physical and emotional neglect associated with alcohol abuse by one or both parents. Although the average age of the children was 8 years, most had experienced multiple placements (the average being four). All of the children had experienced abuse and/or neglect, often suffering multiple forms. The majority had experienced persistent emotional and physical abuse and/or neglect. Several children had experienced prolonged sexual abuse from within the family. The majority of children had contact with their birth-families both prior to and at the time of the planned long-term foster placements. Almost all of the children had established attachments to members of their birth-families. In the previous year the majority of the children had reportedly exhibited behaviour problems at home and/or in school. Educational attainment was lower than average for more than half of the children. Again, almost a half were reported to have health and developmental problems within that period. Clearly, these children were entering their new long-term foster homes from a situation of considerable disadvantage. They also came with established and often complex relationships with birth-family members. The initial study followed their progress for two years after placement (McAuley, 1996a, 1996b; McAuley & Trew, 2000).

At follow-up, the young people (11 males and five females) were keen to share their views and pleased that there was interest in their lives. The file searches focused upon progress and outcomes in the seven developmental areas covered in LAC review forms namely: mental health, emotional, social, and behavioural development; family and social relationships; education; physical health and development; self-esteem, identity, social presentation, and self-care skills. Interviews covered the same areas and also sought views on their experience of care, their relationships with birth-family and carers, their experience of moving from care and leaving care support, and their thoughts on the Children (Leaving Care) (NI) Act 2002. All the interviews took place in settings chosen by the participants.

Following the pathways of these young people who had experienced many years of care yielded rich information. To retain the depth of information generated in this predominantly qualitative study seemed crucial, yet there was a need to preserve the confidentiality of those concerned. The presence/absence of pronounced difficulties/problems while in care/juvenile justice settings were found to vary across the sample, and two groups emerged: the more and the less troubled. Seven were included in the former while the latter comprised the remaining nine. Within the more troubled group were those who had presented serious difficulties throughout or for a considerable part of their lives in care or juvenile justice centres, and some who displayed serious problems while in care but were making good progress before leaving care at 18 years of age. The less troubled group comprised those who had displayed a few moderate problems in care or towards the end of their time in care: it also included some who had exhibited few, if any, problems throughout their time in care.

INTERVIEWS WITH THE YOUNG PEOPLE: KEY MESSAGES

1. Young People Welcomed the Consultation and Provided Rich Reflections

Similar findings have been reported earlier regarding looked-after children and their willingness to participate in consultation (Cleaver, 2000; Shaw, 1998; Skuse & Ward, 2003). The initial consent interviews provided the opportunity to reconnect with them before the more detailed interviews. This gave them the opportunity to choose the location and shape the content of the main interviews. All those who participated were highly committed, at times arranging multiple interviews and providing materials for discussion. Their interviews contained many valuable insights combined with rich reflections. They can act as sources of expertise (Lansdown, 2001), contributing to an improved situation for others in similar circumstances in the future.

2. Long-term Foster Care – Providing a Decade of Stability for Some

Most people interviewed had a positive view of their experience of long-term foster care. This is similar to the findings of earlier studies of foster care (Shaw, 1998; Sinclair et al., 2001). Of particular interest, a considerable number of those interviewed in this study had experienced a decade of stability in contrast to the multiple placements experienced hitherto. Seven of the less troubled interviewed had lived in the planned placements established at the time of the original study. In fact, two were so well integrated into the families that they chose to remain living there several years after leaving care. Others had established their separate homes but remained in close contact with their former foster families. Over the years they had become part of the family, their extended family, and the community in which they belonged. What stood out about the accounts was the fact that they felt so accepted within the family. They described sensing that they were wanted and how much that had meant to them:

> *The last few years of my life have been happy . . . and yet I've gone through the same things with my foster parents . . . the same things that a normal teenager does. I've been treated no differently. I've been treated as if I'm their own son. And I'm sure I've given them a lot of headaches over the years. I've always had the feeling that I've been loved, always been wanted . . . Nobody would know what they mean to me, what they have done for me. They took me out of something bad and gave me something good. They always make me feel special.*
> (Young adult referring to his foster carers)

Feeling cared for and wanted and being treated the same as other children have been seen as crucial to looked-after children in other studies (Schofield, 2003; Shaw, 1998).

Ex-foster children conveyed the foster parents' sense of pride in their achievements in school, interests, and work. Promoting self-esteem is important for the development of a sense of personal control over successes and failures (Daniel et al., 1999). Reinforcing self-esteem has been highlighted as part of responsive parenting with foster children (Sinclair, 2005). Continuous support from foster carers after these individuals were no longer looked after took various forms. If the young people were living near by, they visited for Sunday lunch and, of course, access to the laundry facilities. In the young people's accounts there was plenty of evidence of financial and practical assistance being offered to establish their homes as well as emotional support regarding partner relationships and parenthood. One was particularly overwhelmed with the support he had received with his wedding. In many ways, these foster carers were offering the love and support that parents continue to offer their own children after leaving home. They continued to be regarded as part of the foster family. Schofield's recent study (2003) of adults who had been fostered found evidence of similar relationships maintained over time. There was every indication that these relationships were lifelong.

3. Long-term Foster Care – Providing Relationships of Trust and a Sense of Family Life for More Troubled Young People

There were some important messages emerging from the interviews with four of the more troubled individuals about their foster care experiences. Children who have experienced feeling unsafe or who have been abused by previous parent figures may find it hard to develop trust in new carers and need considerable time (Jones & Ramchandani, 1999). However, recent thinking on discontinuities suggests that there is room for optimism about change over time in a responsive environment (Aldgate & Jones, 2005; Howes, 1999). One young girl in this study, who had suffered severe sexual abuse, found she could place her trust in her second long-term foster mother: *'She talked to me . . . she asked me if I was okay . . . she slept beside me at night-time so I felt safe . . . all the wee, wee things like that.'* In her view, this placement had given her a sense of security. It had lasted for several years and ended, in her opinion, as a result of the premature cessation of therapy. Nevertheless, she had since maintained a very positive relationship with her foster mother. In fact, she viewed her as the only person in whom she would place her trust and her sole support. Given her lack of a network of supportive relationships, this was extremely significant.

Both young people interviewed in prison emphasised the importance of their experience with their long-term foster carers. One had lived with them for several years before moving into training-school. They had maintained contact while he was there and attempted to support him in his transition into the community again. Although there was little contact by the time of interview, his placement with them was very important to him and he expressed regret that he had not tried harder to make it work.

The extent to which the other individual attached significance to his brief foster placement was much more surprising. This was the original study long-term placement which lasted for a year and was his second long-term foster placement. It was also his last family placement in the community before moving into the training-school system at 10 years of age. The foster family had maintained some contact over time. It was obvious that he attached a great deal of significance to their continuing contact. His view was that he experienced normal family life with them and particularly commented on being treated as one of their own children. He expressed regret at not having tried to make it work again with them when they offered respite or a further placement. He attributed this to his inability to trust.

4. Stability in Education

With stability of placement came stability of education for most of those interviewed. This is in contrast to their earlier experiences of multiple moves of school.

As far as could be discerned from the files, the sixteen who participated collectively experienced 56 primary schools (the mean number being 3.5 with a range from one to seven). Generally, the moves were directly related to change of placement and not to the behaviour or learning needs of the children. New placements offered were often not in the area of the schools they had previously attended.

However, a much greater degree of stability was evident at secondary-school level. Twelve of them attended only one secondary school or special school. Four achieved a number of GCSEs. Five attended a college of further education and two went on to university.

The two who went on to study at university were more troubled earlier in their care careers. Their attainments and positive relationships with teachers and peers in school seemed to be related to their growth in self-esteem and improved adjustment. They showed a singular determination to achieve at school and acquire a better life, no matter what effort it would take. 'They expect kids in care to get into trouble in school and I wanted to show that it doesn't have to be like that' (Young person studying at university).

More generally, across the group there was evidence of growing self-esteem associated with interests and achievements in school. All these youngsters had a stable placement in long-term foster care, apart from one who had a stable residential placement. There were numerous references to their good attendance, friendships with peers, and good relationships with teachers. Some struggled academically and had to repeat classes or attend remedial classes. However, two of them became form-captains or prefects. Generally, there were many references to positive interests such as art, drama, computer studies, animals, sports, and dancing. There is some evidence to suggest that happiness in school is not only associated with but directly contributes to better adjustment and placement stability (Sinclair et al., 2005).

In contrast, the four most troubled were not so fortunate, continuing to experience multiple moves of schooling related to successive moves of placement within care, psychiatric, or juvenile justice settings. Perhaps the most striking finding was that these young people had received most, if not all, of their secondary education outside mainstream schooling. This has obvious implications for their opportunities to build friendships with peers and integrate into their local communities.

5. Employment/Education and Housing at Eighteen Years of Age

Most of those studied were in employment or full-time education when they reached 18 years of age. At interview, they were very keen to describe their jobs/courses. Many had obviously worked hard to obtain them. Six were known to be in work or apprenticeships and those who were in full-time study had part-time jobs. One was pursuing an NVQ related to her employment. Another had left a college of further education course and was pursuing a job instead. The young person with special needs was under 18 years of age at the time of interview and was on work experience in a special-needs project. The range of work included employment in an electronic warehouse, a newsagent's shop, a retail warehouse, a café, a painting and decorating firm, a catering business, a factory, and a kitchen manufacturer's establishment. Often they indicated that their foster carers had strongly encouraged them to apply for courses or indeed used local contacts to assist them in obtaining employment. By this stage, most had established themselves in their own homes while some were still living with foster families. Where they had moved into their own accommodation, there were numerous examples of foster families offering practical help such as moving in furniture. Other studies of young adults who experienced long-term foster care have reported similar positive outcomes (Dumaret et al., 1997; Thoburn et al., 2000).

In contrast, two of the most troubled young people were frequently in prison and had no employment nor permanent housing. Another had sporadic employment and was living temporarily with his partner and her family. Another had never been employed but had been caring for her children and had her own home. Less positive outcomes have been reported in the leaving-care literature where high rates of unemployment, homelessness, isolation, and poor academic achievements have been found among care-leavers. However, these individuals have generally entered permanent care later and experienced placement instability (Biehal et al., 1994; Wade, 2006).

6. Contact with Birth-family in Long-term Foster Care

All of the less troubled youngsters generally had regular contact with birth-parents and/or siblings throughout their lengthy period in care. During and just prior to care, four of them had experienced the sudden death of their only known parent or only parent who remained in regular contact with them. Generally, there was clear evidence of strong efforts being made by their social workers and foster carers to facilitate at least monthly visits. It is important to add that for these children, there was no feasible plan for rehabilitation. The purpose of contact, therefore, was to maintain links with their birth-families while living in long-term substitute care. During the interviews they referred to the importance of this contact to them and a few thought that their frequency should have been increased. On the whole, contact was sought by, and was a positive experience for, this group of individuals. Interestingly, what came across from the interviews was the respect shown by the foster carers for their birth-family and their birth-identity. Where there was such respect, the young people deeply appreciated this and seemed to feel even more secure in their placements. Other studies have found that looked-after children generally want contact with their birth-families and often want it more frequently than it actually happens (Cleaver, 2000; Shaw, 1998; Sinclair et al., 2005).

However, for the most troubled ones, contact at times brought further rejection and/or abuse, and the re-enactment of earlier dysfunctional family patterns. For them, contact brought the realisation that their birth-parents continued to blame them for disclosures, and had not accepted responsibility for their behaviour. There is some evidence from other studies that contact with specific people may be harmful for some, particularly to those who had previously been abused (Sinclair 2005; Sinclair et al., 2005).

7. Contact with Social Workers in Long-term Foster Care

The predominant message from the interviews with the young people was that they valued social workers who treated them with respect. They wanted to spend time with them, getting to know them, and sometimes just having fun together. They wanted to know that they could trust them. Several thought that social workers should take the children out more to places they would enjoy to build up a relationship with them. With some of the more established foster placements, some social workers seemed to see the children only during a visit to the foster family. Where this was the case, the youngsters thought that they would have talked to them more readily if they had taken them out. In the absence of an established relationship with them, the questions came across as intrusion and not genuine interest.

There was no doubt that the most troubled and most isolated young people viewed their social workers as central to their lives and, where a relationship of trust was established, this was seen as extremely important to these young people. In the interviews they recalled such relationships, their significance not having diminished over years.

Unfortunately, there was evidence of a considerable number of changes of social worker with three individuals having seven social workers and four others having four or five while being looked after. Clearly, such turnover reduces opportunities for young people to build relationships of trust with their social workers.

8. Social Work Contact Post-care

Across the sample interviewed it was clear that the focus of their energy from their mid-teens was on achieving independence, and in this context they viewed contact with social workers as dependency and therefore not what they would necessarily desire later in care or after leaving care. Again, there was a significant difference in this respect between the more or less troubled individuals. The latter, who were well integrated into their substitute families by the age of 18 and well supported by them afterwards, were understandably not convinced of the need to maintain contact with their social workers. In contrast, the more troubled were also striving towards independence but recognised their continuing need for support and advice. For these individuals, social workers had played a very significant role in their lives and, sadly, in most instances they provided the only supportive relationships they had. What came across from the interviews was the importance again of having someone they felt they could trust to talk to and of whom they could ask advice. The person they turned to might have been their care social worker, a residential worker, an after-care team-worker, or a substance-abuse team-worker. The common denominator was that it was someone they felt they could trust and someone of their choice. Where there was tension, it seemed to be around the involuntary nature of the relationship. For example, one young mother was visited by a social worker on a voluntary basis but she suspected that there was concern about the care of her child. Yet she needed support. In another case, the person was in higher education and dependent upon the financial support offered by Social Services. Although keen to be fully independent, her respect for their earlier support (coupled with insecurity about the future) made her ambivalent. Interestingly, all of the young people were positive about the recommendations of the Children (Leaving Care) NI Act 2002 and in particular welcomed the idea of having a Personal Adviser of their choice.

IMPLICATIONS FOR POLICY AND PRACTICE

1. The Need for Investment in Planned Long-term Foster Care

Long-term foster care, particularly when planned, can provide stable care with the opportunity of life-long relationships (Sinclair et al., 2004). Many children do not wish to be adopted (or are unlikely to be adopted), yet need the opportunity of a stable long-term placement. In this small study we have some evidence of children who had experienced significant trauma and abuse being able to settle and make good progress in such placements. Sinclair (2005) argues that we need to develop a form of foster care that approaches a family for life and which is not seen as second-best to adoption. Investment is needed to increase recruitment, retention, support, and training of foster carers (Sinclair et al., 2005).

2. Family and Child-care Workforce Planning and Investment

The issue of high turnover of child-care social workers needs to be considered from the point of view of the impact on looked-after children and their expressed and understandable difficulty in establishing trust in adults. Commitment to addressing this will mean tackling underlying reasons such as high stress levels, large workloads, and low status, all of which require substantial financial commit-ment. Workforce planning should bear in mind the particular needs of this group of children.

3. Assessment of Children's Needs

The Framework for the Assessment of Children in Need and their Families (Depart-ment of Health et al., 2000) and more recently the *Common Assessment Framework* (Department for Education and Skills, 2005a) place appropriate emphasis on assessment as the key to subsequent planning and intervention to meet the needs of children. Early assessment might well have brought better outcomes for the more troubled young people in this study. Although there have been significant advances in introducing such frameworks in England, Wales, and Scotland (Rose et al., 2006), no comparable framework has been adopted in Northern Ireland. The strategic Framework for Children in Need and their Families currently being developed will hopefully address this significant gap.

4. Developing a Range of Services to Meet the Needs of More Troubled Young People

The first national surveys of the mental health of looked-after children in England, Wales, and Scotland have recently been completed (Meltzer et al., 2003, 2004a, 2004b). Each of these surveys found that prevalence-rates for mental disorders were much higher for looked-after children than for children in the general population. We need to provide a range of services to address this as discussed by Teggart in Chapter 9. Obviously, this poses significant challenges to the current extension of Child and Adolescent Mental Health Services (CAMHS) provision (DfES, 2003). Concern has been raised about access to these services and the level of direct contact. The instability of placements is likely to accentuate these problems. Yet access to CAMHS as part of the support package for long-term foster carers might well make a significant difference as to whether a placement remains stable or not (McAuley, 2006). We do have some evidence from recent research that high-quality, well-supported foster placements can contain young people who would otherwise have been placed in secure accommodation (Walker et al., 2002). Treatment Foster Care (a treatment organisation in the USA) has also been found to be effective, particularly where a systemic approach is adopted with both foster and birth-families (Wilson et al., 2004).

CONCLUSION

A considerable number of children spent significant periods of their childhoods in substitute care. Since the introduction of the Children Act 1989, government policy concerning these children has concentrated on increasing the stability and quality of placements offered to them alongside improving outcomes for individual children to enhance their chances as adults. Long-term foster care remains an important form of substitute care which can provide both stable care and supportive relationships into adulthood. Contact with birth-family members with whom the child has a positive relationship can also be maintained. This is particularly the case if the long-term foster placement is planned.

The cohort in this small study was keen to share the lived experiences of a childhood in substitute care. For most of them, the opportunity to live with long-term foster families had provided them with a decade of stability both in terms of care and schooling. They had grown up in these families and become part of their wider network of extended families and friends. Being part of the family extended well beyond their time as looked-after children, and there was every sense that they had secured lifelong families. Most of these children had experienced abuse, neglect, and multiple changes of placement before entering a permanent one. Bearing that in mind, this is a remarkable achievement on the part of the young people and their foster families.

With the more troubled individuals, their accounts were invaluable in providing insights into their lived experiences of the care and juvenile justice systems. Their care careers were marked by instability in care and school placements. Family relationships were complex and they often experienced rejection. There was little evidence of a comprehensive assessment of their needs, nor of a range of alternative provision to meet those needs. These people recognised that they needed different approaches and would have welcomed the opportunity for therapeutic support and counselling. What came across from listening to them was how isolated they were from family life and community. Social workers, residential carers, and foster carers, who had treated them with respect and with whom they had established relationships of trust, were extremely important. In the interviews they recalled these relationships, their significance not having diminished over time.

REFERENCES

Alderson, P. (2001). Research by children. *International Journal of Research Methodology*, **4**, 139–153.

Aldgate, J., Colton, M., Ghate, D., & Heath, A.F. (1992). Educational attainment and stability in long-term foster care. *Children and Society*, **6**, 38–60.

Aldgate, J., Heath, A., Colton, M., & Simm, M. (1993). Social work and the education of children in foster care. *Adoption and Fostering*, **17**, 25–34.

Aldgate, J., & Jones, D. (2005). The place of attachment in children's development. In J. Aldgate, D. Jones, W. Rose, & C. Jeffery (eds), *The Developing World of the Child*. London: Jessica Kingsley.

Berridge, D., & Cleaver, H. (1987). *Foster Home Breakdown*. Oxford: Blackwell.

Biehal, N., Clayden, J., Stein, M., & Wade, J. (1994). Leaving care in England: A research perspective. *Children and Youth Services Review*, **16**, 231–254.

Biehal, N., Clayden, J., Stein, M., & Wade, J. (1995). *Moving On: Young People and Leaving Care Schemes*. London: HMSO.

Broad, B. (1998). *Young People Leaving Care: Life After the Children Act*. London: Jessica Kingsley.

Butler, I., Scanlan, L., Robinson, M., Douglas, G., & Murch, M. (2003). *Divorcing Children: Children's Experience of Their Parents' Divorce*. London: Jessica Kingsley.

Christensen, P. (2004). Children's participation in ethnographic research: Issues of power and representation. *Children and Society*, Special Issue, **18**(2), 165–176.

Cleaver, H. (2000). *Fostering Family Contact*. London: TSO.

Daniel, B., Wassall, S., & Gilligan, R. (1999). *Child Development for Child Care and Child Protection Workers*. London: Jessica Kingsley.

Department for Education and Skills (2003). *Every Child Matters*. London: The Stationery Office.

Department for Education and Skills (2005a). *Common Assessment Framework for Children and Young People: Implementation Guidance for Directors of Children's Services in Local Areas Implementing during April 2005–March 2006*. London: The Department for Education and Skills. Available at: www.dfes.gov.uk/isa

Department for Education and Skills (DfES) (2005b). *Statistics of Education: Children Looked After by Local Authorities Year Ending 31 March 2004*, vol. 1: *Commentary and National Tables*. London: The Stationery Office.

Department of Health, Department for Education and Employment, and Home Office (2000). *Framework for the Assessment of Children in Need and their Families*. London: The Stationery Office.

Department of Health, Social Services, and Public Safety (2004). *Community Statistics: 1 April 2003–31 March 200*. Belfast: The Stationery Office,

Dumaret, A., Coppel-Batsch, M., & Couraud, S. (1997). Adult outcome of children reared for long periods in foster families. *Child Abuse and Neglect*, **21**, 911–927.

Fein, E., Maluccio, A.N., & Kluger, M.P. (1990). *No More Partings: An Examination of Long-Term Foster Care*. Washington, DC: Child Welfare League of America.

Festinger, T. (1983). *No One Ever Asked Us: A Postscript to Foster Care*. New York: Columbia University Press.

Fratter, J., Rowe, J., Sapsford, D., & Thoburn, J. (1991). *Permanent Family Placement*. London: BAAF.

George, V. (1970). *Foster Care*. London: Routledge & Kegan Paul.

Gorin, S. (2004). *Understanding What Children Say: Children's Experiences of Domestic Violence, Parental Substance Misuse and Parental Health Problems*. Report for the Joseph Rowntree Foundation. London: National Children's Bureau.

Hill, M. (1997). Participatory research with children. *Child and Family Social Work*, **2**, 71–183.

Hill, M., Davis, J., Prout, A., & Tisdall, K. (2004). Moving the participation agenda forward. *Children and Society*, Special Issue, **18**, 77–96.

Howes, C. (1999). Attachment relationships in the context of multiple carers. In J. Cassidy & P.R. Shaver (eds), *Handbook of Attachment-theory, Research and Clinical Applications*. New York and London: The Guilford Press, pp. 671–687.

Jackson, S. (1994). Educating children in residential and foster care. *Oxford Review of Education*, **20**(3), 267–279.

James, A., Jencks, C., & Prout, A. (1998). *Theorising Childhood*. Cambridge: Polity Press.

Jencks, C. (1996). *Childhood*. London: Routledge.

Jones, D.P.H., & Ramchandani, P. (1999). *Child Sexual Abuse: Informing Practice from Research*. Oxford: Radcliffe Medical Press.

Lansdown, G. (2001). Children's welfare and children's rights. In P. Foley, J. Roche, & S. Tucker (eds), *Children in Society*. Basingstoke: Palgrave/Open University, pp. 87–97.

Maluccio, A.N., & Fein, E. (1985). Growing up in foster care. *Children and Youth Services Review*, **7**, 123–134.

Maluccio, A.N., & Pecora, P.J. (2006). Foster family care in the USA. In C. McAuley, P. Pecora, & W. Rose (eds), *Enhancing the Well-Being of Children and Families through Effective Interventions: International Evidence for Practice*. London: Jessica Kingsley.

Mason, J., & Fattore, T. (eds) (2005). *Children Taken Seriously*. London: Jessica Kingsley.

McAuley, C. (1996a). *Children in Long Term Foster Care: Emotional and Social Development*. Aldershot: Avebury.

McAuley, C. (1996b). Children's perspectives on long-term foster care. In M. Hill & J. Aldgate (eds), *Child Welfare Services in the UK: Developments in Law, Policy, Practice and Research*. London: Jessica Kingsley.

McAuley, C. (1998). Child participatory research: Ethical and methodological consideration. In D. Iwaniec & J. Pinkerton (eds), *Making Research Work: Promoting Child Care Policy and Practice*. Chichester: John Wiley & Sons, Ltd.

McAuley, C. (2005). *Pathways and Outcomes: A Ten Year Follow Up of Children Who Have Experienced Care*. Belfast: DHSSPSNI.

McAuley, C., & Trew, K. (2000). Children's adjustment over time in foster care: Cross-informant agreement, stability and placement disruption. *British Journal of Social Work*, **30**, 91–107.

McAuley, C., & Young, C. (2006). The mental health of looked after children: Challenges for CAMHS provision. *Journal of Social Work Practice*, **20**(1), 91–103.

Meltzer, H., Corbin, T., Gatward, R., Goodman, R., & Ford, T. (2003). *The Mental Health of Young People Looked After by Local Authorities in England*. London: The Stationery Office.

Meltzer, H., Gatward, R., Goodman, R., & Ford, T. (2000). *The Mental Health of Children and Adolescents in Great Britain*. London: The Stationery Office.

Meltzer, H., Lader, D., Corbin, T., Goodman, R., & Ford, T. (2004a). *The Mental Health of Young People Looked After by Local Authorities in Scotland: Summary Report*. London: The Stationery Office.

Meltzer, H., Lader, D., Corbin, T., Goodman, R., & Ford, T. (2004b). *The Mental Health of Young People Looked After by Local Authorities in Wales*. London: The Stationery Office.

Minty, B. (1999). Outcomes in long-term foster care. *Journal of Child Psychology and Psychiatry*, **40**(7), 991–999.

Morrow, V., & Richards, M. (1997). The ethics of social research with children: An overview. *Children and Society*, **10**, 90–105.

National Assembly for Wales (2005). *Adoptions, Outcomes and Placements for Children Looked After by Local Authorities: Year Ending 21 March 2004*. Cardiff: National Assembly for Wales Statistical Directorate.

Office for National Statistics (2005). *Statistics of Education: Children Looked After by Local Authorities Year Ending 31 March 2004*, vol. 1: *Commentary and National Tables*. London: ONS.

Parker, R. (1966). *Decisions in Child Care*. London: Allen & Unwin.

Pecora, P.J., Whittaker, J., & Maluccio, A.N. (2006). Child welfare in the USA: Legislation, policy and practice context. In C. McAuley, P. Pecora, & W. Rose (eds), *Enhancing the Well-Being of Children and Families through Effective Interventions: International Evidence for Practice*. London: Jessica Kingsley.

Qvortrup, J., Brady, M., Sgritta, G., & Wintersberge, H. (eds) (1994). *Childhood Matters: Social Theory, Practice and Politics*. Aldershot: Avebury.

Rose, W., Gray, J., & McAuley, C. (2006). Child welfare in the United Kingdom: Legislation, policy and practice. In C. McAuley, P. Pecora, & W.Rose (eds), *Enhancing the Well-Being of Children and Families Through Effective Interventions: International Evidence for Practice*. London: Jessica Kingsley.

Rowe, J., Hundleby, M., & Garnett, L. (1989). *Child Care Now: A Survey of Placement Patterns*. London: BAAF.

Schofield, G. (2002). The significance of a secure base: A psychosocial model of long-term foster care. *Child and Family Social Work*, **7**, 259–272.

Schofield, G. (2003). *Part of the Family: Pathways through Foster Care*. London: BAAF.

Schofield, G., Beek, M., & Sargent, K. with Thoburn, J. (2000). *Growing Up in Foster Care*. London: BAAF.

Scottish Executive (2004). *Children's Social Work Statistics 2003–2004*. Edinburgh: The Scottish Executive National Statistics.

Shaw, C. (1998). *Remember My Messages: The Experiences and Views of 2000 Children in Public Care*. London: BAAF.

Sinclair, I. (2005). *Fostering Now: Messages from Research*. London: Jessica Kingsley.

Sinclair, I., Gibbs, I., & Wilson, K. (2004). *Foster Carers: Why They Stay and Why They Leave*. London: Jessica Kingsley.

Sinclair, I., Wilson, K., & Gibbs, I. (2001). A life more ordinary: What children want from foster placements. *Adoption and Fostering*, **25**(4), 17–26.

Sinclair, I., Wilson, K., & Gibbs, I. (2005). *Foster Placements: Why They Succeed and Why They Fail*. London: Jessica Kingsley.

Skuse, T., & Ward, H. (2003). *Outcomes for Looked After Children: Children's Views of Care and Accommodation*. An Interim Report for the Department of Health. Loughborough: Loughborough University, Centre for Child and Family Research.

Smith, M. (2004). Relationships of children in step-families with their non-resident fathers. *Family Matters*, **67**, 28–35.

St Clair, L., & Osborn, A.F. (1987). The ability and behaviour of children who have been in care or separated from their parents. *Early Child Development and Care*, Special Issue, **28**, 3.

Stein, M., & Carey, L. (1986). *Leaving Care*. Oxford: Blackwell.

Thoburn, J. (1991). Survey findings and conclusions. In J. Fratter, J. Rowe, D. Sapsford, & J. Thoburn (eds), *Permanent Family Placement: A Decade of Experience*. London: BAAF.

Thoburn, J., Norford, I., & Rashid, S. (2000). *Permanent Family Placement for Children of Minority Ethnic Origin*. London: Jessica Kingsley.

Thomas, N., & O'Kane, C. (1998). The ethics of participatory research with children. *Children and Society*, **12**(5), 336–348.

Triseliotis, J. (1982). Long-term foster care: The evidence examined. *Child and Family Social Work*, **7**, 23–33.

Triseliotis, J. (1989). Foster care outcomes: A review of key research findings. *Adoption and Fostering*, **13**, 5–17.

Triseliotis, J. (2002). Long-term foster care or adoption? The evidence examined. *Child and Family Social Work*, **7**, 23–33.

Triseliotis, J., Borland, M., & Hill, M. (2000). *Delivering Fostering Services*. London: BAAF.

UN Committee on the Rights of the Child (2002). *Concluding Observations of the Committee on the Rights of the Child: United Kingdom of Great Britain and Northern Ireland*. Available at: http://www.unhchr.ch/html/menu2/6/crc/doc/past.htm

Wade, J. (2006). Support for young people leaving care in the UK. In C. McAuley, P. Pecora, & W. Rose (eds), *Enhancing the Well-Being of Children and Families through Effective Interventions: International Evidence for Practice*. London: Jessica Kingsley.

Walker, M., Hill, M., & Triseliotis, J. (2002). *Testing the Limits of Foster Care: Fostering as an Alternative to Secure Accommodation*. London: BAAF.

Ward, H., Skuse, T., & Munro, E. (2005). The best of times, the worst of times: Young people's views of care and accommodation. *Adoption and Fostering*, Special Issue, **29**, 1, 8–17.

Willow, C., Merchant, R., Kirby, P., & Neale, B. (2003). *Citizenship for Young Children: Strategies for Development*. York: Joseph Rowntree Foundation.

Wilson, K. (2006). Foster family care in the UK. In C. McAuley, P. Pecora, & W. Rose (eds), *Enhancing the Well-Being of Children and Families through Effective Interventions: International Evidence for Practice*. London: Jessica Kingsley.

Wilson, K., Petrie, S., & Sinclair, I. (2003). A kind of loving: a model of effective foster care. *British Journal of Social Work*, **33**, 991–1003.

Wilson, K., Sinclair, I., Taylor, C., Pithouse, A., & Sellick, C. (2004). *Fostering Success: An Exploration of the Research Literature in Foster Care*. London: SCIE.

CHAPTER 6

KINSHIP CARE AS A ROUTE TO PERMANENT PLACEMENT

Una Lernihan and Greg Kelly

INTRODUCTION

'Across cultures and throughout history people have taken in relatives' children where there was need' (Heger & Scannapieco, 1995). In Northern Ireland, an analysis of the 1991 Census revealed that 11,459 children were living with their relatives with their parents not present in the household. This is more than four times the number of children who were in all forms of State care.

In child welfare, kinship foster care is defined as the care by relatives of children who would otherwise be in foster or residential care. Kinship care is not widespread in society these days. In Northern Ireland, only 274 children were designated as in kinship fostering in 2002. This chapter discusses the capacity of kinship care arrangements to provide permanent placements for children in care. Permanent placements are those that provide care for children into their adult-hood. Permanence means having a sense of security, belonging, family life, being loved, and loving (Thoburn, 1994). Thoburn also highlighted the importance of providing for children's identity needs, ensuring that they know about their birth-family, and about past relationships, that they can fit the present with the past, that they have appropriate contact with important people from their past, and that they are valued as the persons they are. This chapter will consider the capacity of kinship foster care to deliver on this agenda for children who cannot be cared for by their birth-parents.

The use of kinship care to provide for children in State care is a feature of all Western child-welfare systems, but there is enormous variability in its use. Figures as high as 75% (in New Zealand) and 90% (in Poland) have been reported (Greef, 1998), but for most countries between 10% and 30% is the norm. The United Kingdom is at the lower end of this spectrum with 10% only and in Northern Ireland in 2000 there were 274 children who had been in kinship care in an in-care population of 2,382 (11.5%). Given the 'great potential that kinship care has

The Child's Journey Through Care: Placement Stability, Care Planning, and Achieving Permanency. Edited by D. Iwaniec.
Copyright © 2006 John Wiley & Sons, Ltd.

for bridging gaps between child-welfare services and the child's family system, culture, and community' (CWLA, 1994), it is rather surprising that it provides such a small proportion of placements in the UK. This may be attributable to two key influences: firstly, the preoccupation of child-welfare services with child protection (usually protection from the child's own family); and, secondly, the profound impact of the Maria Colwell case in 1974. As we know, Maria was killed by her step-father having been returned to her mother's care from a kinship placement with her aunt, a placement characterised by interfamilial dispute.

Three influences have been important in the developing interest in kinship care in the United Kingdom. Firstly, research has shown that most children return to their birth-families when they are discharged from care:

> For the great majority of children in care, family members are the most important resources available to social workers for it is parents, grandparents, siblings and wider family who are likely to provide continuing and unconditional support. It may be said that some children in care reluctantly go back to relatives because they have nobody else. Nevertheless, whether professionals like it or not, almost all children in care will eventually be restored to their family and our perspectives and interventions need to accommodate that.
>
> (Bullock et al., 1993)

Secondly, the attempt to redress a preoccupation with child protection with a greater emphasis on family support and partnership with parents characterised the Children Act 1989 that became the Children (Northern Ireland) Order 1995. These Acts and the associated guidance instruct social services to investigate and consider the extended family as a first alternative to the birth-parents. Thirdly, changing patterns of family life and increased economic opportunities for women have made it increasingly difficult to recruit and retain traditional foster parents.

The study that forms the basis of this chapter compared samples from 178 fostering households from all 11 Health and Social Services Trusts in Northern Ireland (322 foster carers and 276 children). Selected characteristics of 82 kinship foster care households, 96 traditional foster care households and of the children placed with them were compared. A further sample (14) of kinship carers were interviewed with a particular emphasis on their motivation to care for their relatives' children, the plans for the future care of the children, and their experiences and expectations of social services.

CHILDREN CARED FOR BY THE KINSHIP AND TRADITIONAL FOSTER PARENTS

Data were collected on 122 children in 82 kinship placements and 154 in 96 traditional foster care placements. The proportion of boys placed in kinship care (59%) was greater than that in traditional foster care (46%). It is traditionally more difficult to find placements for boys (particularly as they get older). The children in kinship placements were significantly older (median age 5.4 years compared to 3.4). At the time of the study, the kinship children had been in placement 3.9 years (median length) compared to 5.0 years for the children in traditional foster care. The average age of children in both types of foster care at the time of the study was 10 years. Most of the children in both types of foster care were placed between the ages of 2 and 5 years, with a third (34%) of those in kinship placements being between these ages and even more (41%) of those in traditional foster care being in this age range on placement. The fact that the children were placed so young and had been so long in placement is an indication that these placements had become permanent. Over one in three (35%) (n = 42) of the young people in kinship foster care were over 14 years of age on 1 January 2000, while a quarter (n = 38) of those in traditional foster placements were over 14 years of age. Children in traditional foster care were much more likely to have moved from another out-of-home placement than children in kinship foster care where only 20% had a previous placement compared to 40% of those in traditional foster care. This suggests that children in kinship foster care were very much more likely to be placed directly from home, avoiding many of the damaging experiences associated with the admission to and the instability of public care.

The great majority of children in both types of placements were subject to Care Orders: 81% in the kinship placements and 84% in the traditional foster care placements. It is surprising that only 14% of the children in kinship care were cared for on a voluntary basis. The expectation might have been that the families would have reached a voluntary agreement that was then supported by social services, but this was a rare occurrence.

The reasons for the children's admission to care confirm the essential similarity between the two groups of children in terms of the depth and extent of the problems in their birth-families. Almost all the children in both groups (91% in kinship care and 85% in traditional foster placements) came into care because of confirmed or suspected neglect, the most common form of child maltreatment in the UK and the USA (Iwaniec & McSherry, 2002). The proportions of children across the two groups where sexual and physical abuse were present were also similar. There were strong similarities too in the factors contributing to the breakdown of their birth-families. More of the kinship children had mothers with alcohol problems (58% compared to 43%). The figures for fathers' alcohol abuse were similar in both groups. Alcohol abuse has been identified as a major factor in the admission of children to long-term care in Northern Ireland (Kelly & McSherry, 2002). There are frequently many factors that come together to lead to neglect, e.g. learning disability, mental illness, and the parents' own poor experiences of being parented. In collecting the data it became apparent that 40% of children were in public care due to their mothers' 'personal limitations' and subsequent failure to cope with being a parent. The mothers had an underlying immaturity or inability to take on the considerable responsibilities of being a parent. These mothers, some of whom may have had mild learning difficulties, were unable to put the needs of their children first. They frequently became involved with unsuitable partners and neglected their children, usually not wilfully, but often chronically and severely, by not providing adequate care, and leaving them unattended or with unsuitable carers. The mothers of 40% of each group had been in care themselves, a similar finding to Kelly and McSherry (2002). A key finding was that there were not significant differences between the troubled backgrounds of the children who were in kinship care compared to those in traditional foster care. The kinship foster carers were caring for children for whom all the background indicators were as bleak as those cared for by the recruited and selected traditional foster carers. Both groups were caring for children whose prospects of returning to their birth-families were poor.

THE PLACEMENT OF CHILDREN IN KINSHIP FOSTER CARE

Children in kinship foster care were more likely (48%) to be placed with aunts and uncles than any other relative. Following this, the grandparents were the most likely to offer care (34%). Some 16% of the kinship carers were friends. Only a fifth of children were placed with paternal relatives. Children who were placed with paternal relatives were much more likely to be placed with their fathers' female relatives (aunts rather than uncles). The children's blood relationship was nearly always with the female kinship carer, emphasising the traditional role of women as carers and bearers of responsibility for family matters in our society. The uneven division of responsibility across the genders may be viewed as oppressive to women. This predominance of the mother's relatives as kinship carers is a common feature across the available studies. Otherwise this profile of kinship carers differs from that in other studies. In the USA, over 50% of kinship carers are maternal grandparents and only 33% aunts (Benedict et al., 1996; Brooks & Barth, 1998) – the reverse of this study. It is likely that the pattern of kinship care will reflect differing underlying features of family structures in different societies.

THE MOTIVATION OF KINSHIP CARERS

The interviews with kinship carers elaborated on a number of key and recurrent themes in their motivation. The strongest of these (mentioned by all the interviewees) was family loyalty or duty. Different interviewees described this in different ways, as 'natural instinct', 'emotional response', 'family responsibility', and 'the importance of family caring for each other'. These are illustrated in the following quotations.

> We didn't give it any thought why we took it on, it was just natural instinct, looking after your own. I mean, what do they do elsewhere in the world, in African countries? They don't turn their back. They look after their families. You can't bury your head in the sand, although sometimes you think that might have been a better thing to do.

> I felt that I had a responsibility even without the Welfare being involved. I felt that I had a responsibility and my husband very much so we felt that we had this responsibility towards the youngsters.

A second key motivation was the perception of what the alternative to being cared for within the family would be for the children. There was widespread fear of the children being placed in residential care and a worry that if they were in foster care, they would be moved from placement to placement. In addition, several families felt there was a stigma attached to having children of their relatives in public care. Driven by these forces, many families felt they had no real choice but to look after the children and felt obliged to do so. Several families, however, stated that if a high-quality foster family/or other kinship option had arisen, they would have supported this. For some families no option other than a kinship placement was ever discussed by the social workers involved. In most cases kinship foster carers did not feel that they had actually chosen to foster. Circumstances beyond their control had arisen and fostering their relatives' children seemed to be the only option open to them.

> *If they had just been non-family and just fostering, we would have said it is not for us, but with it being family, we felt morally obliged to give them every help possible . . .*

Other features of the carers' motivation were the relationships they had with the children, and the perception that if they said 'no', a sibling group would have been split up. Six out of 14 of the kinship carers had provided extensive support and care for the children, prior to them coming to live with them on a full-time basis. It was evident that this provided a firm foundation for the kinship fostering relationship. This finding is also supported by Laws (2001). Both studies, despite their small size, had examples where it was the relatives who had urged social services to take action to protect the children.

As in other studies (Laws, 2001), the kinship carers were reluctant to describe themselves as foster carers and did not identify with ordinary foster carers, even when they were receiving the same financial support and a similar social work service.

The elements of motivation illustrated above are almost a wish list of qualities one might seek in carers offering permanent placements:

- a strong commitment to the children based on family bonds;
- a pre-existing attachment to the child;
- a determination to keep children within their extended family;
- an appreciation of and a fear of the fate that might await the children in residential care or traditional foster care.

Additionally must be added the obvious potential of kinship to deliver on the main elements of preserving the child's identity through the continued relationships with the birth-family. However, as will be evidenced below, relationships within and between the paternal and maternal sides of the birth-family can be troubled.

CONTACT BETWEEN THE CHILDREN AND THEIR BIRTH-FAMILIES

One of the most striking differences between kinship foster care and traditional foster care was the capacity of kinship placements to facilitate the child to have consistent contact with their birth-parents as well as contact with a range of other family members and significant others. This is of key importance in the aim to provide the child with the continuity of relationships that should be the hallmark of a permanent placement.

There was a statistically significant difference between the frequency of contact for the children in kinship foster care and their birth-parents, and the children in traditional foster care and theirs. Nearly a half (43%) of the children in kinship foster care saw their mothers on a weekly or more than weekly basis, compared to less than a tenth (9%) of children in traditional foster care. The mothers of 14% of the children in kinship foster care were deceased compared to just 3% of those in traditional foster care. Where mothers were alive, only 7% of children in kinship foster care had no contact with their mothers, compared to 21% of the children in traditional foster care. Very small percentages of both groups had intermittent contact or telephone contact with their mothers, only 6% of children in kinship foster care and 9% of those in traditional foster care families (Table 6.1).

Other research has also highlighted a huge variation in parental contact in kinship care from no contact to shared care arrangements (Laws, 2001). While some research looks at attitudes of foster carers to contact, very little other research

Table 6.1 Frequency of children's contact with birth-mother by foster carer

Type of contact with mother		Kinship placement	Traditional placement	Total
weekly or more	Count	46	11	57
	% within TYPE	43.0	9.1	25.0
fortnightly, 3-weekly, monthly	Count	23	61	84
	% within TYPE	21.5	50.4	36.8
2-, 3-, 6-monthly	Count	9	7	16
	% within TYPE	8.4	5.8	7.0
yearly, 2-yearly	Count		2	2
	% within TYPE		1.7	0.9
no contact, deceased	Count	23	29	52
	% within TYPE	21.5	24.0	22.8
intermittent phone, letter	Count	6	11	17
	% within TYPE	5.6	9.1	7.5
Total	Count	107	121	228
	% within TYPE	100.0	100.0	100.0

quantifies frequency of contact. Studies which have looked at contact have shown a strong correlation between frequent contact and favourable outcomes including a return home to natural parents (DOH, 1991). Research has also shown that attitudes of foster carers as well as practical considerations can militate against contact (Aldgate, 1980; Milham et al., 1986). Similarly, a positive attitude by carers and proximity between foster home and parental home has been shown to increase contact (Triseliotis et al., 1995).

CONTACT WITH BIRTH-FATHERS

Information on contact between children and birth-fathers was limited due to the missing information in many files. More than one in five (22%, n = 22) children in kinship foster care and only 6% (n = 6) of those in traditional foster care were visited on a weekly or more than weekly basis by their fathers. In both groups the majority of children had no contact with their birth-fathers. There was a statistically significant difference between the two groups in relation to contact with birth-fathers. Children in kinship care were more likely to have contact and have it more regularly.

KINSHIP FOSTER CARERS AND CONTACT

The qualitative interviews reflected the quantitative evidence above. There were ten cases where the birth-parent with a blood relationship to the kinship carer was still alive and well. In four of the cases, contact for the foster children was frequent and informal, occurring in the foster home. This was typified by one aunt fostering her brother's daughter who had frequent and informal contact with her father: *'He sees her, he would drop in whenever. He called on Sunday, he feels comfortable in calling any time.'*

In another three cases, contact was still informal but intermittent, occurring every month or every three months. Kinship carers reported more strains in those relationships. In the final three cases there were more regularised contact arrangements. Contact took place outside the foster home, though, and social services were not involved in directly facilitating any of them. In only one of the cases where contact took place outside the foster home was the carer a grandparent, perhaps indicating that grandparents were able to manage contact in their own home better than aunts and uncles. In one case in the early stage of the placement, grandparents were asked by social services to restrict access to their grandson by their son (his father). They found this extremely difficult to do. However, in other instances grandparents communicated the limitations of their children who were the foster children's parents with a caustic realism.

Contact between the parent who was not a blood relative of the kinship foster carers and their child was generally much more problematic. Two of the non-related parents of children in the placements where the kinship carers were interviewed were dead. Another five (all fathers) did not have any contact with their children. In one of these cases, termination of contact was urged by the grandfather (kinship carer) who felt that the father was making a difference between the siblings and causing friction. Six of the 12 non-related parents who were alive had contact with their children outside the foster home. In two cases this was supervised by social services, and in another, transport was facilitated by the Trust. In only one case was there informal contact with a non-related parent, and this was infrequent and intermittent – about three times a year. In this case, the foster carer took the child to see her mother (non-related) and grandparents occasionally. A positive relationship between the kinship foster carers and the non-related parent was not very common. It was only evident in two of the 14 cases interviewed. One carer felt that the Trust social worker had made a mistake in encouraging contact with the non-related parent in light of this parent's limitations and repeated failure to attend contact sessions. The children were being built up for a visit and then let down and disappointed.

The interviews indicated that emotions, positive and negative, were heightened between all the parties when placements were within families. Three kinship foster carers blamed the non-related parent for the whole situation that resulted in the children becoming looked after. On occasion, this strong feeling spilled over into contact arrangements.

> I used to bring them for contact but she used to stand and aggravate out the window . . . so it was basically boiling my blood. I am just lucky that I didn't lose it and freak and do some damage and end up being dragged through the courts.

RELATIONSHIP BETWEEN BIRTH-MOTHER AND FOSTERING HOUSEHOLD

A defining difference between traditional foster care and kinship foster care is the prior relationship between the children and the carers and between the birth-parents and the kinship foster carers. The relationship between the fostering household and the birth-mother and father of the foster children was assessed by means of an audit of the carers' files. The results needed to be interpreted with caution due to the amount of missing information. Information on the relationship between birth-mother and fostering household was only available for just over 50% of the 178 households in the study. It was more evident in the files of the kinship foster care households, as they had child-specific approvals which usually explored the relationship between the birth-mother and the foster carers. Information was available for over three-quarters (76%, n = 62) of these households, while it was only available for just over a third (34%, n = 33) of the traditional foster care households. In the analysis of the data, the relationship was classified as good, strained, or bad by one researcher based on the information in the file.

Results showed a statistically significant difference between the two groups. Two-thirds (66%) of kinship foster care households had a strained (45%) or bad (21%)

relationship with the birth-mother, compared to only a quarter (24%) of the traditional fostering households. Three out of four (76%) traditional fostering families reported a good relationship with the birth-mother, and just a third (34%) of kinship households reported the same. These results must be interpreted in light of the findings in relation to contact. Kinship placements provide more frequent and informal contact but this is more often accompanied by a greater frequency of poorer relationships between the kinship carers and the birth-mother (Figure 6.1).

The interviews with the kinship carers illustrated many of the tensions in the relationship between birth-mothers and kinship carers identified in the quantitative data. Their relationship reaches back into the parent's troubled past. The kinship carers, particularly where they were grandparents, had endured many of the problems that eventually led to their daughters not being able to care for their children. In these situations, high levels of current contact also contributed to the strains.

Missing data were a greater problem for the relationship between birth-fathers and foster carers, but of the 37 kinship cases where information was available, less than half (46%) were rated 'good', 38% 'strained', and 16% 'bad'. This evidence of strained relationships between birth-parents and kinship carers is of concern when considering the viability of kinship care as an option for permanent placement. Clearly, it is undesirable for children to be living for long periods in an atmosphere of tension and hostility that may accompany such relationships. Work on these relationships may need to be a particular focus of support for kinship placements.

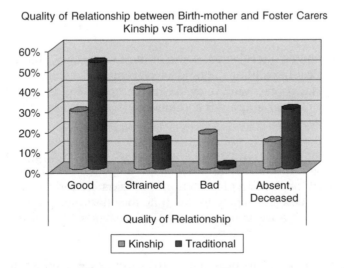

Figure 6.1   Quality of relationship between carers and birth-mother by foster carer type

CARE PLANS

There was a statistically significant difference in the care plans recorded for the children in kinship foster care and traditional foster care. For over half of children in both types of placement, the care plan was to remain in care in their current placement: however, this plan was more evident for those in kinship placements (62%) than for those in traditional placements (57%), there being no significant difference in the length of time in placement for both groups. More children (15%) in kinship foster care had 'return home' as their care plan compared to the children (6%) in traditional foster care.

In most cases the interviews portrayed a picture of kinship carers hoping that there might be a return home for the children, coupled with an acceptance that this was very unlikely, and a willingness to provide a permanent home for them. Over half of those interviewed had the expectation that the children would remain in their care until they were independent, and move out of the family home at an appropriate time (as any natural child would do). For other kinship carers with young children, they looked to adolescence with some anxiety acknowledging that it would be a difficult time.

> We would hope (that she would stay on), but you never know what would happen. She said today that she wasn't leaving until she was thirty – I said, I am sure you will be away out of here before that!

Importantly, the kinship carers invariably felt that the children considered the placement as their home, feeling they could stay there for as long as they wished. While initially many of the placements were temporary, a lot of the kinship carers always knew that they would eventually be permanent. They were able to assess the chances of rehabilitation for the children with the birth-parents, based on their own unique knowledge of the family situation. For the most part they saw little prospect of it. A grandparent commented: 'I don't think that she will ever change, she is not cut out to be the mothering kind. It is all me, me, me!'

In two of the families interviewed, some of the fostered children had grown up and moved on, leaving siblings behind in placement. Despite moving out, they maintained regular contact with their kinship carers, one of the children phoning on a daily basis. The grandparent commented: 'This is always their home; this is where they come to stay.'

In another family, the young person had reached 18 years of age but continued to live with his grandmother, with no plans to move on. In only one case had the young person left the kinship placement in adolescence, and this was to live with an older sibling. These cases help to illustrate the enormous potential for kinship foster care to provide for truly permanent placements for children through to their adulthood and independence.

However, it is important to note that three carers expressed anxiety about the level of support that would be available to them and the children when they were over 18. This anxiety was increased when the children had long-term special needs. In one case where three children had been fostered, the carer felt they could maintain the placement only until the children had left school and got jobs. There was, nevertheless, an impressive sense of permanence about all the kinship placements in the interviews with their carers. This was the children's 'family for life', whether they moved on in their teenage years or many years later.

ADOPTION

Some 18% of children in traditional foster care had adoption as their care plan, this compared to only three in a hundred (3%, n = 4) of those in kinship foster care. The proposed adoption for all these children was by the current foster carers (whether kin or traditional). Interviews with kinship carers showed that adoption was rarely considered as a serious option by them. They echoed findings in American research (Berrick et al., 1994; Thornton, 1991) which concluded that kinship carers' reluctance to adopt was based on the fact that they already had a blood relationship to their foster children. The finality of adoption would mean relinquishing all hope of the children ever returning to their birth-parents, and, importantly, the end of financial and other support from social services for the placement. In addition, kinship carers who were interviewed expressed a fear of the reaction of the birth-parents to adoption as a very final legal solution:

> We wouldn't consider adoption because although her daddy's having problems, he is still her daddy at the end of the day and I don't want to take that from him.

RESIDENCE ORDERS

Under the Children (NI) Order 1995, a residence order settles the arrangements, about the person with whom the child is to be 'resident' and the child is no longer in public care. The child's parents continue to share parental responsibility. It is the most common order giving parental responsibility to non-parents. At face value, it seems to provide a very good solution for those kinship carers who do not wish social services to be so involved in their lives.

Perhaps surprisingly, only slightly more children (17%) in kinship placements had residence orders as their care plan than those in traditional care (13%). The interviews revealed that residence orders were discussed with kinship foster carers by social services in at least half of the families. In general, kinship foster carers, while interested, were apprehensive about the possible repercussions of residence orders for them and the children, both financially and for their ability to access social work support when needed. In addition, like adoption, some kinship carers were concerned about the reaction of the birth-parents to any change in the legal situation. They expressed the fear that it would create further tensions in their relationship. Three of the families supported the children being transferred to residence orders, and this was a reflection of the positive relationship that they already had with social services. They trusted the social worker's recommendation. However, others reacted differently to the suggestion that they should apply for a residence order. They were suspicious that social services were trying to 'wash their hands' of a difficult situation and they were worried how it would be interpreted by the birth-parents.

Kinship foster carers' attitude to alternative legislative arrangements and in particular the move to residence orders for the children seemed to be influenced by three main factors:

1. *Their prior relationship with social services.* In cases where there had been responsive supportive services to the kinship foster carers, a level of trust and respect had been established. This resulted in the kinship foster carers trusting that the Health and Social Services Trust would not advocate a change to a residence order if it would compromise or disadvantage them in any way.
2. *Clarity of the rationale for the change, including the advantages and disadvantages for them.* A continuing problem for kinship foster carers was lack of clarity about their special position within the foster care system, and in particular what their entitlements were in terms of financial help and support. Any attempt to change their status or the status of their foster child brought these issues into sharp relief.
3. *Fear of being left to resolve contentious issues with the birth-parents without the support of the authority of social services.* It was evident that there was ambivalence about social work contact. On the one hand, it was felt as an intrusion on private family life and decisions, yet the withdrawal of support gave rise to anxieties about dealing with contentious issues with the natural parents.

CONCLUSION

Kinship care has been a time-honoured tradition over many centuries, but the inclusion of it as a formal placement option for children in public is more recent. The limited available research on kinship care in the UK research is predominantly positive about outcomes generally and, in particular, its capacity to provide permanent placements. This study provides clear support for these findings; however, caution is needed. Kinship foster care will not be the best placement for all children. The prior relationship between all parties (child, kinship foster carer, and birth-parents) is a strength when these relationships are predominantly positive, but if acrimonious, they can be intensely so. The severe shortage of alternative placements for children and young people should not lead to pressure for the inappropriate use of kinship placements. Kinship foster care is not without its challenges and problems. As the qualitative part of this study confirms, it imposes stress on family systems by changing and redefining family relationships. There can be particular tensions between the birth-parent (especially the birth-mother) who is not related to the kinship carers. There also must be a balanced view taken of the contribution of dysfunction in the kinship carers' family to the birth-parents' inability to care for their children. While acknowledging that the causes of child maltreatment are many and complex, there must be an awareness that some kinship carers (particularly grandparents), through their own parenting, may have contributed to the subsequent failure of their child to parent the child they have later fostered. On the other hand, this study highlighted several examples of the ability of members of the extended family to protect children by urging social services to involvement when they themselves no longer felt that they could protect the child.

One of the great strengths of appropriate kinship foster care, and one that was affirmed by this study, is its ability to provide permanence or a 'family for life' for children or young people. It can take account of the need for continuity of attachment relationships as well as the need for children to permanently belong to a family that is a part of their extended family. It enables children to retain their sense of identity by knowing about their birth-family and fitting together past, present, and future. It often allows children to remain in their home community and area with the network supports these afford. This study found that children in kinship foster care had fewer previous placements than children in traditional foster homes. Interview material supported the view that the kinship carers considered themselves as the child's family for life, and the ending of the formal care episode (in most cases) was not predicted to make any difference to either their living situation or the relationships within the family. This is in stark contrast to many foster care placements. There is, perhaps, not enough emphasis or recognition given to these strengths of kinship foster care in policy and practice, particularly where a narrow view of permanence, that sees adoption as the 'gold standard', is taken.

In reality, many of these kinship placements appeared to have been 'de facto adoptions' – they were the children's families for life. However, they were located within a legislative and administrative system of assessment, boarding out regulations, looked-after children reviews which were formulated on the assumption that the children's stay in care would be temporary and their placement was with strangers. There was little recognition of the difference between these kinship foster parents and traditional, 'stranger' foster parents in the way they were supported and supervised.

There is a growing shortage of placement options for 'looked-after' children. However, kinship foster care must not be considered as a cheap option. If it is to be successful, it needs to be properly resourced and supported. Consideration must be given to the kinship carers and their own children. Children enter kinship care with the same pressing needs as other looked-after children. They need well-supported carers to help them to heal and trust again. Decisions about the best way to do this must be made in consultation with the kinship carers themselves, and should cover a wide spectrum of creative services which respect the extended family network and are not based solely on the parameters governing 'stranger' foster care. There are always risks when children become looked after. The severing of ties with birth-parents (even in dysfunctional families) is a cause of great pain. Relationships and attachments to 'stranger' carers can be notoriously hard to develop. In contrast, kinship care offers for many children a continuity of relationships across the life-span. For many children it will offer the very best alternative to being raised with their birth-parents.

REFERENCES

Aldgate, J. (1980). Identification of factors influencing children's length of stay in care. In J. Triseliotis (ed.), *New Developments in Foster Care and Adoption*. London: Routledge & Kegan Paul.

Benedict, M., Zuravin, S., & Stallings, R. (1996). Adult functioning of children who lived with kin versus non-relative family foster homes. *Child Welfare*, **75**(5), 529–549.

Berrick, J.D., Barth, R.P., & Needall, B. (1994). A comparison of kinship foster homes and foster family homes: Implications for kinship care as family preservation. *Children and Youth Services Review*, **16**(5), 33–63.

Broad, B. (1999). Kinship care: Children placed with extended families or friends. *Childright*, **15**(5), 16–17.

Brooks, D., & Barth, R.P. (1998). Characteristics and outcomes of drug exposed and non drug exposed children in kinship and non-relative foster care. *Children and Youth Services Review*, **20**(6), 475–501.

Bullock, R., Little, M., & Millham, S. (1993). *Going Home: The Return of Children Separated from their Families*. Aldershot: Dartmouth.

CWLA (Child Welfare League of America) (1994). *Kinship Care: A Natural Bridge*. Washington, DC: Author.

Department of Health (1991). *Patterns and Outcomes of Placement*. London: DoH.

Greef, R. (1998). *Fostering Kinship: An International Perspective on Kinship Care*. Aldershot: Ashgate.

Heger, L., & Scannapieco, M. (1995). From family duty to family policy: The evolution of kinship care. *Child Welfare*, **75**(1), 200–216.

Iwaniec, D., & McSherry, D. (2002). *Understanding Child Neglect: Contemporary Issues and Dilemmas*. Occasional Paper No. 2. Belfast: Institute for Child Care Research.

Kelly, G., & McSherry, D. (2002). Adoption from care in Northern Ireland: Problems in the process. *Child and Family Social Work*, **7**(4), 279–311.

Laws, S. (2001). Looking after children within the extended family. In B. Broad (ed.), *Kinship Care: The Placement Choice for Children and Young People*. Lyme Regis: Russell House Publishing.

Milham, S., Bullock, R., Rosie, K., & Haak, M. (1986). *Lost in Care*. Aldershot: Gower.

Thoburn, J. (1994). *Child Placement: Principles and Practice*. Aldershot: Gower.

Thornton, J.L. (1991). Permanency planning in kinship foster homes. *Child Welfare*, **70**(5), 593–601.

Triseliotis, J., Borland, M., Hill, M., & Lambert, L. (1995). *Teenagers and the Social Work Service*. London: HMSO.

CHAPTER 7

EXPLORING REGIONAL TRENDS IN PATHWAYS TO PERMANENCY

Dominic McSherry and Emma Larkin

INTRODUCTION

The Institute of Child Care Research in Belfast has been tracking the placement histories of every child in Northern Ireland, under the age of 5, who was being looked after on 31 March 2000 (n = 375). This major longitudinal study is called 'Pathways to Permanency'. To date, the research has gathered detailed baseline profiles on this population and has also begun to explore how these children and their carers are faring within a range of placement types. The key focus of the research is upon examining the children's pathways to permanency, i.e. returning to their birth-parents, being adopted, or achieving a long-term foster care placement.

The authors are currently developing statistical models, utilising event-history analytical techniques, which will examine the relationship between a range of predictor variables (such as the child's gender, their age when first looked after, length of stay in care, reason for admission to care, number of placements in care), and the child's placement outcome. This type of statistical approach is quite uncommon in this field of research in the UK, but has been utilised quite extensively in the USA (Courtney, 1994; Wells & Guo, 1999; Wulczyn et al., 2002), and to a lesser extent in Australia (Fernandez, 1999). The authors hope to disseminate these findings towards the end of 2006.

This chapter, however, will explore another key issue that emerged within the Pathways to Permanency Study, namely, the extent of variation in permanency outcomes for these children across the different Health and Social Services Trusts in Northern Ireland. There are 11 Health and Social Services Trusts in Northern Ireland with social work responsibilities. These are almost equivalent to local authorities in England and Wales. This variation in approach to the long-term placement of looked-after children raises important questions in

The Child's Journey Through Care: Placement Stability, Care Planning, and Achieving Permanency. Edited by D. Iwaniec.
Copyright © 2006 John Wiley & Sons, Ltd.

terms of the impact that particular placement policies may have on a child's future outcomes, the extent to which they are reflective of either philosophical or local issues, and the subsequent capacity to develop regional placement strategies.

PLACEMENT TRENDS IN NORTHERN IRELAND: POLICY AND PRACTICE

Where possible, it is believed that children should be living with birth-parents as a first care planning option. Indeed, the Children (NI) Order (1995) outlines a duty to promote the upbringing of children by their families by providing a range and level of personal social services in accordance with the children's welfare and safety needs. Professional social work practice in the UK has been attempting to shift from a child protection stance towards a more preventive and supportive model (Walker, 2002). However, there has been difficulty in implementing the family support provisions contained in the 1989 Children Act due to an emphasis on child protection activity by local authorities (Spratt, 2000). In Northern Ireland, a central challenge of the Children (NI) Order (1995) has been to achieve a shift in emphasis from child protection to family support (McSherry et al., 2004; Spratt & Houston, 1999).

It would appear, however, that such a shift in emphasis may have begun to emerge. More recently, the importance of investment in family support measures has been highlighted by the Department of Health, Social Services and Public Safety. The need for a family support strategy to be developed in conjunction with the Boards and Trusts in 2004/2005 was outlined in *Priorities for Action* 2004/2005 (DHSSPS, 2004a), while the 20-year regional strategy (*A Healthier Future*) highlighted the importance of family support services (DHSSPS, 2004b).

If a return home is not achievable, and the children cannot be placed with relatives (see Chapter 6 by Lernihan and Kelly for a detailed review), then adoption is regarded as the next best outcome for children in the looked-after system (Cole, 1985). Northern Ireland has been traditionally slow to embrace the notion of adoption as a permanent placement option for looked-after children (Kelly, 1999; Kelly & McSherry, 2002). However, the way adoption is viewed, utilised, and managed in Northern Ireland has changed in recent years and there has been an increased focus upon achieving permanency for children through adoption by all Boards and Trusts, although not to the same degree.

This increased focus is linked to the recent overhaul of adoption law in the UK. Developments have included *The Prime Minister's Review of Adoption* (Department of Health, 2000a), the ensuing White Paper, *Adoption: A New Approach* (2000b), and the Adoption and Children Act (2002). An adoption and permanence task force was also established in October 2000 in order to develop good practice in terms of promoting stability and secure attachments for vulnerable children and young people and also to ensure that robust arrangements are in place to consider permanence as early as possible in the planning process.

A recent inspection of statutory adoption services in Northern Ireland, *Adopting Best Care* (DHSSPS, 2002), has focused attention upon the existing legislative framework for adoption services. Plans are currently underway for the development of new adoption legislation to put in place appropriate support structures for adoption services, to update the Adoption (NI) Order (1987), and to align adoption legislation more closely with recent legislative developments introduced by the Children (NI) Order (1995) and the Adoption and Children Act (2002) (England and Wales).

As a result of these developments, Northern Ireland has seen a change in the use and practice of adoption. The range of children for whom adoption is now considered as a placement option has broadened to include older children and those who have been looked after for extended periods. There has also been a push for Trusts to encourage foster parents to adopt children who have been in their long-term care (DHSSPS, 2002). Many professionals feel that where strong bonds have formed between the child and the carers, adoption by the foster carers should be encouraged. However, others have cautioned that foster carers may not necessarily be suitable adoptive parents, or the placement itself may not be suitable to meet the child's long-term needs, and have raised concerns regarding the possible detrimental impact of foster carer adoptions, when the numbers of available foster carers are worryingly low (McSherry et al., 2004).

In terms of fostering, a Northern Ireland fostering strategy is due to be introduced in 2006 and will see a major investment to develop fostering services. It is hoped that the strategy will help develop a more cohesive and responsive service, and address a number of current difficulties with foster care provision. These include an insufficient supply of medium- to long-term foster carers, a lack of placement choice, carer recruitment and retention difficulties, insufficient training, and insufficient support to meet the needs of children. The strategy also hopes to address the issue of poor outcomes for looked-after children, particularly when leaving care.

A £6 million five-year strategy has been devised by the four Health and Social Services Boards in order to go some way towards alleviating the approximate £28.5 million funding gap for fostering services in Northern Ireland. It is anticipated that investment in fostering will be streamed into staff recruitment and training as well as employment of additional salaried foster carers to provide specialist service. It is also envisaged that resources will be invested in fostering of additional support and may include initiatives such as a 24-hour helpline to address gaps in existing services, to integrate management of services, provide more specialist response, to set in place long-term planning, and to strengthen provision over the next 2–3 years.

PLACEMENT TRENDS IN NORTHERN IRELAND: STATISTICAL INFORMATION

Adoption

Available figures from the Northern Ireland Guardian ad Litem Agency (NIGALA, 2000, 2001, 2002, 2003, 2004, 2005) indicate that the vast majority of children subject to Adoption Order applications by adoption agencies in the past five years were under the age of 10. The largest numbers of these children were between 2 and 5 years of age. The percentage of children placed by agencies for adoption who were under 5 years of age has remained fairly constant since 2000 with approximate figures ranging between 50% and 60%. There has been a steady decrease in the percentage of children aged under 1 year old who were subject to adoption proceedings from 15% in 2002 to 2% in 2005. These figures show that adoption is no longer weighted towards babies.

While the number of children adopted (placement adoptions as opposed to inter-country or step-parent adoptions) has been erratic from 1999/2000 to the present, an overall increase is evident from the 57 children adopted in 1999/2000 to the 91 adopted in 2004/2005 (NIGALA, 2000, 2001, 2002, 2003, 2004, 2005). When the number of children adopted as a percentage of all looked-after children per year is examined from 2000 to the present, a similarly erratic increase emerges. *Adopting Best Care* recommended a two-fold increase in the percentage of looked-after children adopted from 2.2% in the year ending 31 March 2000 to 4.1% for the year ending 31 March 2001 (DHSSPS, 2002). However, the percentage of looked-after children adopted dropped to 2.6% in the year ending 31 March 2002, and then rose to 4.8% in 2003. A total of 3.3% of looked-after children were adopted in the year ending 31 March 2004 (NIGALA, 2000, 2001, 2002, 2003, 2004, 2005).

Adopting Best Care (DHSSPS, 2002) found significant differences in the rates of adoption within and between Boards. In the year ending 31 March 2001, for example, 9% of looked-after children were adopted in the Southern Health and Social Services Board (SHSSB) compared with 2.4% in the Western Health and Social Services Board (WHSSB). Craigavon and Banbridge Trust had a total of 19% of their looked-after children adopted in the same year compared with 1.4% of the looked-after children in Foyle Trust. Homefirst Trust had the highest number of adoption applications in 2000 (n = 28), 2002 (n = 32), and 2004 (n = 41) (NIGALA, 2000, 2001, 2002, 2003, 2004 2005).

Foster Care

When the percentage of children in foster care as a total of all looked-after children is examined from 2000 to the present, we can see that the mean has decreased slightly from 66% in 2000 to 62% in 2004. When trends are examined for each of the Trusts individually for the years 2000, 2002, and 2004, it can be seen that there was a slight decrease in the percentage of children in foster care in each case. However, it should be emphasised that foster care remains the most utilised placement in each of the Trusts (DHSSPS, 2001, 2003; NISRA, 2004b).

When the percentage of children in foster care as a total of all looked-after children is examined by Trust, regional variation is evident. For example, Craigavon and Banbridge Trust had the highest percentage of their looked-after children in foster care in 2000 (78%) and 2004 (79%). North and West Belfast Trust had the highest percentage in 2002 (72%). Ulster Community and Hospital Trust had by far the steepest decrease in the use of foster care from 2000 and the lowest percentage of their looked-after children in foster care in 2004 (39%) (DHSSPS, 2001, 2003; NISRA, 2004a).

Return Home

There has been an increase in the numbers of looked-after children in Northern Ireland achieving a return home since 2000 (an increase from 19% in 2000 to 21% in 2004). Trends relating to a return home have varied considerably from Trust to Trust since 2000. A decrease in the use of this placement has emerged for some, but an increase has been noted for others. The highest increase in the percentage of children in substitute care placed at home was evident in Ulster Community and Hospital Trust where the percentage increased by 20% in 2000, to 40% in 2002, and 38% in 2004. It also had the highest percentage of looked-after children placed at home in 2002 and 2004, while Down/Lisburn Trust had the highest percentage in 2000 (30%) (DHSSPS, 2001, 2003; NISRA, 2004a). In contrast, there was a decrease in the percentage of children placed at home in Craigavon and Banbridge Trust from 12% in 2000 to 6% in 2004. Indeed, Craigavon and Banbridge Trust had the lowest percentage of children placed at home.

Although variation is evident between Trusts, combined with the figures for adoption and foster care which were described earlier, a pattern can be seen whereby the percentage of looked-after children in foster care has generally decreased while the percentage of adoptions and home placements have increased.

RESEARCH ON REGIONAL PLACEMENT VARIATION

The Department of Health (1998) highlighted the challenge associated with balancing the need for developing local solutions to match situational need while avoiding the pitfalls of 'the postcode lottery' whereby variation within authorities can result in less positive care experiences and opportunities for their respective young looked-after populations.

Oliver et al. (2001) explored English local authority variance on statistical indicators concerning child protection and looked-after children. They largely focused upon variance in key statistics such as numbers of children on the child protection register or numbers of looked-after children. They identified a number of factors that may have contributed to local authority variation. These included technical factors such as problems with data-management systems. The particular circumstances of an authority (such as having a high level of drug misuse) may also have led to particularly high rates of looked-after children. A further category was operational factors relating to the way in which children's services were resourced and delivered (including factors such as the availability of family support services).

Other matters such as availability of services, resources, staffing levels, levels of underlying need, social deprivation, and the underlying ethos and philosophy particular to the organisation, level of turnover, and management regarding the decision-making process have been linked to variation between authorities in relation to rates of looked-after children (Dickens et al., 2005; Packman & Hall, 1998; Stratham et al., 2002). However, less attention has been paid to factors underlying variations in the percentages of children allocated to particular permanent placement types, i.e. return to birth-parents, adoption, and long-term fostering.

Rowe et al. (1989) are one of the few research teams who have investigated variation in terms of placement patterns. They carried out a survey of placement patterns among six local authorities in England including a large city, a smaller metropolitan district, a Midlands county, a Home county, and two London boroughs. When they examined the types of placement employed by these authorities, they found considerable variation in the care experiences of the children despite the authorities working within the same legal framework and within similar resource constraints. Rowe et al. found differences in the amount and type of adoption placements utilised by the authorities in addition to differing rates in the use of foster care. For example, home on trial placements for pre-schoolers ranged from 2% to 14% the percentage of children in foster homes ranged from 26 % to 45%, and the percentage of children adopted ranged from 1% to 7%.

Wulczyn and Hislop (2002) examined placement outcomes for foster children in 12 States across the USA using the Multistate Foster Care Data Archive which is maintained by Chapin Hall Center for Children at the University of Chicago. They commented that 'geographically defined variation can provide important clues about the operation of child welfare programs' (2002, p. 2). They found that urban areas had the lowest rate of return to homes, and highest rates of adoption, and that the incidence rates for children less than 1 year old in urban areas was twice that for the same age group in rural areas, and more than four times the rate for 1- to 5-year-olds. They commented:

> unmeasured child level differences linked to geography may account for these outcomes, but it would be well worth the effort needed to identify the organisational characteristics that contribute to outcomes. In other words, it is rather unlikely that child, family, and community level differences account for all the reasons why some children spend more time in foster care than others do... Since administrative practices and procedures are more amenable to policy interventions, the need to better understand these differences is an inevitable direction for future research.
>
> (2002, p. 21)

EXAMINING REGIONAL VARIATIONS

As mentioned in the Introduction, in addition to examining pathways to permanency for the full cohort, how this may be related to child and family background factors, and comparing how the children are faring in the three types of permanent placement (return home, adoption, and long-term foster care), we were also interested in exploring regional variation in the children's pathways to permanency in the context of the Health and Social Services (HSS) Trust in whose care they were placed.

Methodology

There are 11 Health and Social Services Trusts with responsibilities for looked-after children in Northern Ireland and these are administered by four Health and Social Services Boards (Eastern, Northern, Southern, and Western). For the first phase of the study, a full population of looked-after children under the age of 5 was identified by accessing the Northern Irish Social Services information systems (SOSCARE) for 31 March 2000, for all 11 Trusts. Each Trust maintains its own records relating to the placement of looked after children. Placement information on 422 children was received. Upon cleaning of the data, 27 cases were removed (i.e. children who were not being looked after on 31 March 2000), giving a total of 395 children. Of these, it was possible to access additional information on 375 (95%) through manual searching of social work case files. Given that this additional information was necessary to understanding the children's placement pathways, the sample was deemed to consist of these 375 children.

The type of information that was gathered from the case files consisted of the child's reason for entry to care (type of harm or potential harm to child), the child's and family's background (health and behavioural problems, family constitution, familial economic status, and parental employment), and adverse circumstances (such as alcohol and drug abuse, domestic violence, mental illness, offending, and bereavements). After two years another SOSCARE download was conducted to identify the children's placement on 31 March 2002, and case file searches were carried out for a second time to update the information that had been collected in 2000.

As well as developing this detailed baseline profile on the population, and examining the children's care pathways to the different permanency option, it was also important to examine how the children fared in their placements in comparative terms. This essentially marked the second phase of the study. Here, interviews were conducted with a sample of adoptive parents (n = 53), foster carers (n = 56) of children who remained in foster care, and birth-parents (n = 10) of children who were returned home. During the interviews, carers completed Goodman's (1997) 'Strengths and Difficulties Questionnaire' (SDQ) and Abidin's (1990) short-form 'Parenting Stress Index' (PSI). They then took part in a semi-structured interview/discussion which focused on their views and feelings in relation to

the child's placement history and reason for admission to care; the child's placement history to date; experiences of dealing with social services; contact with the
birth-family or previous carers; the development of bonding with the child and
the child's attachment; the child's place in the immediate and extended family,
and support issues.

The focus of the second phase of the study was not upon identifying changing
placement patterns in the population across time, but upon examining how the
children themselves, and their carers, were getting on. However, it was felt that it
would still be important to get some measure of the children's placement patterns.
This was achieved through direct contact with programme managers in the Trusts
across Northern Ireland, rather than by SOSCARE download. Therefore, the
process of verifying the children's placement occurred between January and
March 2004, rather than on 31 March, as had been the case in 2000 and 2002.

Results

As mentioned earlier, the event-history analysis of placements, and the findings
from the interviews with the carers (both qualitative and quantitative), will be
disseminated towards the end of 2006. Therefore, the following results section will
focus purely upon the regional variation in placement patterns that were found
across 2000, 2002, and 2004.

VARIATIONS IN PLACEMENT PATTERNS OVER TIME

Tables 7.1–7.5 will illustrate the variability that was found between the Trusts
in Northern Ireland over a four-year period (2000–2004), in terms of the use of
non-relative foster care, relative foster care, placement with birth-parents, pre-
adoptive placements, and adoptions. As the numbers of looked-after children in
the full population from Sperrin/Lakeland (n = 20), Newry and Mourne (n = 8),
and Armagh and Dungannon (n = 14) Trusts were relatively small, i.e. less than
or equal to 20, these have not been included in the descriptive statistics. However,
it was felt that the eight Trusts that are presented are sufficient to establish the
extent of placement variability that exists across Northern Ireland.

Table 7.1 shows that in March 2000, 61% of the full population of children
were placed in non-relative foster care, with this dropping to 41% by 2002,
and 22% by 2004. It can be seen that the size of this reduction was almost
identical in both the 2000–2002 (20%) and 2002–2004 (19%) periods. Table 7.1
also shows that this pattern of change was not reflected across the different
Trusts in Northern Ireland. For example, in 2000, Down/Lisburn had a markedly
lower percentage of children in non-relative foster care (40%), relative to most
of the other Trusts, whereas Foyle (76%) and Ulster Community and Hospital
(68%) Trusts showed relatively high percentages of children in this form of
placement.

Table 7.1 Non-relative foster care (%)

Trust	2000	2002	2004	N
Full population	**61**	**41**	**22**	**375**
Causeway	62	35	21	29
Craigavon and Banbridge	61	38	8	26
Down/Lisburn	40	21	10	33
Foyle	76	71	51	59
Homefirst	63	52	13	69
North and West Belfast	49	40	30	43
South and East Belfast	63	33	21	46
Ulster Community and Hospital	68	25	14	28

In 2002, some Trusts were showing quite dramatic drops in the numbers of children in non-relative foster care (such as Ulster Community and Hospital [down by 43%] and South and East Belfast [down by 30%]), while others (such as Foyle [down by 5%], North and West Belfast [down by 9%], and Homefirst [down by 11%]) showed little change. Between 2002 and 2004, most Trusts presented a further decrease of approximately 10%. However, there were relatively large percentage decreases in both Homefirst (39%) and Foyle (20%) Trusts.

By 2004, it could be seen that Ulster Community and Hospital (down by 54% to 14%), Craigavon and Banbridge (down by 53% to 8%), and Homefirst (down by 50% to 13%) Trusts showed large reductions in the percentage of children remaining in non-relative foster care, whereas in North and West Belfast (down by 19% to 30%), Foyle (down by 25% to 51%), and Down/Lisburn (down by 30% to 10%) there were much smaller reductions. It is worth noting, however, that in March 2000 both Down/Lisburn and North and West Belfast Trusts had the smallest percentages of children in non-relative care across all Trusts.

Table 7.2 shows that in both 2000 and 2002 around 10% of the full population were placed in relative foster care, with this dropping to only 6% by 2004. There

Table 7.2 Relative foster care (%)

Trust	2000	2002	2004	N
Full population	**10**	**11**	**6**	**375**
Causeway	4	7	0	29
Craigavon and Banbridge	8	4	0	26
Down/Lisburn	18	9	10	33
Foyle	15	20	15	59
Homefirst	7	4	2	69
North and West Belfast	26	23	14	43
South and East Belfast	2	2	2	46
Ulster Community and Hospital	11	18	0	28

was, however, major variation in the use of this form of placement across the Trusts. The percentage of children placed in relative foster care in North and West Belfast (26%), Down/Lisburn (18%), and Foyle (15%) were much higher than those in South and East Belfast (2%), Causeway (4%), Homefirst (7%), and Craigavon and Banbridge (8%) Trusts.

By 2002, there was very little change to these patterns, with minor reductions where levels were high, and little change where levels were low. The exception is Ulster and Community Hospital Trust which showed quite a large increase between 2000 (11%) and 2002 (18%). By 2004, those Trusts where percentage levels were low in 2000 had very few (Homefirst and South and East Belfast) or no children (Causeway, Craigavon and Banbridge, and Ulster Community and Hospital) placed in relative foster care. However, Trusts such as Foyle (15%), North and West Belfast (14%), and Down/Lisburn (10%), as in 2000, continued to show relatively high percentage levels of children placed in relative foster care.

Table 7.3 shows that 14% of the full population were being looked after by their birth-parents in March 2000. This rose by 8% to 22% by March 2002, and by an additional 5% to 27% by 2004. However, Table 7.3 shows that the pattern of change for the full population was not reflected within the Trusts. In 2000, South and East Belfast (29%) and Down/Lisburn (21%) Trusts had very high percentage levels of children living with their birth-parents compared with Craigavon and Banbridge (4%), North and West Belfast (7%), and Foyle (9%) Trusts.

By 2002, Trusts such as Craigavon and Banbridge (up by 19%), Down/Lisburn (up by 19%), Ulster Community and Hospital (up by 15%), and South and East Belfast (up by 14%) had increased these percentage levels to a greater extent than Foyle (down by 2%), Homefirst (up by 1%), Causeway (up by 7%), and North and West Belfast (up by 9%) Trusts. By 2004, those Trusts where percentage levels were high in 2000 remained high, with some Trusts showing levels over 40% (Ulster Community and Hospital, South and East Belfast, and Down/Lisburn). Of these three, Ulster Community and Hospital showed the greatest increase in the percentage of children living with their parents between March 2000 and

Table 7.3   Care with birth-parents (%)

Trust	2000	2002	2004	N
Full population	14	22	27	375
Causeway	17	24	31	29
Craigavon and Banbridge	4	23	15	26
Down/Lisburn	21	40	42	33
Foyle	9	7	24	59
Homefirst	10	11	18	69
North and West Belfast	7	16	19	43
South and East Belfast	29	43	42	46
Ulster Community and Hospital	14	29	43	28

March 2004 (up by 29%). In other Trusts, percentage levels remained relatively low (Craigavon and Banbridge, Homefirst, and North and West Belfast). It is interesting to note that although Craigavon and Banbridge Trust showed a large increase in children living with their birth-parents between 2000 and 2002 (up by 19% to 23%), this figure dropped quite noticeably between 2002 and 2004 (down by 8% to 15%).

Table 7.4 illustrates that in March 2000, 13% of the full population were living in pre-adoptive placements. This reduced to 7% by 2002, and to only 3% by 2004. However, these trends were not reflected across the various Trusts in Northern Ireland. In March 2000, Craigavon and Banbridge (27%), Homefirst (20%), and North and West Belfast (16%) Trusts had relatively high percentage levels of children in pre-adoptive placements, whereas Foyle (0%), South and East Belfast (4%), and Ulster Community and Hospital (7%) had relatively low levels.

By 2002, it can be seen that the level of children in pre-adoptive placements had decreased significantly in those Trusts where levels were quite high in 2000 (Craigavon and Banbridge, Homefirst, and North and West Belfast). However, there was some growth in the use of this form of placement in Trusts which had low levels in 2000 (Foyle, South and East Belfast, and Ulster Community and Hospital). By 2004, only two Trusts (Homefirst and South and East Belfast) had children living in pre-adoptive placements.

Table 7.5 shows that as one might expect, given that the focus of this study is upon looked-after children, none of the children had been adopted by 31 March 2000. However, by 2002, 18% of the full population had been adopted, with this rising to 38% (up 20%) by 2004. Table 7.5 illustrates that this pattern of change was not reflected across the different Trusts. It can be seen that percentage increases in the numbers of children adopted were much higher in Causeway (35%), Craigavon and Banbridge (31%), and Homefirst (23%), compared to Foyle (0%), Ulster Community and Hospital (14%), South and East Belfast (15%), and North and West Belfast (16%) Trusts.

Table 7.4 Pre-adoption placements (%)

Trust	2000	2002	2004	N
Full population	13	7	3	375
Causeway	14	0	0	29
Craigavon and Banbridge	27	0	0	26
Down/Lisburn	12	9	0	33
Foyle	0	2	0	59
Homefirst	20	7	10	69
North and West Belfast	16	0	0	43
South and East Belfast	4	7	9	46
Ulster Community and Hospital	7	14	0	28

Table 7.5   Numbers adopted (%)

Trust	2000	2002	2004	N
Full population	**0**	**18**	**38**	**375**
Causeway	0	35	48	29
Craigavon and Banbridge	0	31	69	26
Down/Lisburn	0	18	39	33
Foyle	0	0	10	59
Homefirst	0	23	52	69
North and West Belfast	0	16	26	43
South and East Belfast	0	15	26	46
Ulster Community and Hospital	0	14	36	28

By 2004, it can be seen that both Craigavon and Banbridge (up by 38% to 69%) and Homefirst (up by 29% to 52%) Trusts continued to show large increases in the number of children being adopted. In this period, two additional Trusts which had shown relatively low levels of adoption by 2002 (namely Down/Lisburn and Ulster Community and Hospital) showed percentage increases of over 20% in the number of children adopted. Other Trusts which had shown low percentage levels of adopted children by 2002 (namely Foyle, North and West Belfast, and South and East Belfast) showed 10% increases in the percentage of children adopted. Craigavon and Banbridge Trust (which had shown a large percentage increase by 2002) showed a more conservative increase (13%) between 2002 and 2004.

DISCUSSION OF RESULTS

The findings presented here clearly illustrate that the placement trends for the full population of children, in terms of the range of permanency options (i.e. adoption, living with birth-parents, and long-term foster care), are not an accurate reflection of placement practice across the different Trusts in Northern Ireland. Essentially, the tables show that some Trusts appear to have a preference for a particular placement, or combination of placements, for their younger looked-after children.

In terms of foster care, Foyle Trust showed a major preference (51%) for non-relative foster care placement, four years after the initial census point, with birth-parent placement (24%) also quite common. North and West Belfast Trust also showed a continued preference for non-relative foster care (30%), closely followed by adoption (26%). We described earlier that available health and personal social care statistics indicate that Craigavon and Banbridge Trust had the highest percentage of children in foster care in both 2000 (78%) and 2004 (79%), while North and West Belfast Trust had the highest percentage in 2002 (72%). However, it needs to be borne in mind that these figures relate to the total looked-after population, whereas our population was restricted to children under 5 years of age.

Regarding adoption, this was the predominant form of placement in Craigavon and Banbridge (69%) and Homefirst (52%) Trusts, while Causeway showed a preference for a combination of adoption (48%) and, to a lesser extent, living with birth-parents (31%). These findings appear to tie in with the statistics that were provided earlier on trends in the use of adoption across Northern Ireland, which indicated that Homefirst Trust had the highest number of adoption applications in 2000 (n = 28), 2002 (n = 32), and 2004 (n = 41).

In terms of living with birth-parents, this was the most common form of placement in Down/Lisburn Trust (42%, closely followed by adoption at 39%), and Ulster Community and Hospital Trust (43%, also closely followed by adoption at 36%). Only South and East Belfast Trust showed a range of preference across the three placement types, i.e. living with birth-parents (42%), adoption (26%), and non-relative foster care (21%), four years after the initial census point. As described earlier, the health and personal social care statistics for Northern Ireland suggest an increase in the numbers of looked-after children in Northern Ireland achieving a return home since 2000, with Ulster Community and Hospital Trust seeing the most substantial increase in the percentage of children placed at home since the year 2000. Our results would tend to concur with these statistics.

The type of preferences for particular forms of placement highlighted here raises a number of important questions. What is it that is the driving choice of placement across the Trusts in different directions? Why is it that Trusts such as Craigavon and Banbridge and Homefirst Trusts have made major advances towards the use of adoption for looked-after children, while Foyle continues to favour continued placement in foster care? Why is it that Trusts such as Down/Lisburn and Ulster Community Trusts appear better able to both keep looked-after children at home with their birth-parents and to subsequently return children to their birth-parents after a spell in foster care? Are these different approaches reflective of differing placement philosophies, system idiosyncrasies that favour a particular type of placement, or a mixture of both? These questions can only be answered by additional research that would probe the particular placement practices across the Trusts in Northern Ireland in greater depth. The authors are currently developing a research proposal that would specifically address these issues.

It appears that within Northern Ireland, the type of permanent placements provided for looked-after children may be subject to a type of 'postcode lottery', as appears to be the case in England and Wales (DoH, 1998). Essentially, our findings suggest that the type of permanent placement provided for a looked-after child is dependent to some degree upon the particular placement practices of their local Trust. The DoH (1998) raised concerns that this type of postcode lottery may result in less positive care experiences and opportunities for the respective young looked-after populations. This assessment can only be made on the basis of an evaluation of the relative outcomes of the various forms of permanent placement, i.e. long-term foster care, adoption, and return to live with birth-parents. However, very few longitudinal studies have examined this range of permanent placements and compared outcomes (Sinclair et al., 2005; Ward et al., 2006).

The most widely used outcome statistics on public care in the UK are those developed by the UK Joint Working Party on Foster Care (1999). Children who have been in care are: ten times more likely to be excluded from school, twelve times more likely to leave school with no qualifications, four times more likely to be unemployed, sixty times more likely to join the ranks of the homeless, fifty times more likely to be sent to prison, and their own children are sixty-six times more likely to need public care than the children of those who have not been in public care themselves. These figures cannot be dismissed lightly. However, there are problems with them. The fundamental question is 'more likely than who?' The figures compare children who have been in care with the average for the whole population, not children from the same backgrounds who have not been in care. They also tend to associate the 'problem' with having been in care, whereas it may have developed in the years before the child was admitted to care, after they were discharged, or even regardless of their ever being placed in care. Furthermore, research by Ward et al. (2005) noted that despite these suggested shortcomings, many children who have experienced the system view their experiences in a positive light.

Thoburn (1991) demonstrated that, when other variables are held constant, there was no difference in breakdown rates between children placed for adoption and those placed in permanent foster families. Furthermore, Triseliotis (2002) reported a diminishing of the differences in disruption rates between adoption and long-term foster care as older and more difficult children are adopted. However, more recently Selwyn and Quinton (2004) reported very substantial differences between the two. They followed 130 children who had a 'best-interest decision' of adoption as the care plan; however, 46 were not adopted but placed in long-term foster care. At follow-up, 46% of the foster placements had disrupted compared to 17% of the adoptive placements. The children came from similar abusive backgrounds. However, the fostered children were older when they first entered care and when the best-interests decision was made, and were also more likely to have learning difficulties and health problems.

Research that compares the two types of permanent placement consistently reports adoption as delivering better outcomes. Triseliotis (2002, p. 31) reviewed the literature pertaining to both adoption and long-term foster care, and noted that 'compared with long-term foster care, adoption still provides higher levels of emotional security, a stronger sense of belonging, and a more enduring base in life for those who cannot live with their birth parents'. In rigorous comparisons, Sinclair et al. (2005) reported that adopted children were doing better on most outcome variables, although not dramatically so. The researchers attributed this, in part, to the 'family' feeling that adoptive placements generate in children. They noted that the 'difference between adoption and long-term fostering is partly symbolic. Foster carers are not parents, while adoptive carers are' (2005, p.103).

While there has been a major growth in interest and research over the past decade on the lives of children who remain in foster care or are adopted, the experience of those children who return home after a spell in care has received relatively little attention (Bullock et al., 1998). Research that has managed to incorporate the experiences of these children (Aldgate & Bradley, 1999; Cleaver, 2000; Selwyn et al., 2003; Skuse & Ward, 2003; Sinclair et al., 2005) has highlighted two related points. Firstly, the difficulty that is experienced when attempting to recruit these hard-to-reach children, and, secondly, the importance of trying to do so. Although often described as an almost impossible task, Skuse and Ward (2003) managed to interview 39% (n = 49) of their sample of children who had returned home at some point during the tracking period of their study (which was examining children's own perspectives of care and accommodation). The study provides a worrying account of the lives of children returned to their homes, which was typified by a lack of formal support. Older children tended not to remain at home for long, with multiple transitions between different relatives common. The study raised questions concerning the emphasis that is placed on having children returned to their homes, the extent to which these placements are supported when the child does return home, and the efficacy of defining return-home placements as permanent.

CONCLUSION

Clearly, the Pathways to Permanency Study is in a strong position to inform the debate as to the relative merits of the particular permanent placement options, and should inform the development and implementation of regional adoption and foster care strategies for Northern Ireland mentioned earlier. However, it is important to bear in mind that the reasons for variation in placement policy across the Trusts in Northern Ireland is not well understood. These variations may be reflective of differing philosophical and theoretical positions on what is best for looked-after children, and may, therefore, be amenable to change on the basis of strong research evidence that specifies the association between particular long-term placements, and positive outcomes for children.

However, there may also be a range of local issues that may dictate, to some degree, the capacity of any particular Trust to develop alternative placement strategies, even where this may be desired. It would, therefore, be essential for this to be taken into consideration before any attempts were made by central government to impose uniform, regional placement strategies on all Trusts, with associated targets and timescales. It would be important to examine issues at the local level in the first instance, so that support could be put in place to facilitate any proposed changes that were centred around outcome studies, such as the current study, that highlighted which types of placement are best suited to which children. As mentioned earlier, it is hoped that additional research can be conducted to examine these issues in greater depth.

ACKNOWLEDGEMENTS

The authors would like to thank Greg Kelly for his assistance in developing this work.

REFERENCES

Abidin, R.R. (1990). *Parenting Stress Index Manual.* Charlottesville, VA: Pediatric Psychology Press.

Aldgate, J., & Bradley, M. (1999). *Supporting Families through Short-term Fostering.* London: The Stationery Office.

Bullock, R., Gooch, D., & Little, M. (1998). *Children Going Home: The Re-unification of Families.* Aldershot: Ashgate.

Children (NI) Order (1995). Belfast: HMSO.

Cleaver, H. (2000). *Fostering Family Contact: A Study of Children, Parents, and Foster Carers.* London: The Stationery Office.

Cole, E.S. (1985). *Director's Report, Permanency Report.* New York: Child Welfare League of America.

Courtney, M. (1994). Factors associated with the reunification of foster children with their families. *Social Service Review,* **68,** 82–108.

Department of Health (1998). *Modernising Social Services: Promoting Independence, Improving Protection, Raising Standards.* London: The Stationery Office.

Department of Health (2000a). *The Prime Minister's Review of Adoption in England.* London: The Stationery office.

Department of Health (2000b). *White Paper: Adoption, a New Approach.* London: The Stationery office.

DHSSPS (2001). *Key Indicators of Personal Social Services for Northern Ireland 2001.* Belfast: Department of Health, Social Services, and Public Safety. An Roinn Sláinte, Seirbhísí Sóisialta agus Sábháilteachta Poiblí.

DHSSPS (2002). *Adopting Best Care: Inspection of Statutory Adoption Services in Northern Ireland.* Belfast: Department of Health, Social Services, and Public Safety. An Roinn Sláinte, Seirbhísí Sóisialta agus Sábháilteachta Poiblí.

DHSSPS (2003). *Key Indicators of Personal Social Services for Northern Ireland 2003.* Belfast: Department of Health, Social Services, and Public Safety. An Roinn Sláinte, Seirbhísí Sóisialta agus Sábháilteachta Poiblí.

DHSSPS (2004a). *Priorities for Action 2004/2005: Planning Priorities and Actions for the Health and Personal Social Services.* Belfast: Department of Health, Social Services, and Public Safety. An Roinn Sláinte, Seirbhísí Sóisialta agus Sábháilteachta Poiblí.

DHSSPS (2004b). *A Healthier Future: A Twenty Year Vision for Health and Wellbeing in Northern Ireland 2005–2025.* Belfast: Department of Health, Social Services, and Public Safety. An Roinn Sláinte, Seirbhísí Sóisialta agus Sábháilteachta Poiblí.

Dickens, J., Howell, D., Thoburn, J., & Schofield, G. (2005). Children starting to be looked after by local authorities in England: An analysis of inter-authority variation and case-centred decision making. *British Journal of Social Work,* doi:10.1093/bjsw/bch276.

Fernandez, E. (1999). Pathways in substitute care: Representations of placement careers of children using event history analysis. *Children and Youth Services Review,* **21**(3), 177–216.

Goodman, R. (1997). The Strengths and Difficulties Questionnaire: A research note. *Journal of Child Psychology and Psychiatry,* **38,** 581–586.

Kelly, G. (1999). Freeing for adoption: The Northern Ireland social care context. *Child Care in Practice,* **5**(3), 243–250.

Kelly, G., & McSherry, D. (2002). Adoption from care in Northern Ireland: Problems in the process. *Child and Family Social Work,* **7,** 297–309.

McSherry, D., Iwaniec, D., & Larkin, E. (2004). *Counting the Costs: The Children (Northern Ireland) Order 1995, Social Work, and the Courts.* Research Report. Belfast: Institute of Child Care Research, Queen's University.

NIGALA (2000). *Northern Ireland Guardian ad Litem Agency Annual Report 1999–2000.* Belfast: NIGALA.

NIGALA (2001). *Northern Ireland Guardian ad Litem Agency Annual Report 2000–2001*. Belfast: NIGALA.

NIGALA (2002). *Northern Ireland Guardian ad Litem Agency Annual Report 2001–2002*. Belfast: NIGALA.

NIGALA (2003). *Northern Ireland Guardian ad Litem Agency Annual Report 2002–2003*. Belfast: NIGALA.

NIGALA (2004). *Northern Ireland Guardian ad Litem Agency Annual Report 2003–2004*. Belfast: NIGALA.

NIGALA (2005). *Northern Ireland Guardian ad Litem Agency Annual Report 2004–2005*. Belfast: NIGALA.

NISRA (2002). *Children Order Statistics: 1 April 2001–31 March 2002*. Belfast: Department of Health, Social Services, and Public Safety. An Roinn Sláinte, Seirbhísí Sóisialta agus Sábháilteachta Poiblí.

NISRA (2004a). *Children Order Statistics: 1 April 2003–31 March 2004*. Belfast: Department of Health, Social Services, and Public Safety. An Roinn Sláinte, Seirbhísí Sóisialta agus Sábháilteachta Poiblí.

NISRA (2004b). *Community Statistics: 1 April 2003–31 March 2004*. Belfast: Department of Health, Social Services, and Public Safety. An Roinn Sláinte, Seirbhísí Sóisialta agus Sábháilteachta Poiblí.

NISRA (2005). *Children Order Statistical Tables*. Belfast: Department of Health, Social Services, and Public Safety. An Roinn Sláinte, Seirbhísí Sóisialta agus Sábháilteachta Poiblí.

Oliver, C., Owen, C., Stratham, J., & Moss, P. (2001). *Figures and Facts: Local Authority Variance on Indicators Concerning Child Protection and Children Looked After*. London: Thomas Coram Research Unit, University of London, Institute of Education.

Packman, J., & Hall, C. (1998). *From Care to Accommodation: Support, Protection and Control in Child Care Services*. London: The Stationery Office.

Rowe, J., Hundleby, M., & Garnett, L. (1989). *Child Care Now: A Survey of Placement Patterns*. London: BAAF.

Selwyn, J., & Quinton, D. (2004). Stability, permanence, outcomes, and support: foster care and adoption compared. *Adoption and Fostering*, **28**(4), 6–16.

Selwyn, J., Sturgess, W., Quinton, D., & Baxter, C. (2003). *Costs and Outcomes of Non-infant Adoptions: Report to the Department for Education and Skills*. London: DfES.

Sinclair, I., Baker, C., Wilson, K., & Gibbs, I. (2005). *Foster Children: Where They Go and How They Get On*. London: Jessica Kingsley.

Skuse, T., & Ward, H. (2003). *Listening to Children's Views of Care and Accommodation*. Report to the Department of Health. Loughborough: Centre for Child and Family Research, University of Loughborough.

Spratt, T. (2000). Decision making by senior social workers at point of first referral. *British Journal of Social Work*, **30**, 579–618.

Spratt, T., & Houston, S. (1999). Developing critical social work in theory and in practice: Child protection and communicative reason. *Child and Family Social Work*, **4**, 315–324.

Stratham, J., Candappa, M., Simon, A., & Owen, C. (2002). *Trends in Care: Exploring the Reasons for the Increase in Children Looked After by Local Authorities*. London: Thomas Coram Research Unit, University of London, Institute of Education.

Thoburn, J. (1991). Evaluating placement: An overview of 1,165 placements and some methodological issues. In J. Fratter, J. Rowe, D. Sapsford, & J. Thoburn (eds), *Permanent Family Placement: A Decade of Experience*. London: BAAF.

Triseliotis, J. (2002). Long-term foster care or adoption? The evidence examined. *Child and Family Social Work*, **7**, 23–33.

UK Joint Working Party on Foster Care (1999). *UK National Standards for Foster Care*. London: National Foster Care Association.

Walker, S. (2002). Family support and the role of social work: Renaissance or entrenchment? *European Journal of Social Work*, **5**(1), 43–54.

Ward, H., Munro, E.H., & Deardon, C. (2006). *Babies and Young Children in Care: Life Pathways, Decision-making, and Practice*. London: Jessica Kingsley.

Ward, H., Skuse, T., & Munro, E. (2005). 'The best of times, the worst of times': Young people's views of care and accommodation. *Adoption and Fostering*, **29**(1), 8–17.

Wells, K., & Guo, S. (1999). Reunification and re-entry of foster children. *Children and Youth Services Review*, **21**(4), 273–279.

Wulczyn, F., & Hislop, K.B. (2002). *Foster Care Dynamics in Urban and Non-urban Counties*. Washington, DC: Assistant Secretary for Planning and Evaluation, Department of Health and Human Services.

Wulczyn, F., Hislop, K.B., & Harden, B.J. (2002). The placement of infants in foster care. *Infant Mental Health Journal*, **23**(5), 454–475.

Part III

Residential and Mixed Care

CHAPTER 8

DEVELOPMENTS IN RESIDENTIAL CARE IN NORTHERN IRELAND

Dominic McSherry and Emma Larkin

INTRODUCTION

Over the past two decades in the UK, family foster care has assumed a dominant position in terms of the provision of substitute care for looked-after children, with a major decline in residential provision and an almost total restriction in its use to behaviourally challenging adolescents who cannot be accommodated in foster homes. In this context it has been argued that residential care has become a placement of last resort (Little et al., 2005) or a '21st century dumping exercise' (Fulcher, 2001, p. 432). Within Northern Ireland, attempts have been made to move residential care from this 'last resort' position to one of 'positive choice' over a relatively short period (DHSS, 1998). This has stemmed, in part, from a realisation that foster care is not the panacea for child and family difficulties that many considered it to be, and that there will always be a need for a certain level of residential provision. The current focus is upon the development of specialised models of residential care that specifically address the complex needs of the children requiring this type of placement (EHSSB, 2004).

Despite these recent developments, concerns remain that the children to whom these services would be directed are those who would be considered unsuitable for fostering (or for whom foster placements cannot be found), which raises the question as to whether this really addresses the concept of residential care being a less desirable form of provision than family foster care. Furthermore, it remains unclear how the specialisation of residential care provision can address the major problem of improving outcomes for these vulnerable children and young people, given the complexity of behavioural and emotional problems that they tend to experience. This chapter will explore the recent move towards specialised residential provision within Northern Ireland, commonly defined as Intensive Support Units (ISUs), also reflecting on related developments within

The Child's Journey Through Care: Placement Stability, Care Planning, and Achieving Permanency. Edited by D. Iwaniec.
Copyright © 2006 John Wiley & Sons, Ltd.

England and Wales. It will examine their potential to more effectively address the particular difficulties that children and young people requiring them present, and to re-configure residential care as a positive choice, relative to foster care, rather than as a last resort.

SETTING THE CONTEXT FOR CHANGE – RESIDENTIAL CARE IN ENGLAND AND WALES

There has been a dramatic decrease in the number of children and young people entering residential care in England and Wales over the past 20 years, perhaps by as much as 50% (Berridge & Brodie, 1998). It has been argued that factors such as policy and practice shifts towards preventative services, a changed awareness of and attitudes about children's needs, and financial considerations have all contributed to this decline (Gooch, 1996; Hayden et al., 1999; Utting et al., 1997).

As a result of this, many of the children who do enter residential care tend to be older and have more complex problems than in previous years (Frost et al., 1999). Residential care must, therefore, cater for children with a wide range of problem behaviours (Berridge & Brodie, 1998; Sinclair & Gibbs, 1998). Some authorities have reduced their quota of children's homes to very few or even none: a small number of residential placements continue to be made in voluntary and private facilities by these authorities. However, these tend to be very expensive and often involve placing the child or young person at a considerable distance away from the family home (Packman & Hall, 1998). The major reduction in residential care provision has also placed enormous strain on foster care services (Cliffe & Berridge, 1991).

The quality of care provided to looked-after children, including those in residential care, has also come under increased scrutiny in recent years. *The Report of the Review of Safeguards for Children Living Away from Home* (Utting et al., 1997) was instrumental in highlighting areas of concern for children's homes. A key concern was that the mix of young people is seldom taken into account when decisions are made as to where to place a child, and that the consequences of inappropriate 'mixing' can include unsettled and difficult-to-manage behaviour. It was highlighted that inappropriate 'mixing' could lead to children being placed in homes unsuited to their needs and capabilities, leading to potentially harmful consequences both for the child and the unit. An associated concern highlighted in the *Report* was the provision of generic unspecialised care and insufficient choice of realistic placements for each child based on their assessed needs. Almost ten years later, it would appear that the situation has not changed to any great extent.

Interventions in Residential Care

Sinclair (1988) noted that in order to successfully counteract problem behaviours and simultaneously to provide for the more pronounced care needs of such vulnerable children and young people, residential units must provide more than the lowest denominator of care and accommodation. This sentiment is reflected by the Department of Health (DoH, 1998) which stated that residential care should provide a young person with more than just the basics, and should measurably improve his or her quality of life.

There are several ways that staff in residential units can intervene to enhance adaptive behaviour and improve the quality of life chances of the young people in their care. At a basic level, residential care must provide a child or young person with a safe environment (Nunno et al., 2003). Tasks that can fall to residential homes in order to successfully supplement or substitute family efforts include: encouragement of pro-social skills; discouragement of delinquent, anti-social, and disturbed behaviour; and provision of a reasonable upbringing (Sinclair, 2005). In order to be successful and to have the best chances of reducing maladaptive behavioural outcomes, Sinclair (2005) suggested that residential homes needed to be coherent, to provide warmth, and to encourage the acquisition of valuable skills. For long-term success, it has been argued that residential units must also provide effective preparation for independence, given the accumulated evidence which suggests that residential care can often leave young adults ill-equipped for independent living (Parker, 1988; Pinkerton, 2002; Pinkerton & McCrea, 1999).

The terms 'intervention' or 'treatment', when applied to residential care, can be interpreted in a number of ways. Research has indicated that most homes attempt to provide treatment for at least some of their residents (Gibbs & Sinclair, 1999; Sinclair & Gibbs, 1998). However, it has also been noted that 'treatment' is a slippery concept in that it is rarely explicitly defined, and is often assigned disparate meanings and approached in an inconsistent and incoherent manner by those implementing the 'treatment' (Gibbs & Sinclair, 1999).

As one of a number of placement options in substitute care, residential care is, in itself, just one type of intervention and source of treatment for young people who cannot be cared for at home. Once in a residential placement, intervention can be generalised or specified to a child's or a group of children's needs. However, Gooch (1996) noted that trends within children's homes can be characterised by a tendency towards a more generalist service implementation, and less specialisation by sector, with a resulting mix of needs.

Many of the interventions with children and young people in residential care involve dealing with problems such as aggression, restraint, and control (Stevens, 2004). Cognitive-behavioural interventions, including techniques such as social skills training, assertiveness training, self-control, and self-instruction, are being used with increasing frequency to address such problems (Sheldon, 1995; Stevens, 2004). Stevens (2004) examined practice and lessons from American research into the use of cognitive-behavioural interventions with adolescents in residential care and found that, while the evidence appeared to support the use of such interventions, it was difficult to apply these findings to residential settings within the UK without taking into consideration other factors to ensure success, such as support from school, peers, and parents. Adequate assessment of the child or young person, together with adequate staff training and awareness of child development, were also identified as important for the successful implementation of interventions. Furthermore, it was also noted that where these types of interventions are being applied in a residential setting, they tend not to be generalised to other settings where the young people also spend their time, for example, when at school or when visiting their family. This makes progress more difficult as consistency is a critical component for success when applying any behavioural management technique.

Specialised Provision

Rowe et al. (1989) found limited specialist provision in children's homes when compared to other placement options (e.g. foster care). The most common rationale for placement in the children's homes investigated was simply to provide accommodation. Utting et al. (1997) pointed out that specialism in residential care was impeded due to the system being too small for adequate choice with this difficulty exacerbated by an excessive focus on placing children and young people in locations near the family home. Sinclair (2005) outlined four obstacles to specialist provision in England and Wales. First, fewer homes result in a lack of choice both for the young people and for the staff, and in increased difficulty in avoiding a clash of functions and an unsuitable mix of young people in homes. Second, the decline in the sector, and changes to managerial organisation, have created a state of flux. Third, there is an expectation that young people should be placed close to their homes. Independent-sector homes tend to provide more specialist provision, but also tend to be further away from residents' families. Fourth, the creation of small unitary authorities makes it more difficult to provide a spectrum of homes under the local authorities' own control. Sinclair and Gibbs (1998) found evidence of intended specialism in the residential units they investigated. Examples included homes that had attempted to cater particularly for young black men, or young people aged between 10 and 12. However, regardless of intent, the residential care homes investigated tended to house diverse groups.

It is the task of Social Services Departments to encourage the development of sufficient diversity and specialisation using clear specifications and expectations for each unit or home (ADSS, 2006). Nunno et al. (2003) echoed the assertion that specialised knowledge and skills are required in order for staff at residential units to prevent and manage problem behaviour. These authors evaluated and monitored the effectiveness of a crisis intervention system known as 'Therapeutic Crisis Intervention' (TCI) which provides staff with the skills and knowledge to respond to the behaviour and emotions of children. This system was developed from crisis management, prevention, and de-escalation theory, and is based on the premise that adults can help a child to resolve a crisis by responding in a therapeutic and developmentally appropriate manner. It was found that implementation of TCI was successful in reducing the frequency and intensity of critical incidents, and in increasing staff knowledge, confidence, and consistency in dealing with such crises.

Other interventions have focused on the care and management of sexually abused children. Based on their study of understanding and management of abused children in residential treatment, Kools and Kennedy (2002) have shown that intervention with such children should be based on sound developmental principles and care-giver sensitivity. They also argued that staff must be able to recognise and understand behavioural manifestations of past abuse in order to effectively intervene to manage the behaviour. Farmer (2004), in her examination of the management and treatment provided in residential and foster care for sexually abused or abusing children and young people, identified that there were four distinct groups within the population examined and that each of these groups required differing management approaches and placement type. This highlights that even when dealing with a specific sub-group of children and young people in the residential care population, sensitivity must be involved when tailoring intervention and treatment approaches to accommodate multiple and varying needs.

It has been argued, however, that most of the interventions provided for children and young people in residential care could also be provided for children in foster care, without the associated dangers that tend to accompany a placement in residential care, such as bullying, sexual harassment from other residents, and involvement in a delinquent sub-culture (Rushton & Minnis, 2002; Sinclair & Gibbs, 1998). Rushton and Minnis (2002) also pointed out that residential care is unlikely to provide young people with even one positive relationship, and may be harmful to children and young people with attachment disorders. Furthermore, they expressed concern that staff in residential homes often have very little training or contact with specialist child mental-health services to help them deal with the problems that they face.

SETTING THE CONTEXT FOR CHANGE – RESIDENTIAL CARE IN NORTHERN IRELAND

As in England and Wales, due to a combination of family-centred ideology and fiscal considerations which both stressed the benefits of foster over residential care, the 1980s and 1990s saw a major retraction of the residential sector, but this decline was even greater in Northern Ireland. In the ten years between 1986 and 1996, the number of places in both statutory and voluntary children's homes fell by almost 50%, from 688 places to 358. This declined by a further 33% between March 1996 and September 1997. In November 1997, there were 240 places in children's homes, and 42 of these were phased out by the middle of 1998. Consequently, from 1986 to 1998, there was a 70% drop in number of residential places available within Northern Ireland (DHSS, 1998). Essentially,

Northern Ireland had moved to the precarious position of placing all its eggs in one foster care basket (Kelly & Coulter, 1997).

One of the main consequences of this major retraction in residential services, as in England and Wales, was that it only left space for children with the most serious problems, making the residential care task much more difficult and demanding (Murray, 2002). Recognition that this retraction had gone too far came with the launch of a residential recovery plan, entitled *Children Matter* (DHSS, 1998). The key message was that residential care should be designed to meet the needs of the child rather than those of service providers.

The *Children Matter* review (DHSS, 1998) set out to change the perception of residential care in Northern Ireland as a last resort by repositioning residential services within an integrated child-welfare system. A differentiated and specialised model of residential services was developed, incorporating three main types of provision: firstly, 'Specialist Regional Provision' (such as secure accommodation); secondly, 'Sub-regional Specialist Provision' (e.g. homes for children with complex disabilities or units for children and young people with psychiatric/psychological needs or who present significant risks to other children); and thirdly, 'Broadly Based Differentiated Local Provision' (involving short-stay units designed to cope with emergency admissions and which place an intense focus upon returning children to their carers – this type of home would support the wider welfare system, providing children with space to prepare for transfer to another placement or simply to reflect on their behaviour and provide a homely living environment for those children for whom fostering is not an option or who have chosen residential care themselves).

Since the publication of *Children Matter* (DHSS, 1998), there has been considerable progress in developing residential child-care services. On 31 July 2000, Ms Bairbre De Brun, the Minister of Health, Social Services, and Public Safety, formally announced the establishment of the Children Matter Task Force. The task force explicitly endorsed the spectrum of residential child-care provision specified in the earlier review. The Social Services Inspectorate for Northern Ireland (DHSSPS, 2001) highlighted the range of services offered in the 32 children's homes (24 statutory, 8 voluntary) operating in Northern Ireland in the 1999–2000 period: 21 provided observation and assessment; 22 provided respite care; 14 catered solely for children with learning disability; 4 catered for children with a physical/sensory disability only; 12 catered for young people with both physical and learning disabilities; and 9 were hostel/semi-independent units. These figures suggest that some homes offered a combination of these services. However, the report did not specify the exact function of each home. All homes were of mixed religion, only two were single sex (one male and one female only), and most accommodated all age-groups: however, only four catered for children under 4 years of age. Currently, all children's homes are required to have a statement of purpose and a specified age-range. More recently, however, concerns have been raised that placement can still occur on the basis of what is available at the time, rather than what might be most suited to the specific needs of the child (Campbell & McLaughlin, 2005).

The most recent figures provided by the Social Services Inspectorate in Northern Ireland (DHSSPS, 2005) indicated that the percentage (12%) of looked-after children in residential care had remained static since 2001, and that there were still only 304 statutory residential care placements across Northern Ireland, with 82 placements provided by voluntary organisations. This is almost 100 places short of the 400 statutory places recommended within the *Children Matter* (DHSS, 1998) review and suggests that a fresh impetus may be required to meet these objectives.

Specialised Provision

While the Western, Southern, and Northern Health and Social Services Boards in Northern Ireland are currently developing their response to the *Children Matter* review (1998), this chapter will focus in more detail upon developments within the Eastern Health and Social Services Board (EHSSB), where a formal public consultation process has already begun (EHSSB, 2004). The EHSSB has proposed the development of six separate ISUs, each with a capacity for six young people (aged 13–18) with complex needs, to provide residential care that would be more carefully tailored to the needs presented by children and young people in the care system. The proposed ISUs will operate at a level between the differentiated children's home and secure accommodation, and will attempt to address the social, emotional, psychological, and educational needs of these children and young people, using a variety of therapies and approaches (EHSSB, 2004). To achieve this, three specialised units have been proposed: a substance-abuse unit, a therapeutic community, and a behaviour-intensive support unit, and three general units which will cater for young people whose behaviour is unmanageable in their current setting.

Intensive Support Units (ISUs)

The consultation document (EHSSB, 2004) specified a range of criteria for young people to enter ISUs. These were: behaviour in their current setting is unmanageable; behavioural difficulties/authority issues leading to school exclusion; suffering abuse and significant neglect that has impaired their ability to form significant relationships; serious psychological difficulties including depression and anxiety; difficulty with general life situations; behavioural difficulties including physical violence and persistent angry outbursts; history of running away from other care settings; vandalism at previous care settings; self-harm; drugs/alcohol abuse; and difficulties with social situations/forming relationships. These problems would be addressed using a range of therapies (in combination if required), such as: individual and group psychosocial interventions and psychodynamic psychotherapy; behavioural therapy; counselling for substance abuse or trauma; cognitive-behavioural therapy; grief/bereavement counselling; family therapy; systemic therapy; and personal counselling.[1] There would also be group work, activity-based programmes, and support with educational needs.

One of the key objectives of the ISUs is to improve outcomes for the children and young people who use them. The consultation document (EHSSB, 2004) specified

11 main objectives: stabilising individual situations; encouraging constructive placement experience and relationships with staff; increasing engagements by young people with education and improved levels of achievement; improving mental health; enhancing self-esteem and self-image; improving self-awareness and self-control; enabling parents and other carers to effectively support young people and become more confident in managing their behaviour; enhancing the co-ordination of services for young people; improving staff knowledge, skills, and competence in dealing with young people; encouraging social functioning; and facilitating a successful transition to aftercare.

The justification for the proposed units emerged as a result of a 'survey of the social, emotional, and psychological needs of young people in regional care centres' (Murray, 2002), from discussions by EHSSB personnel with other colleagues within psychology, psychiatry, and other specialist services in adolescent care, and was based on available evidence on effective methods of working with young people and adolescents in residential care in Ireland, the UK, and the USA (Berridge, 2002; Brunk, 2000; Jouglin, 2003; Lees et al., 1999; Newman, 2002). However, Little et al. (2005) noted that there is very little evidence that can be drawn upon to make clear recommendations in terms of what types of children are likely to benefit from what types of residential settings. Therefore, in the absence of this evidence, policy and practice are often being guided by ideology. Similarly, Fulcher (2001) commented that most front-line care-givers in residential care 'work from the heart', rather than on the basis of practice and research expertise, and that such an approach 'contributes to a lot of heartache' (2001, p. 428).

DISCUSSION

The ISU model described by the EHSSB (2004) aims to provide an intermediate form of specialist residential provision for children and young people whose needs may be better addressed through a form of intensive support than by the facilities on offer in either broadly based differentiated residential provision or secure accommodation. The introduction of such ISUs raises a number of important issues, both in terms of how such developments would work in practice and in terms of how they would impact upon provision offered at the other two ends of the residential care spectrum.

Firstly, it is difficult to envisage how the complexity of difficult and challenging behaviours that these young people exhibit (and the psychological states from which they emerge) can be disentangled in a way which facilitates this type of focused, specialist provision that is being proposed. It does appear unlikely that the ISUs would be able to address specific problems (such as drug abuse) in isolation, as the literature indicates that there is likely to be a high degree of co-morbidity (e.g. Wingenfeld, 2002).

Secondly, it is important to consider the extent to which the provision of support for children in the differentiated children's homes and secure accommodation will be impacted by that which is provided to the ISU model. As this issue has not been addressed in the consultation document (EHSSB, 2004), it is unclear how this development will impact and be integrated into existing provision. However, there are a number of factors to consider. For example, will there be associated changes to the type and range of services offered in differentiated children's homes or secure accommodation? How will the support needs of children and young people whose behaviour has either *not* become unmanageable or *become* so unmanageable that a Secure Accommodation Order has been deemed necessary be addressed? How will resources be allocated among the three forms of provision? Could this lead to a two- or three-tier residential system? Furthermore, although the consultation document (EHSSB, 2004) does specify the need for residential staff to have a higher level of skills and training in child-care issues than is currently the case, acknowledging the current lack of an adequately trained workforce to provide these forms of specialist treatment (Kilkelly et al., 2004; Rushton & Minnis, 2002), this raises concerns about the possibility of different tiers of staffing, in terms of skills and training, developing across the residential spectrum.

Thirdly, to what extent will the provision of specialised services in residential care ensure that this is not considered a 'last resort' but a 'positive choice' on a placement continuum? It is difficult not to continue to view this form of provision, particularly in the form of the ISUs with their focus upon unmanageable behaviour, as the penultimate option before the true 'last resort' of secure accommodation. Essentially, these are young people who cannot be accommodated in broadly based differentiated residential care. However, this does not mean that it still cannot be deemed a 'positive choice'. Whether this is the case or not will depend on the extent to which this specialised form of residential provision can be demonstrated to improve the young people's current situation and future prospects. Again, we have yet to discover how this move will impact upon the success of broadly based differentiated care in this regard, and its place in the continuum of residential care provision.

It is becoming recognised that interventions should be rooted in evidence-based practice and should have clear evidential support (Dobson & Khatri, 2000; Fulcher, 2001), and that young people in residential care should be provided with services that are effective in producing positive outcomes. However, as there has been very little specific research conducted on the treatment for children and young people in residential care, there is very little evidence available as to the effectiveness of interventions. Rushton and Minnis (2002) pointed out that studies of residential care have rarely been randomised. Furthermore, Bullock and McSherry (in press) commented that the cognitive-behavioural approaches introduced into residential care in England and Wales in the 1990s produced disappointing results for some groups of children. For example, Bullock et al. (1998) examined the care careers of adolescents with emotional and conduct disorders in secure long-stay treatment units. They found that the Youth Treatment Centres that adopted a cognitive-behavioural-focused regime did not do particularly well in terms of behavioural outcomes for severely disordered adolescents. These interventions did not appear to be affecting their deep-seated problems. It could also be argued that where these interventions are being applied by poorly trained staff, then the likelihood of their success is greatly reduced.

Bullock and McSherry (in press) also noted that there is a danger in interpreting the absence of clear research findings on the beneficial effects of residential care that 'nothing works'. They propose two approaches that may establish more encouraging results. Firstly, to look more closely at the link between specific residential interventions and specific groups of adolescents: this requires the development of taxonomies of young people that are linked to a careful scrutiny of interventions (Sinclair & Little, 2002). Secondly, to view 'treatment' in the wider context of the child or young person's needs and the services that best meet these needs. They concluded that young people in residential care will almost certainly present complex cases, and that a variety of approaches may be required. Similarly, Fulcher (2001) argued that it is important to avoid the ideological position which assumes that any family placement is superior to a placement in residential care, i.e. the 'last resort' philosophy. He continued that 'this is not to advocate for using residential group care with every child. The challenge lies in trying to match the most appropriate services with assessments of client need' (2001, p. 431).

CONCLUSION

The Green Paper *Every Child Matters* (2003) has generated momentum among local authorities in England and Wales to create an integrated approach to education and care provision. Although developments are underway to create an infrastructure to support a continuum of service provision for young looked-after children, Northern Ireland still has a long way to go in terms of achieving integrated and specialist service provision for young people in residential care.

The development of ISUs by the EHSSB complies with Phase 2 of the Children Matter Task Force's implementation strategy. Indeed, that significant progress should be made on implementing *Children Matter* (DHSS, 1998) was highlighted as an HPSS priority for action in child care (DHSSPS, 2004). Currently, the organisation, planning, and management of residential child-care services are in a state of flux due to the *Review of Public Administration in Northern Ireland* (RPA, 2005). This will result in restructuring and accompanying changes to the system by April 2008, and appears to be preventing the full implementation of the ISU model within the EHSSB. Although the consultation document acknowledged that the proposals being put forward by the Eastern Board were only a first step in developing some form of specialised provision in residential care, there is clearly a need for any emergent remodelling of services for children and young people in residential care to be rigorously evaluated in order to explore the effectiveness of the new structures and models of care being provided. This echoes the views of

Little et al. (2005) who called for more rigorous evaluation of the impact of residence on child outcomes, as well as greater effort to apply research evidence to policy and practice. One of the planned outcomes in the DHSSPS Public Service Agreement is better life chances for children. Consequently, an evaluation of these new models would assist in determining whether or not the life chances of this vulnerable group of children and young people were improved to any degree.

ACKNOWLEDGEMENTS

The authors would like to thank Professor Dorota Iwaniec and Doctor Rosemary Kilpatrick for their assistance in developing this work.

NOTE

1 Although the range of proposed therapeutic approaches does appear comprehensive, it is surprising that no reference is made to providing art therapy services. These posts are now beginning to be integrated within English County Council CAMHS (Child and Adolescent Mental Health Services) for looked-after children, e.g. Hampshire and Sheffield. More recently, research carried out at Queen's University Belfast demonstrated the effectiveness of art therapy when working with looked-after children (McSherry, 2005).

REFERENCES

Association of Directors of Social Services (ADSS) (2006). *Residential Child Care*.

Berridge, D. (2002). Residential care. In D. McNeish, T. Newman, & H. Roberts (eds), *What Works for Children*? Buckingham: Open University Press.

Berridge, D., & Brodie, I. (1998). *Children's Homes Revisited*. London: Jessica Kingsley.

Brunk, M. (2000). Effective treatment of conduct disorder. *Juvenile Justice Fact Sheet*. Charlottesville, VA: Institute of Law, Psychiatry, and Public Policy, University of Virginia.

Bullock, R., Little, M., & Millham, S. (1998). *Secure Treatment Outcomes*. Aldershot: Ashgate.

Bullock, R., & McSherry, D. (in press). Residential care in Great Britain and Northern Ireland. In M. Courtney & D. Iwaniec (eds), *Residential Child Care: Past, Present and Future. International Perspectives*. Oxford: Oxford University Press.

Campbell, A., & McLaughlin, A. (2005). *Views that Matter: Staff Morale, Qualifications, and Retention in Residential Childcare in Northern Ireland*. London: National Children's Bureau.

Cliffe, D., & Berridge, D. (1991). *Closing Residential Homes: An End to Residential Childcare?* London: National Children's Bureau.

Department of Health (1998). *Caring for Children Away from Home: Messages from Research*. Chichester: John Wiley & Sons, Ltd.

DHSS (1998). *Children Matter: A Review of Residential Child Care Services in Northern Ireland*. Belfast: Department of Health and Social Services.

DHSSPS (2001). *Children Order Statistics: Data from the MH4 Information Return*. Belfast: Department of Health, Social Services, and Public Safety. An Roinn Sláinte, Seirbhísí Sóisialta agus Sábháilteachta Poiblí.

DHSSPS (2004). *Children's Homes: Registration and Inspection Standards. A Consultation Document.* Belfast: Department of Health, Social Services, and Public Safety. An Roinn Sláinte, Seirbhísí Sóisialta agus Sábháilteachta Poiblí.

DHSSPS (2005). *Children Order Statistical Bulletin.* Belfast: Department of Health, Social Services, and Public Safety. An Roinn Sláinte, Seirbhísí Sóisialta agus Sábháilteachta Poiblí.

Dobson, K.S., & Khatri, N. (2000). Cognitive therapy: Looking backward, looking forward. *Journal of Clinical Psychology,* **56**, 671–678.

EHSSB (2004). *The Development of Intensive Residential Childcare Units in the Eastern Health and Social Services Board Area for Young People Aged 13–18 Years: A Consultation Document.* Belfast: Eastern Health and Social Services Board.

Farmer, E. (2004). Patterns of placement, management and outcome for sexually abused and/or abusing children in substitute care. *British Journal of Social Work,* **34**, 375–393.

Frost, N., Mills, S., & Stein, M. (1999). *Understanding Residential Child Care.* Aldershot: Ashgate.

Fulcher, L. (2001). Differential assessment of residential group care for children and young people. *British Journal of Social Work,* **31**, 417–435.

Gibbs, I., & Sinclair, I. (1999). Treatment and treatment outcomes in children's homes. *Child and Family Social Work,* **4**, 1–8.

Gooch, D. (1996). Home and away: The residential care, education and control of children in historical and political context. *Child and Family Social Work,* **1**, 19–32.

Hayden, C., Goddard, J., Gorin, S., & Van Der Spek, N. (1999). *State Child Care: Looking After Children?* London: Jessica Kingsley.

Jouglin, C. (2003). *Cognitive Behaviour Therapy Can Be Effective in Managing Behavioural Problems and Conduct Disorder in Pre-adolescents.* London: What Works for Children Group: Evidence Nugget, September.

Kelly, G., & Coulter, J. (1997). The Children (Northern Ireland) Order (1995): A new era for fostering and adoption services. *Adoption and Fostering,* **21**(3), 5–13.

Kilkelly, U., Kilpatrick, R., Lundy, L., Moore, L., Scraton, P., Davey, C. et al. (2004). *Children's Rights in Northern Ireland.* Belfast: NICCY.

Kools, S., & Kennedy, C. (2002). Child sexual abuse treatment: Misinterpretation and mismanagement of child sexual behaviour. *Child Care Health and Development,* **28**, 211–218.

Lees, J., Manning, N., & Rawlings, B. (1999). *Therapeutic Community Effectiveness: A Systematic International Review of Therapeutic Community Treatment for People with Personality Disorders and Mentally Disordered Offenders* (CRD Report 17). York: NHS Centre for Reviews and Dissemination, University of York.

Little, M., Kohm, A., & Thompson, R. (2005). The impact of residential placement on child development: Research and policy implications. *International Journal of Social Welfare.* doi: 10.1111/j.1468-2397.2005.00360.x

McSherry, C. (2005). Visual notetaking as a vehicle for exploring the transference and counter-transference issues that can occur in art therapy: A study based on working with an adolescent male. Unpublished Masters dissertation, Graduate School of Education, Queen's University Belfast.

Murray, M. (2002). An assessment of the social, emotional and psychological needs of young people in residential care in the EHSSB. Unpublished report.

Newman, Y. (2002). *Promoting Resilience: A Review of Effective Strategies for Child Care Services.* Exeter: Centre for Evidence Based Social Services and Barnardo's.

Nunno, M.A., Holden, M.J., & Leidy, B.D. (2003). Evaluating and monitoring the impact of a crisis intervention system on a residential child care facility. *Children and Youth Services Review,* **25**(4), 295–315.

Packman, J., & Hall, C. (1998). *From Care to Accommodation*. London: HMSO.

Parker, R.A. (1988). Residential care for children. In I. Sinclair (ed.), *Residential Care: The Research Reviewed*. London: The Stationery Office.

Pinkerton, J. (2002). Developing an international perspective on leaving care. In A. Wheal (ed.), *The RHP Companion to Leaving Care*. Lyme Regis: Russell House Publishing.

Pinkerton, J., & McCrea, R. (1999). *Meeting the Challenge? Young People Leaving Care in Northern Ireland*. Aldershot: Ashgate.

Rowe, J., Hundleby, M., & Garnett, L. (1989). *Child Care Now: A Survey of Child Care Patterns*. London: British Agencies for Adoption and Fostering.

RPA (2005). *The Review of Public Administration in Northern Ireland: Further Consultation*. Available at: http://www.rpani.gov.uk/consultdocu.pdf

Rushton, A., & Minnis, H. (2002). Residential and foster family care. In M. Rutter & E. Taylor (eds), *Child and Adolescent Psychiatry: Modern Approaches*. Oxford: Blackwell.

Sheldon, B. (1995). *Cognitive-Behaviour Therapy: Research, Practice and Philosophy*. London: Routledge.

Sinclair, I. (1988). Residential care: Common issues in the client reviews. In I. Sinclair (ed.), *Residential Care: The Research Reviewed*. London: HMSO.

Sinclair, I. (2005). Residential care in the UK. In C. McAuley, P. Pecora, & W. Rose (eds), *Enhancing the Well-Being of Children and Families through Effective Interventions: International Evidence for Practice*. London: Jessica Kingsley.

Sinclair, I., & Gibbs, I. (1998). *The Quality of Care in Children's Homes*. Report to the Department of Health, University of York.

Sinclair, R., & Little, M. (2002). Developing a taxonomy for children in need. In H. Ward & W. Rose (eds), *Approaches to Needs Assessment in Children's Services*. London: Jessica Kingsley.

Stevens, I. (2004). Cognitive-behavioural interventions for adolescents in residential child care in Scotland: An examination of practice and lessons from research. *Child and Family Social Work*, **9**, 237–246.

Utting, W., Baines, C., Stuart, M., Rowlands, J., & Vialva, R. (1997). *People Like Us: The Report of the Review of the Safeguards for Children Living Away from Home*. London: The Department of Health, The Welsh Office, The Stationery Office.

Wingenfeld, S.A. (2002). Assessment of behavioural and emotional difficulties in children and adolescents. *Peabody Journal of Education*, **77**, 85–105.

CHAPTER 9

THE MENTAL-HEALTH NEEDS OF LOOKED-AFTER CHILDREN

Tom Teggart

INTRODUCTION

It is clear that the experience of substitute care in childhood is associated with a range of detrimental effects on well-being and diminished outcomes in adulthood. Viner and Taylor (2005), for example, followed up a cohort of children born in England, Scotland, Wales, and Northern Ireland in 1970. Comparing a sub-group who had been in public care at some stage in their lives with the rest of the cohort, and controlling for socio-economic status, they found that these men and women were less likely to attain high social class, more likely to have been homeless, have a conviction, have psychological morbidity, and be in poor general health. Men were also more likely to be unemployed and less likely to attain a higher degree. Non-white ethnicity was also associated with poorer adult outcomes of being in care.

While a range of negative psychosocial outcomes has been associated with substitute care for a considerable period of time (e.g. Prosser, 1978; Triseliotis, 1989), it is only in the past two decades that research has begun to delineate specifically the significant mental-health needs of young people in the care system. While these findings are unsurprising to many social care staff, for many child mental-health professionals there is a sense that the significant mental-health needs of this group of young people have only recently been discovered. While there is much guidance within the literature regarding screening, assessing, providing intervention, and training and supporting staff and carers, there is not as yet an established best model of service delivery to this group. In respect of the needs of young people in substitute care, the present chapter will do the following.

- summarise recent findings regarding mental-health needs;
- discuss factors that may contribute to high levels of need within this group;

The Child's Journey Through Care: Placement Stability, Care Planning, and Achieving Permanency. Edited by D. Iwaniec.
Copyright © 2006 John Wiley & Sons, Ltd.

- consider to what extent mental-health needs are being met;
- reflect on models of service that may best deliver suitable services.

LOOKED-AFTER CHILDREN AND MENTAL HEALTH

Definition and Prevalence of Mental-health Needs

Published in the seminal report of the NHS Health Advisory Service *Together We Stand* (HAS, 1995), and developed by a multidisciplinary group of child-care, health, and education professionals, parents, and academics, the abilities listed below are a useful definition of child and adolescent mental health:

- to develop psychologically, emotionally, intellectually, and spiritually;
- to initiate, develop, and sustain mutually satisfying personal relationships;
- to become aware of others and to empathise with them;
- to use psychological distress as a developmental process, so that it does not hinder or impair further development.

Children and young people can be said to have mental-health needs if, for one reason or another, they experience impaired ability in any one of these areas. Studies of the mental-health needs of looked-after children have not tended to embrace the detail of investigation recommended by the above definition; rather, they have tended to focus on the presence of symptomatology and diagnosable disorder. The presence of such disorder is, of course, associated with deficits in the areas of ability described, and investigations of the psychosocial outcomes of growing up in the care system (such as those mentioned above) provide convincing evidence of high levels of such impairments among the population of children in substitute care.

In the late 1980s and early 1990s, the high incidence of behavioural problems among young people in substitute care was familiar (e.g. Wolkind & Rushton, 1994), and their vulnerability to developing problems with mental health was increasingly recognised (e.g. Bamford & Wolkind, 1988). Responding to increasing professional and political concern, McCann and colleagues used the Achenbach Child Behaviour Checklist (Achenbach, 1991a) and Youth Self Report Questionnaires (Achenbach, 1991b) to screen all (134) 13- to 17-year-olds in the Oxfordshire care system on a given date (McCann et al., 1996). In a second phase of the study, high scorers on the Achenbach were interviewed using a version of the Kiddie-SADS interview schedule (Kaufman et al., 1997). A 67% prevalence of psychiatric disorder was reported compared to 15% for adolescents living with their own families. Specifically, 96% of adolescents in residential care and 57% in foster care were identified as having psychiatric disorders.

The young people who participated in the McCann study had been in care for an average of 2.9 years. A subsequent study (Dimigan et al., 1999) looked at the prevalence of mental-health disorders among young people on admission to care in the Glasgow area. Utilising the Devereux scales of mental disorders (Naglieri et al., 1993), 70 children with an average age of 9.6 years were assessed on entry to care over a ten-month period. Twenty-five showed severe conduct disorder, 21 had severe attention difficulties, and 18 had autistic-type problems. In terms of emotional difficulties, 11 of the young people had an anxiety disorder, and 11 had serious acute problems (including severe depression). The authors concluded that there was a 'worrying gap' in mental-health care provision as a significant number of young people were experiencing serious psychiatric disorder on entering care but were not being referred for psychological help.

More recently an extensive study by the Office of National Statistics (ONS) (Meltzer et al., 2003) gathered information on more than 1000 5- to 17-year-olds looked after by 142 local authorities in England. The survey covered children who were in residential care, foster care, living with their parents, and 16- to 17-year-olds living independently under local authority supervision. Information gathered included an assessment of 'mental disorders' utilising a measure designed specifically for the study. Table 9.1 summarises their findings with regard to prevalence of mental disorders and includes comparison with the 1999 ONS survey of 10,500 children living in private households (Meltzer et al., 2000).

Prevalence in the looked-after children study was associated with placement type. Two-thirds of children in residential care were assessed as having a mental disorder as compared to around four in ten of those young people living with foster carers or birth-parents and around half of those living independently. Distribution of disorder also varied significantly with placement type. For example, young people in residential care were much more likely to present with conduct disorders than those in foster homes or living with natural parents. Young people living with birth-parents or in residential care were twice as likely to have emotional disorders as those in foster care.

Table 9.1 Summary of mental disorder prevalence figures from ONS studies

	Looked-after children (%) n = 1,134[a]	Private households (%) n = 10,500[b]
5- to 10-year-olds		
Emotional disorders	11	3
Conduct disorders	36	5
Hyperkinetic disorders	11	2
Any childhood mental disorder	42	8
11- to 15-year-olds		
Emotional disorders	12	6
Emotional disorders	40	6
Hyperkinetic disorders	7	1
Any childhood mental disorder	49	11

Source: [a] Meltzer et al., 2003, [b] Meltzer et al., 2000

A range of UK (e.g. Blower et al., 2004; Mount et al., 2004; Nicol et al., 2000) and international needs-assessment studies (e.g. Ajdukovic & Sladovic Franz, 2005; Halfon et al., 2002; Hukkanen et al., 1999; Leslie et al., 2004; McMillen et al., 2005) have supported conclusions about the high levels of mental-health needs among young people in substitute care.

Until recently no such research has been published for the Northern Ireland context. In response to this absence and in view of the need for a local research base to inform policy and practice development (e.g. Koprowska & Stein, 2000), Teggart and Menary (2005) investigated rates of mental-health difficulties among children in substitute care, across five child-care teams in Craigavon and Banbridge H + SS Trust. Sixty-four children were assessed using the Strengths and Difficulties Questionnaire (SDQ) (Goodman, 1997) with multiple informants including carers and teachers as well as self-report for young people aged 11 and above.

Results indicated that more than 60% of 4- to 10-year-olds assessed may have a diagnosable psychiatric disorder. The presence of such a disorder was probable in almost 50%. Among the 11- to 16-year-olds assessed, the proportion likely to have a diagnosable disorder was slightly higher at almost two-thirds of the sample group. A significant number of children appeared in more than one diagnostic category, indicating the complexity of their presentation and probable co-morbid diagnoses.

Young People with Disabilities

McConkey et al. (2004) have observed that debates about the residential care needs of children and adolescents have paid little attention to young people with disabilities. It is suggested that this is partly due to there being little available statistical information about children with disabilities who spend most of their time away from their families (Morris, 1997). This situation pertains despite estimates that as many as 12% of children with disabilities may require to be looked after by a community trust for 90 days or more per year for purposes of respite or treatment (Foundation for People with Learning Difficulties, 2001).

In view of this, McConkey et al. (2004) obtained data on 108 young people aged 1–20 living within one geographical area in Northern Ireland. Of these, 51% were reported to have severe learning disabilities, 29% had profound or multiple disabilities, 10% had mild or moderate learning disability, and another 10% had physical disabilities. Nearly half of the young people were reported to present challenging behaviour, a third experienced severe communication difficulties, and nearly one-fifth had an autistic spectrum disorder.

Despite the fact that there are considerable difficulties in identifying psychiatric or psychological problems experienced by young people with learning disabilities, there is growing evidence that around 40% have significant mental-health needs. This represents a much greater percentage than that found among young people who do not have learning disabilities. In particular, young people with learning disabilities appear to be particularly at risk of developing emotional difficulties and of showing challenging behaviour or conduct disorders (Foundation for People with Learning Difficulties, 2003). In view of the prevalence of mental ill-health among this group it seems reasonable to expect that a significant proportion of those accommodated away from home will have significant mental-health needs, particularly since many among this group may be receiving respite or treatment related to the presence of challenging behaviour. At present, however, there is little published research supporting such an assertion, and processes for identifying, assessing, and treating mental ill-health among looked-after children with disabilities (particularly learning disabilities) appear to be underdeveloped.

Impact of Mental-health Difficulties

While prevalence of mental-health difficulties has been fairly extensively investigated over the past two decades, it is only relatively recently that the impact of mental ill-health on the lives of young people in care has become the focus of some attention. McCarthy et al. (2003) point out that evidence from epidemiological studies suggests that defining significant disorder in terms of symptoms alone does not reliably indicate psychiatric disorder (Bird et al., 1990), and that operational diagnostic criteria usually stipulate that diagnosis should only be made when the relevant symptoms result in significant social impairment or distress (World Health Organisation, 1996). Consequently, they investigated how the lives of looked-after children and their carers were affected by the young people's emotional and behavioural problems utilising an extended version of the SDQ (Goodman, 1999). Seventy carers completed questionnaires, reporting very high levels of impairment in the areas of home life, peer relationships, and learning for the young people in their care. Some 40% had significant problems in three or more of the key areas: home, learning, peers, and leisure. Significant chronicity was indicated with 65% of the group having had significant difficulties for more than one year. The children's difficulties were identified as being a source of significant burden for almost half of the sample of carers and their families.

The response rate in the McCarthy et al. study was not sufficiently large to support confidence in the representativeness of their sample. The single respondent approach is a further limitation. The Teggart and Menary (2005) study described above had a high response rate (approx. 84%) and multiple informants. The study also utilised the extended version of the SDQ and in a further – as yet unpublished – analysis of the data, supports the findings of McCarthy et al. with regard to social impairment, burden on carers/families, and chronicity of difficulties. With the addition of teachers as respondents, a significant degree of impairment to classroom learning was also identified for more than half the sample, with more than half the sample also being seen as placing a significant burden on the class. Mount et al. (2004) demonstrated that burden is an important predictor of high mental-health need. These results, together with the prevalence studies described above, help to underline the importance of developing understandings of the social and mental- health realities of young people in the care system in order that services can best be organised to meet their needs.

UNDERSTANDING LOOKED-AFTER CHILDREN'S HIGH LEVELS OF MENTAL-HEALTH NEEDS

Experiences Prior to Entering Care

Several factors have been suggested to explain the high levels of mental-health difficulties evident among young people in care. Risk factors for developing a mental-health difficulty during childhood have been understood as residing within the separate but interacting domains of the child, the family, and the environment. Risks in each of these domains are elevated for children in care. Richardson and Lelliot (2003) draw attention to statistics collated by the Department of Health on principal issues leading to admission to care. Table 9.2 summarises these statistics for children in care in England for the year ending 31 March 2002 (n = 59, 700). It is clear that the majority of young people in the care system have entered it as a result of abusive, neglectful, or absent parenting.

Stanley (2005) studied a purposive sample, biased towards those with high needs, of 80 looked-after children from two English local authorities. Over 80% had entered the care system as a result of abuse or neglect, with physical abuse being the largest single category (22.5%). Close to one-fifth of the children had had a significant bereavement in their lifetime (including several who had lost their mothers). Domestic violence was evident in the histories of over half of the mothers. Substance misuse was an issue for almost a quarter of the mothers and a fifth of fathers. Nearly a third of mothers had criminal convictions. Some 40% of fathers had convictions, and over 30% had spent time in prison. More than half of the children were either homeless or from homes described as poor. Almost 80% of mothers and 40% of fathers were unemployed. Half the mothers were identified as having a mental-health problem. This figure was lower for fathers but felt to be as a result of their limited contact with social services.

Table 9.2 Principal reasons for admission to care, England 2001/2002

Principal category of need	% of total
Abuse/neglect	62.0
Disability	1.4
Parental illness	6.2
Family in acute distress	6.9
Family dysfunction	10.4
Socially unacceptable behaviour	3.4
Absent parenting	7.2

Source: Department of Health

These statistics demonstrate that many young people in the care system have experience of deprivation and social exclusion. Most young people who become looked after are likely to have entered care from homes that are conflictual, seriously neglectful, or abusive. The detrimental effects of neglect and maltreatment on children have been widely discussed (for a review, see Sneddon, 2003). Trauma and loss are common experiences among this group, and it is likely that a significant proportion of young people already have significant mental-health needs on entry to care.

Attachment experiences with carers may have been disturbed and it has been suggested that such difficulties with attachments can underpin the limited or conflictual pattern of connections that many young people make with care staff and substitute carers (e.g. McWey, 2000; Penzerro & Lein, 1995). As a consequence of long-standing attachment difficulties, the young person's self-esteem and interpersonal, emotional, and intellectual skills may be inadequately developed. He or she may have difficulty making and sustaining friendships. He or she may be experiencing failure at school. Loss of significant relationships is almost always a significant issue, and environmental contributors to emotional and psychological vulnerability – such as poverty, homelessness, and discrimination – are often present. Among the contributions to developing psychopathology within this group is the multiplicity of adverse circumstances and experiences to which many children have been exposed. Research in developmental psychopathology suggests that single individual adjustment problems have limited negative impact on psychosocial development, whereas multiple adjustment problems are associated with a range of negative psychosocial outcomes in later adolescence and early adulthood (Magnusson & Statin, 1998).

Impacts of Entering Care

Clausen et al. (1998) have described how children in foster care are at heightened risk for mental-health problems due to the negative effects of separation from their families. As already described, the majority of young people who come into care have a history of abuse or neglect. Such children are likely to have a history of disrupted attachment with their abusing caretakers. Citing Charles and Matheson (1990), Clausen et al. suggest that removal from home and placement in foster care may cause further distress as the young person may experience: 'feelings of rejection, guilt, hostility, anger, abandonment, shame and dissociative reactions in response to the loss of a familiar environment and the separation from family and community' (Clausen et al., 1998, p. 284).

Richardson and Lelliot (2003) described how coming into care can bring protective factors into the lives of young people who need this type of support – physical safety, better living conditions, fair and consistent rules to live by, understanding and acceptance from attentive carers and residential workers – all of which can support positive emotional and psychological development. However, there are many ways in which foster or residential care does not adequately compensate for family life. Young people from a range of care settings interviewed by Blower et al.

(2004) described how, despite feeling well cared for, their domestic life was unusual in a variety of ways. They differentiated clearly between professional care and familial 'love'. They complained about staff filling in logbooks and about struggling with the need to communicate their needs to carers while wanting to retain a degree of privacy. Some young people also reported being frightened that they might be sexually abused while in care, and this was an impediment for some to developing close relationships with staff and peers.

Furthermore, experiences that young people have in care may contribute to their further isolation, unhappiness, and traumatisation. Sir William Utting's Report, *People Like Us* (Utting, 1997), and a series of research studies conducted by the Department of Health investigating children's experience of being looked after (Department of Health, 1998) have drawn attention to the damaging effects of multiple placements, bullying, and abuse in the care system. Despite the best of intentions, the care system cannot emulate the constancy and security of family life, and many young people in care have been so disturbed by their experiences that the activities and requirements of recovery may seem beyond their grasp.

Impacts of Placement Breakdown

While it is clear that many young people enter care with significant mental-health needs (e.g. Dimigan et al., 1999), there has been considerable debate on the relative impact of genetic risk, adverse experiences before receiving care, and risks associated with substitute care experiences on the subsequent development of mental ill-health (e.g. Roy et al., 2000). An important issue that has received attention is the impact of multiple placements. An association between emotional and behavioural difficulties and elevated rates of placement breakdown has been demonstrated. For example, McCarthy (2004) investigated the developmental histories of children who experienced high levels of placement instability in the care system. Results indicated that those who experienced many moves were much more likely to have displayed multiple problem behaviours prior to entering care than children in a comparison group. There is evidence that disruptive behaviour in children can lead to placement breakdown (e.g. Ward & Skuse, 1999), but placements may also break down for reasons unrelated to the young person concerned (Jackson & Thomas, 1999). Meltzer et al. (2003) found that the likelihood of disorder decreased with the length of time spent in current placement and McCue-Horwitz and colleagues (2001) have demonstrated how adaptive functioning improves after a significant period of settled foster care.

In an attempt to disentangle the relationship between multiple placements and problem behaviours, Newton and colleagues (2000) conducted a prospective study of 415 young people in foster care in California. Results suggest that a history of disrupted placements contributes negatively to both internalising and externalising behaviour among young people in foster care. Numerous changes in placement were associated with a particularly high risk of deleterious effects, but the presence of initial externalising behaviours was the strongest predictor of placement changes, indicating that children who are challenging and aggressive are more likely to be moved from one placement to another. They also found, however, that children who did not present with either significant internalising or externalising behaviours when initially coming into care seemed to be particularly vulnerable to the detrimental effects of placement breakdowns. In particular, this group seems susceptible to internalising behaviours. They may become withdrawn and isolated, and, compared to young people with externalising behaviours, may be relatively unobtrusive, failing to attract appropriate attention, assessment, and support from the relevant agencies.

Clearly, placement disruption can be the result of emotional and behavioural difficulties underlining the need for timely identification, assessment, and treatment to ensure that the risk of disruption is minimised. It also seems to be the case that having multiple placements can contribute to the development of mental ill-health. It has been suggested that experiencing multiple placement changes contributes to an accumulation of disrupted attachments for looked-after children and the development of a lack of trust for others (Stanley, 2005). A child's capacity to form relationships is an important factor in contributing to the development of successful placements (Dance et al., 2002), and children who act out their insecurities and growing mistrust may be unattractive to carers. It is clear that supporting carers and young people to minimise the likelihood of placement breakdown is an important goal to assist with interrupting a cycle that can contribute to entrenched difficulties with young people's mental health.

ARE WE MEETING THE MENTAL-HEALTH NEEDS OF LOOKED-AFTER CHILDREN?

Do Young People Receive the Services They Require?

Many of the needs assessment studies cited above suggest that there is considerable unmet need among young people in substitute care. Social workers in a study carried out by Phillips (1997) believed that 80% of looked-after children on their caseloads required referral to Child and Adolescent Mental Health (CAMH) services yet only 27% were referred.

Recently, research has begun to emerge that suggests this situation is not universal. Nicholas and colleagues (2003), for example, have identified a changing pattern of services to children in residential care in Leeds. An increase in consultation and training available to staff was noted, although ongoing questions of unmet therapeutic needs were also raised. Blower et al. (2004) completed a needs assessment on 48 young people accommodated in the Lomond and Argyle area of Scotland. Twenty-seven of the young people were identified as having significant mental-health problems. Of these, 20 had already been referred to the local child and adolescent mental-health team. In most cases consultation was offered to social services staff following assessment. Waiting times were for the most part long, however, and only six children received any sort of individual treatment from the clinic.

The delivery of services to this population is complex and can encounter obstacles such as the impacts of high staff turnover rates in residential care (Richardson & Lelliot, 2003) or multiple foster placements and unclear planning (Payne & Butler, 1998). In the UK, the Quality Protects initiative provided both impetus and resources for improved services to young people in care (Lewis, 2000). In Northern Ireland, in recent years Trusts have begun to dedicate posts and, in some cases, teams to the provision of mental-health services for young people in care. Developments are patchy, however, and as with so many CAMH service issues in Northern Ireland, there is a lack of regionally coherent planning and investment. Calls have been made for a specific mental-health strategy for looked-after children (e.g. DHSSPS Clinical Psychology SAC, 2002) that would assist the development of tailored, equitable services for this population.

Are Services Provided Equitably?

Leslie et al. (2000) found that race and ethnicity were among the factors predictive of whether young people in foster care in San Diego used outpatient mental-health services. In the UK, research has demonstrated how the prevalence of psychiatric disorders differs across racial and ethnic groups, with non-indigenous people having increased vulnerability for a range of diagnoses (Shah, 2004). While the majority of such investigations has been completed with adults, one study of adolescent psychiatric inpatients found that young people from the black communities (African, Caribbean, and British) were over-represented among those admitted with a psychotic disorder, compared to those from white groups. They were also more likely to be detained under the Mental Health Act, to have been born outside the UK, and to have a refugee background (Tolmac & Hodes, 2004). This suggests that while they may well be subject to discrimination within the system, they may also be more vulnerable to serious mental-health problems because of early life-experiences. There is also evidence that ethnic minority groups tend to have lower rates of treatment for mental disorders (Nazroo, 1997). Extrapolating from these findings, it may well be that young people from ethnic minority backgrounds who are looked after may have increased vulnerability to developing mental-health problems and suffer further impediments to receiving treatment compared with their white peers. Further research is warranted.

The Leslie et al. (2000) study also supported previous research findings that type of placement can influence use of mental-health services, specifically that children residing with kinship carers receive fewer services (e.g. Berrick & Barth, 1994). It has been suggested that this may be the result of lower supervision levels from case workers for children in kinship care. Another interpretation – based on findings that kinship carers tend to be older, and have lower education levels, and fewer economic resources than non-relative foster carers (Gebel, 1996) – is that this may also be a result of kinship carers experiencing greater difficulty with public sector systems than 'professional' foster carers. There are, however, some advantages in kinship fostering as discussed by Una Lernihan and Greg Kelly in Chapter 6 in this volume.

Gender and maltreatment history were further factors influencing service use in the Leslie et al. study. No such investigation of service use appears to have been carried out within the UK. Further research may be needed to investigate to what extent such factors may have relevance for young people in care in the UK and to provide guidance to service providers to ensure equality of access to services.

Are Mental-health Supports for Looked-after Children Helpful?

There is evidence that long-term foster care can be associated with improved functioning (e.g. McCue-Horwitz et al., 2001; Minty, 1999), better outcomes being associated with, for example, placement stability, earlier admission, and later discharge from care and the absence of severe conduct problems. A more recent critical review (Holland et al., 2005) found evidence in favour of sibling co-placement, kinship care, parental participation, professional foster care, and individualised multidimensional treatment for promoting stability and continuity of care. There is, however, little reliable research indicating how such outcomes can be achieved for young people in the care system who have been identified as having significant mental-health problems. While much has been written of late with regard to mental-health provision for looked-after children, the available range of outcome studies to support evidence-based practice remains inadequate (Richardson & Joughin, 2000).

Some encouraging evidence is beginning to emerge with regard to the effectiveness of dedicated mental-health services for looked-after children. For example, Callaghan et al. (2004) report an evaluation of services to 45 consecutive attendees at such a service in the Midlands. The main aims of this service are to be responsive and flexible, provide mental-health assessment and treatment for young people, and consultation to residential and social care staff and foster parents. The evaluation utilised the SDQ and the Health of the Nation Outcome Scales for Children and Adolescents (HoNOSCA). At five months children had significantly improved on a number of the HoNOSCA scales and on the emotional difficulties scale of the SDQ. The service evaluated is one of many established in Britain as a result of increased focus on the mental-health needs of looked-after children since the mid-1990s. While there is much indication in the literature about what might be helpful and much encouragement in terms of progress reports on new initiatives, no long-term outcome data are available; consequently a reliable evidence base for mental-health intervention for looked-after children with significant mental-health problems is yet to be established.

MODELS OF MENTAL-HEALTH SERVICE DELIVERY TO LOOKED-AFTER CHILDREN

What Types of Provision Do Young People and Their Carers Need?

A population that experiences such complex social circumstances and psychological realities requires the availability of a sophisticated array of supports and treatments. The need for individual therapeutic intervention for young people has been detailed. This may include individual and family therapies as well as supports to the wider systems that support young people in substitute care. More specifically, it may include interventions aimed at the remediation of attachment difficulties and recovery from bereavement, trauma, and loss (British Psychological Society, 2004). A small and far from exhaustive sample of some of the types of provision that have been advocated is described below.

As a principle, it has been established for some time that mental-health screening of children on entry to care may be required to identify what specific mental-health problems need to be addressed so that the most effective treatment modalities can be identified and delivered (e.g. Clausen et al., 1998). Useful screening tools have been identified (e.g. Goodman et al., 2004) and, increasingly, systems for operationalising routine screening and assessment are being described (e.g. Bonnet & Welbury, 2004). At present, however, there remains much variation in how these assessments are being carried out, and screening is not yet common practice in all regions.

In terms of therapeutic provision, it has been noted that, at least within residential settings, treatment has tended not to be defined within itself but to consist of all the practices within homes that produce desired outcomes in the longer term (Gibbs & Sinclair, 2000). However, in keeping with a prevailing ethos in CAMHS, specific and circumscribed treatments are increasingly being described. For example, the ubiquitous cognitive-behavioural therapy has been utilised in a variety of settings. Scholte and Van Der Ploeg (2000) found this to be the most beneficial treatment approach in their study of 200 young people in residential treatment in Holland. Caution has also been urged, however, and the needs for accurate assessment, staff training, and the assurance that interventions are always in the best interests of the child have been highlighted (Stevens, 2004).

One of the challenges facing traditional CAMH services is that the most prevalent psychiatric diagnosis among looked-after children is conduct disorder. CAMHS often struggle to provide effective treatments for young people with complex presentations of this diagnosis. The most successful approaches intervene as early as possible, are structured and intensive, and address the multiple contexts in which children exhibit problem behaviour, including within the family, at school, and in the community. This underlines the need for organised inter-agency working which can be difficult to co-ordinate. There is good evidence of effectiveness when young people do receive co-ordinated interventions that address the multiple social systems that sustain their behavioural difficulties (e.g. Hengeller, 1999). In England, a significant project is currently underway, funded by the Department for Education and Skills, to establish this type of support for looked-after children. Referring to the provision as 'Multidimensional Treatment Foster Care', the project currently involves 20 local authorities, and in due course an evaluation of its outcomes will be an important addition to the literature informing service development.

It has also been argued that psychoanalytic psychotherapy may be an essential treatment modality for some young people, due to its focus on the relational aspects of their difficulties (Hunter, 1993). It has also been recognised, however, that not all young people in substitute care will be able to make use of such a treatment. Significant strain can be caused in the process of psychoanalytic psychotherapy to young people and the networks that support them. Careful assessment of both young people and their supports should be made before commencing such a treatment (Barrows, 1996).

The need for training and support of foster carers has been highlighted, and models for achieving this have been described (e.g. Golding, 2004; Minnis et al., 2001), and evaluated (e.g. Minnis & Devine, 2001), although a recent Cochrane Library review of a specifically cognitive-behavioural approach with foster carers failed to find convincing support for its effectiveness (Turner et al., 2005). The literature contains evidence that specialist fostering services can be beneficial for looked-after children who have severe psychopathology (e.g. Clark et al., 1994) and there have been calls for developments beyond 'specialist' to 'professional' fostering, whereby salaried foster carers can receive good training and support to enable them to provide stable and therapeutic homes for young people with significant needs (Testa & Rolock, 1999).

The impact of caring on carers' own mental health has also been discussed in the literature, and the potential need for mental-health support for carers has been highlighted (Lewis, 2000). The emotional impacts on staff of working with looked-after children and the potential for these experiences to inhibit good care practices have also been identified (Emanuel, 2002) as well as the need for training and staff supervision that can address such issues.

How Should We Organise Mental-health Services for Looked-after Children?

As demonstrated above, it is likely that the mental-health needs of looked-after children are not being adequately identified and not enough support and treatment are being provided. A daunting array of treatment and support options is available and, apart from the issue of increasing service providers' capacity to identify and address needs, it is necessary to consider what model of care will be most suitable for planning and organising these services.

Street and Davies (2002) discuss some of the limitations of both social care and medical models as the basis of organising mental-health support and interventions for looked-after children. For example, non-specialist workers may poorly understand child development and mental-health issues. Understanding of young people's difficulties that are not influenced by systemic ideas and analyses may result in the 'scapegoating' of young people for whom the child-care system is not working satisfactorily, and in an over-reliance on the often limited potential of individual therapy or counselling. Organising child mental-health services around a medical model approach – reliant on the presence of symptoms as the basis of referral – tends to result in multiple referrals for assessment and treatment once difficulties and symptoms have already emerged. Street and Davis propose using a 'childhood perspective' to organise services; that is, a perspective which considers developmental processes, and the types and timing of interventions required to support these processes. Organising services along such lines would encourage the alignment of service contacts with key developmental stages, therefore providing more opportunity to engage specialist mental-health workers in issues of prevention.

The tiered mental-health service described in the NHS review *Together We Stand* (Health Advisory Service, 1995) is also, to some extent, organised around meeting needs that are described by the presence of symptomatology. Street and Davis question whether organising mental-health services for looked-after children along similar lines is likely to result in services that aim to promote 'good mental health'. They suggest that a more integrated theory of childhood problems may support consideration of how the tiered CAMHS system can best be linked with the mental-health needs of looked-after children. The model they present is underpinned by contemporary knowledge about systems, processes and problems of attachment, the development of resilience, and individual therapies. Using such a framework to interpret young people's presentations can help contextualise mental-health problems within the developmental requirements of positive mental health.

The authors utilise the work of Cronen and Pierce (1985) on the 'co-ordinated management of meaning' to distinguish contextual levels and patterns of influence within the systems involved in supporting the mental health of looked-after children. According to this analysis, activities at a higher level that influence or give meaning to those at a lower level are referred to as *contextual*. Those operating in the opposite direction from specific to more general are termed *implicative*. Reversing the order to reflect the focus on the individual child, the organisation of influences within the system relating to a looked-after child can be represented as in Figure 9.1.

Implicit in the model is the idea that problems of practice are likely to occur if intervention is targeted at any level without considering needs and impacts within the enveloping levels and contexts. As well as focusing attention on systemic issues, the model's strengths include its non-disciplinary nature and the fact that a developmental perspective can be applied to the first four levels. Using the example of multiple potential pathways to developing resilience, the authors demonstrate how this systemic and contextual model highlights the child's need for relationships within her or his community as well as in the caring system. This

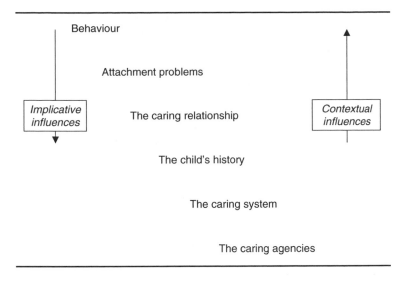

Figure 9.1   Looked-after children: levels of operation
Source: Adapted from Street and Davies (2002)

illustrates the model's capacity to support positive mental-health development, and the clear implication is that specialist professional inputs are not always required.

Given the complex social circumstances and psychological realities of the looked-after child, a model such as this, based on a 'health/developmental' rather than 'medical' or 'social care' approach, may be essential to organise the responses of the individuals and systems involved in providing mental-health care to looked-after children. Services based on such a model would necessarily be multi-disciplinary, and Street and Davis suggest, in view of their considerable skills and training agenda, would operate best from within a CAMHS structure.

CONCLUSION

The present chapter has reviewed a range of research findings that highlight how looked-after children are significantly more vulnerable to experiencing mental ill-health than those who have not been in care. This may be related to their experiences prior to coming into care, and may also be related to the inability of the care system to compensate for the absence of a stable, nurturing family life. Currently there may also be limitations to the care system's ability to identify young people's mental-health difficulties and organise effective interventions. Mental-health services, as they are currently organised, may not be best prepared to intervene to prevent the development of ill-health in some young people, and not all looked-after children who are experiencing distress feel comfortable accessing clinic-based CAMH services.

Much good work is done to support young people in care both by the social care system and by CAMH services; however, it remains unclear to what extent the needs of many young people in the care system are currently being met. A recent ten-year follow-up study has described the experiences of a small number of young people from across Northern Ireland who received long-term care. While only 16 young people participated in the follow-up, accounts of their experiences describe examples of how mental-health services have failed looked-after children (McAuley, 2005). CAMH and learning-disability services were in many cases unavailable to meet assessed needs. There was little evidence of planned work with children, most contacts being in response to behaviour problems in the placement or at school. There was little evidence of CAMH support to carers. And some children were placed in settings that were unsuitable due to the absence of appropriate therapeutic provision. In some cases, the premature ending of therapeutic alliances resulted in young people disengaging from therapeutic services altogether.

Clearly, young people in care require a range of planned, sometimes long-term, mental-health supports. These have not been consistently, or adequately, provided. This situation needs to change if young people are to receive optimal services to support their transition to healthy adult lives. Effective systems for identifying and responding to those who may be described as having mental-health difficulties or disorders are required. There is also a need for services that can more broadly identify need and therefore support interventions that aim to increase young people's resilience and prevent the development of such problems. Central to achieving these goals is assessment of need. This should take place as soon as is practical following admission to care, and should have a systems as well as individual focus. Such assessments can help care workers and foster carers to understand and engage with the contextual and implicative influences which shape young people's development. Support may be provided by a range of people including foster carers, residential staff, social services key workers, and others in the educational as well as statutory and voluntary health-care sectors. This will include, at times, access to therapeutic support from the tiered child and adolescent mental-health system. Further, those supporting young people's mental health who are not primarily mental-health workers require access to training, consultation, and supervision.

It is unlikely that the full range of assessment, planning, and supportive functions described could best be provided through specialist CAMHS. Such services tend to focus on providing treatments, and the range of competing pressures and priorities relevant to specialist CAMHS are unlikely to permit the sort of planned, integrative, prevention-oriented work described. Separate teams of mental-health professionals – populated on the basis of competencies rather than professional background – are required. These can focus on assessment, care and placement planning, training, and consultation with the care system. Such teams should not have a significant clinical remit because of the danger of being overwhelmed by clinical pressures. Rather, young people should continue to have access to CAMHS provision that can be flexibly delivered in ways that engage them.

New mental-health services to looked-after children have been described, and evaluations of these services are beginning to emerge. Useful guidance should become available from such developments to assist service commissioners and providers in developing services into the future. Young people's own views and experiences can be assets to service planning and provision, particularly as methods for meaningful consultation and involvement are increasingly being recognised. On a regional basis there is a need to agree a model for organising services and service development to avoid situations where there is inequity in provision. The allocation of resources must support co-ordinated multi-agency planning to prevent the development of mental ill-health among looked-after children, and to identify and provide appropriate and acceptable treatments for those who have significant needs.

REFERENCES

Achenbach, T.M. (1991a). *Manual for the Child Behaviour Checklist/4–18, 1991 Profile*. Burlington, VT: University Associates in Psychiatry.

Achenbach, T.M. (1991b). *Manual for the Youth Self Report, 1991 Profile*. Burlington, VT: University Associates in Psychiatry.

Ajdukovic, M., & Sladovic Franz, B. (2005). Behavioural and emotional problems of children by type of out-of-home care in Croatia. *International Journal of Social Welfare*, **14**, 163–175.

Bamford, F., & Wolkind, S.N. (1988). *The Physical and Mental Health of Children in Care: Research Needs*. London: Economic and Research Council.

Barrows, P. (1996). Individual psychotherapy for children in foster care: Possibilities and limitations. *Clinical Child Psychology and Psychiatry*, **1**(3), 385–397.

Berrick, J., & Barth, R.P. (1994). Research on kinship foster care: What do we know? Where do we go from here? *Children and Youth Services Review*, **16**, 1–5.

Bird, H.R., Yager, T.J., Staghezza, B., Gauld, M.S., Canino, G., & Rubio-Stipec, M. (1990). Impairment in the epidemiological measurement of childhood psychopathology in the community. *Journal of the American Academy of Child and Adolescent Psychiatry*, **29**, 5, 796–803.

Blower, A., Addo, A., Hodgson, J., Lamington, L., & Towlson, K. (2004). Mental health of looked-after children: A needs assessment. *Clinical Child Psychology and Psychiatry*, **9**(1), 117–129.

Bonnet, C., & Welbury, J. (2004). Meeting the mental-health needs of looked-after children: An example of routine psychological assessment. *Adoption and Fostering*, **28**(3), 81–82.

British Psychological Society (2004). Looked after children: Improving the psychological well-being of children in the care of the local authority. Faculty for Children and Young People briefing paper. Leicester: British Psychological Society, Division of Clinical Psychology.

Callaghan, J., Young, B., Pace, F., & Vostanis, P. (2004). Evaluation of a new mental health service for looked-after children. *Clinical Child Psychology and Psychiatry*, **9**(1), 130–148.

Charles, G., & Matheson, J. (1990). Children in foster care: Issues of separation and attachment. *Community Alternatives: International Journal of Family Care*, **2**(2), 37–49.

Clark, H., Prange, M., Lee, B., Boyd, L., McDonald, B., & Stewart, E. (1994). Improving adjustment outcomes for foster children with emotional and behavioural disorders: Early findings from a controlled study on individualized services. *Journal of Emotional and Behavioral Disorders*, **2**, 207–218.

Clausen, J.M., Landsverk, J., Ganger, W., Chadwick, D., & Litrownik, A. (1998). Mental health problems of children in foster care. *Journal of Child and Family Studies*, 7(3), 283–296.

Cronen, V.E., & Pierce, W.B. (1985). Towards an explanation of how the Milan method works: An invitation to a systemic epistemology and the evolution of family therapy. In D. Campbell & R. Draper (eds), *Applications of Systemic Therapy: The Milan Approach*. London: Grune & Stratton.

Dance, C., Rushton, A., & Quinton, D. (2002). Emotional abuse in early childhood: Relationships with progress in subsequent family placement. *Journal of Child Psychology and Psychiatry*, 43, 395–407.

Department of Health (1998). *Caring for Children Away from Home: Messages from Research*. Chichester. John Wiley & Sons, Ltd.

Department of Health (2002). Statistical bulletin: Children looked after by local authorities year ending 31 March 2002, England (detailed statistics). Available at: www.dh.gov.uk

Department of Health and Social Services and Personal Safety, Northern Ireland, Clinical Psychology Special Advisory Committee (2002). *Services to Meet the Psychological and Mental-Health Needs of Looked-After Children in Northern Ireland. (Consultation Document)*. Belfast: DHSS&PS.

Dimigan, G., Del Priore, C., Butler, S., Evans, S., & Ferguson, L. (1999). Psychiatric disorders among children at the time of entering local authority care: Questionnaire survey. *British Medical Journal*, 319, 675.

Emanuel, L. (2002). Deprivation X 3: The contribution of organizational dynamics to the 'triple deprivation' of looked-after children. *Journal of Child Psychotherapy*, 28, 163–179.

Foundation for People with Learning Disabilities (2001). *Count Us In: The Report of the Committee of Inquiry into the Mental-Health Needs of Young People with Learning Disabilities*. Updates: 4(8).

Foundation for People with Learning Disabilities (2003). *Meeting the Service Needs of Young People with Learning Difficulties and Mental Health Problems*. Updates: 4(10), 1–4.

Gebel, T. (1996). Kinship care and non-relative family foster care: A comparison of caregiver attributes and attitudes. *Child Welfare*, 75, 5–18.

Gibbs, I., & Sinclair, I. (2000). Bullying, sexual harassment and happiness in residential children's homes. *Child Abuse Review*, 9, 247–259.

Golding, K. (2004). Providing specialist psychological support to foster carers: A consultation model. *Child and Adolescent Mental Health*, 9(2), 71–76.

Goodman, R. (1997). The strengths and difficulties questionnaire: A research note. *Journal of Child Psychology and Psychiatry*, 38, 581–586.

Goodman, R. (1999). The extended version of the Strengths and Difficulties Questionnaire as a guide to child psychiatric caseness and consequent burden. *Journal of Child Psychology and Psychiatry and Allied Disciplines*, 40, 791–799.

Goodman, R., Ford, T., Corbin, T., & Meltzer, H. (2004). Using the Strengths and Difficulties (SDQ) multi-informant algorithm to screen looked-after children for psychiatric disorders. *European Child and Adolescent Psychiatry*, 13, supplement 2, 25–31.

Halfon, N., Zepeda, A., & Inkelas, M. (2002). Mental health services for children in foster care. In *A Policy Brief from the Study of Health Services for Children in Foster Care*, 4(Sept.). Berkeley: UCLA Center for Healthier Children, Families, and Communities.

Harman, J.S., Childs, G.E., & Kelleher, K.J. (2000). Mental health care utilization and expenditures among children in foster care. *Archives of Paediatric and Adolescent Medicine*, 154, 114–117.

Health Advisory Service (1995). *Thematic Review: Child and Adolescent Mental Health Services – Together We Stand*. London: HMSO.

Hengeller, S.W. (1999). Multisystemic therapy: An overview of clinical procedures, outcomes and policy implications. *Child Psychology and Psychiatry Review*, 4(1), 2–10.

Holland, S., Faulkner, A., & Perez-del-Aguila, R. (2005). Promoting stability and continuity of care for looked-after children: A survey and critical review. *Child and Family Social Work*, **10**, 29–41.

Hukkanen, R., Sourander, A., Bergroth, L., & Piha, J. (1999). Psychosocial factors and adequacy of services for children in children's homes. *European Journal of Child and Adolescent Psychiatry*, **8**(4), 268–275.

Hunter, M. (1993). The emotional needs of children in care – An overview. *ACPP Review and Newsletter*, **15**(5), 214–218.

Jackson, S., & Thomas, N. (1999). *On the Move Again?* Ilford: Barnardo's.

Kaufman, J., Birmaher, B., Brent, D., Rau, U., Flynn, C., Moreci, P. et al. (1997). Schedule for Affective Disorders and Schizophrenia for school-age children – Present and Lifetime version (K-SADS-PL): Initial reliability and validity data. *Journal of the American Academy of Child and Adolescent Psychiatry*, **36**, 980–988.

Kowprowska, J., & Stein, M. (2000). The mental health of 'looked after' young people. In P. Appleton, J. Hurry, & I. Warwick (eds), *Young People and Mental Health*. Chichester: John Wiley & Sons, Ltd, pp. 165–182.

Leslie, L.K., Hurlburt, M.S., Landsverk, J., Barth, R., & Slymen, D.J. (2004). Outpatient mental health services for children in foster care: A national perspective. *Child Abuse and Neglect*, **28**, 697–712.

Leslie, L.K., Landsverk, R., Ezzet-Lofstrom, R., Tschann, J.M., Slymen, D.J., & Garland, A.F. (2000). Children in foster care: Factors influencing outpatient mental health service use. *Child Abuse and Neglect*, **24**(4), 465–476.

Lewis, H. (2000). Children in public care: Overcoming the barriers to effective mental health care. *Young Minds*, **46**, 17–19.

Magnusson, D., & Statin, H. (1998). Person-context interaction theories. In W.R.M. Damon & R.M. Lerner (eds), *Handbook of Child Psychology*, vol. I. *Theoretical Models of Human Development*, 5th edn. Chichester: John Wiley & Sons, Ltd.

McAuley, C. (2005). Pathways and Outcomes: A ten year follow up study of children who have experienced care. Department of Health and Social Services and Public Safety, Northern Ireland. Available at: http://www.dhsspsni.gov.uk/stats&research/pubs.asp

McCann, J.B., James, A., Wilson, S., & Dunn, G. (1996). Prevalence of psychiatric disorders in young people in the care-system. *British Medical Journal*, **313**, 1529–1530.

McCarthy, G. (2004). The developmental histories of children who experience high levels of placement instability in the care-system. *Adoption and Fostering*, **28**(4), 60–65.

McCarthy, G., Janeway, J., & Geddes, A. (2003). The impact of emotional and behavioural problems on the lives of children growing up in the care-system. *Adoption and Fostering*, **27**, 14–19.

McConkey, R., Nixon, T., Donaghy, E., & Mulhern, D. (2004). The characteristics of children with a disability looked after away from home and their future service needs. *British Journal of Social Work*, **34**, 561–576.

McCue-Horwitz, S., Balestracci, K.M.B., & Simms, M.D. (2001). Foster care improves children's functioning. *Archives of Paediatric and Adolescent Medicine*, **155**, 1255–1260.

McMillen, J.C., Zima, B.T., Scott, L.D., Auslander, W.F., Munson, M.R., Ollie, M.T. et al. (2005). Prevalence of psychiatric disorders among older youths in the foster care-system. *Journal of the American Academy of Child and Adolescent Psychiatry*, **44**(1), 88–95.

McWey, L. (2000). I promise to act better if you let me see my family: Attachment theory and foster care visitation. *Journal of Family Social Work*, **5**(1), 91–105.

Meltzer, H., Corbin, T., Gatward, R., Goodman, R., & Ford, T. (2003). *The Mental Health of Young People Looked After by Local Authorities in England*. London: Office of National Statistics.

Meltzer, H., Gatwood, R., Goodman, R., & Ford T. (2000). *The Mental Health of Children and Adolescents in Great Britain*. London: Office of National Statistics.

Minnis, H., & Devine, C. (2001). The effect of foster carer training on the emotional and behavioural functioning of looked after children. *Adoption and Fostering*, **25**, 44–54.

Minnis, H., Pelosi, A.J., Knapp, M., & Dunn, J. (2001). Mental health and foster care training. *Archives of Disease in Childhood*, **84**, 302–306.

Minty, B. (1999). Annotation: Outcomes in long term foster family care. *Journal of Child Psychology and Psychiatry*, **7**, 991–999.

Morris, J. (1997). Gone missing? Disabled children living away from their families. *Disability and Society*, **12**, 241–258.

Mount, J., Lister, A., & Bennun, I. (2004). Identifying the mental-health needs of looked after people. *Clinical Child Psychology and Psychiatry*, **9**(3), 363–382.

Naglieri, J.A., LeBuffe, P.A., & Pfeiffer, S.I. (1993). *The Deveureux Scales of Mental Disorders*. New York: Harcourt Brace.

Nazroo, J.Y. (1997). *Ethnicity and Mental Health: Findings from a National Community Survey*. PSI Report No. 842. London: Policy Studies Institute.

Newton, R.R., Litrownik, A.J., & Landsverk, J.A. (2000). Children and youth in foster care: Disentangling the relationship between problem behaviours and number of placements. *Child Abuse and Neglect*, **24**(10), 1363–1374.

Nicholas, B., Roberts, S., & Wurr, C. (2003). Looked-after children in residential homes. *Child and Adolescent Mental Health*, **8**(2), 78–83.

Nicol, R., Stretch, D., Whitney, I., Jones, K., Garfield, P., Turner, K. et al. (2000). Mental-health needs and services for severely troubled and troubling young people including young offenders in an NHS region. *Journal of Adolescence*, **23**, 243–261.

Payne, H., & Butler, I. (1998). Improving the health care process and determining outcomes for children looked after by the local authority. *Ambulatory Child Health*, **4**, 165–172.

Penzerro, R.M., & Lein, L. (1995). Burning their bridges: Disordered attachment and foster care discharge. *Child Welfare*, **lxxxiv**, 351–366.

Phillips, J. (1997). Meeting the psychiatric needs of children in care. *Psychiatric Bulletin*, **21**, 609–611.

Prosser, H. (1978). *Perspectives on Foster Care*. Windsor: NFER.

Richardson, J., & Joughin, C. (2000). *The Mental-Health Needs of Looked-After Children*. London: Royal College of Psychiatrists.

Richardson, J., & Lelliot, P. (2003). Mental health of looked-after children. *Advances in Psychiatric Treatment*, **9**, 249–251.

Roy, P., Rutter, M., & Pickles, A. (2000). Institutional care: Risk from family background or pattern of rearing? *Journal of Child Psychology and Psychiatry*, **41**(2), 139–149.

Scholte, E.M., & Van Der Ploeg, J.D. (2000). Exploring factors governing successful residential treatment of youngsters with severe behavioural difficulties: Findings from a longitudinal study in Holland. *Childhood*, **2**, 77–93.

Shah, A. (2004). Ethnicity and the common mental disorders. In D. Melzer, T. Fryers, & R. Jenkins (eds), *Maudsley Monographs* **44**: *Social Inequalities and the Distribution of the Common Mental Disorders*. Hove: Psychology Press Ltd, pp. 171–223.

Simonoff, E., Pickles, A., Meyer, J.M., Silberg, J.L., Maes, H.H., Loeber, R. et al. (1997). The Virginia twin study of adolescent behavioural development: Influences of age, sex and impairment on disorder. *Archives of General Psychiatry*, **54**(9), 801–808.

Sneddon, H. (2003). The effects of maltreatment on children's health and well-being. *Child Care in Practice*, **9**(3), 236–249.

Stanley, N. (2005). The mental health of looked-after children: Matching response to need. *Health and Social Care in the Community*, **13**(3), 239–248.

Stevens, I. (2004). Cognitive behavioural interventions for adolescents in residential child care in Scotland: An examination of practice and lessons from research. *Child and Family Care Social Work*, **9**, 237–246.

Street, E., & Davies, M. (2002). Constructing mental health services for looked-after children. *Adoption and Fostering*, **26**(4), 65–75.

Teggart, T., & Menary, J. (2005). An investigation of the needs of children looked after by Craigavon and Banbridge Health and Social Services Trust. *Child Care in Practice*, **11**(1), 39–49.

Testa, M., & Rolock, N. (1999). Professional foster care: A future worth pursuing? *Child Welfare. Special Edition on Family Foster Care in the 21st Century*, **78**(1), 108–124.

Tolmac, J., & Hodes, M. (2004). Ethnic variation among adolescent psychiatric in-patients with psychotic disorders. *British Journal of Psychiatry*, **184**, 428–431.

Triseliotis, J. (1989). Foster care outcomes: A review of key research findings. *Adoption and Fostering*, **13**, 5–17.

Turner, W., MacDonald, G.M., & Dennis, J.A. (2005). Cognitive-behavioural training interventions for assisting foster carers in the management of difficult behaviour. *The Cochrane Database of Systematic Reviews: Reviews 2005*, **2**. Chichester: John Wiley & Sons, Ltd.

Utting, W. (1997). *People Like Us: A Review of the Safeguards for Children Living Away from Home*. London: Department of Health.

Viner, R.M., & Taylor, B. (2005). Adult health and social outcomes of children who have been in public care: Population based study. *Pediatrics*, **115**(4), 894–899.

Ward, H., & Skuse, T. (1999). *Looking After Children: Transforming Data into Management Information*. Dartington: Social Research Unit.

Wolkind, S., & Rushton, A. (1994). Residential, and foster family care. In M. Rutter, E. Taylor, & L. Hersov (eds), *Child and Adolescent Psychiatry*. Oxford: Blackwell Scientific, pp. 252–266.

World Health Organisation (1996). *Multiaxial Classification of Child and Adolescent Psychiatric Disorders*. Cambridge: Cambridge University Press.

CHAPTER 10

CHANGING LIVES OR JUST CHANGING LOCATION? PLANNING FOR ADOLESCENTS IN SUBSTITUTE CARE

Helga Sneddon

INTRODUCTION

This chapter aims to provide the reader with better understanding of how the needs of children placed in foster and residential care are planned for. The legislative and policy context is described with regard to how it impacts on the planning and placement choices for children living away from home. The chapter then focuses on findings from the *Adolescents in Substitute Care* (ASC) study (Sneddon et al., 2004) which examined the planning process for adolescents placed in residential and foster care in Northern Ireland.

BACKGROUND

All European countries have an obligation for the State to care for children who, for a variety of reasons, cannot be cared for by their families. However, approaches to this differ widely. In the UK, there are several options available for placing children removed from home including residential care, kinship foster care, non-kinship foster care, and adoption. In numerous pronouncements, notably in launching *Quality Protects* (1998) (a three-year programme in England and Wales), the government has stated that the outcomes for many children in public care have been poor and these children do not experience the same life-chances as their peers. Research has consistently shown the deficit in parenting of children in public care (Jackson & Martin, 1998; Utting, 1991, 1997; Ward & Skuse, 1999). The *Quality Protects* initiative made it a priority for social services to achieve better outcomes through the setting of targets for children within the public care system and particularly those looked after by local authorities.

The Child's Journey Through Care: Placement Stability, Care Planning, and Achieving Permanency. Edited by D. Iwaniec.
Copyright © 2006 John Wiley & Sons, Ltd.

Since the 1960s there have been numerous debates on child-care policy and practice (Brandon et al., 1998; Hayden et al., 1999). A major development in the UK was the introduction of the Children Act (1989), the Children (NI) Order (1995), and equivalent in Scotland (1995), which were designed to create 'one primary piece of legislation' for work with children and families, 'embracing several streams of thought and practice' (Hayden et al., 1999, p. 27). These pieces of legislation have attempted to create a more balanced approach in terms of the reasons for intervention into family life and the playing out of relationships between the State, children, and parents before, during, and after interventions (Fox, 1991). The primary aim is for substitute care to produce individuals who have had a secure upbringing that has given them qualifications and social skills, and left them in a good position to make the best of their lives. Any official steps should promote these requirements without infringing the rights of children and parents (Freeman, 2002; Hayden et al., 1999).

A key criticism of children in the care of the State is that their futures are not adequately planned for. Good planning is essential for children and families, given complex family histories and needs that these cases present, and increasing pressure on resources and services. A major thrust of the UK legislation is to set out criteria for assessing children according to need: the regulations require specific aspects of a child's welfare to be reflected in the care plan. These include the child's development, health, and education needs (particularly any issues relating to disability), his or her wishes and feelings, and the type of placement best suited to specified needs. There is an obligation to take account of parental responsibilities and the parents' capacity to provide for the children's needs. Trusts have a duty to enable the child to live with a family member. Where this is not feasible, there is an obligation to place a child looked after by a Trust near his or her home, and with siblings if applicable. Contact between the child and his or her family should be promoted and maintained where possible. There should also be appropriate provision for the child's religious persuasion, racial origin, and cultural and linguistic background. Removal from home is, if possible, to be brief.

Nevertheless, there still seems to be some room for improvement with regard to planning for children living away from home. For example, in 1997, the Northern Ireland Social Services Inspectorate (SSI), in a review of foster care services, recommended that planning for children removed from home could be improved by explicitly stating tasks, assigning them to a named worker, and establishing timescales for their completion. Additionally, greater attention should be afforded to meeting the religious and cultural needs of children placed outside their own community background.

Previous researchers have also expressed concern about the completion of paperwork relating to young people in out-of-home care. For example, Bundle (2001) examined children's home records and child health records for a group of teenagers in residential care. She identified poor use of Looking After Children (LAC) forms and concluded that important information about the health needs of looked-after teenagers, for example, was not known to the staff in the children's home.

In this chapter, planning for children in care is examined and findings are presented from a recent study undertaken in Northern Ireland that investigated social worker case files documenting the care planning of children. In 2002, the *Adolescents in Substitute Care* (ASC) study was undertaken by Sneddon et al. (2004). It aimed to examine the development and implementation of the care plans of children receiving substitute care, and their outcomes one year after placement in either residential or foster care. The study also aimed to identify any issues relating to the collection of the above information from the available documentation in social worker case files.

The sample for the ASC study was selected from a government administrative database (SOSCARE). The study aimed to examine children entering either residential care or foster care for the first time, as well as those who had a previous history in foster care. Data were collected on a sample of 165 of the 259 young people who met the entry criteria. A detailed analysis of the children's social work case files was undertaken, concentrating on the sections that covered the year under investigation. This allowed the collation of information on the children (such as risk factors leading to removal from home, family history, care plans for the child, and the children's characteristics with respect to emotional/behavioural problems, education, health, and social relationships). It was also possible to examine what had happened to the children during that year (e.g. whether they remained in the same placement, and whether any new problems had emerged, whether they had been given any help in terms of treatment and what the effects of these were). Information on children's outcomes at the end of the year was collected via a questionnaire administered to each child's social worker. Issues such as current legal status and placement of the child, the social worker's perceptions of children's progress, and outcomes via measurements in education, health, behaviour, social relationships, and so on were examined. Findings are presented in the following sections, ordered by type of required information that should be documented according to current legislative and practice requirements.

THE PLANNING PROCESS FOR CHILDREN PLACED IN RESIDENTIAL OR FOSTER CARE

Care Plans

One measure taken to improve planning for children removed from home is the recommendation that every child should have a care plan which identifies problems and suggests solutions. Within the UK, there are two *Looking After Children* (LAC) planning forms. The *care plan* establishes long-term arrangements for a young person's future. A care plan should be made before any child/young person is looked after, even if it only covers a few days. The care plan should be completed before a young person is first looked after: in the case of an emergency admission, it should be completed as soon as possible after a placement has been made. Such care plans are supposed to be revised every six months, or when a placement changes, in order to be kept up to date. The regulations within the Children Order require specific aspects of a child's welfare to be reflected in their care plans. These include the child's development, health, and education needs (particularly any issues relating to disability), the child's wishes and feelings when making decisions about its future, and the type of placement best suited to meet its needs. There is an obligation to take account of parental responsibilities and of the parents' capacity to provide for the child's needs.

Worryingly, Sneddon et al. (2004) found that 31% of their sample of adolescents placed in residential or foster care did not have an actual care plan as such, relating to a specific placement within their case files. Nevertheless, there was some information about what was happening to the child and what had been planned in various sections of the case file, such as letters of referral, notes of telephone calls, and so on. However, collating this information into any sort of coherent picture of the plan for the child was difficult and time-consuming. Part of the proposed benefit of summarising planning information into one coherent document such as a care plan is that it makes transfer of information between professionals more accurate and efficient. Given that there is a relatively high turnover of social workers in these cases, information transfer relating to caseloads is crucial to ensure continuity of care. The difficulties facing a social worker new to the case in easily grasping the key details of a case history from the information available in written form are anticipated.

Care plans are supposed to be reviewed on a regular basis (every six months or when a placement changes), and to be updated according to the needs of the child. In our study we found that timescales were specified in the majority of cases (78%), with the majority of children placed in residential or foster care anticipated to be looked after on a long-term basis. Although the inclusion of a contingency plan for situations when a placement breaks down is recommended, information contained in the case files relating to these was often vague or missing.

The Children Order recommends that children and their families should be involved in planning for the future. We found that, in the vast majority of cases, the care plan was discussed with the young person (89%). It was also often discussed with the child's mother (78%). It was less likely to be discussed with the father (37%), siblings (4%), step-parents (2%), or grandparents (2%). For those children placed in foster care, care plans had been discussed with 98% of foster carers. Likewise, for those children in residential care, care plans were usually discussed with the residential worker in 78% of cases. Several arrangements were recorded in order to involve the child and parents in the planning process, the most frequent of which was inviting them to review meetings.

Placement Plans

The *Placement Plan Part 1* contains details of where the child is to be placed, who carers should contact outside of office hours, information the carers need to know about the child in order to provide immediate care (more detailed information goes in Part 2), arrangements for contact, brief details of any behavioural or health problems, and who has authority to give consent for the child's medical care, etc. Unless information is unavailable, all questions in Part 1 of the Placement Plan and Part 1 of the Essential Information Record must be answered before any placement begins, and agreements signed by carers, the social worker, and young people, and parents where appropriate (Arrangements for Placement of Children (General) Regulations, 1996). Wherever possible, all questions in Part 2 of the Placement Plan and Essential Information Record should be answered, and the care plan completed, before a young person is first looked after; in the case of an emergency admission they should be completed as soon as possible after a placement has been made. Part 2 of the Placement Plan must be completed within the next 14 days.

Sneddon et al. (2004) again found disturbingly high rates of non-completion for these forms. Part 1 of the Placement Plan was partially or fully completed for only 65% of the children in their sample of adolescents placed in residential or foster care within a reasonable timescale.

The *Placement Plan Part 2* sets out arrangements for a child/young person's day-to-day care in a particular placement. This includes details of any routines and details of arrangements being made to meet particular needs (such as the child's/young person's physical and emotional health requirements, educational needs, cultural aspects, contact with families, leisure, etc.).

Once again, we found that Part 2 of the Placement Plans was completed for just over half of the children in the ASC study (54% were either fully or partially completed). The ASC study did not examine whether this information is given to carers verbally by social workers rather than in written form at the start of the placement. Nevertheless, giving the carers a written summary of the arrangements would prove a useful reference as the child settles into the placement, as well as ensuring clarity in roles and responsibilities of different individuals.

One example of when the transfer of appropriate information at time of placement becomes critical is when children who have perpetrated abuse and victims of abuse have to be placed together. There is increasing evidence of a problem of sexual abuse of children by other residents in substitute care (Kent, 1997; Utting, 1997). Many adult sexual offenders start their 'careers' during their teens or even earlier (National Commission of Inquiry into the Prevention of Child Abuse, 1996; NCH, 1992). The Centre for Residential Child Care's survey of residential services found that one-third provided placements for young people known to have abused others sexually (1997). Half of the respondents 'suspected' that a young person in their care had abused others sexually. They also found that 31% of services were caring for young people who had been abused together with those who were perpetrators of abuse. Kools and Kennedy (2002) found that registered nurses and child-care workers working in residential care had limited knowledge of the *sequelae* of child sexual abuse. They concluded that developmentally appropriate behaviour of sexually abused children, as well as behavioural manifestations of child sexual abuse, were often misinterpreted and mismanaged.

Although Utting (1991) suggested that, in principle, victims of abuse should be separated from children who are perpetrators of abuse, this is not always possible, particularly since some young people do not reveal their involvement in abuse (either as victim or perpetrator) until after they have been placed (Kendrick, 1998). As one of Lindsay's respondents put it:

> There are enormous difficulties around the practice of working with abused and abusers in the one residential establishment. Abusers have the same basic need for care and attention as those abused, and have often been abused themselves. There is, however, a difficulty in protecting others from them and in dealing with abusive behaviour, which requires different skills and possibly staffing and a different focus.
>
> (1999, p. 410)

Lindsay suggested that new workers, starting on their first appointment, had a 2-in-3 chance of caring for an abused young person, and a 1-in-3 chance of caring for a young person who has abused others. She concluded that in the latter situation they also have a 90% chance of simultaneously caring for both. She was concerned that it is still practice for staff to be employed with no qualifications whatever in the care of such children, and even such qualifications that do exist provide little or no expertise in working within such a complex, sensitive, and risky care environment.

Skinner (1992) recommended that when perpetrators and victims of abuse had to be placed in the same unit, there must be careful assessment of the risks, agreed protection plans, and appropriate levels of surveillance. The abusers should receive intervention to enable them to accept responsibility for their behaviour and learn more appropriate ways of dealing with others. This highlights the importance of providing carers with appropriate information about the child's prior history in order to minimise the likelihood of a victim being placed with an abuser without adequate precautions. The relevant individuals need to have the right information at the right time.

Essential Information Record

The care plan links closely with the *Essential Information Record* and it is therefore important that the latter is kept up to date. Part 1 of the Essential Information Record provides baseline information for carers in an emergency: names and contact details for parents, the child's health conditions, and contacts for doctors, etc. All these questions are supposed to be answered before any child/young person can be left in a placement. The information should be given to carers with the Placement Agreement. Sneddon et al. (2004) found that completion rates for Part 1 of the Essential Information Record were higher than for other required paperwork: Part 1 was fully completed for 69% of the sample. However, for three out of ten children, insufficient information was held regarding whether carers had been given this basic information which would be crucial if an emergency were to arise.

Part 2 of the Essential Information Record contains, for example, information on whether the young person is a parent or has parental responsibility, their NHS number, immunisations, hospital admissions, plus attendances at schools, Child Protection registration, history in care, family history, professional contacts, and similar information. In the case of an emergency admission, it should be completed as soon as possible thereafter.

The recording of this information is important, not only for the child's immediate care such as in an emergency, but also in the more long-term monitoring of its health. Payne (2000) notes that children in public care are at greater risk than other children of organic health problems, including poorly controlled asthma, injuries, speech, and language and developmental delay. They are also at more risk of infectious disease and higher rates of teenage pregnancy. Nicol et al. (2000) found that three-quarters of the young people living in all residential establishments in a geographical region in England had significant health problems including hyperactivity and depression. Others have found that children looked after by local authorities in the UK were significantly more likely than those living at home to experience changes in general practitioner, have incomplete immunisations, receive inadequate dental care, and suffer anxieties and difficulties in interpersonal relationships (Williams et al., 2001). They also tended to receive less health education.

Although they are shown to have more health problems than their peers, evidence suggests that children in public care are also missing out on preventive care such as immunisations, health surveillance, dental care, health education, and health promotion. For example, Bundle (2001) examined children's home records and health records for a group of teenagers in residential care. She found that immunisation uptake was below the national average and particularly poor for BCG and school-leaver tetanus, low-dose diphtheria, and polio boosters. She suggested that the poor uptake of these vaccinations may reflect absence from school and the difficulty of keeping track of immunisations and other health needs when there are frequent placement changes. Incomplete immunisations in looked-after children have also been noted by other researchers (Chernoff et al., 1994).

Grant et al. (2003) found that 74% of the looked-after children in her sample also had unrecognised physical health problems, including serious complaints such as asthma, kidney problems, and epilepsy. Her research suggested that one of the reasons for the under-diagnosis of these problems in looked-after children may be that the children are often moving from placement to placement and diagnosis of such problems needs to be established over a period of time. The appropriate recording of health-related information and transfer of this between relevant individuals therefore become crucial in the care of these young people.

Review of Arrangements

The purpose of a *review of arrangements* is to ensure that day-to-day arrangements meet the child's/young person's needs and that the overall care plan is still appropriate. This review covers the child's development in a number of areas such as health, education, family circumstances, placement, legal status, and similar matters. It identifies things that are going well in addition to areas of concern and what is needed for the future. Reviews of looked-after children are a statutory requirement under the Children (NI) Order (1995) Article 45. As a minimum requirement, each young person's circumstances must be reviewed within two weeks of becoming looked after, within three months of the first review, and, subsequently, at intervals of no more than six months. Only a statutory review can change the care plan. The review form should be completed at each statutory review of the child/young person. Certain parts should be completed before the review, and other parts during or immediately after it. This was the piece of required documentation most likely to be fully completed in Sneddon et al.'s (2004) study: they found that the review of arrangements forms were fully completed for 95% of the children in the ASC study and partially completed for a further 4%.

Preparations and Planning for Leaving After Care

Every year approximately 7,000 to 8,000 young people leave care at the age of 16 or over, and the majority of these young people move to independent living. It is widely recognised that looked-after children and young people who have left care (as well as people in long-term residential or institutional care) are among society's most vulnerable, and, therefore, at most risk of future marginalisation. This can have long-term detrimental effects on their social, emotional, and physical well-being (Focus Ireland, 1998). Other research such as that carried out by Francis (2000) showed that entering into care from a deprived background too often initiates a downward spiral even for young people who were previously doing well. Adolescents ageing out of the child-welfare system are particularly vulnerable to poor health, under-education, unemployment, and homelessness (Collins, 2001).

The Children Act 1989 introduced a duty to prepare looked-after young people for adult life. Preparation, in its broadest sense, should begin at the point young people are first looked after, and is best achieved in the context of placement stability, permitting the gradual development of skills over time, where there is continuity of important links and relationships, where educational progress is positively encouraged, and where preparation is formally integrated into child-care planning (Biehal et al., 1995; Clayden & Stein, 1996). In 2001, the Leaving and Aftercare Bill was passed by the Northern Ireland Assembly to improve the support arrangements for young people leaving care.

Young people are expected to leave care and move to independent living at a much earlier age than other young people in the general population are expected to leave home (Biehal et al., 1992; Garnett, 1992). A majority will move to independent living before the age of 18 compared to fewer than one in ten of their peers living at home (Jones, 1995). While some young people are attracted to the idea of independence and push to leave, moving on is also influenced by a number of factors, including placement breakdown, limitations in the supply of placements, problems in managing challenging behaviour, and traditional expectations about the right time to leave (Biehal et al., 1995).

Not only do young people leave early, but the main elements of transition to adulthood tend to be compressed. Learning to manage a home, gaining a career foothold, and starting a family tend to overlap in the immediate period after leaving care (Biehal et al., 1995; Corlyon & McGuire, 1997; Garnett, 1992). Many young people also receive inconsistent preparation for adulthood, leaving them ill-equipped to face this journey, and, in particular, the needs of some groups of young people – young parents, black young people, and young people with special needs – have not always been consistently met (First Key, 1987; Fletcher, 1993).

Young people are unlikely to manage in adversity without a network of formal and informal support. However, research has shown a tendency for support from social workers and past carers to fall away soon after leaving care (Biehal et al., 1992; Fry, 1992; Garnett, 1992). Direct work with families, including the potential of support from extended family members, has often been given a low priority at the leaving-care stage. In addition, there is evidence that where young people lack positive family support, they are more likely to have poor post-care outcomes and greater difficulties in making and sustaining relationships with others (Biehal et al., 1995).

Leaving-care schemes therefore have an important role to play in preparation programmes for looked-after young people by offering advice and consultancy, developing resource packs, providing training, and through direct work with young people individually or in groups. At the after-care stage, schemes have also been shown to be effective in contributing to more positive outcomes in the life-skills area by providing compensatory support, especially for those who have had less stable care careers.

In order to facilitate the transition from State care into independent living, the requirement is that all children aged 14 or older should have transition plans for adulthood in place. In line with this requirement, Sneddon et al. (2004) found that significantly more children aged 15 in residential care had a transition plan, compared to children of the same age in foster care. This may reflect that it is more common for young people to 'age out' of the residential care system (i.e. stop receiving support because they have reached a particular age), whereas support from foster families can sometimes be phased out over many more years, or continued indefinitely into adulthood.

CONCLUSION

Children removed from home often have complex family histories and needs. There has been concern that their needs must be accurately identified and appropriate interventions offered in a timely fashion. Attention must be given to both the needs of a child at the time of removal from home and the characteristics of the placement that is being considered for it. For example, there should be concern about placing children who have instigated abuse towards other children in the same placement alongside children who have been victims of abuse. However, the availability of key information to social workers about children's history and the pressure on choice of placement can make this a difficult situation to balance. Often, there is considerable time pressure on finding somewhere suitable for the child to live, as the risk at home is too great. This has implications for safeguards that can be put in place if certain groups of children are to be located together.

There is also an issue of the transfer of key information between professionals, for example, if there is a transfer of a child's case from one social worker to another. In the UK, legislation has sought to improve the planning process for these children by specifying documentation that must be completed in order to aid identification of problems, focus the responses to these, and facilitate tracking of problems over time as well as information transfer between key personnel. Unfortunately, in spite of the UK regulations relating to the completion of specified forms, the evidence suggests these are not always adequately completed. For example, Sneddon et al.'s (2004) study suggested that planning for the overall welfare of children entering residential or foster care seemed to be good. However, completion rates of paperwork were problematic, with nearly one-third of children showing no discernible care plans relating to the placement at the start of the year, and little information recorded about other family members. In particular, health-related information was inadequate with just over half of the children with health problems having Part 2 of their Essential Information Record fully completed. Inadequate record-keeping and transfer of information may have a negative impact on the care of these children, particularly in diagnosis of problems where information is required over time.

With respect to paper work, it is important that records are kept up to date regarding children in care and are easily accessible to those that require them. Other research (e.g. Cousins & Monteith, 2002) has shown a relatively high turnover of social workers among younger looked-after children, and it is important that there is continuity in care when changes occur. It may be possible that a more succinct summary document could be developed which would be more likely to be completed. This summary of key points could possibly be kept at the front of the child's case file and regularly updated.

Separate from the transfer of information from social worker to another, or from social worker to carer, ways to facilitate inter-professional communication and working also need to be supported. For example, research over the past 20 years has consistently suggested that the majority of social workers do not consider education part of the core business and consistently give it low ratings as compared with placement issues, maintaining family relationships, and attempting to help children with emotional and behavioural difficulties (Fletcher-Campbell, 1997; Francis, 2000). Rees (2001) suggested that there are still powerful cultural factors to be overcome in this area, notably the historical tendency to think of residential homes as caring for children, with education the exclusive concern of schools and other education services. She also found that most of the residential workers with whom she worked were either ignorant of the low educational attainment of children they looked after or did not see it as a problem. Similarly, others have suggested that the lack of understanding between education and care professionals is one of the main reasons for poor performance. Research examining the education of looked-after children has concluded that the only way to achieve a significant improvement in outcomes is for truly collaborative working between education and social services (Borland et al., 1998; Social Services Inspectorate, 1998).

The support of children after they leave care also needs to be examined, since the available evidence suggests that the experiences of children leaving foster care and those leaving residential care may be quite different in terms of the support that they receive, and their outcomes over time.

REFERENCES

Biehal, N., Clayden, J., Stein, M., & Wade, J. (1992). *Prepared for Living? A Survey of Young People Leaving the Care of Three Authorities*. London: National Children's Bureau.

Biehal, N., Clayden, J., Stein, M., & Wade, J. (1995). *Moving On: Young People and Leaving Care Schemes*. London: HMSO.

Borland, M., Pearson, C., Hill, M., Tisdale, K., & Bloomfield, I. (1998). *Education and Care Away from Home*. Edinburgh: Scottish Council for Research in Education.

Brandon, M., Schofield, G., & Trindler, L. (1998). *Social Work with Children*. Basingstoke: Macmillan.

Bundle, A. (2001). Health of teenagers in residential care: Comparison of data held by care staff with data in community child health records. *Archives of Disease in Childhood*, **84**, 10–14.

Centre for Residential Child Care (1997). *'The Tip of the Iceberg': Sexual Abuse in the Context of Residential Child Care*. Glasgow: Centre for Residential Child Care.

Chernoff, R., Combs-Orme, T., Risley-Curtis, C., & Heisler, A. (1994). Assessing the health status of children entering foster care. *Paediatrics*, **93**, 594–601.

Children Matter Task Force (2001). *The Development of Residential Child Care: A Regional Plan*. London: The Stationery Office.

Clayden, J., & Stein, M. (1996). Self care skills and becoming adult. In S. Jackson & S. Kilroe (eds), *Looking After Children: Good Parenting, Good Outcomes*. London: HMSO.

Collins, M.E. (2001). Transition to adulthood for vulnerable youths: A review of research and implications for policy. *Social Services Review*, **75**, 271–291.

Corlyon, J., & McGuire, C. (1997). *Young Patients in Public Care*. London: National Children's Bureau.

Cousins, W., & Monteith, M. (2002). *The Lives of Younger Looked-After Children*. Belfast: Centre for Child Care Research, Queen's University.

First Key (1987). *A Study of Black Young People Leaving Care*. London: First Key.

Fletcher, B. (1993). *Not Just a Name: The Views of Young People in Foster and Residential Care*. London: National Consumer Council/Who Cares? Trust.

Fletcher-Campbell, F. (1997). *The Education of Children Who Are Looked After*. London: NFER.

Focus Ireland (1998). *Out on Their Own: Young People Leaving Care in Ireland*. Dublin: Oak Tree Press.

Fox, H.L. (1991). *Perspectives in Child Care Policy*. Harlow: Longman.

Francis, J. (2000). Investing in children's futures: Enhancing the educational arrangements of 'looked after' children and young people. *Child and Family Social Work*, **5**(1), 131–143.

Freeman, M. (2002). Children's rights ten years after ratification. In B. Franklin (ed.), *The New Handbook of Children's Rights*. London: Routledge.

Fry, E. (1992). *After Care: Making the Most of Foster Care*. London: National Foster Care Association.

Garnett, L. (1992). *Leaving Care and After*. London: National Children's Bureau.

Grant, A., Ennis, J., & Stuart, F. (2003). Looking after health: A joint working approach to improving the health outcomes of Looked After and Accommodated children and young people. *Scottish Journal of Residential Child Care*, **1**, 23–29.

Hayden, C., Goddard, J., Gorin, S., & Van der Spek, N. (1999). *State Child Care: Looking After Children?* London: Jessica Kingsley.

Jackson, S., & Martin, P. (1998). Surviving the care system: Education and resilience. *Journal of Adolescence*, **21**, 565–583.

Jones, G. (1995). *Leaving Home*. Buckingham: Open University Press.

Kendrick, A. (1998). Bullying and peer abuse in residential child care: A brief review. Scottish Institute for Residential Child Care, Department of Social Work, University of Dundee. Available at: http://www.sircc.strath.ac.uk/research/kendrick1.html accessed 26 January 2006.

Kent, R. (1997). *Children's Safeguards Review*. Edinburgh: The Stationery Office.

Kools, S., & Kennedy, C. (2002). Child sexual abuse treatment: Misinterpretation and mismanagement of child sexual behaviour. *Child Care Health and Development*, **28**, 211–218.

Lindsay, M. (1999). The neglected priority: Sexual abuse in the context of residential child care. *Child Abuse Review*, **8**, 405–418.

National Commission of Inquiry into the Prevention of Child Abuse (1996). *Childhood Matters*, vols 1 and 2. London: HMSO.

NCH (1992). *The Report of the Committee of Enquiry into Children and Young People who Sexually Abuse Other Children*. London: National Children's Home.

Nicol, R., Stretch, D., Whitney, I., Jones, K., Garfield, P., Turner, K. et al. (2000). Mental health needs and services for severely troubled and troubling young people including young offenders in an NHS region. *Journal of Adolescence*, **23**, 243–261.

Payne, H. (2000). The health of children in public care. *Current Opinion in Psychiatry*, **13**, 381–388.

Rees, J. (2001). Making residential care educational care. In S. Jackson (ed.), *Nobody Ever Told Us School Mattered: Raising the Educational Attainments of Children in Care*. London: British Agencies for Adoption and Fostering, pp. 273–289.

Skinner, A. (1992). *Another Kind of Home: A Review of Residential Child Care*. Edinburgh: The Scottish Office.

Sneddon, H., Milner, S., & Iwaniec, D. (2004). The adolescents in substitute care (ASC) study. Unpublished report to funder.

Social Services Inspectorate (1998). *Fostering in Northern Ireland: Children and Their Carers – A Summary*. Belfast: The Stationery Office.

Utting, W. (1991). *Children in the Public Care: A Review of Residential Child Care*. London: HMSO.

Utting, W. (1997). *People Like Us: The Report of the Review of the Safeguards for Children Living Away from Home*. London: Department of Health.

Ward, A., & Skuse, T. (1999). *Looking After Children: Transforming Data into Management Information*. Report for the first year of data collection. Totnes, Devon: Dartington Social Research Unit.

Williams, J.G., Jackson, S., Maddocks, A., Cheung, W.Y., Love, A., & Hutchings, H.A. (2001). The health of those looked after by local authorities: A case-controlled study. *Archives of Disease in Childhood*, 85(4), 280–285.

CHAPTER 11

MAKING USE OF POSITIVE PSYCHOLOGY IN RESIDENTIAL CHILD CARE

Stan Houston

INTRODUCTION

Many children and young people in residential care in the United Kingdom experience significant levels of emotional suffering as a consequence of loss, trauma, abuse, and instability. A brief review of the research confirms this dismal observation. For instance, in a seminal study, McCann et al. (1996) examined the prevalence and types of psychiatric disorder among young people in care and compared the findings with those pertaining to a control group of young people living at home. Worryingly, 96% of subjects in residential units in the cohort presented with some form of psychiatric disorder including anxiety, depression, psychosis, phobias, and anorexia nervosa. This compared with a significantly lower prevalence rate in the control group.

In a comparable study, Mount et al. (2004) examined carers' perceptions of the mental-health needs of young people resident in the care system. Their views were then matched against the findings of a more objective, standardised, mental-health screen. The results showed that carers perceived 70% of the young people to have significant mental-health needs and, in two-thirds of the cases, it appeared that their judgements were in accord with the screen's results.

Adding weight to these findings, Blower et al. (2004), in a combined quantitative and qualitative study, reported that 'a majority of children and young people looked after by our local authority suffer from chronic and disabling mental health problems despite early recognition of their difficulties, attempts at solutions and supportive care settings'. The authors went on to highlight the need for more effective interventions with this very vulnerable client group.

The Child's Journey Through Care: Placement Stability, Care Planning, and Achieving Permanency.   Edited by D. Iwaniec.
Copyright © 2006 John Wiley & Sons, Ltd.

If the above evidence is not fully persuasive, we need only look to Williams et al.'s (2001) survey for further empirical confirmation. These researchers discovered that children accommodated in the care system for more than six months presented with significantly worse emotional and behavioural health compared with children living at home. The salience of this emotional morbidity is revealed by Sinclair and Gibbs (1998) in their wide-ranging study of children's homes in the United Kingdom. In relation to the subjective well-being of the young people reviewed, these researchers found that:

> between a third and two thirds of the residents gave answers suggesting that they were worried, depressed, had a low opinion of themselves or felt they were going nowhere. Eight out of ten felt that they easily became upset or angry. Hardly any described themselves as happy, and a staggering four out of ten had apparently considered killing themselves.
>
> (1998, p. 190)

What is more, we know from longitudinal studies that the consequences of such emotional difficulties are often profound (Buchanan & Hudson, 2000). Impoverished family relationships, poorer school achievement, greater risks of offending, and heightened social exclusion of young people are just some of the possible effects.

Given this picture and its implications, the therapeutic climate within residential care merits much discussion. We know that some models of intervention put forward an eclectic mix of therapeutic responses (e.g. Docker-Drysdale, 1968; Lyman et al., 1989) while others prefer to stay within the confines of one over-arching treatment paradigm (e.g. Bettleheim, 1950; Frost et al., 1999; Hoghugi, 1988; Rose, 1990). Within this broad range of literature some texts have married the therapeutic response to contextual realities to develop treatment modalities such as working in the 'life space' and 'opportunity led work' (Ward, 1993) where group care is viewed as a unique, therapeutic milieu. Other writers (e.g. Whitaker, 1979) have emphasised how treatment needs to be thought of differently with family and community networks playing a vital role in the promotion of emotional well-being.

Important as this canon of work has been, much of it has fallen prey to a deficit-oriented approach to treatment and therapeutic help. In other words, the focus has been on negative factors such as 'trauma', 'abuse', 'adversity', and 'impoverished self-esteem'. Moreover, in looking more closely at the approaches just listed, the influence of an underpinning discourse of psychopathology focusing on offending symptoms (that need to be diagnosed, treated, and eradicated) can be detected. Even the language which professionals adopt seems to reflect this mindset: terms such as 'challenging behaviour', 'children in need', and 'troubled and troublesome' often proliferate in discussions that are held to review a young person's progress (or lack of it).

But there is a danger in all of this of pathologising young people – making them feel different from their peers and in some cases creating self-fulfilling prophecies.

The argument might be that in investing so much attention in negative attributes, one unwittingly reinforces them or, indeed, exacerbates them much like a snow-ball rolling down a hill accumulates both mass and momentum. As Buchanan (2002) tersely suggests, 'labelling a child a "psychiatric case" can be more damaging than the disorder itself'.

By way of contrast, building on the positive dimensions of a young person's life might lead to more efficacious outcomes that do not reinforce stigma. Unfortunately, Western psychology has been unduly influenced by a Freudian legacy that has reinforced the former deficit-orientation in therapeutic work. Eastern philosophies, in marked contrast, put more stress on inherent potential and how it can be realised. In Buddhism, for example, a depressed person is encouraged to let go of his negativity by habituating positive states of mind and by realising his innate worth (Chodron, 2001). The point made here is that background cultural meanings serve to shape the way individuals respond to issues in social life.

In more recent times, though, some of the literature on social work practice with children has turned to the latter, 'positive' direction by focusing on a strengths-based approach (Saleeby, 1997). Here, writers such as Gilligan (1997) and Rutter (1999) have highlighted the value of childhood resilience and its ramifications for policy and practice. Thus, it is argued, building on self-esteem and self-efficacy through supportive school environments, cultural activities, and sporting pursuits appears to accentuate a child's resistance to adverse events. Interestingly, the message is that attending to the protective factors undergirding resilience can inure young people at risk, at least sustaining their emotional well-being in times of crisis or loss.

This approach is 'positive' in the sense that it focuses on the child's existing competences, tries to normalise the helping intervention, and does not mark the child out as different from his or her peers. Taking the point further, if a positive frame of working with young people in need has particular benefits, then it is important that professionals working in residential care embrace it seriously and investigate its potential. This chapter seeks to add to this debate by introducing the reader to a growing movement within the American therapeutic scene known as 'positive psychology' (Seligman, 2005). Positive psychology, in brief, champions the idea of capacity-building over risk management.

To expand on this important perspective, the background and ethos of positive psychology will be outlined and then, in more detail, the work of two of its leading thinkers will be described: Goleman (1995) and Csikszentmihalyi (1990). The therapeutic implications of these thinkers' ideas will then be considered, and suggestions made as to how they might be applied in residential child care.

AN INTRODUCTION TO POSITIVE PSYCHOLOGY

Positive psychology grew out of a new intellectual energy that was committed to the examination of the positive dimensions of human existence. These dimensions were seen to be closely linked with inner subjective experience or ways in which the human subject could adapt to external hardships, and even maintain an inner composure in the midst of them. A living example of this orientation can be found in the approach of the existential thinker Victor Frankyl (1984). A survivor of Nazi concentration camps, Frankyl managed to overcome his daily hardship by realising the power of healing through personal meaning. In this connection, one also thinks of the yogi Atisha's slogan that we should not be swayed by external circumstances when working to develop inner tranquillity (Chodron, 2001). The manner in which we cultivate the time-honoured virtues of hope, serenity, courage, patience, and even spirituality in the face of external afflictions is essentially what is being examined here.

So, rather than investigating psychopathology or becoming engrossed in the latest edition of the mental disorder classification, we are encouraged by positive psychologists to chart what makes life worth living. Let us examine a simple everyday event from this perspective. A female child, aged 7, approaches another child in the school playground trying to establish friendly contact. Unfortunately, she is rebuffed, not perhaps for any significant reason or the manner of her approach, but simply because her intended playmate is having an 'off-day'. But the child interprets her rejection through a negative, internal schema. What then follows is an internal dialogue shaped by feelings of shame and inadequacy. As a consequence, she resolves never to make another approach of this kind in order to defend against further, inner distress. By thinking in such terms, she inadvertently reinforces a negative frame of mind that, in turn, generalises her perceived ineptitude to different interpersonal contexts. Thus, sequences of negative chain effects (Rutter, 1999) are put in motion by this critical incident, damaging opportunities for growth and development.

Now, take a different child facing the same experience. This child interprets her rejection in a wholly different manner. Instead of engaging in self-reproach, she is largely indifferent to the episode. In fact, there is no introspective examination of what occurred because it in no way threatens her internal working model (Howe, 1995). Consequently, she has the confidence to make a second approach to a different child in the playground, this time with a successful outcome.

What, quintessentially, explains the difference in these two children's reactions? Undoubtedly, on the one hand, explanations for children's behaviour have to avoid naïve reductionism but, on the other, there is a crucial characteristic here that may have a heightened explanatory value. To elucidate further, in this partic-ular example the child's inner subjective reaction (her cognitive processing of events) appears to be a formative force in shaping consequent responses by and to her. Furthermore, by pinpointing a particular interpretative schema that has positive benefits, one is able to amplify its strengths. The focus here is on seeking sources of strength, ways of gathering optimism, and connecting with aesthetic experiences that are wholesome and curative. As Seligman and Csikszentmihalyi (2000) appositely put it, 'treatment is not just fixing what is broken; it is nurturing what is best'.

The antecedents of positive psychology's foundational ideas can be found in the humanistic, 'third-way' deliberations of Abraham Maslow (1908–1970). For this pioneer thinker, psychology needed to break free from the biological and instinctual determinism of behavioural and psycho-analytic psychology (hence his third-way approach). In departing from these ingrained canons of psychological thought, Maslow became interested in optimal human experience – a person's capacity to self-actualise. Self-actualising people, according to Maslow, are more likely to experience so-called 'peak experiences' or rarefied moments of heightened awareness, where there is a fusion of component parts of the personality to effect an inordinate integration of the person at all levels.

However, positive psychologists took Maslow's notion of existential well-being further by subjecting it to scholarly standards and grounding it within empirical investigation. Moreover, for proponents of the movement, human well-being was not to be seen as an individualistic pursuit, but rather an issue of civic responsibility. Critically, social policy and governmental reform should be aimed at the widespread prevention of mental ill-health as opposed to micro-interventions directed at tertiary relief. In other words, positive psychologists argued that we should build up social competence and capital through programmes targeted at vulnerable populations.

These theoretical moorings have evinced diverse outpourings. For instance, Buss (2000) has examined the development of positive mind states from an evolutionary perspective, noting how our emotional responses in the present can be understood as functional prerequisites that link back to ancestral times. Taking up this theme of the past, Massimini and Delle Fave (2000) moved beyond Buss's biological focus to explore the impact of psychological and cultural evolution on the expression of human emotions. For these authors, human actors are predisposed to reproduce positive frames of mind, even when faced with a lack of social meaning in society.

Taking a completely different direction, Diener (2000) explored positive psychology through the interplay of a range of domains including social structure, culture, and the individual actor. Crucially, for Diener, happiness correlates strongly with a person's capacity to interpret his or her experience positively in the face of external pressures or demands. Like Diener, Peterson (2000) concluded that optimism plays a vital role in maintaining optimal mental health and Salovey et al. (2000) took this further by making a connection between happiness and physical health. The richness of the movement is also seen in attempts to ground human experience within social process and context. Thus, Winner (2000) linked positive mood to familial experience, a finding that was endorsed widely by other disciplinary inquiries into adversity, risk, resilience, and protective factors (Rutter, 1999). These diverse perspectives are added to in a recently published edited text on positive psychology (Snyder & Lopez, 2005). Here, we find contributions, among other things, on emotion-focused approaches, the role of cognition, spirituality, and attempts to apply positive psychology to specific populations such as people with a physical disability.

But let us now take a more focused look at the work of two of the leading proponents of positive psychology. In doing so, the relevance of their ideas for young people in group care settings who experience enduring emotional pain will be outlined. Let us remind ourselves at this critical juncture that:

> positive psychology promises to get adolescents' internal fires lit, to help them develop the complex skills and dispositions necessary to take charge of their lives, to become socially competent, compassionate and psychologically vigorous adults.
>
> (Kelley, 2004, p. 258)

GOLEMAN AND 'EMOTIONAL INTELLIGENCE'

Goleman began his best-seller (1995) by referring to Aristotle's insight that it is not emotionality in human affairs *per se* that creates problems in everyday living, but how it is expressed. Can we, in effect, bring our intelligence to bear on this key area of our being in the world, asked Goleman, in order to harness its potential to make us happier, more socially attuned beings?

Goleman responded to this rhetorical question by arguing that emotional intelligence exists in much the same way as does cognitive intelligence. Although a relatively neglected area in academic, professional, and popular psychology, he suggested that it has great influence in determining outcomes in life: whom we marry, our success in the world of corporate affairs and business life, and how popular we are with others. In this sense, emotional intelligence is the spark that ignites positive chain reactions within our lives, leading us in ever-increasing circles of influence and steeling us against the effects of adversity. Equally, without it, one might fall prey to negative chain reactions and a sequence of unfortunate experiences. For example, without appropriate emotional scaffolding, a loss of someone special might result in a spiral of denial, drug abuse, further ruptures in key relationships, and eventually a total breakdown of physical and mental health.

But what exactly did Goleman mean by emotional intelligence? To explain the concept, he drew on the work of Salovey et al. (2000) (an important academic pioneer in the field of mental well-being) to elucidate five discernible traits within the person:

- knowing one's thoughts and emotions;
- managing one's thoughts and emotions;
- motivating oneself;
- recognising emotions in others and showing empathy for them;
- forming and sustaining relationships with others.

Let us examine more closely what Goleman has to say about each of these key attributes.

'To know thyself' is a Socratic directive that has permeated Western philosophy and insight-based therapies. Embracing it in full, Goleman noted that:

> [it] might seem at first glance that our feelings are obvious; more thoughtful reflection reminds us of times we have been all too oblivious to what we really felt about something, or awoke to these feelings late in the game. Psychologists use the rather ponderous term metacognition to refer to an awareness of thought process, and metamood to mean awareness of one's own emotions. I prefer self-awareness, in the sense of an ongoing attention to one's internal states. In this self-reflexive awareness the mind observes and investigates experience itself, including the emotions.
>
> (2005, p. 46)

For Goleman, self-investigation must strive to be impartial, neutral, and dispassionate. It must demonstrate a detached curiosity to one's inner thoughts if it is to be classified as intelligent. Such disidentification from the vagaries of mood and emotional engulfment creates a space, it is argued, for intuition and reflective thought to guide action.

Managing one's thoughts and emotions is closely linked to self-awareness. Far too many of us, remarked Goleman, are passion's slaves, having little or no self-mastery over the emotional storms that arrive when fortune is not kind to us. Self-mastery, in this sense, is realised in the ability to regulate negativity, and to control extreme fluctuations in mood that are threatening to the self. One can think here of the effects of unbridled anger and how it damages relationships leaving unhealed grudges that fester with time. The angry outburst might be compared with lifting a hot coal and throwing it at someone: in the process, the assailant burns his own hands while also causing damage to his intended victim. For Goleman, then, foul moods can lead to foul actions, and to be emotionally intelligent means that one is able to master negative mind states such as anxiety, anger, and pessimism. Standing back from the emotionally charged situation, letting go of hostile feelings, and performing relaxation techniques or thought-blocks at appropriate junctures are some ways of enhancing this mastery.

The third component of emotional intelligence (motivating oneself) refers to the capacity to harness drive in the face of difficult challenges in life. What concerned Goleman here is how we marshal enthusiasm, zeal, and confidence to achieve our aspirations. On this particular subject he observed:

> To the degree that our emotions get in the way of or enhance our ability to think and plan, to pursue training for a distant goal, to solve problems and the like, they define the limits of our capacity to use our innate mental abilities, and so determine how we do in life. And to the degree to which we are motivated by feelings of enthusiasm and pleasure in what we do – or even by an optimal degree of anxiety – they propel us to accomplishment. It is in this sense that emotional intelligence is a master aptitude, a capacity that profoundly affects all other abilities, either facilitating or interfering with them.
>
> (2005, p. 80)

Inherent within self-motivation, Goleman wrote, are the mental attributes of hope, positive thinking, and optimism. These attributes, which can be learnt over time, can lead to the belief that some control over circumstances is possible.

Goleman then turned his focus from the world of the self and its inner mastery to the issue of how the self engages with the 'other'. Consequently, his fourth component of emotional intelligence looked at how we recognise and respond to emotions in others. Fundamental here is our capacity to *empathise* with different people in a range of social contexts. The pay-off of this accurate role-taking is much better social adjustment, greater popularity, and heightened extroversion. Not only that, Goleman saw empathic sensitivity as the precursor to moral development. Having deep-rooted feelings for those less fortunate than ourselves inclines one to selfless behaviour.

Lastly, Goleman viewed emotional intelligence as the capacity to handle relationships, by which he seems to have meant being able to respond adaptively and deftly to emotions in others through developing and applying 'people skills' that tune in to the nuances of social encounters. People skills 'are the social competences that make for effectiveness in dealings with others'. Listening, negotiating, exchanging, and managing conflict well are typical of these skills. What Goleman referred to here is social adroitness: we see it enacted when a leader successfully co-ordinates networks of people; alternatively, it is manifest when a mediator resolves conflicts or helps polarised groups to start the process of dialogue. But more than this, it generates insights concerning the inner world of other people, their motives and deepest motivations.

THERAPEUTIC ASPECTS OF 'EMOTIONAL INTELLIGENCE'

Goleman grounded his idea of emotional intelligence within human biology and evolution. As a result, he placed great emphasis on the brain architecture underpinning emotion, its neural physiology and limbic systems. That said, he also focused his analysis on how emotional intelligence is affected within social domains such as the school, work organisations, and, crucially, within families. For instance, the way parents encourage their children to develop emotional intelligence is highlighted as follows:

> there are parents who seize the opportunity of a child's upset to act what amounts to an emotional coach or mentor. They take their child's feelings seriously enough to try to understand exactly what is upsetting them and to help the child find positive ways to soothe their feelings.
>
> (2005, p. 191)

Taking this last point and interrogating it further, in what ways can residential staff, as substitute care-givers, mentor emotional intelligence within the young people under their charge? Unfortunately, Goleman did not offer much help here (preferring instead to direct the application of his thesis to the world of business

[1998]), and so we need to extrapolate from what has been said earlier to outline some responses to the question.

Mentoring might commence with a staff team acknowledging that the emotional domain presents a unique opportunity for growth. That is, in contrast to a perspective which might view young people's emotions as problematic in residential child care (an area to be approached through the lenses of restraint procedures, eviction protocols, and risk management frameworks), staff might instead see the expression of emotional turmoil as an opportunity for developing fragile selves. Clearly, this is no ordinary challenge. Many organisations have developed instrumental cultures that celebrate codes of practice over and beyond the so-called 'touchy-feely' dimensions of intervention. Yet, feelings are facts. Suppressing this reality will only serve to amplify negative abreactions.

If this mindset can be achieved, staff face a further challenge: how to tune in accurately to daily 'emotional events' within the home. For example, a residential team-leader might notice a young person's disappointment when a contact visit is cancelled by his mother; or she may become aware of how an episode of bullying leads the victim to withdraw from others; or perhaps she senses the feelings of shame and confusion that erupt following a pre-emptive sexual experience between two immature children. Sensitivity to such events forms a cradle within which inner resilience and emotional security can develop.

Having the right mindset and sensitivity are the prerequisites for helping interventions. Let us consider one of these at length – educative groupwork. The educative focus can be considered from a number of angles. First, the group might help the members to identify and describe their feelings following emotionally charged events within and outside the home. The identification process is pivotal in generating an inner orientation or a mindfulness of primary emotional states (such as anger, fear, joy, and sadness). Moreover, it kick-starts the process of creating distance, no matter how small, from negative orientations towards self and others. Critically, young people must be taught to undertake this exercise without generating further feelings of self-reproach or blame. If these unintended consequences arise, residential staff (as emotional mentors) must assist young people to become aware of the states of feeling and gently 'let go' of them. Furthermore, there is a danger of slipping into a state whereby other people and situations are labelled rather than the feelings arising from them.

The use of feeling cards (naming a particular emotion or presenting an expressive face through pictorial means) are useful media in this type of work. So, too, is attention to the body and how emotions result in physical manifestations of stress. For instance, young people might be asked to create physical representations of different states of feeling and analyse the experience of doing so. There are also other creative media for identifying emotions in stories, films, and music.

Second, inner attention can be fine-tuned over time so that a distinction can be made between thoughts and feelings. Mental cognition, applying reason to events,

analysing situations, and so on, which constitute the bases of thought, are funda-
mentally different to feeling and emotion which have a more instinctive, visceral
quality involving sensitivities, susceptibilities, and, sometimes, elation. Simple
exercises can help to sharpen critical abilities to differentiate between domains of
consciousness. For example, a range of pre-constructed scenarios can be presented
to the group involving emotional events, say, within the home. Group members
can then be asked to tease out feelings from thoughts. To aid awareness, young
people can be taught to locate feelings within the heart and thoughts within the
head. Cartoon drawings might depict thought bubbles emanating from a character's head compared to heart-shaped drawings from the chest area. Language
can also be reframed. Thus, instead of saying, 'I think I'm scared', the subject
remarks, 'I feel scared'.

Third, the relationship between thought and emotion is another core area for
exploration. Clearly, there is an important interplay between these domains of
experience. By entertaining the thought that 'I over-reacted there', the speaker
subsequently falls prey to feelings of shame and regret. Equally, the corollary
to this is that emotion, in turn, shapes thought. When we experience immediate panic, thoughts of self-preservation may emerge. However, these are subtle
distinctions which might be grounded better in real examples; or through pictorial representations of the thought–emotion interconnection as it plays out in
day-to-day events. Important here is the demonstration of how thought and
emotion both act as critical antecedents to later changes in consciousness. This
interconnection can be explored further by addressing the impact on behaviours.
Sentence completion exercises might help here.

Mood regulation constitutes a fourth, important theme. Being open to one's
feelings, both pleasant and unpleasant, and managing them is what is at stake
here. Group members might be asked to brainstorm a range of effective strategies
for dealing with these types of emotion. Prominent, here, might be physical
exercise or engaging in pleasant distractions. Less effective strategies might also
be listed: for example, watching television or indulging in drugs and alcohol.
Impulse control, observed Goleman, has a number of steps: the first is to stop,
calm down, and think positively (this is a red-light stage); the second is to state
the problem and identify its corresponding emotions, then set a positive goal,
brainstorm potential solutions to it, and think about their consequences (the
yellow-light stage); and lastly, to implement the most beneficial solution (the
green-light stage).

Fifth, taking responsibility for one's feelings should form an essential part of the
educative programme. In this connection, young people should be encouraged to
explore key emotional events in their recent past, attempting to take ownership
of their emotions. So, instead of saying, 'John made me angry', the young person
says out loud, 'I was angry'. This shift in emphasis allows the young person
to realise that they may have greater control of their inner reactions than first
imagined.

The last theme concerns the capacity to read and respond to emotions in others. A range of simple exercises can be employed here: reading others' non-verbal reactions within the group is perhaps the key. Others include role-playing simple situations involving the validation of another's feelings and showing empathy. Refraining from negative judgements or controlling remarks can be modelled by group facilitators to accentuate the learning in these role-plays.

It is important to conclude this section by reiterating Goleman's view that 'temperament is not destiny' and that the activities just described can assist troubled young people to unlearn unhelpful ways of thinking and respond to the inevitable stresses of their lives.

CSIKSZENTMIHALYI AND 'FLOW'

In *Flow: The Psychology of Optimal Experience* (1990), Mihaly Csikszentmihalyi reviewed the importance of 'optimal experience' in people's lives: these are times when subjects report a deep state of concentration and a resulting sense of enjoyment. Literally, they are in a state which Csikszentmihalyi describes as 'flow', a kind of peak experience or entering a zone of complete absorption. Flow, then, is 'the state in which people are so involved in an activity that nothing else seems to matter; the experience itself is so enjoyable that people will do it even at great cost, for the sake of doing it' (1990, p. 4).

Csikszentmihalyi developed his theory of 'flow' through carrying out cross-cultural research on reported experiences of happiness that arise from a wide range of activities such as sports, artistic and leisure pursuits, and cultural practices. Based on this work, he found that 'flow' occurs 'whenever the goal is to improve the quality of life', and so can be applied to practical as well as academic activities. Moreover, it is argued, it can be applied in areas such as psychotherapy, juvenile justice, work with older persons, and occupational therapy with people with disabilities. Importantly, Csikszentmihalyi defended the idea that 'flow' has to be achieved and worked on. It is not a random occurrence, nor a gift of grace, or a genetic endowment, but rather arises in the context of ordered consciousness when realistic, purposeful goals have been set and, crucially, when skills match the opportunities in the social field. On this theme of consciousness, Csikszentmihalyi observed that improvements in mankind are linked to changes in modes of thought. The insuperable role of consciousness is developed further at this point by intimating that it is not the external component of one's life that ultimately brings happiness – for example, fame, status, and holidays abroad – but the quality of inner experience. Csikszentmihalyi drove home the point by highlighting the growing spiritual and psychological malaise within Western, affluent societies. People may be rich in external accoutrements but suffer a poverty of inner experience. Human consciousness, even though it is located within biology and neural architecture, is nevertheless malleable, it is contended. In other words, we possess agency, a capacity to be self-referential and goal-directed. Moreover, we can reframe the meaning of negative events in our lives, and in doing so develop equanimity. What helps us get beyond negative states of mind is our capacity to enter 'flow'.

Csikszentmihalyi enlarged his thesis by reporting on the main elements of 'flow'. First of all, the experience must be challenging and require skill:

> but by far the overwhelming proportion of optimal experiences are reported to occur within sequences of activities that are goal-directed and bounded by rules – activities that require the investment of psychic energy, and that could not be done without the appropriate skills.
>
> (1990, p. 49)

Secondly, 'flow' entails the merging of action and awareness. Put another way, if people can engage in activities that maximise their skills to the point where they attain complete absorption in what they are doing, then a positive state of mind unfolds. Spontaneity results as self-preoccupation wanes. That said, entering 'flow' does not mean that effort is not required, nor does it mean that disciplined mental activity is redundant. Lapses in concentration may well take one out of 'flow'.

A third element defining 'flow' is the presence of clear goals and feedback on activity. Csikszentmihalyi demonstrated the point with the following examples:

> A tennis player always knows what she has to do; return the ball into the opponent's court. And each time she hits the ball she knows whether she has done well or not. The chess player's goals are equally obvious: to mate the opponent's king before his own is mated. With each move, he can calculate whether he has come closer to this objective. The climber inching up a vertical wall of rock has a very simple goal in mind: to complete the climb without falling. Every second, hour after hour, he receives information that he is meeting that basic goal.
>
> (1990, p. 54)

Optimal concentration on the task in hand constitutes the fourth element. It is argued that when we are so fixated on an engrossing activity the unpleasant aspects of life tend to recede. Our inner experience is so ordered by a disciplined attention to the minutia of the temporal focus that neurotic interference is blocked.

Csikszentmihalyi further pointed to the 'paradox of control' as the fifth element. 'Flow' experience lacks the sense of worry about losing control that is typical in many situations of normal life. For example, if a person achieves a sense of 'flow' from playing chess, then if she loses the game, it can be put down to experience; there is no real sense of worry about the outcome. This capacity to 'let go' of outcomes and focus instead on inner control of the process is seen to be liberating.

Lastly, we are assured the experience of 'flow' entails the transformation of time. So, hours pass by in minutes; before one knows it, the activity has been completed. Thus 'flow' has its own time-clock, its own pace. Free from the tyranny of time, there is a more acute awareness of the 'living moment', of staying in the present.

Fears of what the future may bring, or the rehearsal of past emotional trauma, give way to the challenge at hand. Critically, optimal experience becomes an end in itself, what Csikszentmihalyi defined as an 'autotelic' experience.

If these are the characteristics of 'flow', what, then, are the conditions for its manufacture? First and foremost, the challenge presented must neither be too difficult (or it will result in anxiety) or too simple (or it will result in boredom). Getting the optimal level of challenge for an individual's unique range of ability is what is suggested here. Just about enough difficulty sustains attention and leads to a quest to improve abilities.

Another condition is the capacity to concentrate. Thus, someone with a severe attention disorder will find it much more problematic to focus on a chosen task. Or excessive self-consciousness (that is concomitant with shyness) may detract from the quality of lived experience as might the impact of environmental factors – poverty, alienation, unemployment. But Csikszentmihalyi warned against lapsing into fatalism when suggesting that human agents have remarkable powers to remove themselves from the most difficult of circumstances. Quoting Logan (1998), he argued that oppressed members of society can manage to identify activities that allow them to focus on the most minute aspects of their environments (seizing opportunities for actions that match their level of skill), that subsequently enable them to set further self-improvement goals (Csikszentmihalyi, 1990, p. 90).

Csikszentmihalyi's arguments, on face value, appear convincing. Who has not experienced moments of absorption that have allowed for some kind of self-transcendence, limited and rare as they may be? Sports fanatics might allude to key times on the golf course, when the inner game gets into full *flow*. Classical musicians might recount losing self-awareness during the *adagio* sequence of a major symphony. Opportunities to enter 'flow' regularly also seem to pay positive dividends for young people. Thus, both Adlai-Gail (1994) and Abuhamdeh (2000) recount how the regular experience of 'flow' in young people leads to positive cognitive and emotion states. But does the thesis extend to specific populations such as young people in residential care? Responding affirmatively, Nakamura and Csikszentmihalyi (2005) argued that 'flow' researchers have detailed how their findings might be applied successfully by professional helpers to at-risk populations. Specifically, two types of intervention are delineated as worthy of consideration:

- those attempting to shape cultures and environments to allow for the conditions for 'flow' to emerge, while removing barriers to 'flow';
- those where the focus is on assisting individuals to find 'flow' in their day-to-day lives.

Let us consider each of these types of intervention in greater detail, charting how they might apply within residential care.

THERAPEUTIC ASPECTS OF 'FLOW'

We know from research on residential care (Whittaker et al., 1998) that culture within a residential home is a key factor shaping enabling interventions with young people. Culture, in this sense, refers to customs that shape individual identities and provide rules for engagement among actors. Culture allows us to see certain things while limiting other aspects of reality, much like a beam of light illuminates a path but does not foster wider vision of the surrounding terrain.

A residential culture embracing the concept of 'flow' might focus on a wide range of activities providing opportunities for young people to do the following:

- engage in artistic pursuits including painting, sculpting, musical expression, and drama;
- experience their bodies. Yoga and martial arts come to mind here. Experiences of this kind should not be discounted as many young people have become disconnected from physical sensation (Redgrave, 2000).
- experience a range of sporting activities from the very physical (such as rugby) to the cerebral (such as chess);
- access their tradition, culture, and spirituality. These facets of experience stabilise identity and provide roots for coping with the fragmented nature of post-modern society.
- enhance their educational achievement. Much of the literature (Jackson & Sachdev, 2001; Sinclair & Gibbs, 1998) has highlighted the poor educational outcomes for children in care.
- access experiences that are creative and fulfilling. Cooking, for example, involves planning, thinking, sensing, and co-ordinating functions that bring immense pleasure to self and others.

However, such a diversity of opportunity depends on a second characteristic of the residential culture: its capacity to develop and extend social networks surrounding young persons. Introverted cultures – focusing only on the internal management of events – cannot be 'flow'-sensitive. Experience is mediated through language and relationship. It follows, then, that diverse and rich experience hinges on diverse and rich networks. If this idea is accepted, then residential staff must continually screen a young person's social ties, both within what Bronfenbrenner (1979) terms the young person's micro-system (the most intimate domain of informal network, including the immediate and extended family systems) but also his meso-system (the combined effect of various micro-systems). Screening, however, is the preliminary step for one must go on to develop and enhance gaps in social interaction and interpersonal relationship.

That said, opening up 'flow' within a residential home is not just about offering a stimulating range of activities and networks of relationship; it necessitates a limit on activities that lead to boredom, turpitude, and apathy or that provide a 'quick fix' to needs for challenging stimulation. For example, endless hours watching a television set, nights spent wandering the streets, evenings and weekends engaged in the latest computer game, staff too stressed to open up interesting conversation, long, unstructured summer holidays, and drug-induced torpor are all inimical to the experience of 'flow'.

The second type of intervention looks more specifically at each individual's needs. What is being highlighted here is the importance of developing an individually tapered 'flow' plan for each young person within the home. It might commence by screening a young person's past for any episodes where 'flow' was evident or at least the potential for it had been present. Prior to coming into care, a young person might have revelled in fishing expeditions with an uncle; or, he may have volunteered his time at a local animal welfare refuge. Such investigations will need to include not only the young person but also significant others in his network. Identification of activities such as these allows staff to reintroduce them into the present.

However, when screening reveals an absence of 'flow', staff should begin to match a young person's known strengths to possible activities; or, if this is not possible, the investigation should proceed more experimentally (that is, on a 'trial and error' basis). To reiterate, it should be wide-ranging and include artistic, cultural, creative, sporting, and educational outlets. Crucially, though, staff should be aiming for an activity that first of all establishes a basic congruence, or a 'fit' between the activity and the young person's skills and interests. More specifically, it will be vital to adjust two key parameters affecting 'flow': the challenge presented by the activity; and the skill required to perform it. To repeat, 'flow' occurs when perceived opportunities for action are in balance with an actor's perceived level of skills. When the challenge is too high and skills are not commensurate, then anxiety is likely to set in. Conversely, when skills or action capabilities are high and the challenge presented by the activity is too low, then boredom will result. 'Flow', therefore, is a zone where these two parameters are finely tuned.

If such balance can be found, and one should not underestimate the difficulty of achieving it on occasions, then it should be supported through coaching and mentoring the young person in order to maintain 'flow'. Feedback on performance is integral to each of these tasks. That is, praise and encouragement for improvements or for sustained effort in the face of obstacles from those whom the young person trusts ensures that critical reinforcement schedules are in place. Volunteers may be important sources of support in this regard.

'Flow' can also be supported by committing activity-related objectives to paper as part of a 'flow' plan, monitoring outcomes, revising the plan accordingly, and working in partnership with the young person, other agencies, and significant others to maximise potential. If the plan can be followed assiduously, then 'flow' can act as a buffer against adversity, lessening the drift into pathology.

CONCLUSION: POSITIVE PSYCHOLOGY AT WORK

Is it possible for staff in residential care to introduce positive psychology into their daily practice? Surely the very nature of the workplace contra-indicates its application. Emotionally charged incidents abound. Bureaucratic imperatives leave little time for therapeutic work. Lack of 'gate-keeping' in relation to admissions continuously disrupts fragile group cultures. Recruiting and retaining skilled, committed staff are problematic in many areas. At the heart of residential care, some might argue, lies a negative mindset and one far removed from the aspirations of positive psychology.

Such observations are hard to challenge. Yet, what if the tenets of positive psychology, as described earlier, were applied to the organisational management of residential care? What if managerial practices were emotionally intelligent? What if senior managers were committed to providing opportunities for staff to experience 'flow' as part of their daily work? To put the argument more bluntly, managers cannot expect their staff to act positively to the young people under their charge if they manage through a negative psychology, one that is critical, risk-aversive, bureaucratically informed, and obsessed with complaints. Good outcomes for young people are inextricably linked to good outcomes for staff. To sever this connection will only perpetuate what, for many, is a system that is failing many young people and their professional carers.

A healthy work environment that draws on positive psychology exhibits a number of essential characteristics, according to Turner et al. (2005). Firstly, its work practices are characterised by high levels of worker autonomy: having the right kind of control over one's job is essential to job satisfaction. Secondly, active and supportive teamwork must be in place: at a basic level, teams provide identity, companionship, and support. Thirdly, organisations require transformational leaders who exert the right kind of influence, provide inspirational motivation, intellectual stimulation, and individualised consideration to their staff: these attributes, research tells us, are correlated with enhanced well-being in staff.

Such work-based practices must also embrace a range of psychological processes and mechanisms. Trust is fundamental. Commitment to staff well-being is another. A sense of 'felt responsibility' and 'felt belongingness', perceived control of one's work, and flexible role orientation set the foundation for what may be described as organisational citizenship: a sense of having acknowledged rights in the workplace.

Moreover, organisations should strive to be emotionally intelligent. Managers must be in command of their own emotions but also show empathic sensitivity to the feelings of those at the 'front line' of service delivery. It must be remembered that a little empathy goes a long way. Furthermore, staff need to demonstrate emotional intelligence towards each other to achieve desired outcomes. In this regard, Jordan and Troth (2004) showed how emotional intelligence was linked to effective team problem-solving and team performance.

Ultimately, enhanced performance and motivation revolve around staff's access to 'flow' experience within their daily work regimes. Consider the following scenario: a piece of counselling has been undertaken in a skilled manner with a young person attempting a challenging activity. It has so engaged the worker that he enters a timeless zone – a place of ineluctable self-transcendence and fulfilment. The experience of 'flow' is healing and confirming, dispelling earlier doubts about entering the social work profession. But imagine how professional intervention might reach its apogee if both the worker and young person achieve 'flow' together: the worker in her coaching role, the young person in his designated activity. Imagine the synergistic effect of this intermeshed 'flow' for the actors concerned. Positive psychology is the medium through which such outcomes can be achieved.

REFERENCES

Abuhamdeh, S. (2000). The autotelic personality: An exploratory investigation. Unpublished manuscript, University of Chicago.

Adlai-Gail, W. (1994). Exploring the autotelic personality. Unpublished doctoral dissertation, University of Chicago.

Bettleheim, B. (1950). *Love Is not Enough: The Treatment of Emotionally Disturbed Children.* London: Free Press.

Blower, A., Addo, A., Hodgson, J., Lamington, L., & Towlson, K. (2004). Mental health of looked after children: A needs assessment. *Clinical Child Psychology and Psychiatry,* **9**, 117–129.

Bronfenbrenner, U. (1979). *The Ecology of Human Development.* Cambridge, MA: Harvard University Press.

Buchanan, A. (2002). Family support. In D. McNeish, T. Newman, & H. Roberts (eds), *What Works for Children? Effective Services for Children and Families.* Buckingham: Open University Press.

Buchanan, A., & Hudson, B. (2000). *Promoting Children's Emotional Well-Being.* Oxford: Oxford University Press.

Buss, D. (2000). The evolution of happiness. *American Psychologist,* **55**, 15–23.

Chodron, P. (2001). *The Places that Scare You.* London: HarperCollins.

Csikszentmihalyi, M. (1990). *Flow: The Psychology of Optimal Experience.* New York: Harper & Rowe.

Diener, E. (2000). Subjective well-being: The science of happiness and a proposal for a National Index. *American Psychologist,* **55**, 34–43.

Docker-Drysdale, B. (1968). *Papers on Residential Work: Therapy in Child-Care.* London: Longman.

Frankyl, V. (1984). *Man's Search for Meaning.* New York: Washington Square Press.

Frost, N., Mills, S., & Stein, M. (1999). *Understanding Residential Child Care.* Aldershot: Ashgate.

Gilligan, R. (1997). Beyond permanence? The importance of resilience in child placement practice and planning. *Adoption and Fostering,* **21**, 12–20.

Goleman, D. (1995). *Emotional Intelligence: Why it Can Matter More than IQ.* London: Bloomsbury.

Goleman, D. (1998). *Working with Emotional Intelligence.* London: Bloomsbury.

Hoghugi, M. (1988). *Treating Problem Children.* London: Sage.

Howe, D. (1995). *Attachment Theory for Social Work Practice.* London: Macmillan.

Jackson, S., & Sachdev, D. (2001). *Better Education, Better Futures: Research, Practice and the Views of Young People in Public Care.* London: Barnardo's.

Jordan, P., & Troth, A. (2004). Managing emotions during team problem solving: Emotional intelligence and conflict resolution. *Human Performance*, **17**, 195–218.

Kelley, T. (2004). Positive psychology and adolescent mental health: False promise or true breakthrough? *Adolescence*, **39**, 257–278.

Logan, R. (1998). Flow in solitary ordeals. In M. Csikszentmihalyi & I. Csikszentmihalyi (eds), *Optimal Experience: Psychological Studies in Flow Consciousness*. New York: Cambridge University Press.

Lyman, R., Prentice-Dunn, S., & Gabel, S. (eds) (1989). *Residential Treatment of Children and Adolescents*. London: Plenum Press.

Maslow, A. (1968). *Towards a Psychology of Being*. New York: Van Nostrand.

Massimini, F., & Delle Fave, A. (2000). Individual development in a bio-cultural perspective. *American Psychologist*, **55**, 24–32.

McCann, J., James, A., Wilson, S., & Dunn, G. (1996). Prevalence of psychiatric disorders in young people in the care system. *British Medical Journal*, **313**, 1529–1530.

Mount, J., Lister, A., & Bennun, I. (2004). Identifying the mental health needs of looked after young people. *Clinical Child Psychology and Psychiatry*, **9**, 363–382.

Nakamura, J., & Csikszentmihalyi, M. (2005). The concept of flow. In C.R. Snyder & S.L. Lopez (eds), *Handbook of Positive Psychology*. Oxford: Oxford University Press.

Peterson, C. (2000). The future of optimism. *American Psychologist*, **55**, 44–55.

Redgrave, K. (2000). *Care-Therapy for Children: Direct Work in Counselling and Psychotherapy*. London: Continuum.

Rose, M. (1990). *Healing Hurt Minds*. London: Routledge.

Rutter, M. (1999). Resilience concepts and findings: Implications for family therapy. *Journal of Family Therapy*, **21**, 119–144.

Saleeby, D. (ed.) (1997). *The Strengths Perspective in Social Work*. New York: Longman.

Salovey, P., Rothman, A., Detweiler, J., & Steward, W. (2000). Emotional states and physical health. *American Psychologist*, **55**, 110–121.

Seligman, M. (2005). Positive psychology, positive prevention, and positive therapy. In C.R. Snyder & S.J. Lopez (eds), *Handbook of Positive Psychology*. Oxford: Oxford University Press.

Seligman, M., & Csikszentmihalyi, M. (2000). Positive psychology: An introduction. *American Psychologist*, **55**, 5–14.

Sinclair, I., & Gibbs, I. (1998). *Children's Homes: A Study in Diversity*. Chichester: John Wiley & Sons, Ltd.

Snyder, C.R., & Lopez, S.J. (2005). *Handbook of Positive Psychology*. Oxford: Oxford University Press.

Turner, N., Barling, J., & Zacharatos, A. (2005). Positive psychology at work. In C.R. Snyder & S.J. Lopez (eds), *Handbook of Positive Psychology*. Oxford: Oxford University Press.

Ward, A. (1993). *Working in Group Care: Social Work in Residential and Day Care Settings*. Birmingham: Venture Press.

Whitaker, J. (1979). *Caring for Troubled Children: Residential Treatment in the Community*. London: Jossey-Bass.

Whittaker, D., Archer, L., & Hicks, P. (1998). *Working in Children's Homes: Challenges and Complexities*. Chichester: John Wiley & Sons, Ltd.

Williams, J., Jackson, S., Maddocks, A., Cheung, W., Love, A., & Hutchings, H. (2001). Case-control study of the health of those looked after by Local Authorities. *Archives of Disabled Child*, **85**, 280–285.

Winner, E. (2000). The origins and ends of giftedness. *American Psychologist*, **55**, 64–75.

Part IV

Court and Family Support Pathways to Substitute Care

CHAPTER 12

PATHWAYS TO PERMANENCE: ACCOMMODATION, COMPULSION, AND PERMANENCE UNDER THE CHILDREN (NI) ORDER (1995)

Theresa Donaldson

INTRODUCTION

Permanence has been described as the long-term or permanent arrangements which best meet the needs of a looked-after child who is away from home. It has been argued that planning for permanence is making the best choice for an individual child, looking at all the options and considering all the circumstances, including a full assessment of the child's needs (Scottish Executive, 2005). Permanence is best met for the child within its own family and this ideal is reflected in the Children Act (1989) requirement that local authorities make all reasonable efforts to rehabilitate looked-after children with their families whenever possible, unless it is clear that the child can no longer live with his/her family and the authority has evidence that further attempts at rehabilitation are unlikely to succeed. Looked-after children (98) 20 (Department of Health Circular) stressed the need to achieve the right balance between efforts to rehabilitate the child with his/her family and the importance of 'child time' in achieving permanence for the child (Harnott & Humphreys, 2004). It has been emphasised that delay in planning should be minimised as early placement is more associated with success than the placement of older children (Kelly & McSherry, 2002).

In addition to emphasising that children are best looked after within their families and bringing the 'no delay' principle into statute, the Children Act (1989) introduced a number of measures to change the approach of social services to the provision of care. These measures, intended to ensure avoidance of compulsory proceedings wherever possible, included the introduction of accommodation as a 'positive support' to children and families in need. The Act introduced the 'threshold criteria': legal tests to be evidenced before compulsory admission to care was given the approval of the court. The combination of these measures led commentators to conclude that application to court, rather than the provision of care, had become the 'last resort' (Hunt et al., 1999).

The changes to the gateways to care may have been influenced by studies conducted in the 1970s and 1980s (DHSS, 1985). These studies reported fewer negative consequences for the child and the family if admission to care took place through a voluntary agreement, as opposed to compulsory intervention associated with parental hostility and a long period of separation between the child and the family (Millham et al., 1986; Packman et al., 1986). The influence of the Inquiries of the 1980s, particularly Beckford and Cleveland on the emerging legislation, has also been cited (Parton, 1991). However, the European Convention on Human Rights and Fundamental Freedoms (ECHR), although not incorporated into domestic legislation until October 2000, has latterly been noted by a number of authors as having an important effect on the drafting of the Act (Cretney et al., 2002; Fortin, 1999; O'Halloran, 1999; White et al., 2002). The balances incorporated in the Act have been argued to reflect particularly Article 8 of the ECHR (Right to Family Life), but also concern the ability of parents to challenge decisions that affected them reflecting Article 6 (Right to a Fair Trial).

Since the incorporation of the ECHR in October 2000, the court's concern about social services' treatment of parents has appeared in a number of judgments, drawing attention to the imbalance that can occur between action taken to 'safeguard' the child and the human rights of parents under the Convention. These include the judgment of Munby, J., in Re C (Care Proceedings: Disclosure of Local Authority's Decision-making Process) [2002] EWHC 1379 (Fam). Of particular concern in this case were several crucial decision-making 'professional meetings' at which the mother was not in attendance and not represented, nor was there an agenda of what *was to be* discussed or minutes of what *was* discussed. It was held that rights under Article 6 (Right to a Fair Trial) were 'absolute' and were not confined to the 'purely judicial' process: unfair treatment at any part of the litigation process could involve a breach not only of Article 8 (Right to Family Life) but also of Article 6.

The judicial concern about parental involvement in decision-making was reiterated in Re J (Care Order: Adoption Agencies: Adjournment: Adoption Agencies Regulations) (NI) 1989) [2002] NI Fam 26, Gillen, J., stated: 'The Trust should review all areas of decision-making . . . including decisions about initiating care, adoption, freeing procedures . . . which are made without parental involvement.'

In a landmark Court of Appeal case, AR *v* Homefirst Community Trust [2005] NICA 8, before Kerr, L.C.J., Nicholson, L.J., and Sheil, L.J., there was criticism of social services' removal of a child (J) from the mother at birth and subsequent permanent care arrangement. It was 'profoundly disturbing' to the Court of Appeal that the mother's Article 8 rights were not considered at any stage.

In the context of permanence planning, a second judgment by Gillen, J., is particularly relevant and of concern. In the matter of W and M (Breach of Article
8 of the European Convention on Human Rights: Freeing for Adoption Order
[2005] NI Fam 2), the growing frustration of the court was evident in relation to
the treatment of parents by social services. The Trust had not provided written
notification to the parents as required under the Regulations of the decision that
a Freeing Order would be pursued. In refusing to grant the Freeing Order, the
court cited 'material breach of the Adoption Regulations' by the Trust. The court
was satisfied that the Trust had breached the Article 8 rights of the parents and
displayed an 'all too casual approach' to the Regulations and the parents' Article 8
rights. The judgment referred to previous requirements (Re J (Care Order: Adoption Agencies: Adjournment: Adoption Agencies Regulations) (NI) 1989 [2002]
NI Fam 26) for a review of decision-making in adoption with Convention rights
in mind.

The tortuous and lengthy route from admission to care to the making of a Freeing
Order was reported by Kelly and McSherry (2002). The failure to obtain an Order
because of administrative shortcomings rather than that the court deemed an
application for a Freeing Order was not justified, constituted a major criticism
of social work practice but was also a blow to the children and their prospects of
finding a permanent family placement.

The study that will be discussed in this chapter was conducted over an 18-month
period during which the ECHR was implemented in October 2000. The data from
the study indicated that the Article 6 and Article 8 rights of parents were very
tenuous outside the legal process. An exploration of why this should be the case,
despite the increased regulation of social services' contact with families under
the Children Order, will be undertaken through an analysis of social work and
legal processes around cases in the study.

THE STUDY

'The Changing Face of Care under the Children (NI) Order (1995)' was a qualitative
examination of a cohort of 107 children in 58 cases (36 children in 20 cases
subject to Care Order application and 71 children in 38 cases accommodated
at the beginning of the study) that became 'looked after' under the Children
Order between January 2000 and June 2000. The social services' case files were
examined at the time the children were placed 'in care' to record information
on the circumstances of the children coming into care and 18 months later,
between June 2002 and December 2002, to record the care outcome. Case-related
interviews were also carried out with parents and social workers and non-case-
related interviews were conducted with other key informants such as members
of the magistracy and judiciary. In addition, a series of focus groups was held
with solicitors, barristers, guardians ad litem, assistant principal social workers,
and health visitors where the discussion focused on issues emerging from the

study. The children in the cohort were all aged less than 11 years of age at the time the study was initiated.

The findings of the study on the circumstances of the cohort were as follows.

The Circumstances of the Cohort

Multiple Problems Experienced

Data from the study indicated that the provision of accommodation or application for a Care Order was rarely undertaken by social services without a history of service provision. Both Care Order application cases and those accommodated had been known to social services between 1–10 years mean = 3 years) before the child became looked after. It was apparent from the information recorded in social services' case files that the families' contact with social services was inevitably due to multiple problems. These included alcohol abuse (noted as an issue for fathers in 40% [n = 8] of Care Order cases and 37% [n = 14] of those accommodated and for mothers in 30% [n = 6] of Care Order cases and 66% [n = 25] accommodated). The other main causes of concern to social services included mental-health problems (mothers in Care Order cases 45% [n = 9], accommodated 33% [n = 13]; fathers in Care Order cases 20% [n = 4], accommodated 13% [n = 5]). Domestic violence was also an issue in 45% (n = 9) of Care Order cases and 29% (n = 11) of those accommodated.

Despite the families being well known to social services, only vague details about housing and income were recorded in case files. For 90% (n = 53) of children in the cohort, there was no recorded assessment of parent's employment, housing status, or income. Details that did exist were, in the main, embedded in other narrative information, 70% (n = 43) were in receipt of financial assistance from social services and 30% (n = 20) received assistance with housing matters suggesting that problems in housing and finance were areas of added stress for the cohort.

The Child Protection Register

The majority of children's names in the total cohort were registered on the Child Protection Register. The names of the children in the cohort provided with accommodation as a time-limited support tended not to be recorded on the Child Protection Register. Paradoxically, there were cases where the child's name was not recorded on the Child Protection Register, but the harm to the child was severe enough to clearly require application to court.

Notwithstanding this, a high percentage of the cohort was registered:

- 66% (n = 71) of the children in the cohort had their names registered on the Child Protection Register;
- the largest category was that of neglect, 62% (n = 44) of those registered were in this category (39% accommodated, 44% Care Order);

- 21% (n = 15) were in the category of emotional abuse (17% accommodated, 8% Care Order);
- 17% (n = 12) were in the category of physical abuse (14% accommodated, 5.5% Care Order). (Two children in the cohort were registered under both physical abuse and emotional abuse categories.)

The Progression of Children from Accommodation to Becoming Subject to Care Order Application

Of the cohort of 71 children accommodated at the beginning of this study, 33% (n = 24) became subject to Care Order proceedings within the 18-month follow-up period. Of these:

- 15% (n = 11) were accommodated for less than 16 weeks before a Care Order application was made;
- 5% (n = 4) were accommodated less than 32 weeks;
- 11% (n = 7) were accommodated less than 48 weeks;
- 2% (n = 2) were accommodated more than 48 weeks before a Care Order application was made.

The care outcome data also indicated 25% (n = 25) were no longer in care 18 months after the study began and 20% (n = 22) were still accommodated at the end of the study period.

The findings of the study on the circumstances of the cohort indicated a substantial commonality between children provided with accommodation and those subject to a Care Order application in terms of the problems experienced, child protection registration, and the provision of accommodation that was followed by a Care Order application. It has been suggested by other researchers that the provision of accommodation was a significant point of entry to the legal process (Hunt et al., 1999). The issues for the human rights of parents and delay in planning for the child arising from these findings will be discussed in more detail and illustrated through case studies based on the experiences of families in the cohort.

CARE ORDER APPLICATION OR ACCOMMODATION?

The legal process was said to be the 'last resort' by social workers interviewed: however, there was confusion about the use of accommodation in 'safeguarding' cases. What emerged from interviews with social workers was not a clear picture of practice, but of conflicting views, with some viewing the provision of accommodation (whatever the evidence of harm to the child) in the first instance as 'agency policy'. The 'no-order' principle was also cited as a reason for providing accommodation even though the child was believed to have suffered significant harm. Others were of the opinion that a Care Order should be applied for if there were clear evidence to meet the 'threshold criteria' of significant harm.

In the examination of case files for the cohort, although there was a wealth of information, there were few instances of a clear record of the decision that accommodation should be provided or an application for a Care Order made. The findings that emerged from the data about the provision of accommodation in 'safeguarding' cases suggested that parents were in the main not involved in decision-making, both at the time the child was becoming 'looked after' and in cases where the parent wished to remove the child from accommodation. The decision-making at these important junctures appeared to occur during 'in-house' meetings that did not involve the parents.

The use of 'planning' meetings outside the official 'Child Protection Case Conference' or 'Looking After Children' meetings were a feature of social services' practice in the management of Cathy's case.

Cathy's Case

Cathy and her four children were accommodated on an emergency basis in a Women's Aid Hostel. The children's names were on the Child Protection Register under the category of emotional abuse. The family problems recorded in social services' case files included – Cathy's mental-health problems, domestic violence, her partner's alcohol abuse, and Cathy self-harming. There had been continuous social services involvement with the family for three years before the children were accommodated, although there had been sporadic contact with the family over a much longer period. In the hostel, the behaviour of the children began to cause concern and Cathy found it difficult to cope with them. She requested the children be accommodated. It stated in the file that before the children would be returned, Cathy would have to bring about changes, gain her own housing, and apply for resources to assist her coping ability. A Care Order application was made when Cathy requested the children's return after four months in accommodation.

A number of factors appeared to complicate decision-making for social services. These included the domestic violence strongly suspected by social services because of physical injuries to Cathy but which she denied. The home conditions were reported to be very good, and children were well presented. This also seemed to make decisions about the action to be taken by social services more difficult. The case records noted Cathy's reluctance to engage with social services and difficulty in obtaining contact with the family. When Cathy left her partner, she admitted that the level of violence was as suspected by social services. Cathy was angry when she read court reports and could see that evidence of violence was noted by social services over a long period, but that no action had been taken by them. The case records and interviews with staff confirmed that key decisions about application to court were taken at 'professional' meetings not attended by Cathy and presented for ratification at a subsequent Child Protection Case

Conference. The actions taken by social services were puzzling to Cathy as she struggled to extract herself from a violent relationship that undoubtedly had an adverse impact on the children:

> *I put my children into Voluntary Care – I told them it was only for 6 months. I was coming out of a violent relationship – some of the things they had on record. I asked them, did they have all these things on records – why did they not do something sooner? The first thing I went to the Family Centre to read their report – they told me they are applying for a Custody Order – the children are to stay in care for 2–4 years – papers have been sent to London for a woman to make the decision.*

The behaviour of the children was a significant concern in the Care Order proceedings and settling them in the foster placements, where they had been accommodated for four months prior to the application, became an important priority in the care plan. The proceedings lasted 28 weeks and the final care plan stated that the children would remain in long-term foster care. It was also noted that preparation for long-term care could not begin until the court ratified the plan.

The actions taken by social services could be argued to be indicative of the two types of event that Dingwall et al. (1983/1995) identified as consistently precipitating a more investigative treatment of a family. These were (a) withdrawal of compliance and (b) failure of agency containment.

Dingwall et al. argued that 'parental incorrigibility' or 'withdrawal of compliance' to the actions proposed by social services was important for two reasons. Firstly, the authors argued that social services operated within a 'liberal compromise' when dealing with child abuse and neglect. The bulk of the task undertaken by social services was said to be 'uninvited surveillance'. The liberal compromise was that the family would be open for inspection provided State agents viewed what they found positively, unless there was overwhelming evidence of wrongdoing. The importance of parental opposition was argued to be twofold. It cast doubt on the social services' view of the parents' moral character, by refusing to 'go along' with social services they were indicating there was something to hide. Secondly, parents' opposition provided agencies with an excuse for moving against the 'prevailing liberal value' of minimal intervention and to defend compulsory action to their critics by saying they had no choice.

The second of Dingwall and colleagues' events (that consistently precipitated more intrusive intervention) was 'failure of containment' which referred to the extent to which the family problems spread beyond a small circle of front-line workers. The authors argued that agencies whose staff was more insulated from the 'rule of optimism' were more sceptical of 'parents' protestations'.

The circumstances surrounding the applications for Care Orders for Cathy's children suggested the withdrawal of consent to accommodation was the final push needed towards the taking of compulsory measures after a long period of social services contact. Cathy's admission that the level of violence in the home was as social services staff suspected was not in her favour and raised doubts about the priority she attached to the children's needs. The views expressed by staff in the Women's Aid Hostel about the behaviour of the children further inflamed social services' concern about the children and whether they should remain in their mother's care. Cathy's request for accommodation in many ways eased the path to compulsory intervention. Once the children were settled in foster placements and having had confirmation of the level of violence in the family home, it was more difficult for Cathy to convince social services that return to her care was better for the children. When interviewed, Cathy spoke of her distrust of social services and why she had not accepted help in the past:

> Years ago, they offered me help – my mental health was deteriorating. I would not take help off them because I did not trust them. Social workers take your kids off you, they tell you one thing, then they do another. They asked me did I want respite on the children going to nursery – they also arranged for me and my husband to go to the Family Centre – if I had gone with him, I would have got a duffing when I went home

For Cathy and her children, the 'breathing space' provided by accommodation was also an opportunity for social services to strengthen the case that was subsequently presented in court. Cathy was angry that her co-operation with social services contributed to the case against her, and therefore condemned this practice. It appeared from Cathy's case and others that although social workers described the relationship with the parent as a 'partnership', the parents' vulnerability and lack of involvement in decision-making suggested the description belied the reality of the situation for the parent. The actions taken by social workers can be understood when analysed within the framework suggested by Dingwall et al. (1983, 1995), however, they are more difficult to reconcile when considered within the terms of the ECHR and Cathy's Article 8 rights.

PARENTS' 'CO-OPERATION'

In an ideal world, when deciding how to proceed in cases where there were child protection issues, social workers require a clear assessment of the difficulties experienced by parents as well as having access to resources to address areas of concern. These requirements appeared to be in short supply. It appeared from the findings of the study that there were cases where parents were reluctant to accept social services' offers of support although they were obviously 'in need', as was the case for Cathy. Paradoxically, there were situations where parents appeared to be co-operating with social services but this was found later to be a façade that caused drift and delay in planning for the child. This situation appeared to occur most often in cases where alcohol misuse was a major concern.

Angela and Peter's Case

Angela and Peter were known to be alcoholics; both had children from previous relationships they no longer cared for because of their alcohol abuse. They became a couple while having treatment for alcoholism. When Angela gave birth to James, hospital staff reported that they could smell alcohol from her. Following this report, social services very closely monitored the couple's relationship. The case records indicated that between drinking bouts, standards of care for James and hygiene standards in the home were good. Angela and Peter had another two children, Sandra and John. The case records noted that parents were open with social services about their drinking patterns, and this honesty appeared to be rewarded with a level of tolerance, bordering on support for their drinking through the provision of accommodation for the children. During one of Angela's drinking bouts, social services became aware that she had started to drink and efforts to track down Peter and the children to ensure the children were adequately cared for were recorded. The couple were found to both be drinking and the children were accommodated. The couple contacted social services within a number of days, assurances were given that they were both sober, and the children were returned. The case records noted five respite placements in ten months. At the time the case was followed up 18 months later, Care Order applications were lodged after yet another drinking binge. It was noted that the court favoured rehabilitation for the family because of the 'strong bond' between the parents and the children. Several expert reports were requested during proceedings, including a family centre report and a psychiatric report for Angela and Peter. Other reports noted that all three children were developmentally delayed, two were underweight, failure to thrive was queried, yet no organic cause was detected. The care proceedings lasted 44 weeks, and Care Orders were granted: however, the care plan of rehabilitation could not be implemented as the parents' relationship deteriorated and again they both began to drink. Social services pursued permanent care arrangements for the children through freeing and adoption, and within six months of the Care Orders being granted positive moves towards permanent care arrangements for the children were made.

As illustrated by Angela and Peter's case, knowing where to draw the line in a situation where care appeared at times to be 'good enough', yet support of the family involved children 'yo-yoing' in and out of care, was very difficult.

Social services are 'bureau-professional' organisations according to Dingwall et al. (1983, 1995). This means that actions taken by social workers can be viewed as reflecting their role as a representative of an agency, operating within the agency's rules but also as professionals with access to specialised knowledge. Therefore actions cannot be either totally prescribed or totally subject to individual discretion. Dingwall et al. noted that professional engagement in child protection terms was not actually with the ostensible client, i.e. the child, and the interests of children could easily become obscured by the interests of adults to such a degree as to minimise the possibilities of identifying mistreatment. The circumstances for Angela and Peter's young children (James, Sandra, and John) provided an example of just such a scenario where the harm to the children appeared to be given less attention than working in partnership with Angela and Peter. However, the reverse of this argument could also apply, given the difficulty of regulating decision-making in a bureau-professional organisation. In Cathy's case, the overriding concern of those managing the case appeared to be child protection, arguably providing insufficient attention to Cathy's Article 8 rights and giving rise to the judicial concern expressed in the judgments quoted earlier.

The cases cited provide evidence of the daunting task facing social workers in maintaining a balance between ensuring sufficient efforts were made to support the family unit as required by the Children Order and taking action to secure an alternative permanent arrangement for the child if remaining at home were judged to be unacceptable. Such a balance would be difficult even under ideal circumstances. However, it was apparent that resource constraints, particularly in terms of retaining sufficiently qualified and skilled staff to undertake the work, were a major issue. This is well illustrated by the following statement by a social worker:

> The Children Order has highlighted gaps but also raised expectations, and resources are just not there to meet them. Social workers are not stupid – we can see what is needed. I have sat at the back of the court and broken into a cold sweat when I heard the Magistrate order a report or a family aid. The Magistrate sat in court all afternoon in one case until she got the Consultant Adolescent Psychiatrist on the phone to ask for a report and if we ask, we are just told, the court has not requested. The social worker is last in line with other professionals.

As noted, the absence of a clear record of decision-making at important junctures and the in-house meetings held without the parents meant that the reasons court proceedings were initiated were not always clear. It appeared that the social services' perception of parental co-operation was a pivotal factor. However, as also noted, it was not always possible to know how honest the perceived engagement was between the parents and social services. The provision of accommodation as a 'safeguard' was not always clear to the parents until they asked for the child to be returned.

Hostility that could develop when what was happening 'registered' with the parents was also evidenced. This hostility was perceived as a lack of 'co-operation' and could then lead to the initiation of court proceedings, as highlighted in Cathy's case. The parents (of children accommodated and then subject to Care Order proceedings) interviewed accused social workers of wanting to remove the children all along, while social services found it difficult, if not impossible, to overcome parental resistance outside the legal process.

It was noted the children in the cohort experienced periods of accommodation – some for up to 48 weeks prior to the initiation of the legal process. The delay in making permanent care arrangements for such children was therefore significant. There then followed (in some instances) a lengthy legal process lasting between 16 and 56 weeks (mean = 42 weeks), 45% (n = 15) Care Order cases involved 8 court hearings, 25% (n = 8) 8–12 court hearings, and 30% (n = 10) more than 12 court hearings. The length of proceedings in most cases appeared to be due to the number of assessments conducted during the legal process and time taken to agree a care plan that met the approval of the court. There was an 85% increase in the number of assessments concerning parenting capacity undertaken after Care Order proceedings were initiated. A psychologist often conducted the parenting capacity assessments, and there were frequent delays in proceedings. The plan for the child (as recorded in the Looking After Children documentation) at the initiation of proceedings changed from 'time limited assessment (58%) and eventual return to the birth family' (30%) to 'live with relatives (30%) and long-term placement with foster carers with no return anticipated' (64%).

Andrew's Case

Andrew was 6 years old when the Care Order application by social services was made. The application was made after the court expressed concern about his welfare in a contact dispute between his parents, Joan and David, and an investigation under Article 56 of the Children Order was requested by the court. Joan's family had been known to social services, and she spent periods of time in care herself as a child. As the Article 56 investigation was progressing, Andrew was presented at hospital with bruises that were suspected to be non-accidental. A Care Order was applied for, care proceedings lasting 56 weeks were initiated, and Andrew was placed in foster care. The cause of the injuries was unknown but both parents denied responsibility.

In Andrew's case the judge was not able to make a 'finding of fact' in terms of who was responsible for his injuries; however, in order to facilitate the progress of proceedings, both parents made concessions accepting responsibility for the injuries. The 'trade-off' to the parents was that the social services agreed to undertake a further assessment and increased contact of once per week to each parent was granted. The case records noted very serious concern regarding Andrew's behaviour. This was an important issue for the court during the legal process, and an 'attachment-related' disorder was queried in a report submitted to the court from a child psychiatrist.

This pattern of negotiation between legal representatives and concession-making by parents was a feature of the legal process that can cause delay in permanence planning for the looked-after child long after the legal process ended. Such was

the case for Andrew. It was recorded in case files that he experienced six placement moves after the proceedings ended. The increased contact and the further
assessment were commented upon at a subsequent looked-after child meeting
where the Chair suggested a return to court as a move to a long-term foster
placement, viewed as vital, was unlikely with the level of contact that had been
agreed during the proceedings:

> *Judge likes the parties to agree, and that can result in parents thinking that things are*
> *going to happen and they are clearly not – raising expectations of parents and then they*
> *feel down. Sometimes I think it would be better if you went into court and fought it*
> *out – contact becomes the big issue and it should not be a big issue – the child gets*
> *lost.*
>
> *(Social worker)*

The interview with social workers and legal representatives suggested a notable
difference in their perception of and approach to the legal process. In addition
to the resource demands of the court, social workers had to defend the actions
they had taken in bringing the case into the legal process in what were, at
times, very hostile proceedings. Social workers described the damaging effects of
legal proceedings and the efforts required afterwards repairing and rebuilding
relationships. They were critical of the process that demanded further assessments
and more concessions for parents in order to gain agreement to Orders rather than
make a decision on the basis of the children's needs. Legal representatives did
have some sympathy for the ordeal that social workers could be exposed to within
the court; however, they were critical of the social workers' lack of preparedness
for court, and the need in some situations to initiate legal proceedings in order to
gain access to resources. It was clear that although social workers undertook their
own assessment of the situation, this was rarely systematic enough nor included
the specialised inputs of psychology or psychiatry that were inevitably required
in order to reach the standard of proof required by court.

King and Piper (1990) have analysed the legal process and described a clash of
cultures when welfare and law come together. The authors argued that although
significant changes were made to the legal process by the Children Act, including
the strengthening of the role of the guardian ad litem, these changes made very
little difference to the manner in which courts, lawyers, and court welfare professionals conduct their business.

King and Piper's argument was that the law has to convert or 'enslave' the
discourse of other professions into the legal discourse (ultimately a simplification)
in order to deal with them. The core of King and Piper's argument was that the
uncertainty and imprecision of statements produced by child welfare workers
both in relation to what they knew about children and what could happen in
the future made both the statements and the statement-makers even more highly
vulnerable to 'enslavement' within the legal arena. The legal process viewed
the reports provided by the so-called 'psy' professions more favourably as they
assisted the law's search for right and wrong. Lawyers may complain that they
are not given clear answers to questions about the likely outcome for the child: in

such situations the law may demand certainties where they do not exist. It has been argued that clashes between social work professionals and lawyers have more to do with differences in ideological value rather than disputes over the likely outcome (Iwaniec et al., 2004; King, 1997). King and Piper argued that central to the successful conduct of the legal process was the law's ability to conceptualise the world into rights and duties on which it could adjudicate and which swings into action when an individual, personal or corporate, wishes to activate a right or impose a duty.

In following cases through the process managed by social services to the legal process managed by the court, the difference in approach to parents' rights could not be more stark. While there were stresses for parents in attending court and making sense of the process, they were provided with representation and therefore were placed on a more equal footing with social services than had previously been the case for others. On the other hand, the process of concession-making that was a feature of 'court-door' agreements meant that what was best for the child in the circumstances was, at times, pitched against what a good legal representative could extract from negotiations for the parent. The implications of these observations for permanence planning will now be discussed.

IMPLICATIONS FOR PERMANENCE PLANNING

A number of important issues arise from the data in the study 'The Changing Face of Care under the Children (NI) Order (1995)' that have implications for permanence planning for looked-after children. The data suggested that there was little to separate the circumstances of a substantial number of children who became 'looked after' (through the provision of accommodation) from those subject to Care Order applications. Indeed, there was a notable overlap in that 25% of the total sample of children (n = 24) were accommodated prior to becoming subject to Care Order applications.

The re-branding of accommodation as a positive support to parents and children 'in need' may well have reduced the incidence of emergency admission to care. However, there were parents in the study who agreed to accommodation but found out later that return of the child would be the trigger for care proceedings. The vulnerability of parents was apparent in such situations. There has been a debate about the use of coercion in the provision of accommodation (Hunt et al., 1999; Packman & Hall, 1999) and a suggestion that a review of policy should be undertaken (DoH, 2001). The hostility between parents and social services was notable when it became apparent that the service provided as a support was, in fact, a precursor to compulsory intervention. This hostility continued into the legal process, making negotiations between parties more difficult.

The use of 'in-house' meetings, and a lack of awareness of their limited decision-making powers, particularly when parental responsibility was not shared (in the case of RV Tameside Metropolitan Borough Council *ex parte* J [2000] 1 FLR

942, it was noted that when the child was accommodated, the decision-making powers of the local authority were those of 'mundane day-to-day powers of management'), indicated that the processes of children becoming 'looked after' outside the legal process would benefit from a radical overhaul with Convention rights in mind.

A further concern relates to the changes to voluntary care under the Children Order intended to emphasise the importance of partnership with parents: this is the insecurity that is now intrinsic to the service of accommodation as there is no mechanism to move to permanence other than through a Care Order application. The problem of permanence planning in this kind of situation was noted too by Schofield (2000), with social workers advised by their legal departments that grounds did not exist for an application to court even though return home was not a possibility. This situation was exacerbated where there was 'drift' attributable to the local authority's planning process. It was notable that at the end of this study, 20% of the total sample of children (n = 22) remained accommodated without long-term plans for the future. Packman and Hall (1999) also detected a delay in permanence planning for young children accommodated under the Children Act as one option after another was attempted. There was evidence of similar patterns for children in this study. It appears that in the provision of accommodation, the balances introduced by the Children Order intended to ensure that application to court was the 'last resort' can conflict with the objective of achieving permanence for some 'looked-after' children. In addition, parents' Article 6 and Article 8 rights can be vulnerable in this process and this too can have a negative impact on permanence planning at a later stage.

The theoretical analysis of social services' behaviour when initiating compulsory measures provided an indication of the vast difference in the operation of the 'gateways' to care that can both lead to permanent separation between parent and child. Kelly and McSherry (2002) noted that, of the sample of 200 children (for whom Adoption Panels within the NI Health and Social Services Trusts had recommended Freeing Orders [under Articles 17 and 18 of the Adoption (NI) Order 1987 between 4 November 1996 and 30 September 2000]), 32% (n = 70) were 'accommodated' under Section 21 of the Children (NI) Order 1995 or admitted into voluntary care under previous legislation. The authors noted a major factor contributing to delay culminating in the court hearings was that parents contested the case in 75% of the Freeing Order applications. The authors recommended that 'independent counselling mediation and support' to the parents of those children should be considered a priority. The data in the study discussed here suggested that parents might well have benefited from advocacy at an early stage to help to put their cases across and to challenge the actions taken by social services before the case entered the legal process.

Lindley and Richards (2002) have argued the advantages of parental advocacy at a much earlier stage. The authors pointed out that the complexity of the relationship between the parents and social services makes parental participation in decision-making as envisaged in *Working Together* (DoH/Home Office/DfEE,

1999) difficult to achieve. The Article 6 and Article 8 rights under the ECHR and judgments such as those by Munby, J. (cited earlier), emphasise the requirement of procedural fairness. Lindley and Richards argued that the general impression from an initial qualitative examination of the role of parents' advocate was that it helped to engage parents in working with local authorities to address and where possible overcome child protection concerns.

In terms of the conduct of the legal process, the length of time child protection cases lasted and the adversarial nature of cases in the courts were raised recently by DCA (2005) in a *Fairer Deal for Legal Aid*. A number of options are to be considered in a cross-government review of the child-care proceedings system in England and Wales. It was said that one of the options to be considered was an exploration of early low-level judicial interventions to encourage parents to themselves resolve problems, thus avoiding the need for full court proceedings wherever possible and appropriate.

Cleave (2000) argued that 'we are moving rapidly towards an emphatically rights-based culture'. It is crucial, therefore, that the processes infringing on parents' Article 6 and Article 8 rights are Convention-proofed in order to remove potential obstacles to achieving permanence for 'looked-after' children.

REFERENCES

Cleave, G. (2000). The Human Rights Act 1998: How will it affect child law in England and Wales? *Child Abuse Review*, **9**, 394–402.

Cretney, S.M., Masson, J., & Bailey-Harris, R. (2002). *Principles of Family Law*. London: Thomson Sweet & Maxwell.

DCA (2005). *A Fairer Deal for Legal Aid*. (Presented to Parliament by the Secretary of State for Constitutional Affairs and Lord Chancellor by Command of Her Majesty, July 2005, Cm 6591). London: The Stationery Office.

DHSS (1985). *Social Work Decisions in Child Care: Recent Research Findings and their Implications*. London: HMSO.

Dingwall, R., Eekalaar, J., & Murray, T. (1983/1995). *The Protection of Children*. Oxford: Blackwell.

DoH/Home Office/DfEE (1999). Working together to safeguard children: A guide to inter-agency working to safeguard and promote the welfare of children. Department of Health, Home Office, Department for Education and Employment. Published 30/12/1999. http://www.dh.gov.uk/PublicationsandStatistics/Publications/PublicationsPolicyAnd GuidanceArticle/fs/en?CONTENT_ID=4007781&chk= BUYMa8

DOH (2001). *The Children Act Now: Messages from Research*. London: The Stationery Office.

Fortin, J. (1999). The Human Rights Act's impact on litigation involving children and their families. *Child and Family Law Quarterly*, **11**(3), 237–255.

Freeman, P., & Hunt, J. (1998). *Parental Perspectives on Care Proceedings*. London: The Stationery Office.

Gibbons, J., Conroy, S., & Bell, C. (1995). *Operating the Child Protection System*. London: HMSO.

Harnott, C., & Humphreys, H. (2004). *Adoption and Permanence Taskforce*. Available at: www.elsc.org.uk/socialcareresource/publications/adoption/section02a.asp-9k

Hunt, J., & Macleod, A. (1999). *The Best-Laid Plans: Outcomes of Judicial Decisions in Child Protection Proceedings*. London: The Stationery Office.

Hunt, J., Macleod, A., & Thomas, C. (1999). *The Last Resort: Child Protection, the Courts and the 1989 Children Act*, vol. 1. London: The Stationery Office.

Iwaniec, I., Donaldson, T., & Alweiss, M. (2004). The plight of neglected children: Social work and judicial decision-making, and management of neglect cases. *Child and Family Law Quarterly*, **16**(4), 423–436.

Kelly, G., & McSherry, D. (2002). Adoption from care in Northern Ireland: Problems in the process. *Child and Family Social Work*, **7**, 297–309.

King, M. (1997). *A Better World for Children? Explorations in Morality and Authority*. London: Routledge.

King, M., & Piper, C. (1990). *How the Law Thinks about Children*. Aldershot: Gower.

Lindley, B., & Richards, M. (2002). *Protocol on Advice and Advocacy for Parents (Child Protection)*. Cambridge: Centre for Family Research, University of Cambridge.

Millham, S., Bullock, R., Hosie, K., & Little, M. (1986). *Lost in Care: The Problems of Maintaining Links between Children in Care and their Families*. Aldershot: Gower.

O'Halloran, K. (1999). *The Welfare of the Child: The Principle and the Law: A Study of the Meaning, Role and Functions of the Principle as it Has Evolved within the Family Law of England and Wales*. Aldershot: Ashgate.

Packman, J., & Hall, C. (1999). *From Care to Accommodation*. London: The Stationery Office.

Packman, J., Randall, J., & Jacques, N. (1986). *Who Needs Care? Social Work Decisions about Children*. Oxford: Blackwell.

Parton, N. (1991). *Governing the Family: Child Care, Child Protection and the State*. London: Macmillan Education.

Schofield, G. (2000). Parental responsibility and parenting: The needs of accommodated children in long-term foster-care. *Child and Family Law Quarterly*, **12**(4), 345–361.

Scottish Executive (2005). Adoption Policy Review Group – Report Phase I. http://www.scotland.gov.uk/library5/education/apr1-19.asp

White, R., Carr, P., & Lowe, N. (2002). *The Children Act in Practice*. London: Butterworths.

CHAPTER 13

CARE PLANNING IN CARE PROCEEDINGS: A CASE STUDY PERSPECTIVE ON ACHIEVING PERMANENCY

Dominic McSherry

INTRODUCTION

This chapter presents two case studies that were developed as part of a recently completed research study (McSherry et al., 2004). This examined the costs that are incurred by children when social services use the courts to resolve issues with families about the care of children. Costs were defined as dichotomous, being both indirect and direct. Indirect costs were defined by the amount of time that social workers spent on these court cases as well as by the amount of money paid for legal advice. Such issues were considered to reduce more supportive and preventative work in the community, drain financial resources, and decrease the potential for the appointment of additional social work staff. Direct costs were understood as the impact of the proceedings upon the child in terms of establishing a permanent placement (either with birth-parents or alternative carers). The costs of care proceedings to the children involved, both indirect and direct, were found at times to be considerable (Larkin et al., 2005; McSherry et al., 2004, 2005).

The benefit of developing case studies when examining the impact of care proceedings upon children is that they allow the court process to be set in the context of the young person's life before, during, and after the proceedings. Examining the facts of the case before it goes to court allows decision-making that occurs during proceedings to be examined more critically, i.e. do the decisions that are made appear to concur with not only the current situation, but also with the historical evidence that has been gathered? Looking at the child's situation after proceedings also gives a perspective on outcomes, i.e. in what way did the decision-making that occurred during proceedings impact upon the child's future life?

Within the McSherry et al. (2004) study, all 33 Care Order cases that were active during the 2001/2002 period were examined from two Health and Social Services Trusts. This involved an in-depth, unrestricted analysis of social work case files and several key sources of information were regularly utilised. These were: child-protection case conference minutes; looked-after children reviews; social work reports to court and care plans; guardian ad litem reports to court; expert medical reports; Court Orders and Directions; correspondence from Trust legal advisers; correspondence between legal representatives; and correspondence with experts. Two of these cases, i.e. Paula and Jim, were selected for presentation as case studies. They highlight the impact that care proceedings can have for the children involved in terms of establishing a permanent placement either with birth-parents or alternative carers. These case studies also allow for an examination of care planning and decision-making within the court and consider how this may impact upon the child, particularly in terms of the development of attachment relationships with short-term foster carers.

CARE PLANNING

The requirement to draw up a care plan for each child in public care was laid down in the 1995 Children (Northern Ireland) Order. The purpose of such plans was to prevent drift in care and to promote high standards of decision-making and long-term planning. A governmental inspection of care planning in Northern Ireland (DHSSPS, 1999) highlighted the need for continuity of care and carers to enable children to develop appropriate relationships, fulfil their social and academic potentials, and to mature into well-adjusted members of society. The inspection report noted that it was essential for care planning to be timely and goal-directed, and assessed how care plans were being currently implemented. It was found that, while the quality of care plans was improving over time, considerable inconsistency was evident in terms of content and quality. The inspection report (DHSSPS, 1999) emphasised the necessity to place the needs of children at the centre of the planning process and to find ways to limit delay in securing their future.

PARALLEL PLANNING

It has been argued that parallel planning may be a way of avoiding the drift of children within the care system by working towards family reunification while at the same time developing an alternative care plan. Monck et al. (2004) noted that it has been common practice for some time for UK social workers to pursue two plans simultaneously for a child, in case one proves unviable. However, while attempts are made at rehabilitation, the child remains in short-term foster care with carers who may not have been specifically preselected as potential long-term carers for the child. Consequently, the child may have to move to more suitable long-term carers once a decision has been taken that rehabilitation is no longer an option. If the timescale involved in reaching this decision has been lengthy, this may create problems for the child, particularly in terms of the development of significant attachments to their short-term foster carers. However, the benefit of this approach over having only one plan in place for the child (serial planning) is that even in the event that the child does have to move to a different long-term carer, the social workers will have had some time to identify and prepare for this move in advance of any decision regarding rehabilitation. With serial planning, attempts to identify long-term carers would only begin at this point.

CONCURRENT PLANNING

Concurrent planning is often confused with parallel planning because it also involves having different care plans in place for the child, i.e. rehabilitation or adoption. However, the key difference with parallel planning is that, if within a given time period rehabilitation of the child with the birth-parents is not possible, the child will be provided with a permanent family life through adoption with the foster carer who had been caring for the child while rehabilitation was being considered.

Although parallel planning is an improvement upon serial planning, it is less focused than concurrent planning on ensuring the continuity of carer, which is essential for the development and maintenance of attachment relationships. Ward et al. (2003) argued that greater use should be made of either concurrent or parallel planning, given the low fulfilment rate of initial care plans, so as to minimise delay in cases where rehabilitation proves untenable.

A comprehensive review of concurrent planning projects within the UK found that the approach could achieve significant advantages for children, including fewer moves between carers and less time spent in impermanent care (Monck et al., 2003). However, this approach is not without difficulty, as efforts must be made towards both plans simultaneously with the full knowledge of all participants in the case. More recent concurrent planning evaluation projects have shown that rates of rehabilitation can be less than 10% (Wigfall et al., 2005). This figure is not surprising, given that 'the concurrent planning approach was not designed for work with easy cases' (Monck et al., 2004, p. 323). However, it does appear to imply that concurrent planning is heavily weighted in favour of adoption.

PERMANENCY PLANNING AND ATTACHMENT

Kelly and McSherry (2002) noted that although Northern Ireland was quite slow to embrace the 'permanence' agenda, i.e. the belief that children should not spend their childhood in public care but should be either rehabilitated or placed with permanent alternative carers (preferably adoptive parents), things were beginning to change with a marked increase in the use of adoption for looked-after children. A more recent study of pathways to permanency for younger

(0–4 years old) looked-after children in Northern Ireland indicates that this trend towards adoption is continuing, although some Trusts appear to have embraced this permanency option more enthusiastically than others (see McSherry & Larkin, Chapter 7, in this volume).

Permanency planning concepts were heavily influenced by attachment-theory (Thompson, 1998), particularly by findings pertaining to the young child's need for a secure base and how this is impacted by serial-attachment experiences. Stability, continuity, and predictability are at the core of children's emotional well-being, but some looked-after children continue to have little long-term stability in their lives (McSherry et al., 2005). Attachment, i.e. the ability to form secure and lasting relationships to a care-giver, has been viewed as the bedrock upon which all future interpersonal relationships are founded (Bowlby, 1951, 1969, 1973). Research has illustrated that the formation of secure attachment-relationships is an important domain of the interpersonal process, with long-term implications for future developments (Aldgate, Chapter 2, in this volume; Belsky & Cassidy, 1994; Rutter, 1995).

Models of attachment are an individual's representations of their relationships with significant others (Bowlby, 1973). Security of attachment refers to the degree to which a child has internalised experiences based upon continuous exposure to significant others who are perceived as trustworthy, available, sensitive, and loving. Disruptions and frequent changes of care-givers are painful and anxiety-provoking for the child.

Emotional availability and consistency are extremely important in promoting healthy development (Iwaniec, 1995). Emotional security from attachment-relationships (reflected by the child's confidence in the availability, familiarity, and responsiveness of attachment-figures) is central to emotional well-being (Bowlby, 1969). Continuity of attachments in early childhood predicts better peer relationships, fewer behavioural problems in later childhood and adolescence, healthier relationships, and better outcomes throughout life (Rutter, 1995). Attachment-theory, therefore, has been used by child-welfare researchers to explain the severity of problem behaviours among foster children (Leathers, 2002).

CASE STUDIES

The two case studies that are presented here, i.e. Paula and Jim (pseudonyms), are intended to give a detailed picture of the life of a looked-after child before, during, and after care proceedings. In so doing it is hoped that the reader will develop an understanding of the often complex decision-making process that occurs within and outside the court and the impact of these decisions on the child's prospect of achieving a permanent placement. The cases vary in complexity and duration: Paula's care proceedings were relatively straightforward and hence quite timely, whereas Jim's were extremely complex and protracted. These two cases, perhaps, will give a feel for the types of issues and dilemmas that the professionals are faced with on a daily basis, and the type of impact that care proceedings can have upon a child's chances of securing permanency. It is important to point out that there is no attempt being made in this chapter to pass judgement on professional practice in these cases. The case studies are presented to illustrate how care proceedings that have a particular focus upon permanency can achieve positive permanency outcomes for the child, i.e. in the case of Paula, and where there is no particular focus on permanency, i.e. in the case of Jim, there can be quite negative permanency outcomes.

These cases were progressing during 2001–2002 and only reflect professional practice at that time. Since that time there have been several initiatives aimed at improving the progression of Public Law cases through the courts (DHSSPS, 2003, 2004), and it is hoped that the recommendations developed within the research outlined in this chapter (McSherry et al., 2004) will make a similar contribution in this regard.

Paula

Paula's mother was 15 when she was born. At the time social services were concerned about Paula's father (also a teenager), who was abusing alcohol and drugs as well as physically abusing Paula's mother. Immediately after her birth, Paula and her mother went to live with the mother's uncle. Social services continued to monitor the situation (via regular Child Protection Case Conferences), and, at the age of one month, Paula was placed on the Child Protection Register under the category of potential neglect. Things went quite well until just before Paula's first birthday, when her mother and father decided to live together, along with Paula, in rented accommodation. At that time social services were concerned about the parents' lifestyle (parties, etc.), the stability of the parental relationship, and possible alcohol and drug abuse. However, Paula continued to make good progress, and the situation was kept under review. Six months later the concerns remained, and Paula was placed voluntarily full-time with her mother's uncle. Paula was now $1\frac{1}{2}$ years old.

The Trust's plan was to rehabilitate Paula with her parents, but their lifestyle continued to be a cause for concern and they showed no commitment to contact, which was upsetting for Paula. After six months of trying to engage the parents in different assessments (to no avail) the Trust applied for a Care Order so as to establish long-term plans for Paula's future. A range of assessments was specified as being essential prior to rehabilitation. These were: an assessment of the father's drug use; an assessment of the mother's general mental/physical health; a parenting assessment at a family centre; and an assessment at a residential family unit. The Trust suggested that these assessments would take approximately a year. Paula was now 2 years old.

(Continued)

However, both the mother and the father refused to engage in the assessment process. Two months into this process a guardian ad litem's report to court was pessimistic about the parents' capacity to commit to the full-time care of Paula (given their lack of commitment to her to date), and the Trust was advised to reassess the care plan. The guardian suggested that the Trust pursue a parallel-planning approach that considered whether rehabilitation was realistic or achievable within clearly and tightly defined timescales. The guardian argued that if a level of progress compatible with pursuing rehabilitation as a realistic option were not achievable, then the Trust should move to considering permanency in respect of Paula. The guardian emphasised that Paula's needs for stability and certainty were of paramount importance, and outweighed the timescale (one year) being proposed by the Trust in terms of assessment to consider rehabilitation.

Two months later at the next Looked-After Children Review the Trust amended its care plan to include the guardian's suggested parallel-planning approach and ruled out further consideration of rehabilitation if sufficient progress was not made within a specified three-month timeframe of work. Consequently, the Trust included long-term foster care (no return to birth-parent/s anticipated) as a formal component of the care plan. One month later, a full Care Order was granted to the Trust in respect of Paula. The proceedings had taken 20 weeks. Paula was now $2\frac{1}{2}$ years old.

For several months following the Care Order, the mother and father showed some commitment to the required assessments and regularly attended contact. Therefore, the Trust continued with rehabilitation as the main care plan, with long-term foster care as a parallel consideration. However, at the next Looked-After Children Review (held six months later) it was noted that the parents' commitment to the assessments, and to contact, had significantly reduced. It was also noted that Paula had developed strong attachments to her uncle at this stage (she had lived with him for almost two years full-time at this stage), and she appeared uncertain as to who were the significant adults in her life. Consequently, the care plan was changed from rehabilitation/long-term foster care to 'live with relatives' (namely her uncle). Paula was now just over 3 years old.

Paula was almost 4 years old when the next Looked-After Children Review took place. At this stage, attendance for contact was infrequent and a decision was taken to terminate it. When the study (McSherry et al., 2004) ended, Paula was 5 and continued to live in this long-term relative foster placement, and was doing very well. The placement remained long-term fostering rather than adoption as Paula's uncle stated that he needed the financial support provided by the fostering allowance.

Discussion of Paula's Case

Paula's case presents a picture of young teenage parents unable to commit to the adult responsibilities of caring for a young child. The Trust initially spent some time trying to engage the parents in the hope that they would realise that they would have to accept the reality of their situation and change their lifestyle if they wanted to continue to look after their child. Unfortunately, the Trust was unable to engage the parents in the required assessments, and court action was deemed necessary.

This case shows that the focus of the professionals involved differed slightly when it entered the court arena. The Trust was keen to facilitate eventual rehabilitation with the parents and to ensure that the family had the best opportunity to remain intact. This approach was consistent with the requirements specified within the 1995 Children (Northern Ireland) Order of working in partnership with parents and the 'No Order' principle. In their view, a one-year period for assessment may have facilitated this. It needs to be borne in mind that those working on these cases would not have had the benefit of hindsight in terms of actual outcomes to which the researchers were privy. It might have transpired that the parents fully engaged with the assessments and the family was reunited. In that case the Trust would have been fully vindicated in its suggested approach. However, the guardian's intervention put the focus purely upon the child. It was felt that at 2 years old (a critical period for the development of attachments), not to take decisions about the child's future, in terms of establishing a permanent placement, would have been potentially damaging. It transpired that the guardian's analysis was correct on this occasion because the parents did fail to engage in the assessment process, and thus action regarding obtaining a permanent placement for the child was able to begin sooner. Fortunately, Paula had been placed in a relative foster placement by the Trust and the uncle was agreeable for this to become a long-term placement.

In terms of setting the court proceedings in context and assessing any potential direct costs to Paula, it would appear that the proceedings in this instance were actually beneficial for her as they allowed for the issue of her long-term future, i.e. permanence, to be addressed at an early stage, through the introduction of parallel planning, and at a critical period in her development in terms of attachment.

Jim

Jim's mother had been in care throughout her childhood and had mental-health problems. Before Jim was born, his brother had been placed in long-term care as a result of the mother's inability to protect him, with no return anticipated to the mother's care. Three months before Jim was born, a social worker dealing with the case wrote to the Family and Child Care Programme Manager commenting that there was a possibility that the baby (Jim) would not be returning to his mother's care. It was suggested that adoption might be the best plan for the baby, and that attempts should

(Continued)

be made to identify permanent carers who would either foster or adopt the child. The social worker also noted that, given the dilemma currently faced in relation to foster carers wishing to adopt and the difficult issue of attachments developing in these placements, it would be wise to avoid another such scenario by recruiting permanent carers for the baby as soon as possible.

Two weeks before Jim was born, social services held a Pre-Birth Child Protection Case Conference where it was agreed that Jim would be at high risk if he were placed in his mother's care. Subsequently, it was decided that an Emergency Protection Order would be sought immediately upon Jim's birth. Jim was born prematurely by several weeks. The mother was initially happy with Jim, but later became agitated: she expressed the desire to have nothing to do with him and for the child to be adopted. Jim's mother was admitted to a mental-health unit after the birth as a result of psychotic behaviour. Jim was placed on a short-term basis in the same foster home as his 10-year-old brother who was already being looked after long term by this family. The Trust applied for an Interim Care Order in respect of Jim one week after his birth so as to ensure Jim's safety given his mother's continuing mental-health needs, limited intellectual capacity, and lack of insight into her child's needs.

At the Looked-After Children Review held when Jim was one month old, it was stated that there were no initial plans for Jim to leave care and the Review agreed that in relation to Jim's care plan, parallel planning was in his best interests. The Review also agreed that the mother was to undergo all assessments, and if these proved positive and she attempted to make changes to her lifestyle, consideration would be given to Jim being returned to her care. However, if she was not to change her lifestyle and the assessments were not positive, then it would be in Jim's best interests to be placed for adoption. Jim's mother informed the Review that she would not consent to adoption, and wanted Jim placed at home with her. It was agreed that the social worker would gather and present Jim's case to the adoption panel as soon as possible. It was further noted that Jim's foster parents wished to be considered as adopters for Jim, although the Trust were not considering this as an option.

At the Looked-After Children Review held the following week the Trust stated that they aimed to apply for a full Care Order as soon as possible. It was also acknowledged that Jim was not currently in a suitable placement, particularly as his older brother was also placed there on a long-term fostering basis. This Looked-After Children Review established a routine for contact between Jim and his mother of two hours per day, three times per week, depending upon the mother's health.

After one month, the Care Order application was transferred to the Family Care Centre due to the mother's state of mental health, the previous difficulties encountered in relation to her first child, and the need to involve specialist expert witnesses. The proceedings were protracted over the next ten months due to conflicting medical reports regarding the mother's mental-health and parenting abilities, and also as a result of delay in getting parenting assessments completed due to the mother's ill-health. There were two main problems. Firstly, the court had initially instructed the mother's own psychiatrist to give an assessment of her mental state and ability to parent, and this report was inconclusive: consequently, a second psychiatrist had to be instructed. This latter psychiatrist's report noted that during assessment the mother requested adoption for Jim. Secondly, an initial parenting assessment, which was conducted at a family centre, suggested that the mother had positively demonstrated evidence of her parenting ability, and a recommendation was made for contact with Jim to be increased. Social services did not accept this assessment, and requested a further more detailed assessment which subsequently concluded that there was very little evidence to suggest that the mother could provide consistent basic care for Jim.

A Looked-After Children Review held when Jim was four months old noted that the mother was happy for Jim to remain in care but did not want him to be adopted. Concerns were raised that it would not be in Jim's and his brother's interests to be treated differently in the same family, i.e. one adopted and one fostered. The Assistant Principal Social Worker felt that an adoptive placement with the foster parents would not be in the child's best interests, and noted that a Freeing Application was being prepared for Jim. The Review noted that there were no plans to return Jim to the care of his birth-mother, and that he should remain in short-term foster care until a pre-adoptive placement was identified. The long-term plan for Jim was stated as adoption. Dual approved carers were to be identified for fostering and adoption of Jim and he was to be removed as soon as possible to an approved adoptive couple with post-adoptive contact with the birth-mother as part of the care plan. The Review concluded that Jim was young enough for separation from his foster carers and they were not being considered as potential long-term carers for him. This point was reinforced a week later in a letter to Jim's social worker from a social worker working for a voluntary organisation which stated that adoption was clearly in Jim's best interests and that he should be moved from his present placement and placed as a matter of urgency with his new permanent family.

Another letter two months later from the same social worker to Jim's social worker discussed the possibility of presenting Jim's case to the Adoption Panel before the Care Order was granted. The author noted that although adoption plans could not proceed until the Care Order was granted, and

(Continued)

nothing could be done to pre-empt the granting of an Order, there was no reason why concurrent planning (actually meant parallel planning) could not proceed in the meantime. It was also noted that this would be a helpful time-saving device as the plan could be implemented as soon as the Order was in place. The author cautioned that in this instance there would need to be a fair degree of certainty that a Care Order was likely to be granted, but from what was known about Jim's situation, this seemed highly likely.

Two weeks later the same social worker (voluntary organisation) notified Jim's social worker that the voluntary organisation would have suitable adoptive parents for Jim in its lists should there not be any suitable applicants within the Board. A Looked-After Children Review held one month later (Jim now aged seven months) noted that Jim's case was to be presented to the adoption panel that week but that this was at a very early stage and that Jim would remain in short-term care until the completion of his mother's parenting assessment. The Review concluded that the plan for Jim was concurrent planning (illustrating the common confusion between 'concurrent' and 'parallel' planning earlier highlighted).

A care plan presented to court one month later, however, indicted a change of approach and noted that it was the Trust's view that Jim's needs would be best met through continuous foster care. The report pointed out that while the Trust had not ruled out reunification with the mother, it was the consensus of the assessments to date that serious concerns existed in relation to the safety, security, and protection that the mother could provide. The report concluded that the Trust recognised that assessments to date had vindicated a number of their initial concerns, but that there was a need to fully exhaust the assessment process.

A guardian ad litem report to the court one month later pointed out that the Trust had not come to a conclusion with regard to the overall aim of their care plan for Jim, i.e. rehabilitation or permanency via adoption. It was noted that the Court had indicated it would not make a final determination on the application (for Care Order) until a decision was made by the Trust in this regard. It was only after the second parenting assessment was completed (where the mother's ability to provide even basic care for Jim was seriously questioned) that the Trust decided to present Jim's case to the Adoption Panel and to pursue a Freeing Order. At this stage Jim was a year old. A Looked-After Children Review held at this time recommended that Jim should not be returned to his mother's care due to the significant likelihood that he could suffer significant harm, and an Adoption Panel recommended adoption via Article 18 of the Freeing Order. One month later a full Care Order was granted to the Trust and the care plan to pursue adoption was approved.

These care proceedings had taken 55 weeks. The care plan noted that it was likely that Jim would remain looked after until a prospective adoptive placement had been identified and an Article 18 Freeing Order granted. Given that the foster parents had initially presented themselves as potential adoptive parents for Jim, it was decided that a senior practitioner on the adoption team would complete an assessment of Jim's current foster carers' ability to meet his needs via an adoptive placement within six months. However, it was still the Trust's stated intention to find alternative long-term carers for the child. Jim had remained with this family from the first week of his life and was now 1 year old. Throughout this period contact with the mother continued at the initial rate set by social services: however, there were some missed visits as a result of her ill-health. A Looked-After Children Review held when Jim was seven months old noted that he was building up a close relationship with his mother.

The Freeing Order application began four months after the Care Order was made. The Trust was now singularly focused on the foster parents becoming prospective adoptive parents for Jim. However, the application was withdrawn after one year due to difficulties that emerged in relation to assessment of the foster parents. Jim was almost $2^1/_2$ at this stage. At the time that the study (McSherry et al., 2004) ended, Jim was approaching his third birthday. He had been living with this same short-term foster family all his life. The Trust was completing the additional assessment work regarding the Freeing Application. There were no plans for Jim to live with anyone else. It was hoped that the Freeing Application could be reinstated as soon as possible. Jim's older brother continued to live with the same foster family; however, his care plan remained long-term fostering. Adoption was not considered an option for Jim's brother, then in his teens, as he had developed a strong bond with the birth-mother and continued to have frequent contact with her.

Discussion of Jim's Case

The details of Jim's life show that even before he was born social services were concerned that his mother would be unable to care for him long term, as had been the case previously with his brother, and that adoption might be necessary in this instance. The Trust, in its initial care plan, noted that parallel planning would be pursued. It was suggested that if all of the mother's assessments had positive outcomes, Jim would be rehabilitated to her care, if not he would be placed for adoption. This, however, was not parallel planning (as had been suggested in the care plan), but serial planning, even though some early work was done to get Jim's case to the Adoption Panel. If a parallel planning approach had been adopted, as in Paula's case cited previously, the mother's progress would have been monitored at intervals and appropriate decisions taken to ensure a long-term placement for Jim.

The Trust themselves, from early on, felt that Jim's placement was inappropriate given the fact that his brother was already being fostered by this family on a long-term basis and that it would be inappropriate to have two siblings living together with different long-term plans. However, due perhaps to the difficulties that arose in relation to assessments of the mother, the initial short-term foster placement continued to the extent that Jim formed close attachments to these carers. Furthermore, although never stated explicitly in any of the case file materials reviewed by the author, it may also have been the case that the fact that Jim had been placed with his brother throughout this period may have actually been seen as a positive in this instance, with separation, rather than keeping the children together, being deemed to be inappropriate.

It can be seen that it took 55 weeks to get the Care Order for Jim. Much of this time was taken with the assessment of the mother's mental and parenting capacity. The assessment process was exacerbated by the fact that the mother's own psychiatrist had been directed to report upon the mother's mental state and parenting ability and consequently was unable to give a definitive response to the court. This necessitated a further assessment by a second psychiatrist. Furthermore, a second parenting assessment was requested by the Trust after an initial assessment had concluded that the mother had demonstrated positive evidence of her parenting ability. Both these additional assessments (psychiatric and parenting) concluded that the child would be at risk of significant harm if returned to the mother's care, and the question arises as to why it took almost a year to reach this conclusion in Jim's case. Throughout these proceedings Jim remained in a placement that had been deemed from the outset as unsuitable. It was only by good fortune that his short-term foster parents wanted to adopt him. One wonders how long it would have taken to place Jim with prospective adopters if this had not been the case and what impact this might have had.

Viewing Jim's case and the duration of the proceedings in terms of potential direct costs, it can be concluded that the proceedings were costly for Jim in terms of him being placed in a permanent placement with either birth-parents or alternative carers. Although it transpired that plans were eventually made for him to be adopted by his foster carers (with whom he had been placed throughout the proceedings), this was by accident rather than design. Jim's case is a very good example where an early move to potential long-term carers would have been most appropriate, given the mother's past history of inability to parent. This would have avoided the scenario which developed where the child was placed from birth with short-term carers, with attempts to identify potential long-term carers only beginning at the end of protracted care proceedings, after the child had already formed significant attachments to the short-term carers.

DISCUSSION

It is hoped that the two case studies presented here provide a context for understanding decision-making within and outside the court as well as the complex issues and dilemmas that are faced on a daily basis by the professionals involved, without, as has been previously emphasised, the benefit of hindsight. The two cases provide a stark contrast in terms of the impact that court proceedings can have upon a child's life in terms of achieving a permanent placement. The main difference between the two cases can be defined in terms of the focus upon permanency. In Paula's case, the professionals involved ensured that she entered a permanent placement at as early an age as possible. In Jim's case, however, there appears to have been a lack of focus upon ensuring permanency for the child by all the professionals involved, with the principal focus placed upon the assessment process.

A more focused approach to parallel planning might have avoided the type of difficulties that emerged in Jim's case. Parallel planning would ensure that the assessment process was monitored at reasonable intervals and that effective action was taken to ensure that the child was placed, if necessary, with potential long-term carers at the earliest possible stage. However, problems could emerge if the assessment process was inconclusive, and if difficulties were encountered identifying suitable long-term carers. In these circumstances, children might have to remain for very long periods with short-term foster carers, potentially causing problems in terms of the development of significant attachment-relationships, which may eventually have to be broken.

Concurrent planning appears to offer a sensible and child-centred solution to avoiding the type of difficulties that were evident in Jim's case. This type of planning could possibly be extended to include placing children at an early stage with potential long-term foster carers, as well as adoptive parents. This may be an option that would be more suited for children who enter care at an older age and where significant attachments will have already developed with birth-parents.

As mentioned earlier, it is vitally important in concurrent planning that the dual plans of rehabilitation and adoption are pursued with equal vigour, that every effort is made to support the parents, and that the expectations made of them are reasonable and achievable. It is also essential that these types of planning processes involve some objective input, so as to avoid the impression that this is 'adoption by the back door' (Wigfall et al., 2005, p. 8). It is important to emphasise rehabilitation as an equally positive outcome.

One of the biggest problems faced by this type of approach to care planning is recruitment. Detractors of concurrent planning argue that those carers who do become involved in these schemes are first and foremost looking to adopt a child, and that this will always sway the balance of probabilities in their favour. Emphasising that rehabilitation will be pursued as an equally positive outcome to adoption may make it even more difficult to recruit this type of carer. Furthermore, the fact that some carers appear to approach this type of scheme with a view to adoption only to find (in a small number of cases) that the child that they are caring for is rehabilitated, highlights the potential emotional damage that this approach might cause.

One way to overcome some of these issues may be to specify the approach as 'adoption orientated' but only for the small number of children whose future prognosis in the care of their parents is extremely poor. This would be a child-centred approach, aimed at ensuring that those children whom social services deem to be highly unlikely to achieve successful rehabilitation do not experience the type of uncertainty, insecurity, and impermanence that other children have experienced in the care system in the past. This approach would ensure that the birth-parents were clear from the very beginning of the necessity for co-operation in the assessment process, and what the outcome would be if they were not to comply. In these circumstances, if reasonable objectives were set regarding assessments, non-compliance by the birth-parents would indicate that they were not prepared or able to place the needs of their children (to live with their birth-parents) before their own. It could be argued that this, in itself, would reinforce the necessity for such children to be adopted. Certainly, it does appear that Jim would have benefited greatly from such a focused approach to care planning. Hopefully, the recommendation for all Trusts to include objectives and targets for securing the adoption or permanent placement of children in their Children's Service Plans, as specified in *Adopting Best Care* (SSI, 2002), should be helpful in this regard.

ACKNOWLEDGEMENTS

The author would like to thank Greg Kelly for reviewing an early draft of this chapter.

REFERENCES

Belsky, J., & Cassidy, J. (1994). Attachment: Theory and evidence. In M.L. Rutter, D.F. Hay, & S. Baron-Cohen (eds), *Development Through Life: A Handbook for Clinicians*. Oxford: Blackwell.

Bowlby, J. (1951). *Maternal Care and Mental Health. World Health Organisation Monograph Series No. 2*. Geneva: World Health Organisation. Reprinted (1966). New York: Schocken Books.

Bowlby, J. (1969). *Attachment and Loss*, vol. 1: *Attachment*. London: Hogarth Press.

Bowlby, J. (1973). *Attachment and Loss*, vol. 2: *Separation*. New York: Basic Books.

DHSSPS (1999). *Planning to Care: An Overview Report of Care Planning for Children Subject to Statutory Intervention*. Belfast: Department of Health, Social Services, and Public Safety. An Roinn Sláinte, Seirbhísí Sóisialta, agus Sábháilteachta Poiblí.

DHSSPS (2003). *The Children Order Advisory Committee Best Practice Guidance*. Belfast: Department of Health, Social Services, and Public Safety. An Roinn Sláinte, Seirbhísí Sóisialta, agus Sábháilteachta Poiblí.

DHSSPS (2004). *Children Order Advisory Committee Delay Sub-Committee Report 2003*. Belfast: Department of Health, Social Services, and Public Safety. An Roinn Sláinte, Seirbhísí Sóisialta, agus Sábháilteachta Poiblí.

Iwaniec, D. (1995). *The Emotionally Abused and Neglected Child: Identification, Assessment, and Intervention*. Chichester: John Wiley & Sons, Ltd.

Kelly, G., & McSherry, D. (2002). Adoption from care in Northern Ireland: Problems in the process. *Child and Family Social Work*, **7**, 22–24.

Larkin, E., McSherry, D., & Iwaniec, D. (2005). Room for improvement? Views of key professionals involved in Care Order proceedings. *Child and Family Law Quarterly*, **17**(2), 231–245.

Leathers, S.J. (2002). Foster children's behavioural disturbance and detachment from care-givers and community institutions. *Children and Youth Services Review*, **24**(4), 239–268.

McSherry, D., Iwaniec, D., & Larkin, E. (2004). *Counting the Costs: The Children (Northern Ireland) Order (1995), Social Work and the Courts*. Research Report. Belfast: Institute of Child Care Research, Queen's University.

McSherry, D., Larkin, E., & Iwaniec, D. (2005). Care proceedings: Exploring the relationship between case duration and achieving permanency for the child. *British Journal of Social Work*, 10.1093/bjsw/bch362.

Monck, E., Reynolds, J., & Wigfall, V. (2003). *The Role of Concurrent Planning: Making Permanent Placements for Young Children*. London: British Association for Adoption and Fostering.

Monck, E., Reynolds, J., & Wigfall, V. (2004). Using concurrent planning to establish permanency for looked after children. *Child and Family Social Work*, **9**, 321–331.

Rutter, M. (1995). *Maternal Deprivation Reassessed*, 2nd edn. New York: Penguin.

SSI (2002). *Adopting Best Care: Inspection of Statutory Adoption Services in Northern Ireland*. Belfast: Department of Health, Social Services, and Public Safety. An Roinn Sláinte, Seirbhísí Sóisialta agus Sábháilteachta Poiblí.

Thompson, S. (1998). Perspectives on permanence: An attachment perspective. *Representing Children*, **11**(3), 187–199.

Ward, H., Munro, E., Deardon, C., & Nicholson, D. (2003). *Outcomes for Looked After Children: Life Pathways and Decision-Making for Very Young Children*. Research Report. Loughborough: Centre for Child and Family Research, Loughborough University.

Wigfall, V., Monck, J., & Reynolds, J. (2005). Putting programme into practice: The introduction of concurrent planning into mainstream adoption and fostering services. *British Journal of Social Work*, 10.1093/bjsw/bch.250.

CHAPTER 14

THE PARTICIPATION OF LOOKED-AFTER CHILDREN IN PUBLIC LAW PROCEEDINGS

Karen Winter

The Act of 1989 enables and requires a judicious balance to be struck between two considerations. First is the principle, to be honored and respected, that children are human beings in their own right with individual minds and wills, views and emotions, which should command serious attention. A child's wishes are not to be discounted or dismissed simply because he is a child. He should be free to express them and decision-makers should listen.

Second is the fact that a child is, after all, a child. The reason why the law is particularly solicitous in protecting the interests of children is because they are liable to be vulnerable and impressionable, lacking the maturity to weigh the longer term against the shorter, lacking the insight to know how they will react, and the imagination to know how others will react in certain situations, lacking the experience to measure the probable against the possible.

Everything of course depends on the individual child in his actual situation. For purposes of the Act, a babe in arms and a sturdy teenager on the verge of adulthood are both children, but their positions are quite different: for one the second consideration will be dominant, for the other the first principle will come into its own.

(Sir Thomas Bingham MR
Re S (A Minor) (Independent Representation) [1993] 2 FLR CA 263)

INTRODUCTION

In recent years there has been growing acceptance of and attention to the principle of children's participation in decisions affecting them (see Franklin, 2002; special editions of *Children and Society*, 2004, **18**(2), and *Adoption and Fostering*, 2005, **29**(1), for recent and useful summaries of some of the main developments). This principle (which extends to looked-after children whose cases enter the legal process through public law proceedings) has also been the subject of some research

The Child's Journey Through Care: Placement Stability, Care Planning, and Achieving Permanency. Edited by D. Iwaniec.

(Clark & Sinclair, 1999; Clarke, 1995; Hill et al., 2003; Hunt & Murch, 1990; Masson & Winn-Oakley, 1999; McCausland, 2000; Murray & Hallett, 2000; O'Quigley, 2000; Ruegger, 2001a, 2001b; Sawyer, 1995a, 1995b, 2000; Timms & Thoburn, 2003; Tisdall et al., 2002) and debate (Bilson & White, 2005; Head, 1998; James et al., 2003, 2004; Lowe, 2001; Masson, 2002, 2003; Raitt, 2004; Timmis, 2001; Tisdall et al., 2004).

The aim of this chapter is to provide an overview of research, theory, and practice in this area, and, in so doing, to highlight the main provisions and mechanisms for the participation of looked-after children in public law proceedings; the reasons for the increased emphasis on children's participation; the perceived benefits of participation; the results of research focusing on the views of looked-after children about their experiences in this area; and gaps in practice as well as reasons for those. The chapter will end by suggesting ways forward. It begins by considering the term looked after and the lives of the children to whom this label is assigned.

WHO ARE LOOKED-AFTER CHILDREN?

The term 'looked-after child' is a legal construct arising from the Children Act (1989), Children (NI) Order (1995), and Children (Scotland) Order (1995) and refers to all those children in public care or living at home on legal orders (Care Orders). The generic term disguises the heterogeneity of this group of children in terms of age, gender, ethnicity, religion, and class as well as other indicators including: reasons why they become looked after; how long they remain looked after; how many times they become looked after; where and with whom they live; and what their daily care arrangements are (Oliver et al., 2001; Statham et al., 2002).

Current figures indicate that the proportion of looked-after children, taken as a percentage of the total child population under the age of 18 years, varies from 1 in every 100 hundred children in Scotland (SENSP, 2004) through to 1 in every 180 children in Northern Ireland (DHSSPS, 2004) and 1 in every 200 hundred children in England (DfES, 2005). These same statistics also indicate that approximately 40% of looked-after children return to the care of their parents within eight weeks and that, overall, approximately 70% return to the care of their parents within one year. The remaining children continue to be looked after for years rather than months (DfES, 2005). There has been an overall increase in the total numbers of looked-after children because they become looked after at a younger age and remain so for longer (DfES, 2005; Statham et al., 2002).

Research highlights that there is wide geographical variation in terms of children who become 'looked after' (Statham et al., 2002) either as a result of the influence of deprivation (Bebbington & Miles, 1989; Winter & Connolly, 2005), and/or the policies, procedures, and practices implemented by different authorities in response to children and families in difficulties (Statham et al., 2002). In terms of the key characteristics of children assigned the label 'looked after', the research is much less equivocal. A depressing litany of negative indicators accompanies this group of children in terms of their likely family background (Aldgate, 2001; Bebbington & Miles, 1989; Cousins & Monteith, 2002; Cousins et al., 2003) educational experiences, prospects, and achievements (see Harker et al., 2004, for a useful summary), physical health (see special issue of *Adoption and Fostering*, 2002, **26**(4); Hill & Watkins, 2003), mental, emotional, and psychological health and well-being (Broad, 2005), employment prospects, and propensity to criminality (SEU, 2001, 2003a, 2003b).

Overall, the message conveyed is that looked-after children on reaching adulthood have difficulty making a successful transition (Broad, 2005; Dixon & Stein, 2005; SEU, 2003a, 2003b). The SEU (2003a, p. 3), in its report, argues that 'for many, the poor experiences of education and care contribute to later social exclusion: between a quarter and a third of rough sleepers were in care; young people who have been in care are two and a half times more likely to be teenage parents; and around a quarter of adults in prison spent some time in care as children'.

The relevance of these facts and figures in considering the issue of looked-after children's participation in public law proceedings is that before these children even come into contact with the legal process, they are in a position of relative disadvantage by virtue of: firstly, their small numbers; secondly, their experience of and exposure to a constellation of disadvantages which have been with them in their 'pre-care' experiences (Cousins & Monteith, 2002; Cousins et al., 2003; Harker et al., 2004), which are often compounded by their 'in-care' experiences (Harker et al., 2004; Jackson & Thomas, 1999); and, thirdly, the ways in which their circumstances are portrayed to the public at large, cast as they are as troublesome, failing, or both. This results in the additional disadvantage of having to deal with the stereotypes of others as evidenced in work by Morris (2000), NCB (2003), and VCC (2004).

LOOKED-AFTER CHILDREN AND PUBLIC LAW PROCEEDINGS

From this small number of children an even smaller number come into contact with the legal process through public law proceedings. In Northern Ireland, for example, figures indicate that for the period 2003/2004 there were 2,510 looked-after children (DHSSPSNI, 2004) and that within that same time frame the cases of 518 children were involved in public law proceedings (NIGALA, 2005). What this means is that, in Northern Ireland, and with slight variation, approximately one in every 950 children will come into contact with the legal process through public law proceedings in any given year.

As stated by Ruegger (2001a, p. 3):

> public law proceedings are those in which the court's authority, to interfere in what would normally be considered private family business, is sought by the State. The State must demonstrate that the child has suffered, or is likely to suffer, significant harm and that this is attributable to the care they receive from their parents.

Within the framework of the United Nations Convention on the Rights of the Child (UNCRC), this indicates a resonance with two of the principles contained therein, namely children's protection and provision rights or their welfare rights.

The remainder of this chapter will consider looked-after children in public law proceedings within the context of the third principle enshrined in UNCRC, namely, children's participation rights which, within this framework, include children's rights to 'their name and identity, to be consulted and taken account of, to have information, freedom of speech and opinion and to challenge decisions made on their behalf' (Timms, 1995, p. 46). It begins with definitions of participation and a brief account of the reasons behind the increased emphasis on this process.

DEFINITIONS OF PARTICIPATION

A common misconception is that children's participation is synonymous with children controlling adults and telling adults what to do (Alderson, 2000). As Hill et al. (2004, p. 82) observe, some adults view 'children's rights as under-mining adults' authority and rights, with a zero-sum assumption that transferring responsibility to children inevitably takes something away from adults'. This is both a misinterpretation of the term 'participation' and its process in practice (Neale, 2004).

Essentially, the term means taking part in, sharing, influencing, and affecting. As such, the term is multi-dimensional, in practice, relational, and with outcomes determined by the interplay of social processes in which differential power relationships are a central feature. Within this framework it does not necessarily follow that the giving of increased autonomy to a child inevitably leads to the decreased authority of the adult because with the process of participation is a presumption that decisions are reached through a process of mutual discussion, negotiation, compromise, and agreement as a partnership relationship (John, 2003; Neale, 2004).

These themes are reflected in the various theoretical models which exist to depict 'different degrees of participation' and which serve to clarify and check just how far children do participate in decisions affecting them (Alderson, 2000). These models serve to highlight the difference between latent/passive participation through to active participation. These differences are usefully summarised in the four-stage model (Alderson, 2000, p. 113), which is based on the principles contained in Articles 12, 13, 14, and 15 of the UNCRC (1989) and includes being informed, expressing a view, influencing the decision-maker, and being the main decider.

In the context of public law proceedings, case law provides guidance as to what is meant by the term 'participation' and what the ramifications are for looked-after children in terms of their participation in public law proceedings. This is most clearly described by J. Booth in her judgment in the case of Re H (A Minor) (Guardian ad Litem: Requirement) [1994] Fam 11 when she said:

> Participating as a party, in my judgment, means much more than instructing a solicitor as to his own views. The child enters the arena among other adult parties. He may give evidence and he may be cross-examined. He will hear other parties, including in this case his parents, give evidence and be cross-examined. He must be able to give instructions on many different matters as the case goes through its stages and to make decisions as need arises. The child is exposed to and not protected in these procedures... The child will also be bound to abide by the rules which govern other parties, including rules as to confidentiality.

REASONS FOR THE INCREASED EMPHASIS ON PARTICIPATION

The main contributory factors leading to an increased emphasis on participation can be loosely labelled as the four 'C's, namely: changing conceptions of childhood; children's rights; citizenship; and consumerism (Alderson, 2000; Franklin, 2002; Prout, 2005; Roche, 1999; Sinclair, 2004). In brief, our views of the capacities and competencies of children have been challenged by the emergence of new ways of thinking about childhood in which emphasis is placed on children as people, as individuals able to contribute, to influence, to share responsibility, and to form a view (Alderson, 2000; Fawcett et al., 2004; James et al., 1998; James & James, 2004; Prout, 2005).

Furthermore, such views of children are seen by some as a fundamental prerequisite for the full realisation of children's rights, and particularly their participation rights, in practice (Alderson, 2000; Fawcett et al., 2004; James & James, 2004; Roche, 1999, 2002).

At the political level, and as part of the government's aim to deal with the causes and consequences of social exclusion, emphasis has been placed on citizenship through an increase and improvement in participatory mechanisms (SEU, 2001, 2003a, 2003b). Given that looked-after children are identified as one group at risk of experiencing social exclusion, it is not surprising that there has been a concerted effort at developing their opportunities for participation. This is reflected, for example, in the Quality Protects Programme (1998) and core policy documents (CYPU, 2001). In the Introduction to *Learning to Listen* (CYPU, 2001, p. 2), for example, it states that

> [the] government wants children and young people to have more opportunities to get involved in the design, provision and evaluation of policies and services that affect them or which they use... Ultimately that will produce better outcomes for children and young people, as well as stronger communities.

This thrust is further reflected in individual services for looked-after children with policy and practice developments noted particularly in health (DH, 2004;

NCB, 2005); education (Children Act, 2004); and day-to-day care (Adoption and Children Act, 2002; VCC, 2004). As noted, underpinning this approach is, firstly, a desire to foster a culture of citizenship (Neale, 2004; Roche, 1999). Within this framework the benefits of participation are described in terms of the social benefits for the individual (which include enhancing children's protection, social skills, and self-esteem through the opportunity to influence, make choices, understand their own needs and wants, communicate problems, needs, and wishes, and to debate (see Alderson, 2000; Sinclair, 2004; Sinclair & Franklin, 2000) the social and economic benefits for society generally (SEU, 2003a, 2003b).

Secondly, there is a desire to provide for greater accountability and relevance of service delivery and provision by increasing user involvement (DH, 2004). In this context, the benefits of participation lie in the provision of opportunities to make representation with the aim of highlighting deficiencies in service provision, improving their quality, and in preventing institutional abuse. This is of particular importance to looked-after children given, firstly, the findings of several inquiries highlighting the abuse of looked-after children in residential care and their inability to represent their interests by a lack of participatory mechanisms (Fawcett et al., 2004); and, secondly, research drawing attention to the difficulties of young adults leaving care in terms of inadequate social service support and lack of recourse to participatory mechanisms to make known their difficulties and requirements (Broad, 2005).

For looked-after children there are two main expectations emerging from this emphasis on participation. Firstly, they should expect that their views, experiences, and perspectives are going to be properly elicited (regardless of their age and by whatever means they are expressed), and, secondly, that their voices will be given the same degree of validity, significance, visibility, and importance as the views and perspectives of the adults involved in the children's lives (John, 2003). In considering how far these expectations are met in reality, the chapter now considers what mechanisms and provisions exist and how successful they have been.

MECHANISMS AND PROVISIONS FOR THE PARTICIPATION OF LOOKED-AFTER CHILDREN IN PUBLIC LAW PROCEEDINGS

In terms of legal provisions for this group of children, the legislation imposes a statutory requirement on the court and social workers to consider, as part of the welfare checklist, 'the ascertainable wishes and feelings' of children in the light of their age and understanding (Children Act, 1989, section 1(3) (a), Children Order (NI), 1995, section 3(3)). These particular participation rights are part of a broader spectrum (Fortin, 2003; Roche, 2002; Winter & Connolly, 1996) which, under the Children Act (2004), now also includes provisions for the participation of children in need (section 53), and under section 122, Adoption and Children Act (2002), children involved in private law proceedings.

Under Scottish children's legislation, the legal requirement to ascertain a child's wishes and feelings is more demanding in that, under section 6(b), Children (Scotland) Act (1995), 'a person making "any major decision" in exercising parental responsibilities or rights must consider a child's views' (Tisdall et al., 2002, p. 387), and, under section 16(2) (a, b, c), taking account of the child's age and maturity shall, so far as practicable, give the child an opportunity to indicate whether it wishes to express views, and if it does so wish, give an opportunity to express them, also having regard to such views as might be expressed (Raitt, 2004; Tisdall et al., 2004).

As indicated earlier, these participation rights are reflective of the principles contained in three other relevant pieces of legislation, namely: Articles 3 and 4, European Convention on the Exercise of Children's Rights (1996); Articles 12, 13, 14, and 15, UNCRC (1989), and Articles 6 and 8, Human Rights Act (1998). These frameworks all provide for children the opportunity to have their views heard in proceedings about them (Lowe, 2001; Munby, 2004). Within these legal frameworks there is also a series of mechanisms by which the participation of looked-after children in public law proceedings is secured.

Firstly, each looked-after child automatically has party status (Masson & Winn-Oakley, 1999). Secondly, and as a corollary to this, all looked-after children have rights to representation encompassing 'their right to be represented by a Guardian Ad Litem and a Solicitor unless the court considers this to be unnecessary' (Masson & Winn-Oakley, 1999). This system, which operates in England, Wales, and Northern Ireland, is described as a 'tandem model' (Bilson & White, 2005; Masson, 2003; Timms, 1995) and is, according to Timms (1995, p. 81), 'one of the most comprehensive and sophisticated systems in any country'.

Under this system, it is the role of the solicitor to 'act as an advocate for the child ... based upon the child's stated wishes and feelings' (Timms, 1995, p. 104), whereas the role of the guardian ad litem is to both ascertain the wishes and feelings of the child as well as to make an assessment as to what is in the best interests of a child. As noted by Timms (1995, p. 104), when 'what the child wants may not be what the child needs [there is a] divergence between the views of a child and the guardian ad litem'. In such cases there is the possibility of the child and the guardian ad litem being separately represented. A central consideration for solicitors operating under the systems in England, Wales, and Northern Ireland is therefore the question of whether a child is competent to give instruction to a solicitor on his or her own behalf.

In Scotland, there are some similarities for the representation of children in public law cases in that, under s. 41(1) (b), Children Act (Scotland) (1995), Safeguarders can be appointed to secure the interests of children in public law cases and carry out a similar function to guardians ad litem (Hill et al., 2003; Tisdall et al., 2002), but it is less likely that both a solicitor and a Safeguarder will act together. It is apparent that there is a range of mechanisms and provisions regarding the participation of looked-after children in public law proceedings. A crucial issue is their effectiveness. In examining this, the chapter now considers the results of research in which the views of looked-after children were sought.

EFFECTIVENESS OF EXISTING MECHANISMS AND PROVISIONS REGARDING THE PARTICIPATION OF LOOKED-AFTER CHILDREN IN PUBLIC LAW CASES

As indicated in the introduction to this chapter, there is a range of research available which draws attention to the views and experiences of looked-after children who have been the subject of public law proceedings. This research has sought the views of varying numbers of looked-after children ranging from 8 children between the ages of 7 and 13 years (Clark & Sinclair, 1999), through to 20, 28, and 47 children of the same age-ranges in the respective studies by Masson and Winn-Oakley (1999), McCausland (2000), and Ruegger (2001a, 2001b) and, finally, in the study by Timms and Thoburn (2003), the views of 607 looked-after children were obtained. These children ranged from ages 6–18 years with the vast majority falling between the ages of 10–17 years.

Given that we are concerned with the participation rights of these children in the public law court process, the results of this research are best organised around the operational principles of the UNCRC (1989) which include 'being informed; expressing a view; influencing the decision maker; being the main decider' (O'Quigley, 2000, p. 33; see Alderson, 2000; Timmis, 2001). In terms of 'being informed', the research indicates that looked-after children have had varying experiences of receiving information (itself of varying quality) regarding the whole public law court process (Timms & Thoburn, 2003) including: access to leaflets, videos, and other information (Masson & Winn-Oakley, 1999); the roles of the solicitor and guardian ad litem (Clark & Sinclair, 1999; Masson & Winn-Oakley, 1999; McCausland, 2000), for whom the guardian ad litem works (McCausland, 2000); how and why the roles of the solicitor and guardian ad litem differ (Clark & Sinclair, 1999; Masson & Winn-Oakley, 1999); their right to attend court (Clarke, 1995; Masson & Winn-Oakley, 1999); the outcomes of continuing hearings (Clarke, 1995); their access to reports including the guardian's own report (Masson & Winn-Oakley, 1999); and the sharing of the reports with the child's parents (Ruegger, 2001a).

The net result for looked-after children of varying practices and standards of information-sharing by professionals is that there are children who, firstly, feel that they did not receive enough information; who, secondly, did not get a chance to go to court who would have liked to; and, who, thirdly, would have liked the opportunity to meet the judge but did not (Timms & Thoburn, 2003). These results are in spite of developments to improve upon and standardise practice in the area of providing information for looked-after children. In England, for example, looked-after children have, since 2001, had access to information packs called 'Power Packs' (Masson, 2003). While there has been some criticism of the

'Power Packs' (NAGALRO, 2003), their continuing use has been referred to in a positive manner in the second action plan of the Department for Constitutional Affairs (2004). A similar development, with the introduction of Power Packs, has occurred more recently in Northern Ireland (NIGALA, 2005).

With regards to 'expressing a view', the research indicates that looked-after children felt listened to and understood (Clark & Sinclair, 1999; McCausland, 2000; Ruegger, 2001a, 2001b). In Clark and Sinclair's study (1999), comment is made that the children knew that the guardian ad litem was there for them, and appreciated the careful timing of interviews as well as the unhurried nature of the discussion. Other research highlights how some looked-after children were denied an opportunity to express an opinion in the sense that they hardly ever saw (Masson & Winn-Oakley, 1999), or never saw, their solicitor (McCausland, 2000), and did not attend court or meet the judge involved in their case (Timms & Thoburn, 2003). Yet other research describes varying practices concerning the ways in which the wishes and feelings of looked-after children have been incorporated into court reports. James et al. (2004) indicate that some guardians ad litem include quotes from the child while others filter the child's account through the lens of welfare considerations.

Furthermore, research also highlights that children felt comfortable expressing their wishes and feelings to their guardian ad litem, but had little knowledge of what happened to those expressed wishes and feelings afterwards. Some children expressed shock, shame, distress, or anger (Ruegger, 2001a, 2001b) that their parents had gained access to their wishes and feelings via the guardian ad litem's report. Other research highlights the careful attention paid by these professionals in agreeing with a child what aspects of his or her wishes and feelings he or she wished to be included in the report (Ruegger, 2001a, 2001b).

More recent research (Bilson & White, 2005) has argued that guardians ad litem have given little attention to the wishes and feelings of looked-after children in favour of concentrating on the issue of what is in a child's best interests. Their key argument (as articulated in other work, notably James et al., 2004; Masson, 2003; Raitt, 2004; Tisdall et al., 2004) is that the predominance of the 'welfare' model has eclipsed a more 'rights'-based approach in work with looked-after children.

In considering the dual themes 'influencing the decision maker' (who is ultimately a magistrate or a judge) and 'being the main decider', available research generally examines two issues: the attendance of looked-after children at court hearings; and the separate representation of looked-after children who have been deemed competent to give their solicitor instruction on their own behalf. With regards to attendance at court, a consistent finding from the research is that children have expressed a strong desire to attend court but, in the main, were not consulted about whether they wished to attend court and often, therefore, did not actually attend (Masson & Winn-Oakley, 1999; Ruegger, 2001a, 2001b; Timms & Thoburn, 2003). This reflects the approach taken by some in the judiciary where the attendance of children is discouraged (Hale, 2003; Roche, 2002).

With regards to the issue of separate representation, it is, of course, the duty of the solicitor to determine the competence of children to give instruction on their own behalf. In this role they must consult with the guardian ad litem. Ultimately in cases where there is a disagreement, the decision regarding competence is that of the court (Roche, 2002). Research by Sawyer (1995a, 1995b, 2000) indicates concerns about the assessment of the competence of looked-after children. Stevens (2001, p. 89) argues that it appears from Sawyer's research that

> in reaching their decisions Solicitors relied heavily on their own 'feel' for the child's maturity, the benefit or disadvantage to that child of being involved in this way in the proceedings and their own beliefs as to the right of children to be so represented.

In addition, it seemed that there were 'varying attitudes, value judgments and unquestioned influences affecting their practice' (Stevens, 2001, p. 89).

ROOM FOR IMPROVEMENT

In summary, the research indicates that, despite much progress, the voices of looked-after children in public law proceedings remain constrained, if not, in some instances, silent, and that children's involvement in decisions made about them (and thereby their participation rights) have not been fully recognised or implemented (Franklin, 2002; Hendrick, 2003; James et al., 2004; Masson, 2002, 2003; Roche, 2002). In explaining the reasons for this, writers have highlighted two possible contributory factors: firstly, constructions of children/childhood inherent in recent child-care legislation; and, secondly, the constructions of children/childhood inherent in the mindset, social processes, and practices of legal and social care professionals.

With regards to constructions of childhood inherent in child-care legislation, it has been argued that a paternalist perspective is apparent by an overwhelming emphasis on the welfare of the child, that is the provision for and the protection of the child involved (Fortin, 2003; Fox Harding, 1997; Franklin, 2002; Hendrick, 2003; Roche, 2002). Within this discourse, certain aspects of children's rights are prioritised, namely their rights to 'education, health, shelter and a minimum standard of living' (Franklin, 2002, p. 21). These welfare or protection/provision rights are prioritised 'even if this involves restricting children's choices and behaviour' (Franklin, 2002, p. 21). Furthermore, accompanying the welfare discourse is a focus on certain characteristics of children depicting them as 'passive, dependent, vulnerable and in need of protection' (Franklin, 2002, p. 28). The result is an accompanying lack of emphasis on the capacities and competencies of children in their various social settings as well as less focus on their citizenship/participation rights (Bilson & White, 2005; Masson, 2003; Neale, 2004; Winter, 2006).

Similar themes are evident in the views of professionals regarding children and the concept of childhood. There have been many hotly contested debates about when and if children are capable of being involved in decision-making on issues concerning them and what, if at all, their participation rights may look like. Alderson (2000, pp. 65–71) organises these different 'beliefs and feelings' into two groups: those who in principle believe it is the right thing to do and that there are benefits in consulting children; and those who in principle believe it is the wrong thing to do and that there are potential harms in consulting children. She and other writers (James & James, 2004; James & Prout, 1990/1997; Mayall, 2002; Prout, 2005) have drawn attention to the underlying influence of broad theoretical frameworks regarding the concept of childhood in forming these views. Two broad theoretical frameworks are of relevance here: those based in psychology and those based in sociology.

Research has highlighted that social care professionals' views and practices of, and in their work with, children stem from the 'taken for granted' meanings of childhood and understandings of children evident in the Piagetian model of child development (James & James, 2004; James et al., 2004; Taylor, 2004). The Piagetian model is a psychological one in which the social development and competence of a child are inextricably linked to its biological development which proceeds in age-related, sequential, and invariant stages. While there are benefits to this model in terms of addressing the welfare needs of children, the model constrains the participation rights of children because of its insistence on age-related and biologically driven competence which presents 'a deficit model in relation to children, concentrating attention on their limitations and lack of competence' (Taylor, 2004, p. 229).

Research by James et al. (2004) highlights the influence of these views of childhood on children's guardians concluding that children's participation rights are constrained both by the predominance of the 'welfare rights' of children and the use, by practitioners, of a Piagetian child development model which cements rather than challenges this particular approach. As a result, they conclude that

> welfare professionals are unable to acknowledge sufficiently, if at all, what being a child means in terms of that child's experience, agency, and personhood. They cannot therefore enable fully the voice of the child to be heard in family proceedings.
>
> (James et al., 2004, p. 13).

Other research (Sawyer, 1995a, 1995b) has highlighted that solicitors, in considering the competence of looked-after children to give instruction directly and on their own behalf,

> relied heavily on their own 'feel' for the child's maturity, the benefit or disadvantage to that child of being involved in this way in the proceedings and their own beliefs as to the right of children to be so represented.
>
> (Stevens, 2001, p. 89)

In their assessments, age was a factor although not the only factor.

An overview of the role of the judiciary in helping or hindering the participation of children in court proceedings reveals that they too, in general, are also bound, in their decision-making and judgments, by similar views of children and the concept of childhood as held by social care staff (James et al., 2004; Masson, 2003; Raitt, 2004; Roche, 2002). This is illustrated by reference to examples of case law (see Stevens, 2001, for a review). In the case of Re S, for example (quoted at the beginning of the chapter), a commonly held 'world-view' of children is depicted. Furthermore, although, the judgment highlights that tests regarding competence 'are framed with reference to the child's understanding, not his age', the judgment also goes on to state that where 'any sound judgment on these issues calls for insight and imagination which only maturity and experience can bring, both the court and the solicitor will be slow to conclude that the child's understanding is sufficient'.

WAYS FORWARD

As outlined above, there are various social structures and social processes which act to constrain the very voices of the children with whose lives the court is concerned. In seeking to outline ways in which the situation could be improved it is important not to diminish the progress which has been made to date at the levels of the law, policy, research, and practice. However, a multi-faceted response is required by professionals working with looked-after children in public law proceedings (James et al., 2004; Masson, 2003) if we are to reach the situation where the voice of the child is elevated to the same level, and acquires the same visibility, as the voices of so many other professionals who make comment on children involved in public law proceedings. The prerequisites to this approach are outlined below.

Ways of Thinking

Firstly, it is incumbent on all those working with children to become conversant in the many theoretical approaches regarding the concept and nature of childhood. Particularly relevant are the newer sociological frameworks which seek to highlight the fact that 'competence grows through experience rather than with age or ability and very young children can have profound understanding' (Alderson, 2000, p. 131). As well as this, the same frameworks draw attention to the fact that children possess social agency, that is, the ability to construct, determine, and negotiate their social experiences as opposed to being the passive recipient of the input and actions of others.

Research underpinned by these frameworks has demonstrated the abilities, competencies, and capacities of children in a range of settings (Alderson, 2000; Clark & Moss, 2001; Hutchby & Moran-Ellis, 1998a, 1998b; VCC/NCB, 2004). This provides a challenge to our preconceptions about who we think children are, what we think they are capable of, and how we determine our relationships with them and they with us. As argued by James and James (2004, pp. 213–214), this allows for the recognition that 'children are not just social actors, playing a multitude of roles in relation to the increasing range of adults with whom their lives mesh as they move through their own childhoods . . . they are also social agents', that is, individuals making a difference, having an impact.

Taylor (2004, p. 225) argues that professionals should 'engage more meaningfully with the child development literature and use it in a critical and reflexive way in their practice'. This position is supported by Alderson (2000, p. 65) who argues that 'it is vital to examine the beliefs which encourage adults to consult children or stop them from doing so'.

Alderson's work (2000) also highlights that, accompanying the critical review outlined above, it would be helpful for professionals to embark on a similar process with regards to the concept and practice of participation as it concerns children. It is well documented that the meanings, purposes, and perceived benefits of participation are varied (Hill et al., 2004; Sinclair, 2004), and it must be assumed that there is a similar divergence of professional opinion in public law proceedings as to why, how, if, when, where the participation of children should be encouraged. Hale (2003, p. 1) draws attention to this from the perspective of the judiciary when she states 'courts have to distinguish between children as witnesses of fact, and children as participants in the decision-making about their futures'. She goes on to highlight the pitfalls and benefits of the participation of children in court proceedings. Of the benefits, she states that the court

> then sees the child as a real person, rather than the object of other's people's disputes or concerns. Stereotypical notions about children, their needs, their priorities, their qualities and their characteristics are much harder to retain when you're confronted with a real character in front of you. And the child, as is frequently pointed out, is the expert about his or her own life.

It is on these two foundation blocks, firstly, changed perceptions of children and, secondly, the development of a common understanding of participation, that professionals involved in public law proceedings may be able to build new ways of further elevating the voices of the 'looked-after' children. We need to move beyond the current situation in which, as noted by Roche (2002, p. 68): 'the child who is the very reason for the court sitting need not necessarily be heard or seen directly'.

Ways of Working

Our ways of working and responding to this issue should change, premised on the principles outlined above and that:

- children have social agency;
- childhood is socially constructed;
- children of a variety of ages have their story to tell;

- children can express their views, experiences, and wishes if given access to a variety of methods and objects chosen by themselves to communicate these same views;
- there is benefit and merit for children in being involved in decisions made concerning them.

Of particular concern here is to engage with new and dynamic ways of presenting the child's voice in court proceedings. A useful approach, founded on the principles above, is the 'Mosaic Approach' (Clark & Moss, 2001) which has been used to gain the views, feelings, and perspectives of younger children. This represents a multi-method model that incorporates 'a range of symbolic ways' for ascertaining the views and perspectives of children (Clark & Moss, 2001, p. 6), beyond just talking and which, for example, include the use of photographs, video clips, role-play, and drawings. Secondly, it is a participatory model in that the choice of object/activity through which to express views is led by and talked to by the child. Thirdly, it is reflexive in that it engages the listener in an active process with the child which moves beyond just listening to reflecting 'together on children's perspectives, led by the children themselves'. The end product is a portfolio or mosaic comprising of many components representing the perspectives of a child, the interpretation of which is led by the child. A similar model and based on similar principles is outlined in work by Lancaster (2004).

These methods should come as no surprise to those working with looked-after children in public law proceedings in that there is evidence of some guardians ad litem using a range of techniques, not dissimilar to those above, to ascertain the views of these children (Clark & Sinclair, 1999; Norris, 2001). Beyond the advantages to the approach outlined above, it is argued here that there is great potential in the use of such an approach for improving the participation of looked-after children of a variety of ages in public law proceedings via an individual multi-media portfolio.

The particular features and benefits of the multi-media portfolio are described below using the model of participation outlined earlier and including sharing information, expressing a view, and influencing the decision-maker/being the main decider (Alderson, 2000). The model presents greater scope for the development of new ways of sharing information with children about the legal process and the roles of differing professionals within that process. This could include, for younger looked-after children, the development of a set of cartoon characters viewed via the internet or television along the lines of those available in other media campaigns for young children (see Media Initiative for Children, 'Together in the Park', 2005, downloaded from www.mifc-pii.org, November 2005). It could include the use of live role-plays with 'looked-after' children (in and outside court settings) or via actors in video clips (presented via DVD) to share information with older looked-after children about the court process.

In terms of expressing a view, the model encourages a fuller exploration of the wishes *and feelings* of children by its multi-method, child-initiated, and reflexive approach. The issue of a looked-after child's feelings is an important, under-discussed, and under-researched area. Recent debates in the House of Commons regarding the Children Act (2004) make reference to the importance of a child's feelings when it was argued

> Virtually all children will invariably be able to say how they feel. Feelings of anxiety, anger, love, loathing and uncertainty in a child are quite different from a wish that a child might express for this or that particular thing... In many situations it is simply not possible to reach a conclusion about what maybe in a child's best interests until you find out what the child is thinking.
>
> (Lords, Hansard Text for 15 July 2004, 2407 (15–35), Column 1477, re Amendment 40)

Furthermore, its multi-method format presents the opportunity for the proper documentation of such work as it remains a concern that conversations with children regarding their wishes, feelings, and perspectives are not properly (if at all) documented on the case files and reports of social workers (Laming, 2003) or guardians (Bilson & White, 2005; James et al., 2004), who often filter the wishes and feelings of a child through welfare considerations. The end result, the multi-media portfolio, would comprise a compilation of children's own work regarding their wishes and feelings. This could include the use of video clips, photographs, drawings, or paintings to be displayed alongside the child's own interpretation of their work. The portfolio could come in the form of computer PDF files, a PowerPoint format, or on a DVD, for example.

The use of a multi-method and multi-media portfolio could provide a productive focus for an informal meeting between children and the involved judge. This could be facilitated by a guardian or solicitor. The meeting would allow children, if they wish, an opportunity to present, directly to the judge, the content of their own work regarding their own wishes and feelings and to discuss the same. Such an approach would go some way to allowing children the opportunity to participate using methods with which they are comfortable and which may also serve to demonstrate their level of competence and insight into their circumstances beyond what is commonly expected and beyond the straitjacket of the court report.

It may also therefore challenge our conceptions of childhood competence, suspend our disbelief and suspicion regarding the validity of children's accounts, and, as Alderson (1993, p. 158) argues, enable us to countenance the claim that

> competence is more influenced by the social context and the child's experience than by innate ability and to respect children means we must not think in sharp dichotomies of wise adult/immature child, infallible doctor/ignorant patient, but to see wisdom and uncertainty shared among people of varying ages and experiences.

Ways of Responding

With regard to developing new ways of responding, the court report format could be amended to include a section entitled 'The Participation of a Child in Court Proceedings', itself divided into subheadings. These could deal with, firstly, 'sharing information' and allow for professionals to be held to account for what information has been shared with a child, how and by what method it was shared, and what the child's understanding of that information was/is.

Secondly, there could be a subsection on 'expressing a view'. In the absence of any direct input from a looked-after child, the work of those charged with eliciting the wishes and feelings of looked-after children could be the subject of greater evaluation with critical analyses of exactly how the wishes and feelings of looked-after children have been elicited and by what methods; how these have been presented in the court process, whether they have had an impact on decision-making and if so, in what way, and if not, why not?

Thirdly, under the subsection 'influencing the decision-maker/being the main decider', details should be given of efforts to encourage and facilitate a child's attendance at court if that is what he or she wishes. Furthermore, multi-disciplinary discussion needs to take place about definitions and parameters around the term 'participation' and how this could be operationalised in public law proceedings since it is evident that the term reflects a process beyond mere attendance at court. A good starting point could be on research which evidences children's accounts (as well as others involved in their lives) of the benefits and pitfalls of their experiences of participation and what models of participation have most successfully underpinned practice.

At the same time, it would be fruitful for both legal and social work professionals to enter, via a multi-disciplinary forum, a period of critical debate and reflection about measures of competence, the theories of childhood upon which they are premised, and which approach or combination of approaches most usefully and successfully pave the way for greater participation of looked-after children in public law proceedings.

Any good practice guidelines which emerge should start from a positive position regarding the participation rights of looked-after children in public law proceed-ings, starting with considering what they wish they could and should be involved in rather than what we think they could or should not be part of. Such ideological repositioning would be reflected in any subsequently emerging good practice guidelines. These could start with the following:

- with children's consent, any work undertaken by them regarding their wishes and feelings should be made available to the judge in the form of a multi-media portfolio;
- all looked-after children are offered the opportunity to visit the court and meet the judge with the support of a person of their choice – the focus of this meeting could be information gathering for the children and information receiving for the judge in which children are offered the opportunity to share their multi-media portfolio regarding their wishes and feelings;

- consideration is given to those aspects of continuing proceedings that children could be involved in if that is what they wish;
- age is not used as the benchmark to determine any of the above.

The importance and significance of this to professionals and children alike is summed up by Raitt (2004) in her work on the exercise of judicial discretion in private law proceedings, when she states that not only

> does a Judge's choice of method of ascertaining a child's views largely dictate the impact that those views can have on proceedings, but, more importantly, it shapes the child's experience of participation in these proceedings. Ascertaining a child's views should not be reduced to a procedural formality. If, as many have convincingly argued, the judicial interpretation of the welfare of the child ultimately takes precedence over expression of wishes and feelings, then the child's experience of participation becomes all the more critical to that child's sense of being heard.

CONCLUSION

This chapter has set out what is known concerning the participation of looked-after children in public law proceedings. It is argued that while there have been some important developments in this area, there is still room for improvement. Of particular concern is the continuing lack of visibility and lack of involvement of this group of children in the court process. In order to address this, a multi-layered response is required, challenging the structures, processes, attitudes, and views which act together to constrain the voices of looked-after children. As part of this response, the benefits of a particular model, namely the Mosaic Approach, have been discussed. It is argued that the use of this model, to provide a multi-media portfolio of a child's wishes and feelings to the court process, would enable the lives of looked-after children to be in the limelight for positive rather than negative reasons because of its focus on the competencies, capacities, and perspectives of children rather than just their needs. It is hoped that, by increasing the visibility of children's perspectives in the court process, there will be an accompanying paradigm shift both in the ways in which children are viewed by all involved professionals and the ways in which their participation rights are construed and acted upon.

REFERENCES

Alderson, P. (1993). *Children's Consent to Surgery*. Buckingham: Open University Press.

Alderson, P. (2000). *Young Children's Rights: Exploring Beliefs, Principles and Practice*. London: Jessica Kingsley/Save the Children.

Aldgate, J. (2001). *The Children Act Now: Messages from Research*. London: The Stationery Office.

Bebbington, A.C., & Miles, J.B. (1989). The background of children who enter local authority care. *British Journal of Social Work*, **19**, 349–368.

Bilson, A., & White, S. (2005). Representing children's views and best interests in court: An international comparison. *Child Abuse Review*, **14**, 220–239.

Broad, B. (2005). *Improving the Health and Well Being of Young People Leaving Care*. Lyme Regis: Russell House Publishing.

Children and Young People's Unit (2001). *Learning to Listen: Core Principles for the Involvement of Children and Young People*. London: The Stationery Office.

Clark, A., & Moss, P. (2001). *Listening to Young Children: The Mosaic Approach*. London: National Children's Bureau.

Clark, A., & Sinclair, R. (1999). *The Child in Focus: The Evolving Role of the Guardian ad Litem*. London: National Children's Bureau.

Clarke, D. (1995). Whose case is it anyway? The representation of the older child in care proceedings. Thesis, University of Sussex.

Cousins, W., & Monteith, M. (2002). *The Lives of Younger Looked After Children: Preliminary Findings from the Multiple Placements Project*. Belfast: Institute of Child Care Research, Queen's University.

Cousins, W., Monteith, M., Larkin, E., & Percy, A. (2003). *The Care Careers of Younger Looked After Children: Findings from the Multiple Placements Project*. Belfast: Institute of Child Care Research, Queen's University.

Department for Constitutional Affairs (2004). *Involving Children and Young People: Action Plan 2004–2005*. London: DCA.

Department for Education and Skills (2005). *Statistics of Education: Children Looked After by Local Authorities Year Ending 31 March 2004*, vol. 1: *Commentary and Tables*. London: DfES.

Department of Health (1998). *Modernising Social Services*. London: The Stationery Office.

Department of Health (2004). *National Service Framework for Children, Young People and Maternity Services*. London: The Stationery Office.

Department of Health, Social Services, and Public Safety (2004). *Community Statistics: 1 April 2003–31 March 2004*. Belfast: DHSSPSNI.

Dixon, J., & Stein, M. (2005). *Leaving Care: Throughcare and Aftercare in Scotland*. London: Jessica Kingsley.

Fawcett, B., Featherstone, B., & Goddard, J. (2004). *Contemporary Child Care Policy and Practice*. Basingstoke: Palgrave Macmillan.

Fortin, J. (2003). *Children's Rights and the Developing Law*. London: Lexis Nexis UK.

Fox Harding, L. (1997). *Perspectives in Child Care*. London: Longman.

Franklin, B. (ed.) (2002). *The New Handbook of Children's Rights. Comparative Policy and Practice*. London: Routledge.

Hale, B. (2003). It's my life you're practising with. *Association of Lawyers for Children Newsletter*, Issue **30**, 1–11.

Harker, R., Dobel-Ober, D., Berridge, D., & Sinclair, R. (2004). *Taking Care of Education. An Evaluation of the Education of Looked After Children*. London: National Children's Bureau.

Head, A. (1998). The child's voice in child and family social work decision making: The perspective of a guardian ad litem. *Child and Family Social Work*, **3**, 189–196.

Hendrick, H. (2003). *Child Welfare: Historical Dimensions, Contemporary Debate*. London: The Policy Press.

Hill, C.M., & Watkins, J. (2003). Statutory health assessments for looked after children: What do they achieve? *Child: Care, Health and Development*, **29**(1), 3–13.

Hill, M., Davis, J., Prout, A., & Tisdall, K. (eds) (2004). Children, young people and participation. *Children and Society*, **18**(2), 77–176.

Hill, M., Lockyer, A., Morton, P., Batchelor, S., & Scott, J. (2003). Safeguarding children's interests in welfare proceedings: The Scottish experience. *Journal of Social Welfare and Family Law*, **25**(1), 1–21.

Hunt, J., & Murch, M. (1990). *Speaking Out for Children*. London: The Children's Society.

Hutchby, I., & Moran-Ellis, J. (1998a). Situating children's social competence. In I. Hutchby & J. Moran-Ellis (eds), *Children and Social Competence: Arenas of Social Action*. London: Falmer Press, pp. 7–26.

Hutchby, I., & Moran-Ellis, J. (eds) (1998b). *Children and Social Competence: Arenas of Social Action*. London: Falmer Press.

Jackson, S., & Thomas, N. (1999). *On the Move Again?* Ilford: Barnardo's.

James, A. (1998). Foreword. In I. Hutchby & J. Moran-Ellis (eds), *Children and Social Competence: Arenas of Social Action*. London: Falmer Press, pp. vii–x.

James, A., & James, A.L. (2004). *Constructing Childhood: Theory, Policy and Social Practice*. Basingstoke: Palgrave Macmillan.

James, A., & Prout, A. (1990/1997). *Constructing and Reconstructing Childhood: Contemporary Issues in the Sociological Study of Childhood*. Basingstoke: Falmer Press.

James, A.L., James, A., & McNamee, S. (2003). Constructing children's welfare in family proceedings. *Family Law*, **33**, 889–898.

James, A.L., James, A., & McNamee, S. (2004). Research – turn down the volume?: Not hearing children in family proceedings. *Child and Family Law Quarterly*, **16**(2), 189–207.

James, A., Jenks, C., & Prout, A. (1998). *Theorising Childhood*. Cambridge: Polity Press.

John, M. (2003). *Children's Rights and Power. Charging up for a New Century*. London: Jessica Kingsley.

Laming, L. (2003). *The Victoria Climbie Inquiry*. London: The Stationery Office.

Lancaster, Y.P. (2004). Listening to young children: Promoting the 'voices' of children under the age of eight. In Rt Hon. Lord Justice Thorpe & J. Cadbury (eds), *Hearing the Children*. Bristol: Jordan Publishing Ltd.

Lowe, N. (2001). Children's participation in the family justice system: Translating principles into practice. *Child and Family Law Quarterly*, **13**(2), 137–166.

Masson, J. (2002). Case commentary: Securing human rights for children and young people in secure accommodation. Re K (a child) (secure accommodation: right to liberty) and Re C (secure accommodation order: representation). *Child and Family Law Quarterly*, **14**(1), 77–101.

Masson, J. (2003). Paternalism, participation and placation: Young people's experiences of representation in child protection proceedings in England and Wales. In J. Dewar & S. Parker (eds), *Family Law: Processes, Practices and Pressures*. Oxford: Hart Publishing.

Masson, J., & Winn-Oakley, M. (1999). *Out of Hearing: The Representation by Guardians ad Litem and Solicitors in Public Law Proceedings*. London: John Wiley & Sons, Ltd.

Mather, M. (ed.) (2002). Special issue: Promoting children's health. *Adoption and Fostering*, **26**(4), 2–112.

Mayall, B. (2002). *Towards Sociology for Childhood*. Buckingham: Open University Press.

McCausland, J. (2000). *Guarding Children's Interests. The Contribution of Guardians ad Litem in Court Proceedings*. London: The Children's Society.

Morris, J. (2000). *Having Someone Who Cares? Barriers to Change in the Public Care of Children*. London: National Children's Bureau.

Munby, J. (2004). Making sure the child is heard: Part one – human rights. *Family Law*, **34**, 338–358.

Murray, C., & Hallett, C. (2000). Young people's participation in decisions affecting their welfare. *Childhood*, **7**(1), 11–25.

NAGALRO (2003). *Response to the Consultation on Power Packs*. London: NAGALRO.

National Children's Bureau (2003). *Let's Get Positive: Challenging Negative Images of Young People in Care*. London: National Children's Bureau.

National Children's Bureau/Department for Education and Skills (2005). *Healthy Care Programme Handbook*. London: National Children's Bureau.

Neale, B. (ed.) (2004). *Young Children's Citizenship*. York: Joseph Rowntree Foundation.

NIGALA (Northern Ireland Guardian ad Litem Agency) (2005). *Annual Report 2004–2005*. Belfast: NIGALA.

Norris, G. (2001). Direct work with children. In M. Ruegger (ed.), *Hearing the Voice of the Child: The Representation of Children's Interests in Public Law Proceedings*. Lyme Regis: Russell House Publishing, pp. 44–55.

Oliver, C., Owen, C., Statham, J., & Moss, P. (2001). *Local Authority Variance on Indicators Concerning Child Protection and Children Looked After*. London: Institute of Education.

O'Quigley, A. (2000). *Listening to Children's Voices: The Findings and Recommendations of Recent Research*. London: Joseph Rowntree Foundation.

Prout, A. (2005). *The Future of Childhood*. Abingdon: Routledge Falmer.

Raitt, F.E. (2004). Judicial discretion and methods of ascertaining the views of a child. *Child and Family Law Quarterly*, **16**(2), 151–164.

Roche, J. (1999). Children: Rights, participation and citizenship. *Childhood*, **6**(4), 475–493.

Roche, J. (2002). The Children Act 1989 and children's rights: A critical reassessment. In B. Franklin (ed.), *The New Handbook of Children's Rights. Comparative Policy and Practice*. London: Routledge, pp. 60–80.

Ruegger, M. (ed.) (2001a). *Hearing the Voice of the Child. The Representation of Children's Interests in Public Law Proceedings*. Lyme Regis: Russell House Publishing.

Ruegger, M. (2001b). Children's experiences of the guardian ad litem service and public law proceedings. In M. Ruegger (ed.), *Hearing the Voice of the Child. The Representation of Children's Interests in Public Law Proceedings*. Lyme Regis: Russell House Publishing, pp. 33–43.

Sawyer, C. (1995a). *The Rise and Fall of the Third Party: Solicitors' Assessments of the Competence of Children to Participate in Family Proceedings*. Oxford: Centre for Socio-legal Studies, Wolfson College, University of Oxford.

Sawyer, C. (1995b). The competence of children to participate in family proceedings. *Child and Family Law Quarterly*, **7**(4), 180–195.

Sawyer, C. (2000). *Rules, Roles and Relationships: The Structure and Function of Child Representation and Welfare Within Family Proceedings*. Oxford: Centre for Socio-legal Studies, Wolfson College, University of Oxford.

SENSP (Scottish Executive National Statistics Office) (2004). *Children's Social Work Statistics 2003–04*. Edinburgh: Scottish Executive National Statistics Office.

Sinclair, R. (2004). Participation in practice: Making it meaningful, effective and sustainable. *Children and Society*, **18**(2), 106–118.

Sinclair, R., & Franklin, B. (2000). *Young People's Participation*. Quality Protects Research Briefing. London: Department of Health.

Social Exclusion Unit (2001). *Preventing Social Exclusion: A Report by the Social Exclusion Unit*. London: SEU.

Social Exclusion Unit (2003a). *Tackling Social Exclusion. Achievements, Lessons Learned and the Way Forward*. London: SEU.

Social Exclusion Unit (2003b). *A Better Education for Children in Care*. London: SEU.

Statham, J., Candappa, M., Simon, A., & Owen, C. (2002). *Exploring the Reasons for the Increase in Children Looked After by Local Authorities*. London: Institute of Education.

Stevens, S. (2001). Assessing the competence of the child to give instructions: The solicitor's role. In M. Ruegger (ed.), *Hearing the Voice of the Child. The Representation of Children's Interests in Public Law Proceedings*. Lyme Regis: Russell House Publishing, pp. 78–95.

Taylor, C. (2004). Underpinning knowledge for child care practice: Reconsidering child development theory. *Child and family Social Work*, **9**, 225–235.

Thomas, C., & Thomas, N. (eds) (2005). Listening to children. *Adoption and Fostering*, (Special Edition), **29**(1), 2–119.

Thorpe, Rt Hon. Lord Justice, & Cadbury, J. (2004). *Hearing the Children*. Bristol: Jordan Publishing Limited.

Timmis, G. (2001). CAFCASS: A service for children or a service for the courts? *Family Law*, **31**, 280–287.

Timms, J. (1995). *Children's Representation*. London: Sweet and Maxwell.

Timms, J., & Thoburn, J. (2003). *Your Shout! A Survey of the Views of 706 Young People in Public Care*. London: NSPCC.

Tisdall, K.M., Bray, R., Marshall, K., & Cleland, A. (2004). Children's participation in family law proceedings: A step too far or a step too small? *Journal of Social Welfare and Family Law*, **26**(1), 17–33.

Tisdall, K.M., Cleland, A., Marshall, K., & Plumtree, A. (2002). Listening to the views of children? Principles and mechanisms within the Children (Scotland) Act 1995. *Journal of Social Welfare and Family Law*, **24**(4), 385–400.

Voice for the Child in Care/National Children's Bureau (2004). *Start with the Child. Stay with the Child*. London: Voice for the Child in Care/National Children's Bureau.

Winter, K. (2006). Widening our knowledge concerning looked-after children: The case for research using sociological models of childhood. *Child and Family Social Work*, **11**, 55–64.

Winter, K., & Connolly, P. (1996). Keeping it in the family: Thatcherism and the Children Act 1989. In J. Pilcher & S. Wagg (eds), *Thatcher's Children: Politics, Childhood and Society in the 1980's and 1990's*. London: Falmer Press, pp. 29–42.

Winter, K., & Connolly, P. (2005). A small scale study of the relationship between measures of deprivation and child care referrals. *British Journal of Social Work*, **35**, 937–952.

Part V

Messages from Research

CHAPTER 15

MESSAGES FROM RESEARCH

Dorota Iwaniec and Helga Sneddon

INTRODUCTION

This book sets out to outline recently completed research findings regarding children in substitute care and the legal routes to alternative care granted by the courts. Research discussed in this book was conducted after the *Quality Protects* (DOH, 1998) governmental initiative was introduced in order to examine the effectiveness of the proposed improvements and changes into looked-after children's lives. This concluding chapter will highlight some of the key points which have emerged. Although most of the studies were conducted in Northern Ireland, they are relevant to the United Kingdom, and indeed further afield.

The general objective to provide stability and security for children who are unable to live with their parents for a range of reasons is recognised in many countries on both sides of the Atlantic: permanency in these children's lives is the most natural way to meet basic needs and to encourage a sense of belonging, not only when they are small and dependent, but also when they grow up. Having a home for life is a great comfort to all people, but this is of particular importance to children who have experienced insecurity for a considerable time. Many chapters in this book refer to the issue of permanency and ways it can be achieved (e.g. through adoption, long-term fostering, or kinship care).

PATHWAYS TO PERMANENCY

The driving idea of *Quality Protects* was to improve the quality of care for looked-after children, emphasising secure attachment to the carers and the commitment and competence of the latter to provide effective upbringing for the duration of childhood. Permanence in care provision was the government's major target in order to avoid drifts from placement to placement and discontinuity of attachment-behaviour, resulting in serious emotional disturbances, social disen-gagement, instability, and developmental deficits. The permanence idea was legislated for and regulated through adoption, 'special guardianship', and long-term foster care. The aim was to reduce the breakdown of foster placements and to inhibit frequent movements of a child to short-term placements because of ill-informed care planning or lack of suitable resources. *Quality Protects* also argued for better support for young people leaving care. Long-term foster care remains an important form of substitute care provision providing permanency, stability, and supportive relationships into adulthood (McAuley, Chapter 5 in this volume; Schofield et al., 2000; Sinclair, 2005; Sinclair et al., 2005; Thoburn et al., 2000).

Outcomes of longitudinal studies and the growing literature dealing with long-term foster care suggest that if a placement is well chosen, well matched to the child's needs and temperamental attributes, and the child feels wanted and supported (as well as having a space for his/her own thoughts and ideas), such a placement can be successful and satisfactory, providing a permanent base long outlasting the statutory time in care (McAuley, Chapter 5, in this volume; Sinclair et al., 2005b).

Not all placements are successful, however, and there are many reasons for this (e.g. incompatibility between foster carers and the child, extremely disturbed behaviour, inadequate or unsuitable therapeutic help, difficulties in adaptation, and inability to build new relationships and attachments, as well as unappealing personality). On the foster carer's side, there might be too many high and unre-alistic expectations, lack of patience or sense of humour, emotionally undemon-strative behaviour, and a critical approach to socialisation and social learning.

Many foster parents find it difficult to deal with the emotional state of traumatised children (who might present indifferent, aggressive, or guarded expression of feelings), and as a result do not get satisfaction from their caring efforts. Addition-ally, if foster children's behaviour has negative effects on the foster parents' own children and disrupts family functioning, then, in such circumstances, placement break-up is almost unavoidable (Lernihan & Kelly, Chapter 6 in this volume; McAuley, Chapter 5 in this volume; Triseliotis, 1989). Placement break-ups have been observed over the years to be the most serious problems experienced in the fostering service: they disrupt stability and attempts to build permanency for the most needy children. It is easy to blame foster parents or fostered children for the unsatisfactory outcomes for both parties, and it is essential to investigate what is needed to make the task of fostering better informed and better supported, placing children with suitably chosen foster carers, and seeking the children's expression of choice as to where they want to live (older children, for example, may prefer residential care). These issues are fully discussed by Kilpatrick in Chapter 4, Winter in Chapter 14, and McSherry and Larkin in Chapter 8 in this volume. Children's participation in the decision-making seems to go a long way in making placements work satisfactorily, avoiding frequent break-ups, and building pathways to permanency.

Colette McAuley's ten-year follow-up study of 19 foster children provides a sense of optimism that foster homes can become permanent sources of help and support after statutory placement ends. Like other success stories, these individuals were very young when they entered foster care: they integrated well into family life, were successful at school, were able to build trustful relationships with their foster families, and had easy and appealing personalities. It is encouraging to learn that even those for whom foster placement proved unsatisfactory, they appreciated the help and support which they received while in foster care.

The support and help of social workers have been found by many researchers to be a contributory factor to successful outcomes, both for foster children and those in residential care (McAuley, Chapter 5 in this volume; Utting, 1997). Those lucky enough to have the same social worker for a considerable time attending to their worries and needs felt supported, listened to, and helped. Constantly changing social workers proved to be a negative factor in terms of encouraging children to believe they had someone known to them on whom they could rely.

KINSHIP CARE

The care of children by members of the extended family in the absence of natural parents (because of death, illness, or other problems) is as old as mankind itself. The records of ancient civilisations (such as those of Rome, Egypt, or Greece) mention kinship care, which in one way or another survives and is being practised to this day. However, due to many factors (e.g. social changes, demographic shifts, mobility, and the availability of unrelated foster placements and residential care), kinship care has dramatically declined in the UK since 1945.

Relatively little research has been done in the UK in relation to kinship care, but what has been carried out describes the commitment necessary to provide care for the children of a close relative (who may prove unco-operative and even hostile), as well as the difficulties of obtaining adequate support and help from social services (Greef, 1998; Laws, 2001; Richards, 2001).

Far more is known about kinship care in the United States. In 2000, 3% of children (of whom two-thirds were under some form of legal order) were living with relatives: however, these carers received less support, supervision, and fewer services than did unrelated foster carers (Lynch & Browne, 2000). Una Lernihan and Greg Kelly, in Chapter 6 in this volume, share outcomes of kinship care and traditional foster care research conducted in Northern Ireland on 122 children in 82 kinship placements, and 154 in 96 traditional foster care provisions. They found that kinship care was more stable in terms of the number of movements, and provided continuity of attachment to familiar figures, sense of identity and belonging, and permanency for life. The carers were usually maternal aunts and uncles, and, in fewer cases, grandparents. It was surprising to read that most children in kinship care were subject to Care Orders, and only 14% of them were cared for on a voluntary basis. Most kinship carers were financially supported by social services and provided with help and advice as needed. Kinship carers felt that it was their duty to look after these children and could not envisage placement with strangers. Of course, kinship care is very much encouraged by the Children Act and provides better prospects for permanency and sense of belonging to the blood-family.

Kinship care, however, is not free of problems, as the relationships between extended-family carers and the child's parents can be extremely difficult. Additionally, within a new family the child in question must find its place and acceptance by all. It is easy to see how a 'Cinderella' syndrome can develop if care is not taken and the case is not supervised. On the whole, kinship care can be a good option for a child if the placement is well supported and supervised. As most children in public care tend to return to their families after statutory care ends, it may be wise to try harder to place more children with kinship carers, with suitable allowances, regulations, and help in place.

PERMANENCY THROUGH ADOPTION

It is strongly believed that if there is not a realistic possibility of the child's being rehabilitated into the parents' care, then the next best option is adoption. The trend to promote adoption on a large scale emerged from extremely negative outcomes for children in public care. Radical changes in permanency planning have been driven by the Prime Minister's initiative: *Adoption: A New Approach* (2000) and the Adoption and Children Act (2002) are the results of extensive research and deliberations of what is best for children in order to prevent drifts in care and to speed up the adoption process.

Dominic McSherry and Emma Larkin (Chapter 7) present findings from their cohort study of 375 children and the placement pathways. Increases in applications for Freeing Orders (as well as successful adoption cases) were considerable, taking into account the very low rate of adoption in Northern Ireland. However, there were also significant differences within and between Boards and Trusts, indicating the conservative response to seeking Freeing Orders without parental agreement. With the emphasis on the European Convention of Human Rights, adoption without parental agreement will become more difficult, as illustrated by Donaldson (Chapter 12). Of course, adoption is not always the best option for all children in public care. Long-term fostering (especially for older children who do not want to be adopted), or residential care for those who are difficult to foster, are the subjects of current developments promoted by the governmental Strategy for Children and Young People, reported in Chapter 8. New investment in fostering services is needed in order to increase the number of foster placements, training for foster carers, the provision of salaried specialist foster parents, and more and prompt support for carers. Only by adequately preparing foster parents in dealing with, at times, extremely troubled children in their care can the stability of fostering be improved. Fostering, without the injection of new money and considerable extension of the support system, will not improve. It is encouraging to see constructive movements towards better service provision in order to secure permanency for children in State care.

BUILDING ATTACHMENTS AND BONDING

The importance of a child's attachment has been long recognised by both researchers and practitioners, although sometimes misunderstood. Aldgate (Chapter 2) explores how attachment-behaviour relates to only one specific aspect of a child–care-giver relationship (that activated through fear), and how this is different from general affectional behaviour towards the carer. It is important to understand that attachment-behaviour in the child is separate from, but parallel to, the behaviour of the care-giver who is seen by the child as an attachment-figure. The child's attachment is influenced more by the sensitivity and consistency of the care-giver's response to its security-seeking behaviour, rather than the emotional feelings of the carer towards the child. In light of this, Aldgate argues that, in relation to looked-after children, it is not necessary for substitute carers initially to feel an emotional connection with the children for whom they care, so long as their care-giving behaviour is consistent with a sensitive response to the attachment-needs of those children, and they have emotional investments in the child's outcomes.

Current thinking also suggests that children who have been cared for by many people may present evenly spread patterns of attachment, and that different attachment-relationships may affect various different domains of development. Nevertheless, research suggests that the process of making new attachments is similar, whenever it occurs. This does not negate, however, the importance of providing stability in children's lives and maintaining a young person's sense of identity and belonging. Work with children and new carers must minimise the trauma of separations and losses and aim to facilitate the development of new attachments that are complementary rather than competitive (Fahlberg, 1994). Aldgate argues that workers should stay the course with children as long as possible, and that, if they leave, transitions should be made smoothly with appropriate support. The theory of socio-genealogical connectedness also provides a useful perspective on attachment when contact is not possible between a child and its family (Aldgate, Chapter 2). Rather than emphasising actual contact between individuals, more emphasis is placed on the information about attachment-figures that children possess, particularly the degree to which children identify with their parents' backgrounds.

Although it is still widely believed that childhood patterns of attachment will be carried into adult life, there is now a better understanding of subsequent discontinuities. As Aldgate notes, the care-giving response for many looked-after children will call for heightened sensitivity and persistence, especially in cases where children have difficulty in developing trust. Children with previous damaging attachments need to have those attachments discontinued by having the support of experienced substitute care-givers (who are themselves secure in their adult attachments and can respond sensitively and consistently to the children). These carers need to be aware of these issues and need to be provided with adequate support and training.

Larkin (Chapter 3) examines the carer–child relationship from the perspective of bonding and the emotional tie from parent or carer to child. Bonding is generally believed to be a bi-directional, reciprocal process that develops through positive feedback and satisfying interactions between the attachment dyad. Several potential adverse consequences have been identified for children whose parents have encountered bonding difficulties (including reduced capacity to form meaningful emotional bonds with others, interpersonal difficulties, fragile sense of self, poorer coping strategies, and increased risk of developing psychological disorders). Perceived difficulties with the bonding process can be potentially distressing and isolating for the parent, and are linked to problems such as finding interaction with the child unrewarding, lessened motivation to care for the infant, and decreased willingness to invest effort in meeting and prioritising the child's needs.

Larkin explores the bonding process between adoptive mothers and their adopted children. This is thought to be aided by factors such as the degree of mental preparation for the adoption of the child, the amount of engagement in fantasies regarding the child, physical closeness, nurturing, and joint activities. It is also influenced by the child's characteristics in terms of history, age, background, culture, language, and past attachments. Pressures on the bonding process include destructive or negative behaviour, detachment or rejection by the child, and depletion of energy and resources. The parental identification of the child as their 'own' is also important in the bonding process, and Larkin explores the implications of this for situations where there has been a lack of clarity as to the length of the placement in relation to fostering with a view to adoption, and the difficulties for carers in not knowing whether they have a child for now or a child for life.

CHILDREN'S RIGHTS AND PARTICIPATION OF CHILDREN IN PUBLIC LAW PROCEEDINGS

Kilpatrick (Chapter 4) and Winter (Chapter 14) explore issues around looked-after children's rights. Research indicates that despite progress in some areas, there is still room for improvement with respect to children's rights and the participation of children in public law. Winter examines what exactly is meant by children's participation, and notes that a common misconception is that children's participation is synonymous with children controlling adults and telling adults what to do. Rather, she argues, the term means taking part in, sharing, influencing, and affecting decisions reached through a process of mutual discussion, negotiation, compromise, and agreement in a partnership relationship. There are different degrees of participation, ranging from being informed, expressing a view, influencing the decision-maker, and being the main decider. The aim should be to elevate the voice of the child to the same level and visibility in proceedings as the voices of the other professionals who make comments on these children's lives.

Kilpatrick (Chapter 4) presents evidence of children's rights in different alternative care settings and court proceedings. There are examples of children's rights being underplayed or ignored when children are removed from the family home, notably in relation to key principles of best interests, non-discrimination, and participation in decision-making. Within the CRC (Children's Rights Convention) there is a need to ensure that there are effective, child-sensitive procedures available for all children and their representatives, including child-friendly information, advice, and advocacy, as well as support for self-advocacy. There must also be access to independent complaints procedures and to the courts. Kilpatrick argues that the scarcity of foster placements of all types results in a lack of choice for children when being placed, and thus the child's wishes, best interests, and/or needs are not met. In residential care, lack of placements may result in inappropriate groupings of children in the same unit that can put highly vulnerable children at risk: this can be further complicated by the high turnover of staff and lack of skilled practitioners (a similar situation exists in secure accommodation).

Winter (Chapter 14) suggests that for a looked-after child there are two main expectations emerging from an emphasis on participation. Firstly, children and young people should expect their views, experiences, and perspectives to be properly elicited (regardless of their age and by whatever means they are expressed), and, secondly, that their voices will be given the same degree of validity, significance, visibility, and importance as the views and perspectives of the adults involved in their lives. She argues for a multi-faceted response by professionals in public law proceedings: all those working with children need to become conversant with the many theoretical approaches regarding the concept and nature of childhood, so preconceptions of who we think children are, and what they are capable of, can be challenged; a common understanding of participation needs to be evolved; and a multi-layered response needs to be developed to challenge the structures, processes, attitudes, and views that act together to constrain the views of looked-after children.

Winter outlines the usefulness of the 'Mosaic Approach' in encouraging a fuller exploration of the wishes and feelings of children by its multi-method, child-initiated, and reflexive approach: employment of multi-media portfolios would have many benefits including the opportunity for the proper documentation of such work when currently such records may often be filtered through welfare considerations. Use of the multi-method and multi-media portfolio could provide a productive focus for an informal meeting between children (if they wish) and the involved judge in public care proceedings which could be facilitated by the children's guardian or solicitor: it would also offer children the opportunity to participate using methods with which they are comfortable and which may also serve to demonstrate their level of competence and insight into the circumstances beyond what is commonly expected. Winter also suggests that the court report format could be amended to include specific sections on participation.

CARE PLANNING, ASSESSMENT, AND INTERVENTION

Looked-after children often have complex family histories and needs, and can be more vulnerable to experiencing problems than are those who have not been in care. Many of these problems may stem from experiences prior to entering care, but there are also concerns that difficulties may be exacerbated by a care system that does not adequately meet their needs, particularly with respect to mental health. In the UK, legislation has sought to improve the planning process for these children by specifying documentation that must be completed. Sneddon (Chapter 10) presents evidence that, although the planning for the overall welfare of children entering residential or foster care appears reasonable, the completion rates of paperwork held in social worker case files are problematic. This could make it more difficult to identify problems and focus responses to needs, to provide key information to carers at time of placement in order to ensure adequate safeguards, to facilitate the transfer of information between professionals (such as when different social workers are involved), and to facilitate tracking of problems over time. Sneddon suggests that a more succinct summary document could be developed that would be more likely to be completed by social workers. This summary of key points could be kept at the front of the child's case file and regularly updated.

Many professionals are currently concerned about limitations in the present care system's ability to identify young people's mental-health difficulties and to organise effective interventions (although the extent of met and unmet need has not been fully quantified). Teggart (Chapter 9) argues that current systems need to better address ways of identifying and responding to children and young people who may be experiencing mental-health difficulties. Central to this is the assessment of need (which must be structured and focused on the individual case) to take place as soon as is practical following admission to care. Support interventions need to aim to increase young people's resilience and also to prevent the development of problems. Rather than expecting the specialist CAMHS (Child and Adolescent Mental Health Services) workers to provide a full range of assessments, planning, and supportive functions, Teggart suggests that separate teams of mental-health professionals are required to complement the CAMHS service. He suggests that these separate teams should be composed on the basis of competencies rather than on professional background, and should focus on assessment, care, and placement planning, training, and consultation to the care system. The primary clinical remit would remain with CAMHS, which could then concentrate on flexible service delivery in ways to engage the young people. Houston (Chapter 11) also comments that much of the therapeutic work for children in residential care has adopted a deficit-oriented approach to treatment and therapeutic help, and a more positive strategy would be helpful in order to shift thinking and practice towards an increase of capacity rather than merely risk management. Treatment is not just fixing what is broken: it is nurturing what is best (Seligman & Csikszentmihalyi, 2000).

LEGAL AND VOLUNTARY PATHWAYS TO SUBSTITUTE CARE

The philosophy behind the aims of the Children Act (1989) (among other things) was to redirect child-welfare work from focusing almost exclusively on child abuse and protection to more holistic child-centred work addressing a wide range of children's needs. Family support was seen primarily as a means to help parents who experienced child-rearing difficulties, and, by so doing, reduce or even eliminate the necessity of legal intervention. Short-term voluntary accommodation of children with substitute carers constitutes family support, which also emphasises intervention with agreement from, and in partnership with, parents.

The Children Act (1989) also stresses that children should be brought up by their parents whenever possible and without resort to legal proceedings. That belief is reflected in the following:

- the new concept of parental responsibility;
- the local authority's duty to provide support for children in their families;
- the local authority's duty to return a looked-after child to the family unless this is against his/her interest.

Meeting the above requirements and observing principles of accommodation under the family support proved to be very problematic in practice. Quite often short-term accommodation became long-term placement without a clear care plan, the children becoming alienated from their parents, getting attached to 'temporary' carers, and getting more confused as to whom they belonged. Parents, as a rule, find themselves trapped in a no-win situation: on the one hand, having power to discharge the child into their care; but, on the other, being told that if they do so, social services will start legal proceedings to obtain a Care Order. In many studies, decision-making (as to when to accommodate a child, for what purpose, for how long, and what is required from the parents for the child to be returned to their care) has been found to be unclear and poorly communicated to the parents (Donaldson, 2003, and Chapter 12 in this volume; Hunt et al., 1999). In many instances, accommodation has been used as a stepping-stone to care proceedings.

Donaldson's study (Chapter 12) revealed that parents were not always informed about social services' intention to take the case to court, or the parents were coerced into agreeing to accommodation. Such practice, of course, is considered an abuse of Article 6 and Article 8 of the European Convention of Human Rights.

Theresa Donaldson brings to our attention findings from her study of 107 children (36 children in 20 cases subject to Care Order applications and 71 children in 38 cases of accommodated children). Both Care Order application cases and those accommodated had been known to social services, on average three years, before becoming looked after. Most children were on the Child Protection Register. The largest category was that of neglect for both accommodated and Care Order cases. The findings indicated substantial co-morbidity between the groups and that the provision of accommodation was a significant point of entry to the legal process. These findings are in line with other studies in this area (Donaldson, 2003; Hunt & Macleod, 1999; King, 1997). In Donaldson's study, the use of accommodation was found to be inappropriate: evidence of significant harm was high and the likelihood of a required change in parenting was low. More worryingly, parents seldom seemed to be involved in care planning for their children, and not sufficiently informed as to what was going to happen to them in the long run. Decision-making appeared to take place during 'in-house' meetings and did not involve parents. The consequences of such practice are illustrated by Cathy's case in Chapter 12. Again, putting unrealistic emphases on working in partnership with parents (where possibilities of and willingness to change are remote) can only obstruct securing child welfare and lead to delay (as in Angela's and Peter's cases). Donaldson provides evidence of the daunting task facing social workers in maintaining a balance between supporting a family unit (as required by law) and taking action to secure a permanent placement for a child (if remaining at home has been judged unacceptable).

It needs to be remembered (and observed in practice) that there is rapid movement into a rights-based culture, so it is crucial that Articles 6 and 8 are taken into consideration to remove possible obstacles in securing permanence for children when deemed necessary. The 'No Order' principle and emphasis on family support are often given as reasons for not making a firm decision early on to apply for a Care Order, and making endless allowances and justification for damaging parental behaviour. The difficulties faced by social workers in court work cannot be underestimated, as they have to deal with conflicting demands (e.g. the Rights of Children *versus* the Human Rights of Parents, 'No Order' principle *versus* the 'No Delay' principle, and ensuring that the welfare of the child is paramount). It should also be borne in mind that lack of appropriate and adequate resources to facilitate the complex needs of children and their parents is a perennial problem.

DIFFICULTIES AND COSTS OF LEGAL PROCEEDINGS

The legal process of care proceedings is costly in both financial terms and professional time. It can also be emotionally costly for children because of unnecessary delays in decision-making. Attachments are often formed in what was supposed to be short-term care and then broken when a child is eventually placed in a permanent home. However, it needs to be remembered that care proceedings, or freeing for adoption, are extremely serious matters and cannot be rushed for the sake of saving time or money: some delays are also necessary for making appropriate and fair decisions. Nevertheless, some of the lengthy proceedings are hard to justify as they do not serve the best interests of the child, and substantial amounts of money and time are spent waiting for various additional reports (which may not add much to the required evidence).

Social workers feel that they are undermined by courts, and receive differential treatment when giving evidence in comparison to other professionals.

Undoubtedly, there is uncomfortable tension between social workers and the legal profession: the former often feel that their credibility is devalued and that they are expected to provide evidence which nobody could provide; and the latter frequently consider that social workers cannot prepare cases analytically based on sound evidence. Dominic McSherry in Chapter 13 illustrates some of the problems associated with timely and sound decision-making regarding children's lives, both prior to taking a case to court and then difficulties associated with proceedings. He draws attention to the necessity of having a concurrent plan for each child in order to avoid delays in securing permanent placement. The case studies illustrate the shortcomings of all concerned and discuss ways in which problems might be solved.

CONCLUSION

Children enter care for a multitude of different reasons, but all have experienced difficulties in their lives. It is widely recognised that early experiences can influence later outcomes, but this is not inevitably so. Given the right opportunities, support, and help, these children can show considerable resilience: many of the authors in this book have highlighted the importance of engaging and building on these young people's strengths and moving away from labelling them solely by their care experiences. Aldgate (Chapter 2) highlights the need to move towards recognising that looked-after children are ordinary children, albeit in extraordinary circumstances. Whatever difficulties young persons may have encountered during their childhood, they need not be condemned by their experiences: they can be viewed as having *survived* their past, rather than forever being victims whose pasts will hold them back (Schaffer, 1992). Houston (Chapter 11) writes of the shift towards taking a more positive approach in describing and engaging with looked-after children, changing the mindset that focuses on negative factors such as 'trauma', 'abuse', adversity', and 'impoverished self-esteem', and modifying professional terminology that labels them as 'children in need', 'troubled and troublesome', and showing 'challenging behaviour'. He argues that building on the positive dimensions of a young person's life might lead to more efficacious outcomes (that do not reinforce stigma) by emphasising the child's existing competencies, normalising the helping intervention, and not marking the child out as different from his or her peers. Winter (Chapter 14) argues that increased use of child-centred techniques (such as the 'Mosaic Approach') would enable the lives of children to be in the limelight for positive rather than negative reasons because of its focus on the competencies, capacities, and perspectives of children rather than just their needs. There is an urgent requirement to reinstate direct work with children as an essential part of the social work role. The needs and experiences of both young people and professionals in the legal processes need to be examined to redirect attention away from bureaucratic procedures to focus on children and their needs and why they are in court in the first place. Everyone could benefit from mutual training so that they know what is expected of each other's roles and responsibilities. This would also cut the length and cost of proceedings.

In the UK, foster care has become for many children the placement of choice when they are unable to continue living with their birth-families, with a corresponding decline in residential provision. Since the late 1990s there has been an increasing realisation that residential care should be viewed as a placement of choice for some young people, rather than as a service of last resort. As McSherry and Larkin (Chapter 8) describe, the current focus in Northern Ireland is on developing specialised models of residential provision, or Intensive Support Units (ISUs), that specifically address the complex needs of the children requiring this type of placement. The emphasis is on designing residential care to meet the needs of the child rather than those of the service-providers. Although the effectiveness of proposed changes to residential and foster care are not yet clear, one thing is certain for the future: sadly, there will always be a need for the State to care for some of the most vulnerable children and no work can be done without adequate resources, staffing, training, and the appropriate policies. We have to learn as professionals to listen to and hear the children's wishes, preferences, and feelings, and always remember that it is up to us to help those children to reach their potential and be prepared for life.

REFERENCES

Department of Health (1998). *Quality Protects*. London: The Stationery Office.

Donaldson, T. (2003). *The changing face of care under the Children (NI) Order 1995: A prospective study of decision-making and care-outcome for looked-after children*. Unpublished PhD thesis, Queen's University Belfast.

Fahlberg, V. (1994). *A Child's Journey Through Placement*. London: British Agencies for Adoption and Fostering.

Greef, R. (1998). *Fostering Kinship: An International Perspective on Kinship Care*. Aldershot: Ashgate.

Hunt, J., & Macleod, A. (1999). *The Best-Laid Plans: Outcomes of Judicial Decisions in Child Protection Proceedings*. London: The Stationery Office.

Hunt, J., Macleod, A., & Thomas, C. (1999). *The Last Resort: Child Protection, the Courts and the 1989 Children Act*, vol. 1. London: The Stationery Office.

King, M. (1997). *A Better World for Children? Explorations in Morality and Authority*. London: Routledge.

Laws, S. (2001). Looking after children within the extended family. In B. Broad (ed.), *Kinship Care: The Placement Choice for Children and Young People*. Lyme Regis: Russell House Publishing.

Lynch, M.A., & Browne, K. (2000). Conclusions: Future challenges in child protection. In K. Browne, H. Hanks, P. Stratton, & C. Hamilton (eds), *Early Prediction and Prevention of Child Abuse: A Handbook*. Chichester: John Wiley & Sons, Ltd.

Richards, A. (2001). *Second Time Around: A Survey of Grandparents Raising their Grandchildren*. London: Family Rights Group.

Schaffer, H.R. (1992). Early experience and the parent–child relationship: Genetic and environmental interactions as developmental determinants. In B. Tizard & V. Varma (eds) (2000), *Vulnerability and Resilience in Human Development*. London: Jessica Kingsley.

Schofield, G., Beek, M., & Sargent, K. with Thoburn, J. (2000). *Growing Up in Foster Care*. London: BAAF.

Seligman, M., & Csikszentmihalyi, M. (2000). Positive psychology: An introduction. *American Psychologist*, **55**, 5–14.

Sinclair, I. (2005). *Fostering Now: Messages from Research*. London: Jessica Kingsley.

Sinclair, I., Baker, C., Wilson, K., & Gibbs, I. (2005). *Foster Children: Where They Go and How They Get On*. London: Jessica Kingsley.

Thoburn, J., Norford, I., & Rashid, S. (2000). *Permanent Family Placement for Children of Minority Ethnic Origin*. London: Jessica Kingsley.

Triseliotis, J. (1989). Foster care outcomes: A review of key research findings. *Adoption and Fostering*, **13**, 5–17.

Utting, W. (1997). *People Like Us: The Report of the Review of the Safeguards for Children Living Away from Home*. London: Department of Health.

INDEX

Note: page numbers in *italics* refer to information contained within tables, page numbers in **bold** refer to diagrams.